THE HANGING OF FLOSS

Book I
VIOLENCE

For Dee
with love from William

William Gates 9.3.98

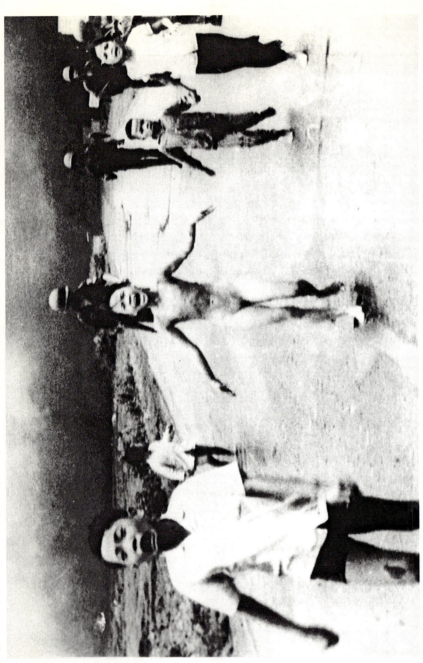

The horror of the Vietnam war was driven home to the American people in this 1972 photo. A ten-year-old Vietnamese girl, Phan Thim Kim Phuc, running down a country road has ripped flaming clothes from her body after being burned by napalm. (Photo: Alan Downes, courtesy of The Associated Press Ltd.)

William Gates

THE HANGING OF FLOSS FORSYTH
Book I: Violence

First published in paperback in 1997 by
Destination Way
PO Box 7700
London SW1V 3XQ

Copyright © William Gates 1992

ISBN 0-9525896-0-5

British Library cataloguing-in-print data
applied for

Maps drawn by Maureen Churchman

Typeset in New Century 11/13pt by
Scriptmate Editions
Manufacture coordinated in UK by Book-in-Hand Ltd
20 Shepherds Hill, London N6 5AH

Events in this book are based on fact. Most of the
characters used to portray events are fictitious.
Whenever possible, to ensure privacy, the names of
living characters have been changed.

THE HANGING OF FLOSS FORSYTH:

Ye whose hearts are fresh and simple,
Who have faith in God and Nature,
Who believe, that in all ages
Every human heart is human,
That in even savage bosoms
There are longings, yearnings, strivings,
For the good they comprehend not,
That the feeble hands and helpless,
Groping blindly in the darkness,
Touch God's right hand in that darkness,
And are lifted up and strengthened;
Listen to this simple story ...

ACKNOWLEDGMENTS

I am grateful for permission given to use material in copyright. In making the following acknowledgements I hope I have not, inadvertently, left anyone out.

The First World War

Allies

Michael Goldsmith, Janes Information Group, for the use of *The War the Infantry Knew* by Captain J. C. Dunn.

Penguin Books Ltd. for the use of *The First World War: An Illustrated History* by A. J. P. Taylor, Hamish Hamilton/Rainbird, 1963, (UK); The Putnam Publishing Group, New York (USA).

A.P. Watt Ltd. on behalf of the Trustees of the Robert Graves Copyright Trust for the use of *Goodbye to All That* by Robert Graves.

Leo Cooper Ltd. For the use of *Christmas Truce* by Malcolm Brown and Shirley Seaton.

Grafton Books (Collins Publishing Group) for the use of *For the Sake of Example* by Anthony Babington.

Germans

Der Angriff Publications for the use of *Fritz* by Fritz Nagel (PA).

The Bodley Head Ltd. for the use of *All Quiet on the Western Front* by Erich Maria Remarque (UK).

Pryor, Cashman, Sherman & Flynn, New York, for *Im Westen Nichts Neues,* copyright 1928 by Ullstein A.G.; copyright renewed © 1956 by Erich Maria Remarque.

All Quiet on the Western Front, copyright 1929, 1930 by Little, Brown and Company; copyright renewed © 1957, 1958 by Erich Maria Remarque. All rights reserved (USA).

The British Library for advice on Germans on the Somme (League of Nations): Philip Gibbs (PA).

The Second World War

B. T. Batsford Ltd. for the use of *El Alamein* by Michael Carver.

J. M. Dent for the use of *El Alamein — Desert Victory* by John Strawson.

Independent Broadcasting Authority and Thames Television for advice on London Blitzes (PA).

Lt. Col. T. A. K. Dillon, the Gloucestershire Regiment, for the use of *Rangoon to Kohima* by Terence Dillon.

The Gloucestershire Regiment for the use of *Cap of Honour* by Scott Daniell.

David Williamson, Debrett's Peerage Ltd., for the use of *Personal Tribute to Derek Mond* by Lord Cherwell, 1945.

Vietnam War

Michael Bilton, Yorkshire Television, for the use of extract from 'A Half Told Story', *Sunday Times Magazine,* April 30, 1989. Copyright Michael Bilton and Kevin Sim.

Periods Leading Up to the Wars

Mills & Boon Ltd. for the use of *The Story of a Nobody* by Ian Dewhurst.

B. T. Batsford Ltd. for the use of *Kaiser Wilhelm II* by John Röhl and Nicolaus Sombart.

George Weidenfeld & Nicolson Ltd. for the use of *The People of England* by Maurice Ashley; also for the use of *King Edward VII.*

Methuen & Co. for the use of *The Common People* by J. F. C. Harrison.

Blackie and Son Ltd. for the use of *Palace and Hovel* by Daniel Joseph Kirwan (Ed. A. Allan).

Royal Archives, Windsor Castle, for information on New Thames Bridges, Prince of Wales, 1933, and Diamond Jubilee Procession, Queen Victoria (CN).

General

The Macmillan Press Ltd. for the use of *A History of England* by Keith Feiling.

Virago Press for the use of *Bowen's Court* by Elizabeth Bowen(UK). From *Bowen's Court* (second edition) by Elizabeth Bowen, copyright 1942, 1964; renewed 1970 by Elizabeth Bowen. Reprinted by permission of Alfred A. Knopf, Inc. (USA).

Brian Vine, *Daily Mail,* for the use of *The Cost of Belligerence,* 1986, by Ruth Leger Sivard.

Blackie & Son Ltd. for the use of *The Song of Hiawatha* by H. W. Longfellow.

The Librarian, Lambeth Palace Library, for information on LET LIGHT PERPETUAL SHINE UPON THEM, from an ancient Latin hymn (CN).

Mrs. Nicolete Gray and The Society of Authors on behalf of the Laurence Binyon estate for extract from *For the Fallen* (September 1914) by Laurence Binyon.

Embassy of the Republic of Fiji for advice on *Ratu Cakobau* by Deve Toganivalu, The Fijian Society (CN).

For the use of material regarding the murder of Allan Jee, 1960: The Times © Times Newspapers Ltd. 28.6.60, *Daily Telegraph, Daily Express, Daily Mirror, Daily Mail, Evening Standard Company*

Ltd., Middlesex Chronicle (Argus Group). Also (no longer in circulation): *The People, News Chronicle, Evening News.*

Acuff Rose Opryland Music Inc. for the use of 'All I have to Do is Dream' by Boudleaux Bryant © Acuff Rose Opryland Music Inc. Lyrics reproduced by permission of Acuff Rose Opryland Music Ltd. (UK); House of Bryant, Gatlinburg, Tennessee (USA).

I would also like to thank the Imperial War Museum; the Tank Museum, Bovington; Mark Bostridge, official biographer of Vera Brittain; Paul Fussell, Donald T. Regan professor of English Literature, University of Pennsylvania, and author of *The Great War and Modern Memory,* for their considerable help and advice. I am indebted to Matthew Evans, chairman of Faber and Faber Ltd. for advice on the use of Memoirs of a Foxhunting Man by Siegfried Sassoon; to Maureen Churchman for her maps on the First World War and the battle of El Alamein; to Fraser Gray for his photographs; to Terence Charman, Department of Printed Books, Imperial War Museum, for checking the First World War and Second World War sections; also to the Lord Chancellor's Office for giving permission, and the General Office, Central Criminal Court, for providing facilities, enabling me to copy from the transcript of the Forsyth trial.

PA: source not traced, permission assumed.
CN: copyright permission not required.

Forsyth had been dead ten minutes when I left Rose. I had bumped into her, unexpectedly, half an hour before the execution. Meeting Rose in this way gave me this slightly nervous inclination to be chatty, to say how nice it was to meet up with her again after all these years. It's a long time, thirty years, but I have never forgotten those lovely summer days when as teenagers — or rather when she was a teenager, because she was fourteen and I only eleven — we lay in the long grass by the sandpits reading from books Rose had stolen. She had stolen them from a shop at the back of Hampton station. The old lady who kept the shop was deaf and nearly blind, which was why it was such a good place to go for our books. I say our books because Rose didn't steal all of them. I stole one which was this cheap edition of Longfellow's *The Song of Hiawatha*. We read Hiawatha again and again because I loved it and Rose loved it. The book would only have cost sixpence if I'd paid for it, so I didn't feel too bad.

I took it while the old lady was talking to Rose. She was a sweet old lady who had this great love for children, believing implicitly in the words of Jesus when he said: "Suffer little children to come unto me, for of such is the kingdom of heaven". She just believed that, basically, all children are innocent. She may have been right because we didn't think at the time we were doing wrong. It was like a game really, getting away with a book without the old lady finding out; a bit of a one-sided game on account of her blindness and deafness, but you only realize these things when you get older. She was particularly fond of Rose because Rose had this great love of books, and the old lady would chat to Rose for ages about poets like Matthew Arnold and Dryden and John Donne, and about writers like Hardy and Galsworthy and the Brontës, and so on. She taught Rose quite a lot about English literature, which wasn't difficult to do as Rose had such an insatiable interest, particularly in the poets. I don't know what would have happened if the old lady had caught us, but she never did. She died quietly one Christmas Eve, so Rose and I called it a day because we couldn't believe there would ever again be anyone as nice as she was, or as blind or deaf, or someone thinking that all children are basically innocent.

Where Rose got her love of books from I couldn't say. She lived in this hovel in Green Lane and I don't think her mum or dad could read or write. Or if her father could write, he could just about fill in a betting slip. There were six other children. They were a pretty illiterate lot. The only one who'd really done well and made money was her brother Teddy. He'd made quite a lot of money from armed robbery or something like that, and he was also mixed up in the protection business. It all came out later, when he was caught. Of course I didn't know this at the time, but I had a great admiration for him because he'd done so well and got on. He had, too, a beautiful car and on his little podgy fingers were gold and diamond rings. Maybe if Rose hadn't been very poor she would have bought the books; not that you have to be very poor to want to steal. I had this great friend who was very rich and who on occasion had this great urge to steal. I didn't know he had the urge until he told me about it one evening.

We were dining at the Savoy, just the two of us. We'd had a couple of dry martinis each and a good claret, then brandy with our coffee, and he got into this very confiding mood. He regretted it the next day because he rang up in a bit of a panic and said he'd been joking and not to take any notice of what he'd told me. Actually I didn't take any notice, but I'd believed all he said because when he said it, it seemed to come from the heart. You can tell, in a way, when things come from the heart and people are telling the truth.

Anyway, he said he sometimes got the urge, particularly when he was in a shop or store. He was so rich he could have bought everything ten times over, but I suppose it just seemed more fun to steal something. Of course, unlike Rose and me when we robbed the old lady, he didn't actually steal anything but kept his need to wishful thinking. It could have been that my rich friend looked on stealing in the way Rose and I had regarded it, as just a game; but the difference was that in the 1930s, Rose and I were young and we were both poor. When my friend told me about his temptation it was just after the Second World War when I was up at Oxford and nearly thirty and he was two years younger than me; so with him it couldn't be said that when, for no apparent reason, he got this urge to steal, behind it lay the basic innocence of a child.

When I drove past Wandsworth Jail on that bleak, wet November morning in 1960, it had just gone half past eight. I saw the small crowd: the little old man carrying his placard with the white chalked words ACCORDING TO THE LAW OF GOD HANGING IS ALL WRONG, the old woman dressed in black saying Hail Marys over and over again outside the prison gates, the policemen on duty standing outside the prison or sitting in police cars nearby. So curious to see more, I pulled up on a side road, walked back, and became, to this extent, involved in the hanging.

I saw Rose and recognised her immediately even though it was thirty years since we had last met. I said, "Hullo, Rose," and she said, "Hullo,

Willie," and the way she spoke it was as if nothing had happened in between to change our childhood friendship. Then she introduced me to her husband. I shook him warmly by the hand and thought what a silly little man, until she explained that Henry was a vicar. I mean a vicar is a vicar even if you are short and heavy with a large nose, a red face, and a bit of a squint in one eye. It's simply that a dog collar seems to make all the difference. Not that he was wearing his dog collar, but once I knew his calling, he got the respect I feel should always be given to the cloth. I tried to think of something sensible to say, but could only come up with the usual trite remarks about the weather.

As a matter of fact, it was quite good weather for an occasion like this: clouds and rain and a damp, chilly wind. I could see why Rose had married Henry. He was educated. You could tell this by the quality of his voice. He had, too, this very forceful way of speaking. I only just had time to shake hands when he said: "Have you come to protest?" I didn't like to say I had come out of nosiness, so I said yes, that is what I had come for. Then he said, still in this very forceful way: "I'm glad to see you here, sir; the more people who stand up to be counted the better." I nodded my agreement and took it that all the people here outside the prison, except the policemen on duty, were standing up to be counted; because even if you were all for the hanging of these young thugs, it wouldn't seem right to be walking about now looking pleased when only a couple of hundred yards away, on the other side of the prison wall, a condemned youth had fifteen minutes of life left.

Although Henry was small, I could see he knew how to put things over. He reminded me, in this way, of my rich uncle. Actually he reminded me of my uncle in two ways: the forcefulness with which he spoke and the fact that he was religious. It would, of course, have seemed strange if Henry, being a vicar, wasn't religious, but my uncle, as chairman of our family business, wouldn't have the same need. However my uncle, when his mind wasn't on the business, or sometimes when it was, spoke to anyone he happened to see — managers, drivers, engineers, pasteurisers, butter makers, the yard sweeper, laboratory staff — explaining about Armageddon and the New Jerusalem, Christ Jesus and Salvation, and when everyone could expect the second coming. From time to time his prophecies appeared in photo-copied booklets with titles such as *The Time of the End–Part III* and *End of the Days–Part IV*. These were published and distributed by the print division. Sometimes he would send out a form which anyone could fill in and return if further booklets weren't required, but although most people found the booklets boring and couldn't be bothered to read them, none of the forms came back. This was because my uncle was chairman, although the reason he sent out the forms was not to find out who didn't want to read his booklets but to save unnecessary postage. He was a careful man, not in a mean way, which many rich people are, but shrewd as if he saw everything, including the road to eternity, in terms of profit and loss.

So standing there, on that bleak November morning, thinking about Henry and my uncle and how alike they were in attitude and mannerisms yet so totally different in appearance — my uncle being tall and good-looking with his distinctive military bearing — thinking about this I suddenly became aware of a woman sobbing. She was a young woman, plump, attractive, with rosy cheeks, dark hair, and dark eyes, about twenty-two or twenty-three. She stood with her head bowed, a white handkerchief clasped to her face, and I could see by the way her body was shaking that her grief was deeply felt, almost uncontrollable, needing only a touch to break into hysteria. This sobbing produced a curious kind of tension, curious because nothing outwardly had changed except the words on the old man's placard were half washed off by the rain. But there was no shouting, no fuss, no violent demonstration, only the few who had come to mourn and to protest standing waiting, the old woman all the time reciting her Hail Marys, the police not moving, doing their job, just another day's work, Henry looking drawn, Rose dressed tastefully in black, a head and shoulders taller than her determined husband.

Often in times of stress you can think of something quite trivial, and when the moments up to the time of execution could be counted on one hand I began thinking how soft and pleasing Rose's voice had become. Not that her voice had ever been harsh, but she had lost the faint cockney accent, the slight thinness, and in place of this was a delicacy, a refinement that over the years had become so much a part of her personality that it now sounded quite natural. As a matter of fact, now I come to think about it, even as a teenager all those years ago Rose had this tendency towards refinement. Although she came from a very poor background, there was nothing coarse about her; also, I had never known her envious of others. She believed firmly that birthright was by design, not accident, and that if you were born poor there was nothing to stop you doing what her brother Teddy had done and become rich. Of course, at that time, Teddy hadn't been caught, so I couldn't say what Rose's feelings were later.

Not only was Rose not envious of those who had the splendour of great wealth and the power wealth brings but she enjoyed reading about them, which was one of the reasons I borrowed two books from Mr Mackintosh. The Mackintoshes lived at the end of our road. Mr Mackintosh was a young schoolteacher and looked on Karl Marx in the way most people look on Jesus. Outwardly Mr Mackintosh was very easygoing; little things that worried most people didn't seem to bother him. The Mackintoshes had one little daughter, Naomi, aged five. In the summer months Naomi was allowed to run around naked, which didn't please other people in our road who hadn't the same progressive views. Quite a lot of poison pen letters were written to the Mackintoshes, but they didn't seem to take much notice. One day they asked my mother if I could baby-sit and that's how I got to know them. They were very kind to me: Mrs Mackintosh would leave me a nice supper and Mr Mackintosh gave me half a crown, a lot in those days. They did this each time I went.

In the sitting room were shelves and shelves of books: books on education, family life in the London suburbs, life in India's slums, a new approach to psychology, crisis in society, the American poor, children in need, and books by and on Rousseau, Kant, Hegel, Nietzsche, and others. Looking back at it now, it amuses me that Rose, who was not the least bit troubled by stealing books, insisted we treat the two Mr Mackintosh lent us with the greatest care and return them as soon as possible.

Because Rose was so keen to return the two books, we interrupted our second reading of Hiawatha. We didn't mind doing this because we'd only just started, getting no farther than the lines beginning: "Ye whose hearts are fresh and simple," which, when I come to write this book on the hanging of Floss Forsyth, I shall use for the title page. I had found the two books when thumbing through others on Mr Mackintosh's bookshelves; he said I could borrow them for as long as I liked.

One book was about Queen Victoria and the poor people of London, the other about Fiji and Fijian customs and traditions and how Fiji, through the white missionaries, became civilised and was then handed over to the Great White Queen. Rose was very keen on royal families and had a particular affection for King George V and Queen Mary, who were reigning over us at that time. We began with the book on Queen Victoria, and Rose read aloud about the Queen; then I took over and read to her about all the poor people and how some poor people became rich.

The Queen, it seemed, had an enormous bed. This was at Windsor Castle. The bed was large enough to hold three people the size of the Queen and was hung with red velvet and yellow silk. The counterpane, quilted blue-and-pink satin, was bordered with purple velvet and gold lace and had the royal arms embroidered in the centre. The pillow slips had trimmings of Valenciennes lace half a yard wide hanging from their open ends. Covering the bed was a velvet canopy lined with blue-and-

15

white satin from which hung down heavy folds of Mechlin lace. A few feet from the bed stood a little table of ivory inlaid with gold and lapis lazuli. This table was supported by a tripod elegantly worked in solid silver. At one end of the room was a sideboard of most intricate carving. On one of its shelves stood green Venetian glasses. The carpets in the room were so soft and luxurious that anyone coming in would have the feeling of sinking into them. There was also this delicious odour of cologne, roses and musk, the Queen's favourite scents, which she liked to have dabbed on the counterpane.

In the morning she drank two cups of coffee. She was also, particularly before Prince Albert died, a good eater. For breakfast she liked veal cutlets well done. Also sweetbreads. She would often eat a pound of veal at breakfast. The serving of breakfast involved an intricate pattern of behaviour. A lady-in-waiting would place a cup of coffee on the ivory table then stand away at a respectful distance, and when the Queen was ready to eat, the lady-in-waiting would bring the dish ordered for that day. Most of the ladies-in-waiting had to remain standing, but one or two favourites, such as the Duchess of Atholl and Lady Diana Beauclerk, when they weren't actually serving the Queen, were allowed to sit down.

The sense of mystery and enchantment in the room was broken only when the Queen's eldest son came in drunk. Then there would be a row. These rows happened quite often because the Queen's son liked drinking. He also liked women. And gambling. He particularly liked women who had come up the hard way, who because of their determination to succeed were able to mix on fairly equal terms with fashionable society. Many of these women had been paupers, as poor as Rose was in the 1930s when she and I were reading these books to each other. The women the Queen's son liked, and who had been so poor, were mostly girls with pretty faces who began by hiring lodgings for themselves in places such as Pimlico, Fitzroy Square, Portman Street, Howard Street, Winchester Street, Sutherland Street, Gloucester Street, and other respectable localities. They paid two or three sovereigns a week for a suite of apartments, furnishing the rooms at their own expense, and they kept a servant to do the cooking and washing. Some of the girls spent as much as five hundred pounds on their apartment. The equivalent today would be several thousand pounds. They ordered costly furniture, pictures, mirrors, ormolu clocks, tapestry carpets — and there were many other items of luxury to be found in their apartments.

A favourite place for meeting was the Cremorne Gardens in Chelsea. Also the Goodwood race meeting. At the races these girls were often accompanied by the young nobility. You could see there one young woman,

16

sitting toying with her fan, who five years before had been a working girl, wretchedly paid, eking out an existence in an Oxford Street shop at seven shillings a week. Now the diamonds on her fingers alone would purchase a comfortable villa. She wore, too, an exquisite pearl necklace given to her by the Queen's son which had cost all of five thousand pounds. He was very kind in this way, in helping girls who had been paupers. Now, every day, this young woman rode in Rotten Row almost touching the Princess of Wales as they passed close to each other. She was also to be seen at other fashionable resorts: the opera, the Chiswick Flower Show, and, in the company of the noblest ladies in the land, at Kensington Gardens. She had a sumptuous villa in St. John's Wood, while in her stables were fifteen blood animals for the saddle or for driving, gifts from her many aristocratic admirers. She knew stable talk and betting ring slang and the jargon of the hunt. One young lord, following the charitable example of the Queen's son, settled on her an annuity of two thousand pounds. She was a brilliant horsewoman and went to meetings in a shire when the hounds were assembled. Once in the Bois, magnificently dressed and mounted, she met the Empress Eugénie, who was also out riding. She bowed to the Empress, who, thinking this acknowledgement was from a lady of rank, bowed graciously in return.

Of course, most of the people who were poor stayed that way. It was much worse being poor then than it is today. A lot of children ran around with dirty faces and in ragged clothes. They begged for coppers and searched dustbins for food. In some of the dustbins they found crusts which they could mix with oats to make good porridge. Often their faces were prematurely aged, and many of them turned to crime. At this time there was one law for the rich and one for the poor. There wasn't supposed to be a separate law, but that is how it worked. When a youth of eighteen, who was poor, went on trial at the Old Bailey for defrauding his employer of a hundred and fifty pounds, he was sentenced to twelve years' penal servitude. At the Mansion House a young man, whose father was the senior partner in one of the city's largest banking firms, was found guilty of defrauding his father of fifteen thousand pounds. When the time came for sentencing, the Lord Mayor, having consulted the defendant's counsel, decided that this young man had suffered enough and released him. Then the Lord Mayor dealt with a poor youth caught pickpocketing, and sentenced him to eighteen months' imprisonment for stealing fourteen shillings.

Not all poor children turned to crime. Many got up at five o'clock in the morning and went to Farringdon Market. There they bought watercress, split it into small bundles, and worked all day, often up to midnight, trying to sell these little bundles. If they were lucky, they could earn a few shillings a week.

In Soho Square and other places, small, dirty, rosy-cheeked children would play happily the whole day through; nevertheless, the Queen's capital city was one of the worst places in the world for vagrancy. It was vagrancy of the worst kind. About a hundred and fifty thousand men, women, and children out of a total London population of less than three and a half million lived in workhouses. As well as these there were about fifteen thousand casuals who roamed the streets and slept in the recesses of the Thames bridges or in old boat-houses and other such places, wherever they could find a rough shelter.

Haggard men and women, teenagers of eighteen and nineteen, pregnant girls, children ten years and under, with no more meaning to society than any bundle of rags kicked to one side, carried on their tired shoulders the burden of destitution. Born and bred in the gutters, there most of them stayed, and on any night you could see a child dressed in a tattered old calico gown bending over a small fire made from dried pieces of driftwood and toasting a large potato. Near her, on the stone steps of the bridge, an old wizened man would be lying asleep snoring, stirring uneasily as a gust of wind hit the arches. Then again you would find two women who had lost their jobs, the old one earning two and sevenpence halfpenny a week for making penny baskets to carry fish home, the younger woman getting eight shillings a week as a lace maker.

In and around Regent Street and Pall Mall and around the cafes, small, wary, half-naked children collected cigar ends from ash heaps and crusts of bread from dustbins which they put into little bags made from potato sacks. These children sold the cigar stumps, sometimes making tuppence a day. The healthiest of the paupers were the street acrobats. Exercise and fresh air made them this way, but many were injured and some died from their falls.

At night, in murky streets where gas lamps burned feebly, breakfast stalls served tuppeny worth of bread and butter and a bowl of tea to rough-looking fellows. In the same early hours, at Covent Garden market, servants and pages in their liveries, who were from some of the best known families among the London aristocracy, bargained for bouquets to go on their mistresses' tables. In Covent Garden the coffee was good and hot, the penny baked potatoes fresh and smoking from the oven. Young street boys, who ran an errand for a penny, would hold your horse, catch a flying hat, and steal a cabbage or potatoes from the stalls. You might see one of these boys, aged about fifteen, his hands in the pockets of his ragged trousers, negotiating a potato with the stall holder, and doing this with all the aplomb of a VIP negotiating a business deal. But the boy had slept rough in the market all night. His coat was ragged and soiled, his hair full of straws from the market gardener's basket used as a pillow. The market was full of beggars, with the young girls splitting their huge bundles of watercress into the little bundles. Many of these beggars were ragged children sent by their parents to cadge enough coppers for tuppence worth of gin. For the poor there was little difference between night and day. In dim back streets, in London's sprawling slums, children fought to survive. Many did not and died of starvation and disease. It was the law of the jungle, and the weakest of the Queen's subjects went to the wall.

But there were more important matters than getting rid of all this poverty and squalor at home, so at this time Britain sent the greatest number of missionaries abroad to convert the heathen.

Some of the missionaries went to Fiji, where the King of Fiji, Roko Tabaiwalu, ruled. Once he became king and had an immense concentration of power, he began slaughtering his subjects. He did this mostly for enjoyment, but sometimes for practical purposes. When visiting a distant land, before setting sail, he would send on warriors to slaughter a number of men there; this was because it was bad luck to lower the sail before killing some of the inhabitants; also, when it was time to return home, he could use some of the bodies as rollers to preserve the keel of the canoe at launching. When the canoe was in the water, the bodies were cooked and eaten. The king's favourite method of eating his subjects was the cattle-eating style of Abyssinia. In Abyssinia a living animal furnished meal after meal before its death. This was because meat tasted a lot better when cut from a living animal. Every few days the king gave orders for the killings; then the bodies were taken to Rewa and portioned out for food. On one occasion the king ordered the Nakelo tribes to present yams at Natogadravu. While the tribesmen were doing this, the king's warriors surrounded them, killing nearly two hundred people; afterwards they made a great feast when the bodies were cooked and eaten.

In 1817, on the island of Bau, there was born a prince, and the birth of the little prince gave much pleasure. As in England, the birth of a prince was an important occasion, and there were a lot of ceremonies which culminated in a series of feasts: the feast when the child was first washed in water brought in from the sea, the feast when the little prince first turned over by himself, the feast when he first crawled, and other feasts of a similar nature. Tended by the queens of Rewa and nourished in the king's house amidst the warmth of the swampy city, the child grew quickly, becoming strong and agile. Bau, with its mixed Tonga-Fiji population, was the best city to be in.

The prince, a Bau chief of the first importance, ranked with the gods, and he grew into manhood with his every wish gratified. If he wanted an airing, a man had to carry him on his shoulders; if he wanted to sleep, women fanned him and soothingly pressed his feet; if he was angry with his nurse, he could strike her; if he quarrelled with his playmate he could bite, strike, and maim with impunity. If a slave accidentally interrupted him, the prince could draw his bow and put an arrow through the intruder. When he was seven years old, his father, Tanoa, became king. Up to this time he had remained at Bau and had taken little interest in political life. He liked angling, swimming, gaming, eating, drinking, playing, and sleeping — all the things any rich, well-brought-up little boy would do. In fact, the prince did not enter political life until 1832, and he might not have done so then, but a revolution took place which he, with great strength and courage, put down. So he grew into manhood resolute, fearless, a great leader.

The white missionaries told the king and the prince it would be better if they stopped eating their own people and instead drank the blood of Christ; if they did this it would please the Great White Queen across the water. The prince replied that it was all very well saying that, but just as the Great White Queen had her customs and traditions, and attached great value to the practice of these in her own kingdom, so the Fijians had theirs, and since eating people had been traditional in Fiji from early times, he saw no reason to discontinue. It was easy for the missionaries to criticise, but white men could get all the beef they wanted from animals.

One day the Superintendent of the Wesleyan Missions called to see the king. It had not been an easy journey. There was a strong wind, the tide was out, and a lot of rain made it unpleasant wading through the mud, so that he and his crew had great difficulty getting to the canoe. Also, he was nearly boiled by the vertical rays of the sun. The island of Bau was scarcely a mile in length and, with the exception of the summit which was used as a deposit for all dirt and refuse, the island was covered in irregular streets. Most of the houses were modest and not always clean, but they gave privacy. The principal feature of Bau was the great temple which stood in an irregular square on a basement a few feet above ground level. Its roof was nearly three times higher than the walls, beautifully thatched and ornamented with coconut plaits, the long external ridgepole decorated with white cowrie shells. The building stood on a raised platform and was surrounded by a few trees and graceful foliage. Under one of the trees lay the large *lali*, the sacred drum beaten at festivals and sacrifices. Overshadowing this was the place where the bodies of victims were dedicated to the Kabou, the evil spirit. After the dedication, the bodies were handed over to those who had to cook them in preparation for the banquet. At this place the lower branches of the tree had been cut away to a height of about ten feet from the ground. This had been done to accommodate eighty or so corpses slain in battle and heaped on the spot ready for dedication and cooking.

The temple was interesting, particularly inside, where a cloth screen covered the sanctuary while on the ground lay a few neck pillows, also an elephant's tusk which had been presented by a trader many years before to King Tanoa. Because whales' teeth were greatly valued and used as an indeterminate currency, the elephant's tusk, with all its ivory content, was especially valuable. Many smaller temples, like chapels, similarly adorned, could be seen in different directions, all of which showed an organised system of religious worship.

Over towards the hill two blocks of stone shaped like two pillars were almost overgrown with grass. It had been intended to use these as a monument to the king's father. If they should be used in this way, then two human beings, at least, would be required as a sacrifice, it being traditional that in works of this nature, when the house of the ruling chief was being built, a man must be buried alive at the foot of each post. This was to ensure the stability of the monument or building. But in magnitude and grandeur the king's house surpassed anything the missionary had seen in these islands. It was a hundred and thirty feet long and forty-two feet wide, and in the centre were massive columns with strong, curious workmanship in every part.

The king received the white missionary graciously, clapping his hands, which is the highest mark of respect, then beckoned to the missionary to sit beside him. After he had sat down, the missionary spoke about Christianity and his wish that this should be taught in Bau. The missionary's words seemed to appeal to the king, who listened courteously, and the missionary, pleased with such a sympathetic hearing, and in a happy and hopeful frame of mind, took his leave of the king and went on to see the king's son.

The missionary found the prince seated in an attitude of respect, waiting to receive him. As the missionary entered, the prince rose, unfolding from his waist a train of white native cloth some ten yards long. He invited the missionary to sit in a chair near him. The missionary could not help but admire the appearance of the prince, the most powerful and energetic of any in the Pacific. He was large, almost gigantic in size, his limbs were beautifully proportioned, and his countenance, with far less of the Negro cast than among the lower orders, was agreeable and intelligent. His immense head of hair, smoke-dried and tinged brown, was covered with gauze, giving him the appearance of an Eastern sultan. His magnificent chest was bare, showing the natural colour of his skin, and his simple dress was in contrast to the wealth that surrounded him. He looked every inch a king.

Not far from the prince sat his favourite wife, a stout, good-looking woman. With her was a boy of eight or nine. At a respectful distance a crowd of crouching courtiers surrounded the prince. This crouching posture had to be adopted not only when sitting but when moving about in the royal presence.

Stories about the prince's courage and daring were legendary, and the missionary knew that, best of all, the prince loved war. He made war whenever he found an opportunity and whether or not there was any particular reason for the fighting. It was because of his love for war that the prince hardly ever bought clothing or stores from merchant vessels; instead he ordered cannon, muskets, balls, powder, and lead. He kept a large quantity of ammunition, sometimes having in stock a thousand kegs of powder and five thousand muskets.

One morning, accompanied by a carefully chosen body of armed Bauans, the prince arrived at a slumbering town. At cockcrow he gave the signal for attack, and there followed a terrible slaughter. Men awoke only to die. The prince brought back captive women and children, some for slavery, some for target practice, some to be eaten. On another occasion the Moturiki tribe killed nine Kavula people. The Kavulas appealed to the prince for payment. He, accompanied by his warriors, went to Moturiki, where he ordered different towns to come before him and pile yams. Surrounded by the Viwa chiefs and some of their attendants, he sat down to receive the tributes of the assembled towns. A procession of young men from the towns, each man bringing one or two yams to lay at the feet of the prince, passed in single file. As the procession was drawing to a close, the prince looked up; the warriors, seeing this prearranged signal, rushed on those passing at that moment, killing nineteen young men. The prince then ordered the yams to be taken on board while the Bauans dragged the bodies to the canoes. The two vessels, with yams and freshly slaughtered meat, left in triumph for Bau. On their way back they came on a single canoe. This they immediately attacked, killing the nine people in it, and so observed an ancient Fijian custom of killing anyone crossing their path during a war excursion.

On another occasion the captain of a British warship had offered to take the prince out to sea; so, accompanied by missionaries, the prince embarked in his boat for Ovalau. There was very little wind, and they were rowed for twenty miles up to the ship at Levuka. It had not been a comfortable journey because the boat was full of spears, clubs, pottery, and other objects, but the prince looked very dignified seated in the stern sheets, his head decorated with a new turban of smoke-coloured gauze beneath which projected a long tortoiseshell pin resembling a knitting needle. He used the pin for scratching his head as no fingernail would be long enough to reach through the thick, curly hair.

On board ship the prince and the missionaries went to their quarters to watch target practice. The target, a hammock with the figure of a man painted on it, was fastened to a conspicuous rock on the beach at a distance of about eight hundred yards from the ship. When the prince saw the smallness of the target, he expressed incredulity at the possibility of striking such a mark. The senior missionary handed him a spyglass, and the prince, standing on the bowsprit out of the way of the smoke, put the spyglass to his eye. The firing began, and the second shot struck the figure on the head. After this, scarcely a shot missed its mark, and a very few rounds were sufficient to knock the target to pieces; the target was then replaced by two more in quick succession. Even the short time needed for the replacement proved too much for the prince, and in a state of great excitement he begged the captain to wait. Pointing out first a man on the beach and then a canoe with several people on board, the prince remarked that these were much better targets than the inanimate figure painted on the hammock. Much to his surprise, the captain refused to use these people as targets; so the prince made another request that the captain should try more shots in the direction of his enemies in Lavoni. This, he said, would prove that they were in reach of him. Again the captain refused, so the prince contented himself with the firing as it was.

Sometimes, before killing people, the prince liked to torture them. During an engagement at Viwa two men were taken alive and sent to Kaba to be killed. On their arrival at Kaba, the prisoners were ordered to dig a hole in the earth so that an oven could be built. They were then sent to fetch firewood for the roasting of their own bodies. After this they were told to wash and were given a banana leaf, which they were ordered to make into a cup. Then a vein in each prisoner was opened and the banana leaf filled with blood. In the presence of the two men the Kaba people drank the blood. After this the prince ordered that the arms and legs of the prisoners should be cut off, cooked, and eaten. When the limbs were nicely roasted some of the cooked flesh was offered back to the prisoners, but they weren't hungry. When the prince and his warriors had eaten the arms and legs, the prince ordered fish-hooks to be fastened into the prisoners' tongues. The tongues were drawn out as far as possible, cut off, roasted, and eaten. As the two men were still alive, incisions were made in their sides and their bowels were taken out, which ended their sufferings. By this deed and many others like it, the prince covered himself in glory.

The prince welcomed the missionary with a few courteous words, then sat down again and waited for the missionary to speak. The missionary told the prince of lands he had visited and the object of the Wesleyan Mission. Then he added: "There is another matter, sir, which causes us and causes the Great White Queen deep distress." The prince waited politely for the missionary to explain, and the missionary continued: "I have been informed that after a war, captured women and children are brought back to Bau to be eaten, and that some of the children are first fastened to trees so that your own children can use them for target practice, killing them with bows and arrows and so learning to shoot straight and become warriors."

The prince said: "That is so. It is the custom of Fiji to train our children for war in this way."

The missionary replied: "It would be seen as a mark of friendship to the Great White Queen, as well as to ourselves, if you would prevent further killing of your people and so stop using them as food for banquets and other celebrations."

The prince, being a prince, and conscious of good breeding, thanked the missionary then explained again that it was all very well for white people to remonstrate when they had plenty of beef, but the people of Fiji had no beef except men.

After this the prince asked the missionary if he would like to stay and eat with him. The missionary accepted and was impressed by the cleanliness observed in serving the food. Boards, like small butcher's trays, on which the food was served, were spotlessly clean, each board covered with banana leaves. The food, rolled up in small balls, was also covered with green leaves. There were several different dishes, each in its own tray and each, when the food was eaten, removed by a little boy who crawled up to it and crawled back again. Then water was brought so that the prince and his guest could wash their hands and mouths. Nearby several chiefs were sitting in a crouching position. When the meal was over there was a general clapping of hands.

The missionary thanked the prince and urged him to think seriously about becoming a Christian. The prince answered: "If I am the first to become a Christian among my people I shall be the first in Heaven, shall I not?"

The missionary replied: "If you love God the most, and serve Him best, you may have a higher place in Heaven."

The prince paused for a moment, then said: "What will become of the bodies of those who have been eaten and of those who have been buried? Will they rise again from the dead?"

The missionary answered: "Your body, and the bodies of all whom you have eaten, and the bodies of all who are in the graves, will rise again at the day of judgment; and if you and they have not repented you will all be condemned and cast into hell-fire."

The prince remarked: "Ah well, it's a fine thing to have a fire in cold weather."

Then the missionary, before taking his leave, said: "There is one other Fijian custom which I would like to mention. It is the strangling of wives on the death of a chief. I would beg you, sir, to put a stop to this cruel practice."

The prince answered: "With us, the strangling of wives on the death of the chief is a sacred duty."

The missionary was silent for a moment, then said: "When the Lasaliau chief, Gavidi, was killed in the war with Verata, one of our missionaries, Mr Calvert, went to Bau hoping to prevent the strangling of Chief Gavidi's widows. Unfortunately, Mr Calvert was too late; when he arrived he saw, to his great sorrow, the bodies of three women whose lives had already been sacrificed so that they might accompany the spirit of the departed chief. I also understand, sir, that you personally assisted in the strangling of Chief Gavidi's mother. In fact, Mr Calvert found you fast asleep not long after you had pulled tight the death cord on the old lady."

The prince, whose manners, no matter what mood he might be in at these formal occasions, were always most polite, said good-humouredly: "What is wicked in wanting wives to accompany their husbands?" The missionary frowned, for he knew that the prince, always conscious of his royal inheritance and so a stickler for maintaining the traditional values of his country, and who regarded ancient Fijian customs as sacrosanct, exerted a powerful influence on friends and foe alike.

When we finished reading about the Great White Queen and about Fiji, I returned both books to Mr Mackintosh. Rose thought it really great that we had done so much for Fiji in sending missionaries to stop them eating people, even if there was all this poverty in England with children dying from starvation and that sort of thing. But as much as anything, she enjoyed reading about the lady who had risen from being a pauper to mixing on equal terms with nobility.

Rose said she couldn't imagine anything more exciting than being able to ride in Rotten Row so near to the Princess of Wales and being acknowledged by the Empress Eugénie. It seemed, both to Rose and to me, really great. Although she didn't talk about it all that much, I know she had this feeling of admiration for people who bettered themselves, especially if they had been very poor and became very rich. I felt the same way, which is why, as I have mentioned, I admired Rose's brother Teddy. I mean no one could have been poorer than any of Rose's family. They were so poor that even other poor people in the nearby council estate looked down on them. As a matter of fact, everyone looked down on the people who lived in the Green Lane hovels.

The hovels in Green Lane, like those houses in Bau that we had just been reading about, had this one advantage, which was privacy. Although built of brick, they were, in structure, not unlike the detached prefabs put up in the Second World War and, set back from the road as they were, there was quite a lot of space between them. I suppose Green Lane was more like a road than a lane, although at this time, in the 1930s, it was pretty rough, full of pot-holes, and not made up. Some of the pot-holes were quite large, and when it rained they filled with water, and sometimes cars that went too fast got stuck in them. Cars went up and down quite frequently. At one end Green Lane made a T-junction with the main Staines road; at the other end it led into Burgoyne Road, where at number thirteen was our house. Green Lane was a dreary place in winter and uninspiring in summer; at least that is how it used to be when Rose and I, in those summer months, lay in the field beside the sandpits and read to each other.

It was less than a month after we read Mr Mackintosh's two books that Rose's little brother Bobby got drowned in the sandpits. It upset Rose, of course, but it upset Teddy more. At the funeral he broke down and cried. Rose told me about it. She said that when Teddy saw the small coffin lowered into the ground, he collapsed and had to be helped away from the grave.

This happened just before Bobby's ninth birthday, and I remember feeling extra sad when Rose told me that, for a birthday present, Teddy had bought Bobby a beautiful new bike. It also seemed funny to me, at the time, that a grown man should behave in this way. I had this same strange feeling about a man breaking down when, some years later, in fact it was Christmas 1943 in the wardroom of HMS *Manatee*, I saw this RNVR lieutenant do what Teddy did, start to cry. He was a big man, in his mid-forties, grey-haired, nice-looking, and he broke down suddenly and for no apparent reason. Two other officers got hold of him, one on either side to support his arms, just as the two prison officers later supported Forsyth for that last little walk, and the officer was led away. I stood, clasping my gin and tonic, watching him go, his head bent, his shoulders heaving, and I couldn't understand it any more than I understood why Teddy, although he felt so deeply the loss of his little brother, being grown up couldn't control his grief. I used to think then that tragedies were only really almost unbearable when they happened to rich people. This was because poverty and suffering seemed to go together; so Bobby drowning, and to a certain extent our paper boy being run over, which occurred the same week Bobby was drowned, although it was terrible that these accidents should have happened, had beneath the distress and feeling of loss an inevitability somehow rooted in class. I felt this way with the paper boy, but felt it even more so with Bobby.

Although the paper boy, too, was very poor, everyone liked him. He was quiet, well-mannered, clever at school, and working for a university scholarship. He was just thirteen when he was killed. I saw the accident, which was where our road joined Cavendish Road. The paper boy was wheeling his bike towards the corner when a Cantrell & Cochrane lorry, backing round, ran over him, crushing his chest. He just said: "Oh, Oh, Oh," and lay on his back, quite still, gazing up at the blue sky. He had this funny glazed look in his eyes which I had seen once before in a dog that had been run over. As the dog lay dying I saw the brightness fade from its eyes and then this glazed look, a kind of nothingness look, the same look which the paper boy had. When I saw the dog die, it wasn't very nice and gave me an eerie feeling. I didn't get this feeling with the paper boy because I didn't realize he was dead until the doctor came twenty minutes later, put his stethoscope onto the paper boy's chest, shook his head, and went away. After this a blanket was pulled over the paper boy, covering his face.

A week later, in our local paper, there was a photograph of the funeral. For a paper boy it was quite an impressive funeral, with his scout troop lining part of the route. A lot of people went to the funeral, and there were lots of wreaths and flowers. The vicar said that although it might seem a waste of a life when there was so much promise, the Lord sometimes, for reasons He knew best, called people back to Him. I could see what the vicar was getting at, although, being at the time eleven and a half, I did wonder if it was because God had a paper round that needed doing; but whatever it was everyone was sad about the paper boy and nothing was said about Bobby. This was probably because Bobby was not only an urchin but was always in trouble. He played truant and swore and threw stones at animals, tied cats' tails together, and generally made a nuisance of himself in the way urchins do.

Mention was made in the paper of Bobby getting drowned, but there was no photograph and no report of the funeral. For all I know it could have been a relief to some of the people that he was no longer around.

It upset Rose losing her little brother. At first she cried a lot. She loved Bobby and didn't look on him as an urchin. Then she got to talking more about her older brother, as if Teddy's success might, in some way, compensate for the awfulness of the tragedy. Neither Rose nor I knew, at this time, how Teddy made his money, but in any case we didn't give it much thought. We only knew that he was rich, nice to everyone, and that he visited his parents often. I thought it very good of him to visit his parents as often as he did; they weren't a very prepossessing couple, nor was Rose's old wizened gran who lived with them. For this reason I can't remember ever going to Rose's house. From the first time I met Rose when I went to Sunbury Council School we always met out.

I used to see her family quite often when I was waiting for her or walking past the house. Her father was a small, weedy man with hunched shoulders, nearly always dressed in an open-neck, collarless flannel shirt with his braces hanging down over brown corduroy trousers that were tied just below the knees, the way workmen wore them in those days. Not that I had ever seen him work. Rose said he sat around most of the time and rolled his own cigarettes, and she said he was very knowledgeable about horses. Rose's mother was a large woman, large and fat with untidy grey hair, a coarse skin, and small fleshy lumps on her chin and neck. She shuffled rather than walked, and although she took no interest in her own appearance, she was up at four every morning scrubbing, polishing. She kept her place spotless. Rose's gran, too, played her part in this obsessive need for cleanliness, for in the summer months, sitting outside with one or other of the younger children standing meekly in front of her, the old woman was often to be seen searching a child's hair for lice. I had once seen Rose having her hair searched in this way. It was when we first came to this part of Sunbury.

Sometimes, when I was waiting for Rose in Green Lane, I would meet Teddy. He always stopped and spoke and wasn't the least bit condescending; in fact, he had this gift of making you feel you were the only person who mattered and that meeting you gave him genuine pleasure. And yet it wasn't that he had a particularly impressive appearance; he was short, stocky, powerfully built, with blue eyes, thick lips, and a mass of brown, curly hair brushed back. He had a thin moustache and wore expensive rings: a gold ring, a ruby ring, and a ring with a large flashing diamond. But in spite of Teddy's apparent good nature, his open, breezy manner, and the way he always seemed to be affable, he wasn't a person to cross swords with. He had this terrible temper. How I got to know about it was because once, with his bare hands, he killed a dog.

It was quite a strong dog, a cross between an Airedale and a retriever or something like that. It was when Teddy was living at home, and the dog, a stray, woke everyone up with its yowling and barking. Teddy lost all control of himself, threw a coat over his vest and underpants, went out, caught the dog, half strangled it, then picked it up by its hind legs and smashed its head against a tree. After this he walked across to the sandpits which were two fields away and threw the animal into the water. Some time later Rose told me that Teddy was sorry he'd done this. It was just that something seemed to snap and he had this terrible temper, which he mostly managed to control.

After the war, when I was working for our family business, I met with a similar situation when Bert from Covent Garden lost control of himself and got two years for hitting a policeman. Bert was different from Teddy in that he didn't have Teddy's terrible temper and was, on the whole, fairly placid. I suppose it is that in each one of us there is this breaking point, for although Teddy killed the dog, he wasn't unkind to animals, not in the way that Bobby was unkind when he pulled the wings off butterflies, put lighted matches under bees, tied the tails of cats together, and buried a kitten alive. So it made more sense to think of it as the dog's fault for barking late at night, which in a way was what happened to Bert when a young couple, rowing in the early hours, woke most of the street.

But whatever Teddy did I could never think of him as cruel when he always showed such kindness to Rose and me. Twice he gave me money, the first time sixpence and the second time a shilling, a lot for a small boy in those days. It gave me this really warm feeling towards him, not only because he'd been generous but for some reason I can't explain. Twice, too, he took Rose and me out for rides. Once in his Chrysler and then in an 8-105 Auburn which Teddy wanted to try out. He was quite excited about it and took a lot of trouble explaining that, being a simply constructed straight-eight, it was a fast car that did most of its work in third or top. He showed us the built-in starter and switch mechanism and demonstrated the three forward speeds and how the gears were changed by the central lever. It had a top speed of nearly eighty miles an hour. The engine ran smoothly and quietly, there was good suspension, and the saloon held the road properly. Rose and I found it very comfortable. When we left Green Lane we hadn't even noticed the pot-holes.

The first time Teddy took us out, which was in the Chrysler, we drove to lower Sunbury. We went over the railway bridge where I had seen the dying dog, down Green Street, and at the bottom turned right into Thames Street. The evening sun was on the river as we passed Wilson's boatyard. On the other side of the road was the Lord's house. It was very large, the size of a country mansion, but because this part of Sunbury was built up it stood in less than half an acre of land. The house was enclosed on three sides by a high wall, not unlike the prison wall at Wandsworth. The Lord's house, together with the few other large houses in the area, has long since been pulled down and replaced by housing estates and a police training college. Where one family lived, fifty or more families have their homes.

You couldn't see much of the Lord's house because of the high wall, but one side of the house was protected simply by a deep basement passage and tall railings with oval spikes, so that if you looked down through the railings, down to where there was a large scullery window, you could see, standing behind a huge old-fashioned sink, four or five servant girls, steam rising up into their faces as they sweated away, scrubbing at greasy pots and pans. They stood in a row, uniformly dressed, the only relief to their drab black dresses the little white frilly caps perched on their heads. Once, as they stood slaving away, their serious faces physically young, mentally old, I saw one smile. She was Rose's age, about fourteen or fifteen, and she caught my eye as I walked by, so I smiled and she smiled and I saw two dimples appear in her cheeks, rosy cheeks in a peaches-and-cream complexion, an asset that even the Lord's lady might have envied. And the smile itself, that wistful fleeting expression was, for me, a glimpse into a private world and has remained with me, a camera shot in the mind, a recorded moment, still pristine clear as if the image has shrugged off the half thousand million moments that must have brushed its surface since.

And when I think about this I think, too, of all the great banquets the Lord gave — the delicious food, exquisite china, crested silver, superb wine in priceless cut glass, the men dressed formally in white ties and tails, the ladies in expensive evening dresses, some wearing glittering diamond tiaras. Rose told me that all the servant girls in the service of the Lord were employed full time, and she thought they were paid about six shillings a week.

Teddy was quite keen on large houses and the people who lived in them. He knew a lot about famous people and spoke about them in an intimate way as if he was on, or almost on, equal terms with them. A week after Teddy had been to the Derby, where the Aga Khan's horse won, he told Rose and me how he had stood close to members of the Royal Family. Rose said excitedly: "How close? As close as we are to you?"

Teddy nodded in a way which didn't say yes and didn't say no, but left us with the feeling that he had been very close indeed, and this feeling was confirmed when he went on to say how lovely Queen Mary looked in a rose-beige cloth coat with fox collar and cuffs and wearing a toque of the same colour with pink, mauve, and blue pansies on the brim; Princess Mary, too, in a stunning apple-green coat frock with a sable stole and kemp straw hat and wearing a diamond racehorse brooch; the King in a black frock coat and with a black silk hat. Also there were the Prince of Wales and the Duke of Gloucester and the Aga Khan with his son Prince Ali Khan. Teddy was very good at giving these descriptions and he said it had been a lovely day for the race, pleasantly warm and not too hot, with a slight heat haze over the course. The way he described it gave me this wonderful exhilarated feeling in picturing a world of colour, beauty, and splendour so far removed from the squalor, poverty, and ugliness seen in and around the suburban streets where Rose and I lived.

Perhaps it was because I was so young, still a schoolboy, that I was impressed by Teddy's grand talk. I certainly did not suspect him of the slightest exaggeration, and even if I had done so, any lingering mistrust would have been dispelled when, on the afternoon of 3 July 1933, the Prince of Wales opened Hampton Court Bridge.

The prince was due to open the bridge at five-thirty in the afternoon. It was a day of sunshine and crowds. Fifty thousand people stood on the Middlesex and Surrey sides of the new bridge, while hundreds of eager schoolchildren dressed in smart school uniforms lined the roads leading to the bridge. All of them were from local schools, including Hampton Grammar, where I was a pupil. We had been marched there earlier in the afternoon. I stood next to Andy Francis. Andy couldn't keep still. He was looking from right to left, and fidgeting; then he said: "I've never seen a real prince before." I told him that it would be the first time I had seen one, but I think for Andy it was also the last time because nine years later, returning from a bombing mission over Germany with a bullet lodged in the base of his spine, he was pulled half paralysed from the cockpit to die a hero's death. I don't know if he was decorated posthumously for this, but I expect he got something.

Before coming to open our bridge, the prince opened two others, one at Chiswick and one at Twickenham. At Twickenham a workman had been presented to the prince, but all the important people were waiting at our bridge in a specially constructed pavilion where there was this beautiful view over one of the loveliest stretches of water. The pavilion not only gave the prince this outlook over the river, but also a clear view of the red-brown roofs and chimneys of Hampton Court Palace. To the left of the pavilion the British Legion, with standards, had mounted a guard of honour, and at five-thirty exactly the prince arrived. As he stepped from his car, wearing a light grey lounge suit with a dark red carnation in his button-hole, and wearing a straw boater, he was greeted by loud and prolonged cheers.

The prince inspected the guard of honour, then all the distinguished people were presented to him, after which the clerk of the committee read the address of welcome, saying that the royal visit was regarded by them all as recognition of the high value attached to these great schemes of public improvement. Amplifiers carried the address to the many thousands of people crowded in at both ends of the bridge. In his reply the prince said he was glad to have come. He said the bridge would give easier access to the beautiful heritage of the Thames side, and he was glad to think the construction of these bridges and the formation of the approach roads had given welcome employment to many fellow citizens. He hoped the building trade would benefit by the demolition and widening of existing streets. All these things, the prince said, added to his gratification at being here this afternoon. However, I think the prince must have got fed up after this, because when I had my only glimpse of him, which was when he was leaving, a little lonely figure sitting in the back of his chauffeur-driven car, he looked tired and bored.

After the prince had left, the police cleared a way for distinguished guests leaving the pavilion. I stood quietly watching as some of them walked over the bridge. I saw Sir Charles Pinkham, the chairman of the joint committee, and Sir Reginald Blaker, the MP, and then I saw this tall, strikingly beautiful lady whose photograph had been in our local paper from time to time. I knew she had a titled husband but I couldn't immediately think of her name. Her husband had done a lot for youth clubs and she had presented trophies, judged at competitions, that sort of thing.

All these important people looked impressive, the men in smart summer suits, the ladies in elegant dresses, a dignified blend of gaiety and formality suitable for such a marvellous royal occasion. Then I saw Teddy. He was walking on the other side of the tall lady, chatting and joking in a way that is only possible between people who are on intimate terms.

Teddy looked elegant, too, in a grey chalk-stripe suit with a pink rosebud in his buttonhole, and with a straw hat not unlike the one the prince wore. And not only was Teddy talking to this tall lady in this very chummy way, but she was talking back to him as if there had never been a time when they weren't the closest of friends.

I am glad now that when I bumped into Rose on the morning of Forsyth's execution I didn't ask after Teddy, because it wasn't until some years later, when I had gone to see Patrick, that I discovered how Teddy had become rich and influential. When I found out about this, Teddy was still inside.

My first meeting with Patrick was when he came to Oxford just after the war. He had come to see a friend with whom he had started a literary magazine. It sold reasonably well here and in Europe, but not enough to cover costs. It lasted eighteen months.

Then in 1960 Patrick disappeared. He was away for two years in Thailand, but no one knew he'd been there until he came back, because he didn't tell anyone he was going. He just threw everything up, being theatre and film critic for two national newspapers, writing plays and books, with two of his plays having been performed, and one book, a beautifully illustrated history of ballet, published. He left without even a goodbye and that was that. I suppose he ought to have been reported missing, but he'd always been a bit odd the way he behaved — moody, unpredictable, eccentric — so that when he threw up these really good jobs on national newspapers, which is not something you'd expect anyone to do lightly, no one took any notice; and when he returned with his head shaved and all calm and philosophical, people just said: "Hullo Patrick, good to see you," as if he'd never left Fleet Street. But more extraordinary than what he did, leaving so suddenly without one goodbye, was the change in his personality when he returned. He was quiet, relaxed, controlled, not the least bit restless, and certainly not touchy and moody like he used to be. Before he went he was always, literally, banging his head against the wall and threatening to commit suicide.

In Thailand Patrick had gone to live with his Teacher, a Buddhist monk whom he had first met at a smart temple in Bangkok. Not long after Patrick arrived, the Teacher, a small, thin man with a straggly moustache who came from a wealthy Chinese family, renounced all worldly possessions and went to live in the jungle, in a little temple that had one ugly statue of Buddha and where few people came — a horrible place, Patrick said. This temple, which was no more than a hut, stood near a river that had been condemned by the irrigation authorities, and at dusk mosquitoes came out and bit Patrick. He had never been so miserable in his life. The place was poor and was miles away from anywhere, which was why they had no visitors to speak of. Patrick thought it remarkable that the Teacher, having come from this wealthy upper-class family and having held an important position in the smart Bangkok temple where he taught undergraduates, should have retreated to such a terrible place in the jungle where it was hot, steamy, and depressing. Added to all this, the Teacher suffered badly from leprosy, and although his family had tried to persuade him to go back, the Teacher said that what mattered to him most was his independence.

Although Patrick respected the Teacher whose words were very important to him, Patrick loathed the place, and being bitten by mosquitoes got him down, until in the end the Teacher said that Patrick must make up his mind whether to stay or leave. Patrick asked for time to think things over. Then some monks brought a civilian to stay the night. This civilian, like the Teacher, had leprosy but it was a different type of leprosy. The Teacher's leprosy was where scales from the skin drop off the body, while the civilian had the dreaded lion leprosy, where the fingers and hands drop off and the face changes.

When he saw the civilian, Patrick had this overpowering experience, seeing in the lion leprosy an image of death. And he remembered as a child, when he was five or six, being scared of death, being frightened of the moon, knowing that it had been there long before he was born and would still be there after he was dead. Frightened, too, of the ego being dead and then realising, after he recalled all this, that the Teacher, when telling him to make up his mind, was actually saying: "You stay here and be dead to the world," which was what Jesus said, too, because becoming totally independent ends up like this, like this Teacher in this dreadful temple in the steamy jungle where you no longer value other people's advice and you have no preference. Patrick knew that listening to other people's advice is often like listening to parrots in a zoo, but he said he couldn't go on living in the jungle, becoming totally independent; he wasn't ready for it. So he returned to Bangkok and started discussing timetables, the weather, skin rashes, constipation, ordinary worldly things, and in 1962 came back to England. For six months he reviewed novels for a film company; then he gave up reviewing and began teaching simple English to mentally handicapped children. At the same time he made educational films for television and wrote, and had published, a reading book for dyslexic children. He also became a prison visitor, which was how he met up with Teddy.

In 1974 Patrick's Teacher died. This had a profound effect on Patrick, and he thought again about the meaning of total independence, which is a search for tranquillity and peace of mind. In this he was helped by notes he'd made in cheap exercise books from the sayings of his Teacher, and of all these sayings the one he remembered most was that independence, which means not relying on other people, can never be properly understood.

A BOOK WITHIN A BOOK — I

SAILING BY

Secret Place

A search, an adventure, no cover-up, no looking over one's shoulder at other people, no thinking about what other people may think. An analysis of oneself, one's motives, one's fears. A search for the truth. A search for freedom, for order and purpose. A book of notes, of notes from notes, of interviews, of memories, too. A book of books, of wisdom learnt from those who point the way. A book of thanks for those whose views on background, breeding, class, and chance judged matters old and new. A book of dreams, of kings and queens, a book of yesterday. I asked them why, why we are here, they tried but could not say. They went away, the wise, the good. I understood. They tried but did not know.

Dedication

To those who helped, who gave their views, the psychiatrists, psychologists, priests, doctors, philosophers, princes, paupers, social workers, teachers, those who knew Forsyth and those who knew of him — kind sympathetic people who, when I explained what I was trying to do, must have known, as I now know, that it is difficult enough exploring the mind of your nearest and dearest, let alone trying to open up the innermost thoughts and feelings of a dead boy.

Indolence

Sitting dreaming, thinking of Oxford days, I picked up my 1949 diary and indulgently, soporifically, read, at random, these entries:

Wednesday February 16, Oxford

It has been glorious spring weather today, and all the crocuses are out, so are the snowdrops in Wadham, and the daffodils are nearly out. The trees are in bud and the birds preparing to nest.

Tuesday February 22, Oxford

This evening Angus Ogilvy took me to the Grid Iron dinner. Everyone was very drunk and became rowdy. My port was knocked over and went onto my trousers; Andrew Younger broke a picture, climbed under the table, and upset more wine and coffee. Afterwards I tried to drive off in the president's car, but he caught me. Then a lot of us went to Wadham. Robin Warrender was chased by Arthur, the porter, for pulling up wallflowers; Tony Berry tried to get everyone to join the Labour Club, and someone wrecked Norman Mim's room. Altogether it was very rowdy.

Wednesday February 23, Oxford

This morning I awoke, after a dreadful night, with a headache and a hangover. I went to the Ritz this afternoon and saw The Guinea Pig, a picture of a working-class boy who gets a scholarship to a public school.

Friday February 25, Oxford

I took Mr Bliss (my tutor) to lunch at the Carlton and we talked about my first novel. He said it was very bad, but the one merit I had was that I could tell a story. Mr Bamborough (my literature tutor) said later that to be able to tell a story and to acquire a good style do not necessarily go together.

Saturday February 26, Oxford

I went to Elsfield and had lunch with Lady Tweedsmuir. It was very pleasant and most enjoyable. The ride there was delightful along the by-pass and up the little road to Elsfield.

Tuesday March 1, Oxford

This evening Angus Ogilvy, Julian Earl, David and Brian Blacker, Peter Hemphill and Ian Maxwell-Scott came into Bobby's room. Everyone was very merry. I went to the B.R. near the station for supper this evening. One man in the B.R. drank his tea from a plate, which I thought a good setting for a book — or part of a book.

Thursday March 3, Oxford

The papers are headlining a gruesome murderer who has just been caught, by the name of Haigh.

Saturday March 5, Oxford

I went to Eton by bus and an old man sat next to me who started to chatter away. At the end of the journey I discovered that he was Sir Percy Marsh, who was at Wadham 1900-1905. I saw Ivan Terestenko, Mark Dent-Brocklehurst, and Timothy Boyd Maunsell. Ivan is now in the library in his house (Wickhams), and he and I looked at the canes with which they beat boys. Eton is a wonderful school.

Sunday March 6, Oxford

At the chaplaincy this morning the Rev. J.J. Bevan spoke of heaven as a conception that cannot be described. One might as well attempt to describe a beautiful sunset to a man who had been blind all his life.

Thursday March 24, Oxford

It has been a beautiful day, warm and sunny. Wadham is full of coloured flowers and blossoms.

Friday April 1, Oxford

I listened to Mr Churchill speaking from Boston. He certainly has a marvellous delivery.

Friday April 8, Oxford

Bobby arrived from Paris at 1:00am and climbed into college through the window of my room.

Saturday April 9, Oxford

I went to a reception party for the return of the Warden, who has been six months in America. Dr Bowra had lunched with Mr Churchill on the passage back and told us some very amusing stories.

Thursday April 14, Oxford

Today I am thirty years of age.

Saturday April 16, Oxford

It has been very hot today and the blossoms are out on the trees. There is one tree in the back quad of Wadham that is covered with mayflowers. This evening at Black Friars the Friars were wearing their white habits.

Wednesday April 20, Oxford

Angus Ogilvy came in to see me this evening. I was very interested to hear the views of Angus on society. He felt that in spite of all its superficial glamour and attractions it was really worthless, and that there were more important matters in life.

Monday May 2, Oxford

Edward Boyle came round to Bobby's room where there were already

Peter Hemphill, Richard and Nicholas Pemberton. We discussed our usual topics with him, life, death, and religion.

Sunday May 8, Oxford

I went to the chaplaincy this morning and heard a conference given by Archbishop Matthew, the brother of Father Gervase. Father Gervase introduced me to him afterwards, but the archbishop behaved rather oddly and didn't speak to me at all — I wondered afterwards if it was because I did not kiss his ring.

Friday May 13, Oxford

Along the Banbury and Woodstock roads the colourful blossom of May trees is dying, but instead the fresh green leaves look delightful, vigorous and cool.

Sunday May 15, Oxford

The Warden introduced me to Evelyn Waugh and Christopher Hollis, MP.

Friday May 20, Himbledon Manor, Droitwich

Bobby and I arrived here this evening. Patricia and Meriel Hill Richard's sisters, were here, and his mother, Lady Sandys, came in later. There is an Admiral Sir Richard Hill staying here, a brother of Lord Sandys; we have been swopping naval yarns.

Saturday May 21, Himbledon Manor, Droitwich

We went over to Ombersley Court, another home of the Sandys. Lord and Lady Beauchamp joined us for lunch. Lady Beauchamp is Danish and very amusing. Lady Sandys went away in the afternoon to a Guide meeting. The weather is lovely — warm and sunny — and the country around here is very picturesque, with tracts of woodland around the villages.

Tuesday May 24, Oxford

I was shown a letter written in 1927 by a graduate of Oxford who had gone to Manchester. The graduate was complaining of the hard, business-like way in which Manchester worked compared to the glorious and noble traditions of Oxford. In 1927 I was at Fulwell Council School.

Saturday May 28, Oxford

Angus Ogilvy told me that he was offered the job of ADC to the Duke of Gloucester if he (Angus) had remained in the Guards.

Wednesday June 1, Oxford

This evening I had drinks with Julian Earl, John Baring, and Brian Blacker in Julian's room in Trinity. John said that only the aristocracy should be educated, as if the lower classes were educated they only became dissatisfied. I met Angus Ogilvy later and he agreed with this.

Saturday June 4, Oxford

Timothy Gilmour-White drove me to Eton for the Fourth. In the afternoon the weather cleared and it became a warm and soothing June day. I wandered over the playing fields and watched the fashionable parents and their pretty children in black tails and top hats. I had tea with Timothy Boyd Maunsell in his room.

Sunday June 12, Oxford

I listened to the Liberals speaking at an open-air meeting in St. Giles, but they were rather dull. Then the Communists were having a meeting. They were much more fun and I stayed until 9:00pm listening to them.

Thursday June 16, Oxford

I met Angus Ogilvy in the Broad, and we sat on the wall outside the New Bodleian and watched old Ada selling bananas from her barrow. It was very sunny and warm.

Monday June 20, Oxford

It was the seven hundredth anniversary of University College and the Prime Minister (Mr Attlee) came. I spoke to him.

Wednesday June 22, Oxford

I saw Sir Stafford Cripps among those who were being given honorary degrees.

Thursday June 30, Rhinefield, Brockenhurst

I arrived at Brockenhurst this afternoon and was met by Mrs Walker-Munro in the Rolls. In the car was Tom Walker-Munro with his Nanny. So many of the family are here. It is a pity that such places as Rhinefield are becoming a thing of the past, and yet I can never stay here without thinking of the very poor and uneducated and how unfair life is.

Friday July 1, Rhinefield, Brockenhurst

Another quiet and restful day here, with lovely warm weather and the forest looking quite beautiful around the house. This evening I took Molly Walker-Munro to the Bachelor's Ball in the village and we joined Mrs Pleydle-Bouverie's party; she is Edward Montagu's mother, and Edward and his sister Caroline were there as well.

Saturday July 2, Cold Hayes, Liss

I arrived here from Brockenhurst. Colonel and Lady Doris Blacker were very amusing. Julian Earl was here: he, David, Brian, myself, and three girls all went to the Emmetts' dance at Amberley Castle.

Sunday July 3, Barnes, London SW13

I got up, breakfasted, and then talked to Colonel Blacker for the rest of the morning. Lord Selborne came to lunch and he told me about his grandfather, the great Lord Salisbury. Captain Kennedy, who is also staying here, is writing Lord Salisbury's biography. After lunch Lady Doris took Lord Selborne and me over the farm, and although it was hot and I was rather tired, I enjoyed it very much. I arrived back in Barnes in the evening and met on the station a man who had been at Hampton Grammar School with me. He was booking office clerk.

Friday July 29, Oxford

The English results came out and I have failed.

Tuesday August 2, Goring-by-Sea

Mr Taylor and I went on the shore this morning. The tide was out and we walked along on the soft sandy mud, paddling through pools that were thick with dank brown seaweed. I could smell the fresh salt of the sea air; a stiff breeze blew and ruffled my hair. Bramwell Gates rang me this morning. He is chairman of Cow & Gate, and I have to see him on Thursday. He said he was very sorry about my degree.

Sunday August 7, Hunts Cross, Liverpool

I travelled here today and am staying for two months while I train with Dunlops in management and production.

Thursday August 11, Hunts Cross, Liverpool

Mr Symes gave me a talk on the managerial side. We discussed education in this country, which Symes said is the worst in the world. Haigh was executed yesterday morning. I wonder if he has met the people he murdered?

Sunday August 14, Hunts Cross, Liverpool

Last week R. (my room-mate) condemned the News of the World as being a filthy paper. This week he read it from cover to cover and remarked every five minutes what a terrible paper it was.

Saturday August 20, Hunts Cross, Liverpool

I walked down by Dunlops, over some fields, and to the river. It was beautiful there, quiet with no one about and the setting sun made a red path over the calm water.

Monday August 22, Hunts Cross, Liverpool

Russia and Yugoslavia are quarrelling.

Tuesday August 23, Hunts Cross, Liverpool

It is so hot and close.

Thursday August 25, Hunts Cross, Liverpool

Today I stood in the middle of the factory and looked around me. Here, among the throbbing, roaring, hissing, screeching machines, were sweaty, dirt-soaked men working for their very existence. As I stood here and watched these grimy people toiling for long weary hours, I thought of Oxford, with its lovely old buildings, its great tradition, the peace and calm of the college gardens and the rivers.

Monday August 29, Hunts Cross, Liverpool

I started in the cycle tube department today. The naphtha fumes and white powder get into one's lungs and make one very sleepy.

Tuesday August 30, Hunts Cross, Liverpool

I went for a walk during the lunch hour down to the river. It was quite lovely on the beach — calm and peaceful. It was good to get away from that stuffy factory, the stifling heat, and fumes from the rubber and naphtha and the chalk one continually breathes.

Saturday September 3, Gawthorpe Hall, Burnley

I arrived here this afternoon to stay with Anne and Tom Shuttleworth, and as Tom had to go to a meeting in Blackpool, we all went there. In the Majestic Hotel we met Geraldo (the famous dance band leader) and the Mayor and Mayoress. We had a most wonderful dinner, with good wine, and the Mayor joined us. The Mayor began by calling Tom and Anne "my lord" and "my lady," but he got so drunk and cheerful towards the end that when we left he said to Anne: "Good night, Anne." It was a most enjoyable day.

Sunday September 4, Hunts Cross, Liverpool

After breakfast I joined Anne and Tom in the nursery and we all played with Charlie. This afternoon we sat out in the grounds and read; it was so calm and peaceful.The sun shone and made the grounds warm and cosy. I arrived back at 8:00pm, back to R. I am reading Darwin's *Descent of Man* at the moment.

I should have left the diaries alone, because what I intended to do was finish this chapter on my rich uncle and show how he and his two brothers built up our large family business, which became a household name. Cow & Gate: The Food of Royal Babies. But even when I had finished browsing through the diary, I stayed in this dreamy mood and began thinking about all the babies we had fed, and how some babies like Forsyth have one inheritance and others like the Queen have another. I know we all end up the same way when I suppose nothing matters, but it's getting there I find interesting. And if, in this book within a book, I am to tell the truth, I have to say straight away that I think it better to be born rich than to be born poor. If you are born poor you can become rich, but the chances are not very great, so it is better to be born rich if possible and own large houses and lots of land. This is what I have found. All the rich people I have stayed with, those who own large houses and lots of land, they are all very glad that they were born that way.

When I say I intended writing about my rich uncle and our family business, I did get down a few words. Nineteen, to be exact, which can be stretched to twenty-three if you include the punctuation. The nineteen words I wrote were: "My rich uncle sent me a note: Dear Willie, please see this man and report back. God bless you."

I know that a person who doesn't profess to being a writer could have written more, and I know that if I hadn't started dreaming, thinking how some people are born one way and some another, I would have finished the chapter. But my trouble is I not only dream, I like dreaming, because in dreams you can be what you think you ought to be, which is usually a lot better than being what you really are.

I wish I wasn't a dreamer. I wish I could be like people who get to the top. Like those great sportsmen who not only have talent and aptitude but work for what they want. If I could be like them and work and work and work, I would have done long ago what Patrick said I should do, which was to write this book on Forsyth. Yet I would, if I could, forget all about Forsyth and leave him at peace in his quiet prison grave. But the image of death remains as sharply etched on my mind now as on the morning of his execution, when I stood with Rose and her husband outside Wandsworth Jail.

Patrick, being a writer and a critic, knew I could have written this book on Forsyth because not only is it in my mind from beginning to end but I can feel it, feel it inside me as if the characters are there walking about: Forsyth, Major Dunleavy, Lord Mountbatten, Lord Butler, Pierrepoint, Bert from Covent Garden, so many people who have come and gone and the few who have stayed. And this book, which would have been a book within a book, where there is no cover-up, no looking over one's shoulder at what other people may think, I would dedicate also to my friends, to Rose and to Patrick, to all those who think as I do, feel as I feel, go where I go, who will be with me at the end when I set out, alone, on the long last journey to the great lakes and the wild prairies, the forests and the meadows, a journey that may have begun many years ago when Rose and I, in those balmy days of summer, lay in the warm grass by the sandpits reading from my little stolen sixpenny edition. Hiawatha, my friend, my companion, my guide!

To write this book, to adequately interpret my thoughts, I would like to have been a poet. But I am not a poet, I never will be a poet, I haven't a poet's mind. As a matter of fact, since, in this book within a book, there is no cover-up and it is the truth I am after, I have to say that I don't think I am a writer. I mean writers write, and however much I might like to pretend, nineteen words, most of them copied from my uncle's letter, so that there is not even one original thought, are not very much for a whole evening's work.

Perhaps I inherited this weak side of my character from my father. Victoria Glendinning, in her book on Elizabeth Bowen, wrote quite penetratingly about him. She doesn't say very flattering things, but there isn't much you can say about him that is flattering unless you are telling lies. Two years before he died from sclerosis of the liver, when he was fifty-eight, he was sacked. He would have been sacked long before this if he hadn't been working in our large family business, and if the directors who were his cousins hadn't been very religious. These directors, except for my rich uncle, who, as I have already explained, was a prophet, were Plymouth Brethren. Quite a few of these old family businesses have a religious background like, for instance, the Quaker Cadburys, which is not a bad thing; because when my uncles found out my father was cooking the books and pocketing the money, instead of sacking him immediately, they prayed for him. But when their prayers remained unanswered, and even the chance of a miracle began to fade, they had to call it a day. There were ten thousand other employees who weren't crooked, and nepotism can only go so far.

It's no good pretending I don't feel badly about not being a writer because I do, although there is this to be said: that when you face up to things and come to terms with yourself, there is this great feeling of freedom, of release. You don't have to go on reaching for what isn't within your grasp. Whether I found all this out for myself, about not being a writer, or whether it was because of what Arthur said, I'm not sure.

I had gone over to see Arthur one mellow autumn afternoon in 1981 and was sitting with him on the patio of his south London suburban home, looking at his latest funeral arrangements. For years Arthur had worked on these arrangements, which included a memorial service to be held on the fourth Thursday after he'd been buried. It's always been in the back of my mind to find out why he decided on that Thursday, but I've never got round to asking him.

Arthur regarded the working out of his funeral arrangements as a pastime, a hobby which he took seriously in the way that other people who have their own hobbies follow football, or collect stamps or play the cello. The only other person I knew who had this same interest in how he was to be buried was Lord Mountbatten. Of course, Arthur, being only a bank clerk, couldn't have a gun carriage, troops, and that sort of thing, but he shared Lord Mountbatten's enthusiasm and had, in common with the admiral, a capacity for thoroughness and an eye for detail, so that the finale for each, although a state occasion for the one and the local church and cemetery for the other, was a moving and dignified tribute. Each man had also an inner arrogance that enabled him to disregard the feelings and criticisms of others, a natural ingredient in the great leader, but with Arthur simply that he didn't give a damn for the opinions of those who thought his preoccupation with death morbid and bizarre — an attitude that was excusable since his wife and three children accepted such a preoccupation as part of their happy, stable family life.

When I had looked through Arthur's latest alterations and additions, I showed him lines I had taken from *The Song of Hiawatha*, lines I thought he might like to incorporate in his service. He took the sheet on which I had written them out, glanced at it, handed it back, and said: "Read them to me, Willie. I want to hear how they sound."

So I held up the piece of paper and read aloud:

"Great men die and are forgotten,
Wise men speak; their words of wisdom
Perish in the ears that hear them
Do not reach the generations
That, as yet unborn, are waiting
In the great, mysterious darkness
Of the speechless days that shall be!
On the grave-posts of our fathers
Are no signs, no figures painted:
Who are in those graves we know not,
Only know they are our fathers."

When I had finished he sat quietly for a moment or two, then nodded and, without further comment, took back the piece of paper.

I must say I envied Arthur and admired him for his singleness of purpose. This dedication to a task is something I've tried to forge within myself, but it isn't easy. I mean, I make all these notes on people who have it — particularly those in the sporting field, where grit, sweat, and determination are visibly reflected and expressed as the great men and women battle towards success — and I hang on to every word uttered by them: McEnroe, the perfectionist; Barry Sheene, who will only put his best into anything and who says the winner is the one who tries the most; Tom Watson, ice-cool, making the last, all-important putt which gives him victory; Mary Decker in the Helsinki Games, gritting her teeth as she throws herself over the finishing line to win; Torvill and Dean, practising professionally eight hours a day for Olympic and world amateur championships.

In his own way Arthur had what they had, an uncompromising toughness, so that just as McEnroe ruthlessly slammed in the ball to win and Mary Decker, victorious at the finishing line, showed the whiteness of her teeth, Arthur went on regardless, experimenting with hymns, poems, proverbs, arias, quotations, prayers. He juggled, substituted, altered, deleted, explored, reshaped until he found a pattern that satisfied him, each pattern complete in itself. He then stored them away to be slotted in, when needed, for interpretation, as he saw it, of the great universal yearning that is mankind's dream of a foothold beyond the grave. I did once ask him if he'd given himself a time limit, whether, since few of us know when we are going to die, he might assume three score years and ten and aim for that; but he said it was an on-going thing, and if he died before it was finished, then, like Schubert's "Unfinished", there would still be plenty of meat, so to speak, which he hoped would show he hadn't wasted his time. I suppose it was this dedication to his task of expressing his own vision of eternity, and the discipline he had imposed on himself all these years with such thorough research and wide reading, and seeing in me a lack of these essential qualities, that he was able to tell me, in the nicest possible way, when I again mentioned the book on Forsyth I intended to start soon, that I would never be a writer.

It was shortly after I had read those lines from Hiawatha that he told me this. I was feeling relaxed, sitting out on his patio looking idly at the soft autumn colouring in the garden. His wife was in the kitchen humming a just-in-tune melody that, happily, was soon drowned by the dishwasher, while from the upstairs window, from his younger daughter's stereo, came a 1958 release, a catchy tune now sung by Bobbie Gentry and Glen Campbell: "All I Have to Do Is Dream."

Arthur said: "Why can't they play anything quietly? Why must she have it blaring out like that?"

He said this good-humouredly, for in spite of deep convictions, or perhaps because of them, he was a kind, tolerant person. I had never known Arthur in a bad mood. So when I said: "You know, Arthur, a lot of these young people's songs have really deep meanings. I mean it's quite true, isn't it, dreaming is nice, but you can easily dream your life away."

After I had said this, it did come as a bit of a shock when, with an impish grin, Arthur replied: "Yes, Willie, and that's why you'll never be a writer." Still half smiling, he went on: "You talk about writing, you tell all your friends you want to write, but you don't do anything about it."

After the shock of hearing this, although I realized immediately he might be intending to prod me into some sort of action which didn't make me feel too badly, I knew it must have been difficult for Arthur, who was a doer, to know what it was in my make-up that stopped me getting on with what I most wanted to achieve. Nobody likes having to face an unpleasant truth, but, as I say, it didn't needle me in the way it might have done if put less kindly. For a moment or two I sat looking at him, an average man, average height, average build, brown eyes, hair grey at the edges, fresh, almost ruddy complexion, small moustache, neatly dressed even in casual clothes, and with this rather precise way of talking as if everything had to be carefully thought out beforehand.

I had first met Arthur in the latter part of the 1950s when I was working in our family business. I had gone to see his wife, who complained when she found a dead centipede in the bottom of her milk bottle. The centipede was harmless, as it would have been sterilized in the bottle-washing process, but it was important to get back the bottle before the health authority could use it as evidence in a prosecution. She was very nice about it and gave me the bottle; then we sat talking, and I discovered that her nephew had been a boy seaman at the time I was an ordinary seaman in HMS *Glasgow* just before the war. I remembered him well. I was nineteen at the time; Tommy was sixteen and a homosexual. He hadn't become a homosexual through being in the Navy, which happened to so many sailor boys; he was born one. For as long as he could remember his feelings were for older men. He told me this late one evening, when we were standing on the upper deck looking at the moon, which appeared to be tearing across the sky as scattered black clouds were swept by a strong wind over its surface. Behind us, dockyard cranes were no more than tall, stooping shadows in the semi-darkness, and the only sound, apart from the wind blowing around the bottom of the funnel shaft and sometimes rattling the halyards, was the oily water swishing gently against the ship's side a long way down. In spite of the gusty wind, it was peaceful and calm, and there were certainly no thoughts in our minds of the dreadful war only a year away — a conflict that would leave Tommy's pretty face scarred and ugly after he'd been too near an exploding shell, and leaving him to die before he was forty.

We stood there for a time, relishing, in a way, the familiar pungent dockyard smell of tarred rope carried by the night breeze or, as it was that night, the rather gusty wind, and we talked about our homes and our families until we heard the shrill piped command over the loudspeakers for boys to stand by their hammocks. The command had scarcely finished when Tommy, coming perceptibly closer, held up his face and said: "You can kiss me if you want to, Willie."

It took me back a bit, but I recovered quickly and said I didn't in any way wish to upset him, but I had only ever kissed girls, and although he had this pretty face, not unlike a girl's, I didn't really fancy doing it — though had I known at the time how much terrible suffering would come his way, perhaps I should have done.

Then I heard Arthur's voice saying: "You know, Willie, dreaming is all in the mind." Arthur, being a kind person, was, I am sure, concerned in case he'd hurt me by telling me what he had, because he then said: "The last time you came here you said you wanted to show me some newspaper reports on the Hounslow murder, the one you want to write about. Did you bring them?" I said yes, I had brought them, but I was only half listening, because I could still hear in my mind the words of that song: "All I have to do is dream. Dream, dream, dream. I can make you mine, taste your lips of wine; the only trouble is, gee whiz, I'm dreaming my life away."

I showed Arthur the newspaper reports which I had edited. This edited version seemed to me to form a story in itself and showed, in fact, the beginning of Forsyth's short journey to the scaffold:

MURDER HUNT

Scotland Yard began a full-scale murder hunt for the killer of 23-year-old Allan Jee, an engineer, of Hall Road, Isleworth.

Detectives think that robbery may have been the motive which would make it a case of capital murder but this has not yet been definitely established.

Allan had become engaged on Friday. He was brutally struck down by his killer on Saturday night.

His sweetheart, 18-year-old Jacqueline Herbert, of Hartswood Road, Stamford Brook, Shepherd's Bush, broke down when she was told of Allan's death today.

Allan, an ice skater and a member of the Aldwych Speed Club at Richmond Ice Rink, was attacked while taking a shortcut home across a Southern Region footbridge at James Street, Isleworth.

He had been to see Jacqueline at her home. She went with him to the bus stop. They kissed; he said goodnight, and caught the bus home.

While taking the shortcut at the end of his bus journey, the attacker — it may have been a gang of thugs — beat him across the head with a cosh. Allan was found shortly before midnight.

He was rushed to West Middlesex Hospital, but he never regained consciousness.

Detective Superintendent Frederick Hixson, CID Chief of T Division, immediately set up a murder hunt.

Detectives searched the scene of the attack for the murder weapon as other CID men began widespread inquiries in the district.

As Jacqueline wept uncontrollably in her bedroom today, her father said: "It is a tremendous tragedy. They met at Richmond Ice Rink about two and a half years ago.

"Allan asked me on Friday night if I and Jacqueline's mother would give our blessing to their getting married.

"I said we would gladly do so. Then the four of us went out for a quiet celebration drink at the local. That was the last we saw of him."

Evening News
27 June 1960

ATTACK AFTER ENGAGEMENT: FOOTPATH PROTEST

People in the district complained last night of inadequate lighting along the footpath.

Daily Telegraph
28 June 1960

COUPLE PLANNED TO WED

Jacqueline said last night: "I don't know why anyone should want to harm him. He didn't have an enemy".

The mystery is: Why was Allan killed? The little money the young engineer had on him was found in his pockets.

Daily Express
28 June 1960

FATAL BLOW ON DAY HE WAS ENGAGED

Police wish to trace anyone who was near Chatsworth Crescent and James Street, where the body was found, between 10:45 and 11:45 on Saturday night.

The Times
28 June 1960

ENGAGED, HE IS LEFT TO DIE

His father, Mr Alfred Jee, said yesterday: "Who could have done this? We have no idea. Allan was a quiet lad. He never looked for trouble."

Daily Mirror
28 June 1960

DID YOU SEE ALLAN ON WAY HOME?

Police today appealed to courting couples to help them in their bid to find the killers of 23-year-old Allan Jee.

Detectives today made house-to-house inquiries in the area and interviewed scores of housewives and men in an attempt to find a motive for the murder of Allan.

It is thought that a gang of about three men ambushed Allan Jee.

The attackers were probably disturbed by approaching footsteps and ran away. It is thought that the murder took place after a lamp-post light was deliberately turned off a few feet away.

Throughout the night detectives with police dogs searched a recreation ground and the allotments area for clues.

Evening News
28 June 1960

MURDER HUNT: "A LONG JOB"

Det.-Supt. Frederick Hixson, who leads the murder hunt, said it looked like a long and painstaking investigation.

Evening Standard
28 June 1960

DYING MAN: POLICE SEEK HOODLUMS

Twenty extra detectives have been ordered to round up local roughs in the Hounslow area.

News Chronicle
29 June 1960

SILENCE BARRIER IN MURDER HUNT

After interviewing more than 500 persons living around the murder spot at Isleworth, police are confident that some people are withholding information.

Detectives today called at houses in Hounslow and took three youths to Hounslow police station. After questioning by Det.-Supt. Fred Hixson, the youths were allowed to return home.

Evening News
29 June 1960

ALLAN EDWARD JOHN JEE

Allan served in the RAF for two years on National Service until last February, spending 16 months in Cyprus. Once he had a narrow escape during the EOKA trouble when a booby-trap bomb went off in a washroom.

"It seems terrible to think that he came through all that trouble safely only to be killed like this near his home," said his mother. Letters of sympathy have been reaching her by every post.

Allan, who planned to marry in about two years when he had saved enough for a home, had a promising career as an engineer in a London firm. He came to Hounslow as a baby when his parents moved into their present home 21 years ago and was educated at nearby Chatsworth School and the Bulstrode School, Hounslow. He was a choirboy at Holy Trinity Church for five years.

The inquest on Allan Jee was opened yesterday at Ealing by the West Middlesex Coroner, Mr H.G. Broadbridge. Alfred Henry John Jee, Capstain Setter Operator, of 31 Hall Road, Isleworth, identified his son, who, he said, was a trainee engineer, living at home.

Dr R.D. Teare, pathologist, of St. George's Hospital, said the cause of Jee's death was bruising of the brain due to fracture of the skull.

As a full-scale murder hunt was launched by police in Hounslow this week, Allan Jee's parents sat in their home and asked themselves: "Why did it happen?"

For this was apparently a murder without a motive.

Allan Jee — a decent, hardworking boy "without an enemy in the world."

The attackers had darkness on their side for the street lamp was out at the spot where Allan was found.

The body was discovered within minutes of the crime by a Hounslow youth who was retracing his steps when he came on the inert figure. He went to a nearby house and gave the alarm.

Allan's 51-year-old mother, Mrs Doris Jee, said: "I saw him go off with his fiancée on Saturday afternoon. I watched them get on a bus at the top of the road to go to Richmond, and he waved to me from the bus. Then I caught the bus the other way to go to Hounslow.

"The next time I saw him was lying in West Middlesex Hospital on Sunday. I was shocked to learn he had been terribly beaten. He had a terrible black eye, and he lay there unconscious, having a blood transfusion. I stroked his poor forehead.

"The hospital said he was critically ill, and I couldn't sleep that night for worry. In the middle of the night they came to tell us he was dead.

"We keep asking: Why, why, why? And any minute I think that perhaps it hasn't happened and he will walk up the path."

Middlesex Chronicle
1 July 1960

YOUTHS SHADOWED IN HUNT FOR KILLER

Detectives hunting the killer of Allan Jee were last night seeking three men and a youth seen nearby whom they wish to question. Police issued descriptions of two of the men and the youth.

Daily Mail
1 July 1960

MURDER HUNT — CID SEEK THREE MEN

The descriptions are:

A man in his early 20s, 5 ft. 8 in. tall, medium build, and wearing a dark suit.

A man aged 20 to 30, 6 ft. 1 in. tall, well built, with dark, greasy hair, and wearing a short duffle coat.

A youth about 18, 5 ft. 6 in. tall, slim build, fair hair, and wearing a blue herringbone jacket and long pointed shoes.

Detectives are anxious to trace the three and are also appealing to anyone who was in the area where Jee was found to tell the police of anyone they saw on Saturday night.

Evening Standard
1 July 1960

SENSELESS MURDER

Last week 40 weary detectives were still pursuing their seemingly hopeless task to find a clue to the murder of 23-year-old Allan Jee.

Already they have seen nearly 3,000 people in the Hounslow area of London. They have called at every house within half a mile radius of the spot where he was found battered into unconsciousness.

It is not too difficult to form a theory of what happened on that ill-lit path. Allan Jee was, perhaps, picked on by a group of Saturday night roughs either as a victim of a petty hold-up, or just as a target for their taunts.

He, no doubt, resisted, and was overwhelmed by a rain of blows. It is almost certain that there was no intention to kill.

In all probability, it was as simple and terrible as that.

The People
17 July 1960

When I got home that night I sat down at my desk with the typed pages of the edited newspaper reports in front of me; then took up my pen and sat staring at the writing — a thick pad, two hundred leaves, narrow faint ruling — and I read again the nineteen words which were all I had written when my thoughts wandered off in the direction of the Oxford diary. Arthur telling me what he did gave me the impetus to go on with what I had started, so I added a few more lines to the nineteen words, then sat back and studied the whole paragraph, which now read:

'My rich uncle sent me a note: "Dear Willie, please see this man and report back. God bless you." My uncle is not only rich, he is religious. He thinks he is a prophet. He may be a prophet for all I know, except that what he prophesies doesn't happen. Up to now it hasn't happened, but this doesn't mean it won't happen in the future. So from this point of view he could be prophesying correctly but getting his dates wrong. My uncle is not only rich and a prophet, but he is chairman of our family business.'

Having written this, I should have gone on, but I sat twiddling my pen, fiddled with the typed pages of the newspaper reports, then heard once more the words of that song: "All I have to do is dream. Dream, dream, dream." Then, and I suppose this was an excuse for indolence, I started to wonder who, apart from me and possibly Arthur, would be interested in the life and death of Francis Robert George Henry James Forsyth, teenage killer, of 20 Clare Road, Hounslow, educated at Isleworth Grammar School and Spring Grove Secondary School, who passed his 11+, became a road-worker, then, in June 1960, kicked to death Allan Edward John Jee, and, his reprieve having been refused, was executed. And it wasn't as if young Forsyth was anyone who mattered, just a backyard Caesar from the working class, a small-time crook, clever at school, touchy, hating to be laughed at, violent, fond of his parents, king of the roost but with no sense of loyalty or allegiance to authority, aggressive, the leader of a gang whose association with violence found its climax in a brutal murder. Yet there were those who respected him, liked him, were sorry for him, those who hoped that when he took the last few steps to the scaffold he went bravely. Perhaps, beneath his aggressiveness, his insecurity, his need for recognition, he was brave. He had to face, at an early age, what few at any age have to face, knowing the exact moment of death.

But to get back to my writing and what I should have done and all that I haven't done, I did talk this over with Patrick. As a matter of fact, I have talked it over with him quite a few times because Patrick knew my weaknesses; also, being a writer himself, he was able to say quite a lot about writing. Actually he said quite a lot about lots of things; about super-ego, values, dependency, love and caring, childhood, change of attitude, habits, God, stimuli and reaction, symbolism, emotions, all that sort of thing. He had learnt a lot from his Teacher, but he had also read widely. He had books scattered around his room. Some he'd borrowed from the library; some he'd bought second-hand; some were cheap paperback editions with such titles as *The Eye and the Brain*, *The Science of Animal Behaviour*, *New Horizons in Psychology*, *The Theory of Evolution*, *Objective Knowledge*, *Social Behaviour in Animals*, *The Dancing Bees*, *The Psychology of Perception*, *Child Care and the Growth of Love*, *The Year of the Gorilla*.

Perhaps it was reading books like these that made him sad. He was always sad, the way he spoke and the way he looked and in his attitude to life generally. I have met a lot of philosophers and psychiatrists and psychologists, and they all seem sad. I mean, they never seem all that happy. Even if they aren't as sad as Patrick, they don't smile very much, or tell light-hearted jokes like most people do.

Not long after Patrick returned from Thailand, in the summer of 1963, I went to see him. He had come back to his attic room in Lowndes Square. It was a nice room, neatly though not elaborately furnished, with a divan bed and a table by the window on which stood a green plant. There were also a couple of chairs, a cupboard, a chest of drawers, and, against the wall by the door, an expensive stereo set. Before he went to Thailand his shelves had been full of books; now these had all gone, and in their place, scattered about on the shelves and on the table, were the books I have mentioned. Also on the top shelf were two piles of exercise books in which he had written the sayings of his Teacher. On the bottom shelf, propped up against the wall at the back, were coloured postcards mostly from abroad. One was a picture of a squatting Buddha.

Patrick looked the eccentric he was. About five feet eleven, he had a full pale face, thick lips, grey eyes, glasses, and had the whole of his head close-shaved. At this time, in his late forties, in spite of frugal eating, he was inclined to heaviness. But the fixed sad expression on his face was deceptive, for it hid to all but close friends and colleagues a clever, penetrating, critical intellect. It seemed as if, for him, the world's ills were only just tolerable because of his constant preoccupation with seeking a solution to the burden they imposed, and when he did attempt a smile, which was rare, it was more an expression of resignation to the inevitable than a feeling of happiness.

Although spotlessly clean, Patrick dressed shabbily. His old tweed jacket had leather patches on the elbows and on the rim of the sleeves; his dark green pullover, when he wore it, was torn under one armpit and frayed at the bottom; his grey flannel trousers, which he usually wore, were creased in the wrong places; and his shoes, when he was not wearing sandals, were, although always polished, invariably down at the heel. He was one of those people for whom nothing seemed right. In summer it was too hot and he came out in rashes; in winter he sat huddled over his one-bar electric fire longing for the warmer weather. Any noise, however small, upset him: a wireless too loud, the heavy reverberations of a jet overhead, a dog barking in the street below, any sudden sound, a thump, a bang from the flat underneath. When in London, he yearned for isolation, for an escape into as near total silence as possible; in Thailand, when he got near to this with his Teacher in the jungle, he found a need for ordinary human frailties, not because he missed these as such but because they were part of ordinary comforting companionship, the mental and physical stimulus of which he missed so much when they weren't there.

When I called on him in that early summer of 1963, it was the start of many discussions, about writing and about matters which interested us both. He told me about Thailand, that he'd stayed there for nearly three years but the climate was terrible; that there were these two monsoons a year and, in between, this terrible humidity. He said he came out in rashes all the time, and he spoke in this sad way with this sad, sad voice. And he went on looking sad as if disaster was always just around the corner.

Patrick said that for some of the time in Thailand it wasn't too bad. When he lived with his Teacher in the jungle, he slept on the floor, finding it more comfortable than sleeping in a bed. And the food wasn't too bad. He'd lived on rice and fish. The country is full of water, the fish easy to catch. Plenty of fruit, too; you can pick it off the trees. Mangoes, plenty of mangoes. This was in Bangkok. In the country it's more difficult. The Buddhist life was a Spartan kind of existence, primitive in a way once you get away from the ritual and the colour of the robes. And you get this marvellous peace of mind, which is what it's all about: finding peace of mind, finding true happiness.

It was a long job. Thailand had to make the jump from the seventeenth and eighteenth centuries into the twentieth century in about thirty years. There was a kind of vacuum all over southeast Asia. The people there are curious, Oriental. To them Buddhism is what the Church of England means here. The old people preserve the ritual; the young think it's mostly mumbo jumbo. This is because young people are educated, they despise the monks as peasants. They need the rituals when they are born, when they marry, and when they die, like we do in the Church of England, and it is not always because we believe in it but because we have to observe the right thing to do at the right time.

The monsoons were terrifying. Very unpleasant and terrifying. Terrible storms about every hour and heavy clouds all the time. The monsoon season lasts about four weeks. Nevertheless, he'd learnt a lot from the Buddhists, from sharing their way of life, although what he'd come back with was not Buddhism as it is generally understood, which is no more than a replacement for any other system, chiefly Catholicism, the robes and rituals of Buddhism having the same superficial attraction, for it is the rituals that make people stay with it; it was from being with his Teacher in the little hut in the jungle that he'd learnt most, because it was there he'd been taught to rely on himself, on his own resources.

It was after he had finished telling me about Thailand and we got on to the subject of violence and aggression in young people, and in particular the violent aspect of hanging, that Patrick said: "Willie, you ought to write about Forsyth. I think you should."

So although, nearly twenty years later, Arthur had said more or less the same thing, it was Patrick who first put the idea in my mind. I then began to make notes and interviewed many people, among them Albert Pierrepoint, who, until he resigned the position in 1956, was Britain's chief executioner. On 12 March 1978, confirming a meeting we had arranged in London, Albert wrote: "I am about 5 ft.7 in. tall, will be wearing a white topcoat, and a dark grey trilby hat, and carrying a black overnight case. Looking forward to seeing you on 3 April."

Sitting over coffee, in this pleasant, clean hotel near Euston station, I spent the whole morning discussing with Albert his role as hangman. He had hanged quite a few people, mostly murderers, but also one or two traitors and all the Belsen crowd. At the end of the meeting I handed him twenty-seven pages of typed questions, leaving room on the right-hand side of each page for his answers. He told me that some of the questions were subject to the Official Secrets Act; the rest he answered fully, so that I was able to get, clearly in my mind, this picture of young Forsyth's execution:

THE CONDEMNED CELL

After sentencing, Forsyth would be sent straight from the Old Bailey to the condemned cell, where he would remain for the whole of the 6 weeks and 3 days.

The furnishing of the condemned cell consisted of a single bed and an ordinary wooden table with three or four chairs and a wardrobe. The table was bare and stood in the centre of the cell. The floor was wooden. There were no pictures on the walls.

The condemned cell was one room approximately sixteen feet square. There was a window letting in daylight. The cell was lit by sealed electric light and had central heating.

In the centre of the wall between the cell and the execution chamber there was a communicating door. This door opened back into the cell, but was hidden by the wardrobe until the morning of execution. The condemned cell door was double-locked with one key. There was no difference in locking procedure for the morning of execution. The executioner would want to get in quickly.

There were two condemned cells next to one another, with a communicating door and a toilet in between.

EXECUTION CHAMBER

The trap doors were in the centre of the floor. In the right-hand corner, as you entered the chamber from the communicating door, there were side stairs that led to the pit. Except for the scaffold, the execution chamber was bare.

The execution chamber, which was the same size as the condemned cell, was spotlessly clean at all times.

During the time of Albert Pierrepoint the execution chamber was painted cream with a two-inch black band running in the centre of the four walls. The chamber was bright with windows letting in daylight. There was sealed electric light in the chamber as all cells were lit in this way.

The ceiling of the execution chamber was not solid, just another cell on top.

TOP CELL

The top cell had no special features; it was nothing in particular, just empty and bare and the same size as the others.

Going across this cell was a great beam. Fastened to the beam was a four-inch chain and attached to this chain was the rope.

THE LAYOUT OF THE CELLS

The execution complex consisted of a three-storey set of cells:

The ground floor: the pit.

The first floor: the condemned cell and execution chamber.

The top floor which carried the great beam.

In Wandsworth the execution complex was in the centre of the prison.

TREATMENT OF THE PRISONER

As soon as Forsyth was in the condemned cell, the medical officer would carry out an ordinary medical inspection to make sure that the prisoner was fit to hang.

He would be able to go to bed when he liked. He would be taken out for exercise about lunchtime or in the evening when all would be quiet. In Albert Pierrepoint's time no wireless was allowed in the condemned cell, but it was later allowed; nor was there then TV.

He could write as many letters as he liked, within reason, and, with the governor's permission, to anyone he chose.

The light in the condemned cell was left on all night with two officers in the same room.

He would be allowed a daily ration of alcoholic drink. He could have special food, but only on the doctor's orders.

He would be put straight into prison drab; this is prison dark grey and shoes without laces. The clothes belonging to Forsyth, which he would be allowed to wear on the morning of execution, were probably kept in the laundry.

Although Forsyth could go to the chapel if he wished, it would not be whenever he liked. When he did go he would be accompanied by a prison officer who would normally stay with him. The prison chaplain was the only person allowed to be alone with him. The prison chaplain could take confession in the condemned cell or in the chapel, and he would then be alone with the prisoner.

The governor, the medical officer, and the chief officer would visit Forsyth daily, sometimes twice daily. The governor would, if it was possible, make one of these visits last thing at night. He would never be alone with Forsyth. The visits would be made all the time Forsyth was in custody.

The governor, as soon as he was informed that the reprieve had been refused, would visit Forsyth in his cell and tell him the news. The governor would probably be accompanied by the chief officer. Once a reprieve was refused, the only chance of escaping the death sentence was through the House of Lords, but this would be very rare.

Forsyth would not be allowed to have as many visitors as he liked. The governor would be responsible for all visitors.

Two officers would look after him. The officers would work three eight-hour shifts. The prison officers would try to make Forsyth as happy as possible, and over a period of six weeks they would become friendly, so it is possible they would call him by his Christian name or even use his nickname. The governor might also call him by his Christian name.

Forsyth would be watched all the time, even when he was sitting on the toilet. He was never left alone, so there was never a minute during the whole of his time in the condemned cell when he had any privacy.

There would be no difference in the treatment of Forsyth from the time he was refused a reprieve to his execution. Treatment would remain the same during the whole of his 6 weeks 3 days in the condemned cell.

THE CONDEMNED PRISONER'S BEHAVIOUR

In the condemned cell the prison officers would play games with Forsyth. This helped to pass the time away.

Usually, from Albert Pierrepoint's experience, the prisoner was very brave. He was usually friendly with the prison officers and polite to the governor and other supervisors.

THE EXECUTIONER AND HIS ASSISTANT

The executioner and his assistant had to arrive at the prison before 4:00 on the day before the execution.

The executioner's rooms could be a visiting room or anywhere in the prison, but always seemed to be in the same place and were always comfortable. The sitting room could be an office, fitted with office furniture; it would be a bright room with a window, a room where you could see into the prison yard. All the prison was centrally heated. The rooms, when not used by the executioner, would be used by other people.

The executioner and his assistant would wait until the governor sent for them. The governor was always pleased to see them, and would send for them as soon as possible.

The executioner would test the apparatus when Forsyth was out of his cell, probably when he was at exercise.

The executioner usually had a choice of ropes, one new and one old, but this was regarded as confidential. The choice of rope was left to the executioner.

The Judas hole, a prison term for a spy hole, was in the top part of the cell door about eye level. It passed through the door with a cover on the outside. Forsyth would be able to see the Judas hole but would not be able to see anyone looking through it.

The executioner would be able to observe Forsyth in his cell, and when he was at exercise. In the cell Forsyth would probably be playing games or talking to the prison officers. The executioner was not permitted, nor would it be his wish, to observe Forsyth in the chapel.

ON THE MORNING OF ECXECUTION

The executioner and his assistant were awoken at approximately 6:30am. If the execution was set for 9:00am, at approximately 8:55am the executioner was told that the sheriff had gone to the governor's office. The sheriff came from outside the prison. The executioner and his assistant would go to the execution chamber a few minutes before the time set for the execution (either 8:00am or 9:00am). They would be accompanied by a prison officer leading the way. Forsyth would be waiting in his cell. The final adjustment to the length of rope needed for the drop would have been made. If the rope needed shortening, this was not done by putting a knot in it; other methods were used. White chalk was used

for the relining of the T-mark on the scaffold. The executioner sometimes slightly shifted the cross planks on either side of the T-mark,
making one final adjustment to make sure the prisoner would not hit
the cross planks when falling.

THE EXECUTION

On the morning of execution, it was up to the prison officers as to what
time Forsyth would be woken.

On rising, Forsyth would dress in his own clothes.

About one hour before the execution the chaplain would go to the condemned cell. The chaplain would be robed as if conducting a service. If
Forsyth wished, he could pray with the chaplain.

The prison officers, who would also be the escorting officers taking
Forsyth to the scaffold, would be chatting to him for much of the time,
trying to take his mind off what was going to happen.

The chief officer would unlock the door of the condemned cell to let in
the executioner. The signal for the unlocking of the cell door would be
given by the under-sheriff ten seconds before the time of the execution.
Forsyth would have a good idea of the time.

Albert Pierrepoint had never seen a calming drug or brandy given to
the prisoner prior to the execution.

When the executioner went into the cell, the chaplain would probably
be talking to Forsyth. In the execution chamber the chaplain would stay
in the background.

Forsyth would be given no special shirt to wear for the execution, nor
would the executioner roll down the collar of the shirt Forsyth was
wearing after his wrists had been strapped.

When the chief officer had opened the cell door, he would walk quickly
to the wardrobe and move it away from the communicating door. The
communicating door was opened immediately the chief officer moved
the wardrobe, which was as soon as he entered the cell on the morning
of execution.

The distance for the executioner to reach Forsyth, on entering the condemned cell, was about three to five paces.

As Forsyth was escorted out to the scaffold he would see the noose
hanging in front of him.

If the prisoner resisted when being taken to the scaffold, it would not
be necessary to use force. There are other means, but these Albert Pierrepoint has never had to use.

The executioner and his assistant were in no particular dress. They
could wear anything they chose.

The official witnesses, the governor, sheriff, and others, would be
standing just inside the chamber door out of the way of the executioner.

These official witnesses were called the sheriff's party, because the sheriff of a particular county where the murder occurred was in full charge of the execution. The executioner was engaged by the under-sheriff, but the sheriff was always in charge and was responsible for any execution.

The chaplain would be standing at the back of the chamber. He would not be reciting prayers.

When Forsyth was on the drop, the escorting officers would be level with him. If he was calm, there would be no special hold.

Each plank was to the side and clear of the trap.

Each escorting officer, with his disengaged hand, would be holding on to a supporting rope for safety.

Forsyth's feet were aligned to the T-mark by the executioner, who would have told him where to stand.

As soon as Forsyth was aligned on the drop, the assistant executioner would pinion his legs.

The white cap was just a linen bag with no holes in it.

The wash-leather on the rope, on that part of the noose which goes round the neck, is to stop the noose from opening and slipping over the prisoner's head. The rubber claw grip, pulled along the rope to hold it, is just to keep the noose in position. The noose around the neck is ordinary, not too tight.

For Forsyth, and everyone waiting, the execution would be over before most of them realized it. Albert Pierrepoint has heard people say that they never saw what happened. If the execution was set for 9:00am, the sheriff's party would go into the execution chamber at ten seconds to nine. The execution took anything from ten to twelve seconds.

The actual drop was timed for as near 9:00 as possible.

AFTER THE EXECUTION

The executioner would go to the pit immediately after the execution. He would then open Forsyth's shirt to prepare for the examination of the body by the medical officer.

The medical officer would follow the executioner down into the pit, and would then examine the body by putting the cup of his stethoscope onto Forsyth's chest. Although Forsyth would have suffered instantaneous death, his heart would be beating for about ten to twenty seconds, getting fainter, but it would be impossible to revive him.

With a good execution the body hangs perfectly still without any movement or twitching.

When the cap and noose were removed there should be no mark or swelling on the neck. The neck would be absolutely clear; if not, the officials would want to know why.

When the white cap was removed, whether the prisoner's eyes were open and staring or whether they were closed differed in each case.

Forsyth's head would not be over to either side.

After the medical officer's certification of death, Forsyth's body would immediately be taken down.

The body was not always measured, and the prisoner would only be completely stripped of all his clothes if a post mortem examination was desired. The clothes taken from the body were usually burnt.

The burial of the condemned prisoner usually took place in the lunch hour. The burying of the prisoner's body in lime was stopped nearly a hundred years ago. All bodies were respected at all times.

The coffin was a standard prison coffin made of plain wood.

Forsyth's relatives would not be allowed any say in the burial. Forsyth would be buried in the grounds of the prison beneath the lawn, which is a private piece of land. Prisoners were sometimes buried three to a grave.

Albert Pierrepoint has never seen a plate with the prisoner's initials and date of execution on the prison wall, near to where the prisoner is buried.

As soon as the execution was over, the executioner and his assistant would return to their rooms for breakfast.

OFFICIALS INVOLVED IN THE EXECUTION

The sheriff and the under-sheriff

The governor

The medical officer

The engineer

The prison officers guarding the prisoner, two of whom were the escorting officers

The executioner and the assistant executioner

The chaplain.

I suppose, in one way, since I have all these notes from interviews and research, it is an achievement to have done so little, particularly as Patrick not only suggested I write this book on Forsyth but showed me the way. I can remember now, as if it had been yesterday, sitting in the Lowndes Square attic with Patrick facing me, the bright light coming in through the window behind him as he said in this very sad voice: "A writer must go whole-heartedly into writing; a writer is someone who breaks through symbols and sees people, so in any great work the individual is seen, also happiness or something that involves pain and suffering. And if, Willie, your image of people comes from a two-dimensional view instead of three-dimensional, you are missing out as a writer. Remember, too, that if you present something to the public, they have a right not to like it. In writing you've got something to say that's you, and when you've said it, you send it out into the world, and if it fails, go on. All that anyone has to give is themselves, nothing else to sell. All writing is a process of self-discovery, and this is why writing is difficult. Some people write for sheer gain; you, Willie, do it to please yourself. The battle is between technique and content. Learn technique until it becomes second nature. Technique must be in the service of expressing something. Technique must be to make clear what you are trying to say."

I should have taken Patrick's advice. I know this now. Having all these notes and having everything in my mind, I could have written not only this first volume but the second, third, fourth, and perhaps fifth on the life and death of Francis Robert George Henry James Forsyth. I could also have finished that chapter on my rich uncle, ending with an account of the battle that led up to Dunkirk, following this with an account of my meeting with Mr Solomon and hearing from Mr Solomon the surprising news that Bert, known to everyone as the gentle giant, and who had been decorated by the King for heroism in Burma, was doing two years for an act of violence completely out of character. I could have written this and a lot more, but it's no good complaining; you are what you are, and I suppose there is some comfort in knowing you can't be the only one with these bad habits, that there are other people with weak characters who are dreaming their lives away. Dream, dream, dream; but if you go on dreaming long enough, your dreams become your real world and the real world an illusion:

In the drowsy, dreamy sunshine
In the never ending summer

A dream of greatness. No toil, no agony, no sweat: the toil, agony and sweat that comes with writing. A journey of dreams:

Here the sunshine of the meadow.
Here the shadow of the forest,
Here the wind among the branches,
Here the groves of singing pine trees

And as I journeyed on towards the great lakes, the prairies, and the meadows, I thought about space and freedom, knowing now, in this dream, what space and freedom must have meant to those who, throughout history, have been denied it: the persecuted, the tortured, the oppressed, the six million Jews and others in German concentration camps waiting to go to the gas chambers. But scarcely had this vision faded when it was replaced by another, that of a young man:

Red with blood of youth his cheeks were
Soft his eyes, as stars in spring time

I saw him some way off, walking slowly beside one of the great lakes, in the distance the giant forests, and I was glad I was not alone. But the young man must have been farther away than I thought because as the day wore on, and the afternoon grew heavy with heat and silence, he seemed to get no nearer. I started to walk towards him, for I knew that once in the forest he would vanish forever, and that it would then be too late to say what I had to say; but the more I walked towards him the more he kept his distance.

And even in all this space, with the great prairies and cornfields and the great lakes stretching away towards the distant forests for as far as the eye could see, even in all this vast space, and having experienced the freedom which space can give, I began to feel restricted, confined, and I was unable to move quickly enough. My feet were dragging, and I had this awful fear that at any moment he would vanish and I would never see him again, and I felt intensely sad, for although he was slim, strong, supple, his head hung awkwardly to one side, and although Albert Pierrepoint said that after execution the head would not be over to either side, it was seeing this deformity that filled me with pity. So I called out: *Wait, don't go, please don't go.* He didn't hear, or if he heard he took no notice. I called out again: *Please don't go, I have something to tell you.* Still he took no notice, and I knew there was nothing I could do, that he had to go and the opportunity to say what I wanted to say would be lost forever.

And what I wanted to tell him was that there is always hope, that there is a way out of suffering, that I knew this for certain because Patrick had shown me the way. I wanted him to know what everyone in the world should know, that there is this hope, that in despair, in frustration, in violence, in neglect, in cruelty, in loneliness, even in dying, there is a way out. Patrick had told me that the way is not easy but that to get out of suffering is the main purpose of existence. And I knew then that had I written this book — the one I wanted to write, the one on Forsyth that Patrick and later Arthur said I should write, this book that is all in my mind — if I had done that, I could have shown the way, shown this young man that no matter what he had done, love, compassion, and understanding are indestructible, and so I would have redeemed myself. But sadly, inevitably, his head over to one side, he walked away:

In the glory of the sunset

In the purple mists of evening,
To the regions of the home-wind
Of the north-west wind, Keewaydin,
To the Islands of the Blessed.
To the kingdom of Ponemah
To the land of the Hereafter!

My rich uncle sent me a note: "Dear Willie, please see this man and report back. God bless you." My uncle is not only rich, he is religious. He thinks he is a prophet. He may be a prophet for all I know, except that what he prophesies doesn't happen when he says it will happen. Up to now it hasn't happened at all, but this doesn't mean it won't happen in the future, so from this point of view he could be prophesying correctly but getting his dates wrong. My uncle is not only rich and a prophet but he is chairman of our family business. Although our family business began in 1750, when we owned a small grocery shop in Guildford High Street, it was not until 1885 that we started marketing cream in little brown jugs, using our label showing a cow looking over a gate. It was a pure, rich, thick cream and was bought by the best people, including Queen Victoria and the Prince of Wales.

It is very good working in a large family business, because you can reach the top quickly. To do this you have to be a close relative, a son or nephew, but it is one of the best ways of getting on. The note which my rich uncle sent me was dated 10 April 1960. I got it on the Tuesday morning, and on this Tuesday morning I was standing in my office, looking out of the window across Kennington Park Road and into Cleaver Square where there was an art school; and I was thinking it would be very nice to be an artist: a painter or writer or sculptor or composer, because even when you are in a large family business getting rapidly to the top, the grass on the other side always looks greener.

The day had started well, bright and not too cold, and Janice, my nineteen-year-old secretary, was back, having had a week's leave to celebrate her engagement. Janice was pretty. She had an elfin face with light brown eyes and a few freckles. She thought everything was funny. I mean, anything you said to Janice she seemed to treat as a huge joke. Once, after a firm's dinner and dance, in a dark corner, I kissed her. She put her tongue furiously in my mouth and slipped my hand inside her dress. It worried me a bit not only because I was much older — forty-one to be precise — but I got to thinking about this business of doing it on your own doorstep. Anyway, Janice came in the next day all bright and breezy, and it seemed she had just met this boy and they had got serious, and when I asked suspiciously how she felt, she laughed, so I didn't pursue it.

Inside my uncle's note was another note, undated. This other note was written on pages torn from a cheap exercise book. Actually, it was more than a note, it was an epistle. It surprised me when I read it, not only because of its length, but because it was written in good English: correct grammar and punctuation, and balanced sentences. The last time I got one of these notes from my uncle I made up my mind it would also be the last time I would visit one of these doss-houses to interview a bum who had my rich uncle on his list as an easy touch. Somehow I couldn't convince my uncle that although I would agree we ought to believe that all of us are brothers in Christ, there are exceptions.

Even today, many years later, when I think about it, I remember the surprise I felt, almost shock, when I read the epistle. It was completely out of the ordinary: literate, legible, starkly honest. None of those obsequious phrases used by other bums when begging: "God bless you, sir; the Holy Mother of Jesus be with you; God bless your honour." So when I had finished gazing out of the window, I went in to see Janice, who had the office adjoining mine, and I told her that I had decided not to visit our Hounslow branch that afternoon, but would go to the doss-house and see Julian Dunleavy, who was the author of this epistle I have mentioned.

When I looked at Janice I could see that spring was in the air. She already had this blushing bride look. She looked up and said in an excited voice: "Twenty thousand pounds are being spent on spring flowers for Princess Margaret's wedding."

I said: "Oh good! Twenty thousand pounds? That should buy a lot of flowers." And I am talking about the year nineteen hundred and sixty.

Janice, of course, was very wedding-minded. She probably saw Princess Margaret's wedding as a projection of her own. For better, for worse, for richer, for poorer, in sickness and in health; it was written in bold handwriting all over Janice.

Then she said. "It's so exciting and so romantic. I never thought she'd marry. And to meet just an ordinary sort of person. A photographer!"

I'm the last one to want to spoil things for anyone, but I felt it best to put the record straight: "He's not an ordinary person, Janice. He went to Eton, and his mother's a Countess." Then, waving my uncle's note at her, I said: "Will you cancel the Hounslow visit, and I'll go and get this sorted out."

Janice said: "I thought you weren't going to do it any more. You said you would just pretend you'd been."

I said: "You are quite right, but this is different. Did you read

Dunleavy's letter?" Janice said yes, she had read it, and I remarked: "It's not like any of the letters we've had before, from any of the other bums."

Janice said brightly: "But a begging letter just the same."

I nodded. "Yes, a begging letter just the same."

Then Janice added: "I couldn't make out what he meant at the end, when he said only a coward is truly brave."

I shrugged. "I didn't understand it myself, but it doesn't seem to have bothered the Chairman." Thinking about this, I went back to my own office, picked up the begging epistle, and read it through once more:

Dear Colonel,

I write to ask for your help. I do so reluctantly but I am in greatly reduced circumstances. I do not want to mislead you: I am not a practising Christian.

All I can say by way of introduction is that we were fellow soldiers. I, like you, was at Dunkirk. That glorious retreat! The French were convinced that the Maginot Line, and north-west of the Maginot Line in the forested Ardennes, was impassable for armour.

The British had spent nearly eight months preparing temporary defences south of the Belgium border, planning to move up to the Dyle River with nine BEF divisions and twenty-seven French divisions. We hoped, of course, that the twenty-two Belgian and eight Dutch divisions would blunt the German attack.

Well, it wasn't to be. Rundstedt broke through to the Channel in ten days. Six days later the Belgians surrendered and our government ordered the evacuation of the BEF. I was with the last British and French forces on June 4, that historic day when we hoped to rescue 50,000 men but brought back 337,000, of which 115,000 were Allied troops, French, Belgian, and Dutch. As I have said, I am not a practising Christian, but I am sure that God was with us that day.

Fog and smoke hindered the Luftwaffe. The RAF threw in every available squadron, blasting the Hun out of the sky The way our boys fought! It was magnificent. They fought courageously, desperately, to protect the beachhead. They killed the enemy. They should have killed more.

I heard later that among all the shooting and bombing and carnage, you got down on your knees, on the beach, with your men, and you prayed, not from fear but because you believe in His goodness and mercy; and I met men later who testified to the immense moral uplift which your action gave them. For at a time like this, in such moments, only a coward is truly brave.

Sincerely — Julian Dunleavy

On the way to the doss-house I was thinking to myself that there is something to be said for being a bum. They don't have to worry like the rest of us. I felt, too, that summer is the best time to be one; then you can sit drinking your meths in comfort in the warm fresh air. And in the back of my mind I had this image of Dunleavy sitting in the sunshine on the pavement outside the doss-house, his back against the wall, just as I had seen other bums sitting, with a brown beer or cider bottle, looking happy and relaxed, as if they were on holiday in Brighton.

I parked the car in Covent Garden not far from the doss-house, pausing to read again Dunleavy's letter. It didn't give me any fresh thoughts, so I walked the short distance into the narrow cobbled street which was the address of the doss-house Dunleavy had given in the letter.

The street was so narrow that it seemed just a slit between tall buildings squeezing out daylight on either side. It was behind Drury Lane and led into Kingsway. I had no trouble in spotting the doss-house. There were two bums sitting outside. They had this stupid look on their faces which they all seem to have. I saw that the place was called a crèche. There was a board fastened on the red brick wall which said that the building was a crèche, and underneath this board was another board which had painted on it in bold gold sanserif: NO BARKING. I felt that this was rather unkind of the crèche; then, going nearer, I saw that someone had altered the "P" into a "B".

Looking down at the two bums, I called out in a very friendly voice: "Good afternoon, gentlemen. Would one of you be Mr Dunleavy?"

One of them looked up at me and leered, while the other took a swig from a quart beer bottle. The one who took the swig was young, with thick black wavy hair hanging down the back of his neck. The other, whom I judged to be in his late fifties, had a stained green porkpie hat pulled down over his ears. Both were unshaven; both looked very decrepit in ill-fitting greasy clothes. The jacket worn by the older bum was torn.

Then the younger one said in a soft Irish brogue: "Can you spare a shilling, sir?" I searched my pocket for change. I couldn't find a shilling so reluctantly gave him half a crown. In a quaint way he made as if to touch his forelock, the ingrained servant touch, then he said: "Pete's inside, sir. He'll help you."

Inside the crèche I found Pete. He was a young man in his early twenties. He was nice-looking, bearded, the light of Jesus in his brown eyes. I found him sitting behind a cheap green-baize-topped card table placed just inside the entrance in a corner near the lift shaft. The lift was one of those old-fashioned cranky affairs, just a little more advanced than the kind you pull up and down with a rope. I asked: "Are you Pete, the gentleman in charge here?" He said yes he was Pete, and he was in charge here, and if he could help me in any way he would be only too pleased. I thanked him, took out Dunleavy's letter, and said: "Mr Dunleavy has written to my uncle. Would it be possible for me to have a word with him?" I emphasized the "mister" to show that, as far as I was concerned, class distinction was out. I mean, even a bum is entitled to some dignity.

Pete said: "You mean the major. No, he's not here, not today. He might be in tomorrow."

I couldn't believe my own ears so I asked Pete: "Did you say major? A real major?" Pete said: "What other majors are there?" I was about to say that there are drum majors, Salvation Army majors, major domos, but I felt this to be facetious, although it irked me that he could call any man who had sunk low enough to be a bum, a major. So I just said: "If I call back this evening can I see Major Dunleavy? He does live here, doesn't he?"

Pete said: "I think you misunderstand. This is for the homeless during the day. There are other places where they can sleep." I said yes I knew that, and I was thinking of the embankment and underneath the arches, where on any night you can see them wrapped in newspapers, their feet tucked into cardboard boxes. Pete continued: "Those other places close in the morning and open in the evening; so we give them shelter during the day, otherwise they'd be out on the streets."

This too irritated me, that people like Pete could feel sorry for these layabouts. I said: "So Major Dunleavy is not here. Thank you for your time. I'll call again if I may"

Pete replied: "Any time." And this irritated me more, because nothing seemed to rattle him.

It had been for me, a time-wasting afternoon, but I was keen to leave on a friendly basis, so I said: "It's much nicer having the light summer evenings now the clocks have gone on." But he just shook his head non-committally. Outside I acknowledged a wave from the bum who had taken my half crown. Then, as I was in the area and so as not to make the journey completely useless from the business point of view, I decided to call on Mr Solomon.

Mr Solomon was the owner of a wholesale fruit company. He had a branch in the Borough Market and a branch in Spitalfields Market, but Mr Solomon himself could usually be found in Covent Garden, where he had his office. Whenever I saw Mr Solomon, it reminded me of a picture I saw in a newspaper in the early 1930s. It was a picture of a middle-aged Jew squashed into a small wooden cart, sitting with his legs bunched up, his arms pressed into his sides. The expression on the Jew's face was one of hopeless resignation, the look people have when deep fear has given way to acceptance of the inevitable. He sat looking out from his cart at nothing in particular. Surrounding the cart were young laughing Nazis, and you could see they were taunting the Jew. Two of the young Germans held ropes attached to the cart and were in the act of pulling it through a busy shopping street in this German city. At the time, because I was then thirteen or fourteen, the Jew seemed old, but he was probably only in his early forties, younger than Mr Solomon was now.

Mr Solomon, in 1960, would have been in his late fifties, but what made the Jew in the cart look older was his big flowing beard and the black trilby hat he was wearing, whereas Mr Solomon was clean-shaven and, in a way, quite young-looking. In the picture, the Jew in the cart didn't look badly fed, but it was just the way he sat there, all bunched up, that was sad, and being taunted by these young Nazis. At the time, although they had on military-style uniforms with swastikas, I didn't look upon them as Nazis; I just thought they were ordinary Germans, and it seemed unkind they should be mocking this poor Jew.

But why the picture reminded me of Mr Solomon, or rather why Mr Solomon reminded me of the picture, was because he had the same unhappy expression. Of course, the Jew in the cart had a reason for being miserable since his fate, although he may then only have had a premonition of the Holocaust, was to be the gas chamber; but Mr Solomon, as far as I know, had never been pulled along in a cart or had this kind of treatment. The few times I had seen him driving to or from the market, he had been in his silver Rolls-Royce. You would think that being in a Rolls-Royce would make Mr Solomon happy, but always he had this mournful, pensive, faraway look, an expression many Jews seem to have and which must be because of the terrible burden of persecution carried by their race throughout the centuries.

By the time I got to the market most of the stalls were closed, but Mr Solomon was there. He was only happy, in his melancholy way, when he was within sight and sound of money. The sight was the buyers pulling out wads of notes to pay cash for fruit and flowers, the sound that of the till opening and closing in an atmosphere of light chitchat.

When I got there, Mr Solomon was standing, as usual, with his legs slightly apart, as if he needed this width to support his plump body, and as he was busy, talking to a customer, I looked around for Bert. Seeing Bert always gave me the same feeling of permanence which you can get from seeing Big Ben, or looking at Nelson's Column, institutionalized objects fixed in one's mind as images of changelessness made permanent by time and familiarity.

Bert was ten years older than me, and since leaving school, at the age of fourteen, he had worked first for Mr Solomon's father, then for Mr Solomon. Bert had been doing this same job, standing on this same pitch, for nearly forty years.

But to my great surprise there was no sign of Bert. It surprised me because I knew he'd had his holidays, and I couldn't ever remember him being away through illness, not once. And it would not be possible to miss Bert, who was not only tall, well over six feet, but broad-shouldered and heavy, a large man in every respect; and by large I mean not only physically but in his outlook, for he had a quiet, gentle manner and spoke always in a soft pleasant voice, answering often with a courteous nod of the head and, when agreeing with you, which he usually did, with a friendly smile. So it was quite a shock, I can tell you, when, having waited for Mr Solomon to finish talking to his customer, I went up to him and asked: "Where's Bert, Mr Solomon?" and Mr Solomon, pursing his thick lips, looked at me for a moment, then said: "He's still inside."

I pretended that I hadn't understood and said: "Inside? Inside where?"

Mr Solomon answered: "Inside prison. But he'll probably come out on parole."

For a moment I thought Mr Solomon must be joking, but when I saw he wasn't I asked: "What's he gone inside for? Fiddling?"

Mr Solomon, equally shocked at the suggestion, said: "Bert, fiddling? No, no. Nothing like that. Bert wouldn't fiddle. Dear me, no. He assaulted the police. That's what he did. First of all, he hit this bird, which was stupid, but assaulting the police was the serious charge, and he was lucky to get away with two years."

In utter astonishment I listened to Mr Solomon, then I said: "I find this quite incredible, Mr Solomon. How did it happen?"

One of Mr Solomon's assistants came up, asked him something, then picked up two trays of apples and carried them off. Mr Solomon said: "Well, boy" — and just for a moment he almost smiled — "so Bert not only assaults a young lady but he flattens a policeman. You ask me how it happened. I will tell you."

He paused, as if to chew over what he had to say, then continued: "If you ask me what made him do it, then I can't tell you. Except he was provoked by some crazy cow hootin' and tootin' on her horn at midnight outside her boyfriend's house, not only waking up Bert but disturbing the whole street."

My thoughts went back to Teddy getting up in the early hours and smashing in the dog's head, but Mr Solomon was saying: "Of course, she wasn't to know that Bert has to get up at three; nevertheless, the crazy bitch goes on hootin' and tootin', and the next thing she knows is that Bert has appeared in his pyjamas, pulls her screaming from the car, and gives her a backhander across the chops." Again there was almost a smile. He went on: "Well, in a way that was good, but silly of Bert. You can't take the law into your own hands. So Bert leaves her there shrieking and yelling, and of course there's faces at all the windows. Then the bird's boyfriend comes out — it seems they've had an up and a downer, but all is forgiven and now he's on her side. Someone shouts at the boyfriend to fuck off, so he gets the needle, goes back, and phones for the police. Altogether there's a right old rumpus."

Mr Solomon paused once more, shouted instructions to another assistant, and although I knew it was well past closing time and I didn't wish to detain him, I was interested to hear more about Bert, and he seemed keen to tell me.

He went on: "So Bert goes back to bed, but by now he is very tired and very irritable on account of being an early riser. Well, he just gets comfortably to sleep when the front doorbell goes and keeps on going, and this is more than Bert can stand. So he rushes to the front door, pulls it open, sees two blokes standing outside, and before the nearest one can open his mouth Bert has landed him one right in the guts. Later Bert said he didn't realize he'd hit a policeman, but no one believed him because they was in uniform and you couldn't help knowing. Needless to say, it wasn't long before the front doorbell goes again, and this time there are more coppers and they are not taking chances. Bert is arrested. At the magistrates' court it was stated he got his black eye, broken nose, and general bruising resisting arrest. He went to the London sessions and got two years. He was lucky to get away with that."

I nodded and said: "Yes, he was very lucky. GBH is a serious offence, especially when it involves the police."

Mr Solomon went on: "It was not only that he had an unblemished past — model citizen, good husband and father — but there was his war record."

I asked: "So there's never been anything like this before?"

"Good as gold. Never lifted a finger to anyone. Fed all the stray cats, that sort of thing. A good boy."

To me it didn't seem right that Bert should be in prison. Not, mind you, that I condone assault and battery, far from it, and not even when you are provoked like Bert was. So I said: "Well, I don't understand it. I've known Bert a good long time. It's certainly the most extraordinary thing that he should have acted like this. How long have I been coming to this market? Six, seven years? In all this time I've never seen Bert anything but happy and friendly." I shrugged and went on: "Even if the sentence was, in the circumstances, lenient, two years can be a long time. As you say, he'll get parole." I paused again then added: "I know from experience, Mr Solomon, I know what it's like. When I was fifteen and a boy sailor at HMS *St. Vincent* — this was before the war — it was like being in prison. Loss of freedom, that's a terrible thing. When I was there, one boy came up to me holding this little packet. He'd got lime from a building site when he was on weekend leave, and he begged me to put the lime in one of his eyes to damage his sight so that he could get out of that dreadful place. Another boy tried to commit suicide by jumping from the mast a hundred and sixty feet up, but he fell into the safety net. In that place, it was a boys' training barracks, a day was a month, a month a year; that's what prison must be like. You never think the day will come when you'll get out into the open. And the awful thing is that if you are shut up too long, you don't care any more and may even be afraid of going out." Mr Solomon nodded sympathetically. Then I said: "Bert was lucky. He certainly was lucky. I suppose, to a certain extent, the judge must have been on Bert's side."

Mr Solomon, rubbing his plump chin, said: "I think it was his war service that helped. Did you know that Bert was decorated for gallantry? Not that he talks about it. He's too modest. Much too unassuming. That's Bert's trouble, really. But whatever he lacks in the gift of the gab, his missus more than makes up for it. She don't stop."

I asked: "What was he decorated for?"

"I told you. It was for gallantry."

"Yes, I know. But what did he *do* ?"

Mr Solomon said: "I'll tell you the best thing to do, boy. Ask his pal Jack. He comes every week to collect Bert's money and takes it over to Bert's missus. It's very good of Jack, although he don't have much else to do."

Looking surprised, I said: "Then Bert gets paid while he's in prison?" Mr Solomon answered: "We don't have to pay him, but we do. He's a good boy. Naturally, he can't have the money in prison.

"His missus don't like coming here, not while he's inside. So that is why Jack comes for it. Jack was out in Burma with Bert. You can ask Jack about Bert's war service. He'll tell you. Bert got his medal in Burma. He was a sergeant and was behind the Japanese lines. Can you imagine a worse situation? Stuck in the middle of the jungle. I can tell you, boy, just to have been there entitled you to the VC."

In a slightly lighter tone, Mr Solomon went on: "Mind you, Bert hated those little yellow bastards. They was evil, he said. An evil race. They worshipped the Emperor like he was God. On the surface, if you meet them in peacetime, they are well-mannered, all very courteous, bowing and smiling, you kiss my arse and I'll kiss yours. But what they done to China was terrible. They can kill and torture with a ruthlessness beyond belief. Bert always said they was a formidable enemy. He didn't underestimate them. But he said they would lose the war. He said this quite a few times. He said he knew right from the beginning, when they attacked Pearl Harbor, that they would lose, just as the devil always loses. That is what Bert said. In fact, when he went there, went to Burma, he was so convinced about this, that they would lose, he made everyone feel ten feet tall and proud to be British."

Mr Solomon took out his hanky and wiped the back of his neck and said: "It was just the way Bert talked and behaved, never showing fear, never wavering in his belief that we would win, that gave his men heart." He stopped and scratched his ear, then said expansively: "I'm a Jew, but it don't matter what you are as long as you got something to cling onto. Believe me, boy, it's when you see death staring you in the face — and a time comes when it does just that — if you got something to cling onto, any straw, you can accept dying calmly."

I warmed to Mr Solomon. Not that I had ever not liked him, but what he had just said sounded big, really great, having, in common with all things immortal, some kind of universal application. He looked at me morosely. "Well, boy, I've got to lock up. Go and see Jack; he'll tell you about Bert. Give him a ring at home. He'll be pleased to see you. He lives by himself. He don't do much. He got a bullet in one of his lungs, in Burma, and can't walk very far. Gets a bit breathless. That's why he likes coming here. He can take his time and it's an easy journey. I'll get you his phone number." Mr Solomon went away for a moment or two, then returned with a scrap of paper on which he'd scribbled the telephone number. But nearly three weeks went by before I could find the time to go over and see Jack.

When I telephoned Jack I got through to one of those communal coin boxes, and the woman who answered had to go and fetch him. He got to the telephone, puffing a bit, but was very pleased when I told him I'd like to come and talk to him about Bert. So I went over to Streatham, where he lived, the following evening. Jack had this large bed-sitting room reasonably furnished with a divan, chest of drawers, cupboard, two armchairs, upright chair, and small square teak table. On the table stood a teapot and some cups. A yellow screen partially hid a washbasin. On top of the chest of drawers were three photographs, one in a cheap gilt frame, the other two in wooden frames. One photo was of three smiling children and a plump smiling woman; another was of a dog, an Irish setter; the other showed a Royal Army Service Corps group in 1940s uniforms.

Looking at Jack I could see that he was not unlike Bert in build but not as tall. He had a square face with a thin scar that stretched from his chin halfway up his right cheek. Although he had thinned a bit on top, his hair, dark and brushed neatly back, still had a youthful touch. His carefully trimmed moustache was a slightly lighter colour, not fair, but not dark like his hair. He had an upright figure and the same spick-and-span appearance I had noticed in his room the moment I stepped into it. I could feel the background of army discipline, not that of the conscript but of the professional soldier. The only concession to age seemed that forced on him by the wound: a wheeziness which made him draw in short breaths frequently. When he shook hands his grip was firm. He indicated the armchair and asked if I would have a beer. I declined, so he insisted on making coffee. I sat down and he brought the coffee over to me. For a little while we talked about the weather and his visits to Covent Garden; then we got onto the subject of Bert.

As Jack didn't say anything about Bert being inside, I didn't mention it either. I said: "You and Bert were in Burma together?"

Jack said: "We were there when the first Jap bomb fell. That was in 1941. I remember it well. The explosion was quite unexpected, as you can imagine. We threw ourselves flat. A few minutes later, when I looked round, all the Burmese had disappeared — vanished. I don't know where. So had the Indian police and all the air raid wardens."

I said: "You mean they were killed or injured?"

Jack answered: "I mean, sir, they ran. But don't ask me where; I never saw them again." He sat looking at me, then said: "After this there were heavy raids on Mingaladon and Rangoon. There was also an attack on Rangoon on Christmas Day. It left the city badly damaged, and afterwards Rangoon was quite a strange place. Hideous, really. A city of the dead, deserted by the masses, empty except for the scavengers and starving animals. By March the Japs had penetrated in great numbers across the eastern frontiers, from Siam into Burma. There were only two roads north from Rangoon, the main road to Mandalay through Pegu and Toungoo, the other lying to the west through Prome and the Burma oil fields. After violent fighting to the southeast on the Sittang River, the Japs cut the Mandalay road to Pegu, leaving only the Prome road open from Rangoon. But on 7 March — I always remember the day — we got orders to evacuate Rangoon. Me and Bert helped blow up the oil refineries at Seikgyi and Thilewa. I remember, when I saw the black smoke mushrooming up over the jungle, feeling sad yet knowing it was all for the best. The Japs came into Rangoon the early hours of 8 March, and that's when we began a fighting withdrawal."

Sitting back comfortably in the armchair, one leg crossed over the other, listening to all that Jack said, I couldn't say it was enjoyable, this story of violence, of starving people and starving animals, of total disruption with fleeing rootless refugees, men, women, and children. Only Jack's enthusiasm made it compelling listening. It was easy to see, as he recounted incident after incident, that he was back in uniform, in the jungle, alongside his comrades.

He went on: "Well, sir, as you can imagine, the administration had collapsed, and in one way or another me and Bert became involved in all the major battles: Taukyau, Letpadan, Paungde, Padigon, Shwedaung, Mongwa, and I never saw Bert afraid of anything. I remember once, when we'd been under heavy machine-gun fire near a road block and suffered lots of casualties, what was left of the platoon retreated past a hut in the woods. A party of Burmese in the hut opened fire, killing two of our men. Bert went forward with the platoon lieutenant while the rest of the platoon raked the trees with machine-gun fire to clear out the snipers; then Bert came back and with the others helped to annihilate a Jap machine-gun section. This was in the face of some pretty murderous fire from the enemy."

Jack moistened his lips and said: "I'll tell you another thing about Bert; even in the most terrible conditions — and you'd go a long way to find worse than these — he kept his sense of humour. After the engagement, when we were all sitting sweaty and dirty and dead beat, old Bert went round making everyone laugh. That's how it was with him. Even on the long march — when we withdrew northwards, covering some hundred and forty miles from Taukhyam to Prome — Bert was happy, cracking jokes, all the time cheerful, and at a time when we felt more like dying from exhaustion. But I'll tell you this, sir, many of those who survived would also tell you they owed it all to Bert. He had this way with him, making the retreat seem like a victory. You have to remember that the climate at that time of the year was nearly at its hottest, so you can imagine what it was like in that terrible jungle; but there was Bert's patrol, covering a wide frontage with little support, and Bert never letting up telling us — us, the survivors — that the Japs were only yellow trash, and anyone who had this idea they were supermen, a myth that had built up after they'd overrun southeast Asia, could think again."

All the time Jack spoke there was this underlying breathlessness, but the more he recounted the more he seemed to want to say. He continued:

"You also got to remember the Japs hadn't suffered a reverse, not one; not until we ambushed them in the village of Letpadon. What happened in Letpadon was this: we had created a successful diversion and then assembled unnoticed under a railway embankment near the town. There we had eight medium mortars mounted on armoured cars, and four medium-machine guns in carriers. The battle began, and in one minute a hundred and twenty mortar bombs exploded among the buildings; at the same time machine-guns from the right flank shot up the nearest houses and school. Then our lads went in, cleaning up the houses in the centre of the town."

Jack's square moustached face broadened into a smile. He coughed, cleared his throat, and said: "You should have seen Bert. It was a sight for sore eyes, to see those little yellow bastards trying to get away into the jungle and Bert with his men picking them off as they ran into the open." Jack stopped again. All the talking he was doing was not without increasing effort, but his enthusiasm never waned. He went on cheerfully: "I remember as if it was yesterday how we slaughtered those trapped in the school building. Our captain tossed the first grenade through one of the windows and there was bloody chaos, Japs running in all directions trying to get out. Some came into a stream of bullets from our Bren gun; others, jumping from second-storey windows, had their guts ripped out by our lads bayonetting upwards. We surrounded the building, threw more grenades in, and the annihilation of those who remained inside was soon complete. While we slaughtered that little lot, other platoons, including Bert's, working their way up the main street, shot down and bayonetted more Jap soldiers. The Japs by now were all hysterical, and were running in all directions." I drank the remainder of my coffee. Jack paused, then said: "You never seen anything like it, sir. Quite a few of the Japs, who were only half dressed, escaped into the jungle, but our lads were in full cry, charging the ones left behind, those who were trying to make a stand. We killed the lot. But although we won that battle, the retreat continued, and I remember waking up one still moonlit morning and seeing our lads flat out from exhaustion asleep under the trees. We'd bivouacked about two miles from Paungde. I remember that morning well. We had a quick breakfast and prepared for action; then we saw a motor-car coming out of Paungde. At first we thought it was flying a Red Cross flag. But the flag wasn't the Red Cross, it was the Japanese rising sun. Just as we noticed this, three machine-guns from the car opened up on us, but we quickly returned the fire, covering the car in a hail of lead. We killed two Jap officers and seriously wounded another officer and a private. Then our men, covered by mortars and machine-guns, left their vehicles and went in to attack the town. First they threw grenades into the bamboo houses, then Molotov cocktails, then with the enemy inside they left the houses to burn. I saw Bert; I saw his section moving towards a house. Then I saw him turn and with his Bren gun bring down four Japs who were getting into firing position. He just turned his gun on them and got the lot."

Only pausing to ask me if I'd like another coffee, which I declined, Jack continued: "By this time a new force of Japs had crossed the Irrawaddy river to the west of the Prome road, and had come between our main column and the rear guard. The enemy had also occupied Schwedaung. As we approached the village, air attacks intensified, but the street in Schwedaung was under continuous fire from our mortars and small arms. I counted three dive-bombing attacks as our men fought their way through. Bert's section got to the outskirts of the village; they laid up there under cover of darkness until they thought it safe to rejoin the battalion, which meant a difficult march across country over difficult hills. Although there were many wounded, with no fresh supplies, and everyone exhausted, Bert never showed strain. He must have felt terrible, like all of us did, but he never showed it. Even in the terrible fighting, in that dry and waterless region to the east of Yenangyaung where most of the Burma Army were trapped, he was still perky. If we couldn't all be singing, Bert certainly made us feel that much better. Nothing seemed to matter to him. Nothing frightened him. When most of us would have given one of our eyes to be out of the hell of that awful jungle, and given almost anything else to feel again on our faces the soft cool touch of an English spring or autumn, there was Bert, larger than life, charging around, calling out: 'Come on lads, let's have you. We'll show those yellow bastards. Come on, come on! Those bastards won't have to worry about hari-kari when they get the feel of our bayonets in their guts'."

Sitting listening to Jack, I found it difficult to think that the man he was describing was the same Bert, the big quiet fellow I knew, who for years had stood placidly, efficiently selling Mr Solomon's fruit in Covent Garden. But for Jack the real Bert was this war hero whose capacity for courage and bravery seemed limitless. Then Jack said: "He has a heart of gold, has Bert. One of the best. I remember the time we found Yenangyaung deserted. The houses stood high up on the Irrawaddy. Beautiful bungalows, sir. Beautiful. Inside we found wardrobes full of clothes, children's books and toys in the nurseries, even crockery left on the dining room tables. This really upset Bert. As a matter of fact, it made us all feel sad. Bert was looking at some of the kids' toys and he said to me: 'Jack,' he said, 'when I get back after the war to dear old England and the politicians start telling us the hatchet is buried and we're all friends again, and telling us we mustn't live in the past — when that time comes there'd better not be a fucking Jap anywhere near me'." Jack shrugged, as if he himself had kept a neutral position on this issue, and said: "Anyway, after that Bert went with two companies that were sent to Monywa to try and check the enemy's advance northward. Well, just as the sun went down, firing came from the houses on the west bank of the Chindwin. The Japs had arrived and were less than eight hundred yards away. Bert's section, all the lads weary and with sweat and dust on their faces, came in from the south. Facing the might of the Japanese army were about a hundred of our men, a comparatively small force of one battery of .77mm artillery, one mountain battery, one company of Indian engineers, one section of carriers from the Cameronians, two columns of the Burma Frontier Force, and a squadron of tanks."

Jack stopped again. More and more I admired the way he remembered everything in such detail. Then he said: "In Budalin, a village about forty miles north of Monywa, our lads took up positions. While the bulk of our force waited for the Japanese, Bert went out with a patrol. During the afternoon, it was the afternoon of 3 May, there was a tank battle, and just before dawn on 4 May the enemy launched their main attack. They came in, supported by tanks, from the southwest." Jack rubbed the bottom of his chin. "I can see those little devils now, screaming and yelling and firing shells and mortar bombs into us. They got a direct hit on our leading tank, which caught fire. Well, there was bedlam, I can tell you; and what with all the noise and our tanks having to pull back, the Indian unit panicked. A couple of Indians — they were kids, hardly out of their teens — started firing indiscriminately. They did it from sheer terror, but Christ knows what it might have cost us in casualties, because they were firing at their own side. Of course, they didn't know they were doing it. What might have happened is anyone's guess, but Bert saw straight away what was happening, and, cool as a cucumber, he just creeps up on them from behind and quick as lightning puts his rifle in turn to each of their heads and blows their brains out. Bang, bang, and it was all over. A matter of seconds. I've never seen anything like it. But I can tell you, sir, it was a tricky situation, and cool of Bert. Don't forget the state those kids were in. Sheer blind terror. Anything could have happened. If either of them had heard Bert and turned, Bert would have got a bullet in the guts."

Jack shifted his position slightly in his chair, then said: "There was no time for even a rough burial, so we left the bodies to rot. Out there, in that sultry climate, they decompose pretty quickly, although there wouldn't be much left once the scavengers had got to work."

I asked: "Did Bert have *have* to shoot them?"

Jack stared reflectively at the window, from which could be seen the grey roof of the house opposite. He looked back at me and said slowly: "Bert had to shoot them. There was nothing else he could do."

I said: "Couldn't he have overpowered them in some way? I mean, they were only boys."

Jack shook his head. "No, sir, he couldn't. There was no other way. It's easy to think what you might do when there's no threat, but when you've got a couple of crazed kids firing at anything that moves — and I can tell you, sir, frightened people can be very dangerous — you don't stop to think about it, you make up your mind quicker than yesterday and just do what you have to do." I didn't feel easy about Jack's explanation, but I accepted it, and Jack continued: "Our lads reached Ye-u at six o'clock in the evening. From Ye-u we went to Kaduma, then to Pyingaing, and on to Thetkegyn. We arrived at Thetkegyn at midnight 8/9 May. Then we moved on to Kalewa across the Chindwin. We'd travelled eighty miles, and our lads had to march for long stretches through bloody treacherous jungle in the most terrible heat. All the time we were only just in front of the enemy. Well, about five miles from the Chindwin we destroyed all our vehicles and crossed the river on launches. By the time we got over that jungle-laden mountain barrier, the one that lies between Burma and Assam, we were bloody weary, but we pushed on towards the Tamu Pass, which is 6,500 feet above sea level, and all this time we were carrying the wounded. There were thousands of refugees trying to keep up with us, but to make matters worse, cholera broke out, and by now I thought we'd had it; only you can't break the British spirit."

I nodded and said: "No, that's one thing you can't do."

Then Jack said: "Weary though he must have been, Bert still went round laughing, joking, making light of everything, rallying those who seemed on the point of giving way to utter exhaustion. I saw him a couple of times helping refugee children. Poor little sods, it wasn't their fault their country was overrun. Well, by the end of May we'd reached the new supply road which had been built along the old mountain tracks, and so we got to India."

I was just beginning to wonder how much longer Jack could go on for, as his breathing was becoming more and more laboured, when with a shrug and wry smile he said: "And that was it, a lot never made it. We were the lucky ones."

Nearly two weeks went by before I again visited Covent Garden. Mr Solomon was in his usual position, standing with his legs slightly apart, watching buyers come and go, sometimes speaking to them, sometimes leaving it to members of his staff to discuss their requirements. And it was then I remembered I hadn't asked Jack to tell me about the gallant act that had earned Bert his decoration, but before I could ask Mr Solomon he said: "Jack was here Friday. He told me you'd been to see him. You did him a lot of good. That boy has never got used to being a civilian. The one thing that's kept him going is his time in the army."

I said: "Yes, he certainly knows his history." Then I added: "He knows it better than anyone I've ever met. All the dates and names of places, got them off pat. Remarkable, really. He thinks the world of Bert."

Mr Solomon said: "I don't know if Jack told you this, but in court Bert was called a hero. Bert's counsel said anyone who went around like Bert did, in those appalling conditions, couldn't be anything less than a hero. That's what his counsel said, and you know, boy, these people have a way of putting it over." Wagging his finger, he went on: "I'll tell you this: everyone who heard Bert's counsel agreed one hundred per cent with what he said. One hundred per cent. Everyone. Because what Bert did in that stinking Burma jungle was heroic. They could have let him off with a caution and no one would have minded."

I said: "I'm sure you're right, Mr Solomon, but even a hero can't go round bashing up policemen."

Mr Solomon answered: "No, boy, indeed not. I quite agree. But it surprised me that Bert never got the VC. If anyone deserved the VC it was Bert." He put one hand lightly on my shoulder and said: "That counsel of Bert's was good. He had a lovely voice. Why, even the judge was nearly in tears at the end." Mr Solomon winked. "It's not so much what you've done, as how you are represented. That's the important thing, to get the right bloke speaking for you. All these judges are very patriotic; so when Bert's counsel got going on all that Bert had done for king and country — and it's not just what he said but how he said it — it was very moving. Very moving indeed."

I asked: "Did you go, then, Mr Solomon? Did you go to the trial?"

"No, boy. No, I didn't. But I heard all about it. If they'd wanted me to speak on Bert's behalf, I would have been there. Straight away. But he had so much going for him, I couldn't add anything significant. No, they didn't ask me."

I said: "So the judge was sympathetic."

Mr Solomon said: "In a way he was. Of course, what Bert had done was bad, there was no getting away from that. Jack went to the trial. He was there the whole time. Not that it was a long trial. Bert wanted to plead guilty, but his solicitor wouldn't let him, and in the end Bert agreed." Mr Solomon added emphatically: "Good job he didn't. They might not have said all those nice things."

"They would, Mr Solomon. They'd have said a lot in mitigation."

Mr Solomon said: "Bert never talks much. They must have got it all from his missus. She's got verbal diarrhoea." He rubbed the end of his nose and went on: "Jack said the judge was very nice. Benevolent-looking. Not that you can always tell by looks. Anyway, this judge told Bert that if it wasn't for Bert's exemplary record, the sentence he was about to impose would have been very much longer. The judge said it was sad that a man with such an outstanding record of war service, a man whose courage and determination in those appalling conditions must always remain an example of all that is noblest in the service of the Sovereign, a man who, up to this unfortunate time, had been a model citizen, it was sad that such a man should find himself in the dock, guilty of these serious charges. Then the judge said that although he would take into account Bert's war service and give what must be, in the circumstances, a lenient sentence, violence was on the increase, particularly among young people; and if people like Bert, for whatever reason, or however provoked, resorted to it, then anarchy could follow. The judge said that in no circumstances could violence be tolerated, so Bert must think himself fortunate that he was being dealt with comparatively leniently."

I remarked: "Well, that makes sense." Then I felt this moment a good opportunity to ask Mr Solomon what it was that Bert had done to get his medal, but before I could do so someone called out to say that Mr Solomon was wanted inside, and he immediately excused himself. I felt I'd taken up enough of his time, so I said goodbye and left as he raised a podgy hand in acknowledgement.

So I never did find out which of all Bert's gallant acts earned him his medal: whether it was for bayonetting the Japs at Letpadan, or going forward with the lieutenant to kill the Burmese who were firing from the hut in the wood, or the time he led his section through the dive-bombing attacks on Shwedaung, or whether it was that moment when, in Budalin, with great courage and resourcefulness, he blew out the brains of two terrified Indian youths.

I wrote to my rich uncle and told him I hadn't been able to see Dunleavy, but, to my surprise, I had discovered that Dunleavy was a major. My surprise was not that Dunleavy was a major, but that being a major he was now a bum. In my letter to my uncle I didn't use the word "bum" because my uncle, being religious, looked on everyone as just another human being.

About three weeks after I'd been to the doss-house — in fact it happened to be Princess Margaret's wedding day, the great day Janice had been waiting for — my uncle called for me at our London office and said he was taking me out to lunch. He did this sometimes, called unexpectedly. As soon as I got into his Bentley he asked me how things were going. He always asked this, and I always told him everything was fine. That is what he wanted to hear so that is what I told him. Then, as soon as he could, but without making it look as if the business side wasn't important, he got onto religion.

The religious part of these outings was boring, but I always got a good lunch. In fairness I have to say that my uncle, who was chairman, hadn't the very narrow outlook which his brothers, who were also on the board of directors, had. The brothers were all Plymouth Brethren; they had inherited this from their father, Bramwell, who had been chairman almost up to the time he died, when he was in his eighties. One of the brothers, my Uncle Arthur, became an exclusive Plymouth Brother. Being exclusive means you can't mix with anyone else who isn't exclusive, not even other Plymouth Brethren, if they don't think the way you do. At this time there were quite a few thousand people in our family business, but as far as I can remember there was no one who thought the way my Uncle Arthur did. Also, because Uncle Arthur was in charge of engineering and because we were a substantial business in this country and abroad, a lot of people came under him; so although he would rather have kept to himself, he couldn't help mixing a little.

On one occasion I flew with him and other executives to our creameries in Ireland. Uncle Arthur sat all by himself in the rear of the plane and didn't talk to anyone. One of the creameries to be visited there was where my father was manager. My father wasn't keen on these visits by directors even though he was related. The reason he wasn't keen was because he used to cook the books and pocket quite a bit of the creamery profit. He was good at that sort of thing, cooking books. During the war he built up a very successful black market butter trade. He sold quite a lot of the company's butter on the black market, even getting some of it over to this country. He also had this great gift of making everything he did seem right. He looked on his black market butter in a sort of philanthropic way, as if he was doing everyone a favour, letting those who were able to afford his prices have an almost pre-war supply. The poor people couldn't afford his prices, but he said that didn't matter because what they'd never had they wouldn't miss, therefore he wasn't doing anyone out of anything. That is how he saw it.

But with Uncle Arthur, who liked sitting by himself at the rear of the plane, I do know that my father would have been quite pleased if Uncle Arthur had stayed this way — that is, keeping to himself and not talking to anyone — because when Uncle Arthur got to the creamery, he always asked a lot of awkward questions. At the same time the books would be examined and discrepancies remarked on; only as my father was exceptionally good at lying, and had this vivid imagination, and could lie without thinking, his explanations sounded just as natural and sincere as those of any less gifted person telling the truth. I suppose that just as some people have vocations to be priests or doctors or teachers, my father's vocation was lying and cheating. If he had done for our family business what he did for himself on the black market, and in cooking the books, he would have made a considerable contribution to the group profits.

So on this day, which was Princess Margaret's wedding day, I was sitting beside my uncle in his Bentley, half listening to him, and for a little while he did talk about the business, telling me about his plans for expansion into Australia, which included the building of a large manufacturing plant along the lines of the one we already had in Canada; and he spoke about progress at home and abroad, for we had these agencies in most countries in the world, including China. He went on to say that the Australian development should be of particular interest to me as the directors were thinking of suggesting I go out there for a time, because we already had a member of the family in Canada and it was felt to be a good idea to have the family name in Australia. But when I say I was only half listening to my uncle, this is not because I am not interested in our family business. I am very interested even though, in 1959, our family business merged and died.

Once, when I was sitting alone with my uncle in the drawing room of his Guildford house, he spoke briefly of the name and its history, telling me about the little shop we had owned at 20 High Street, Guildford, where, in 1750, we began selling groceries. In 1850 the business, still at 20 High Street, belonged to Charles Gates, and in 1871, the year that the trade unions became legal, Charles advertised to the people of Guildford that he had an agency for Gilbey's wines and spirits. Ten years later he was advertising himself as grocer, and included in the advertisement the wares of four well-known brewers.

In 1882 Charles died and was succeeded by two sons, Charles Arthur and Leonard, and in 1883 the brothers were advertising themselves as tea and coffee merchants under the name of C.A. and L. Gates. In 1884 the advertisements of the brewers reappeared, but a year later, quite unexpectedly, these advertisements were dropped. It seems the reason for this was that one day, as the brothers were leaving the shop, they tripped over an old soak lying prostrate on the pavement outside. The thought of what they were doing so horrified them that they immediately brought up from the cellars the rest of the drink and tipped it into the High Street gutter. After this they decided that they would never again deal in wines, spirits, and ales.

This action led to considerable loss in profits, and it was then they realized that the spacious premises, with its yards and stables, could easily be used as a dairy, so they changed the name of the business to the West Surrey Dairy, which became the West Surrey Central Dairy Company Ltd., and later changed its name to Cow & Gate.

In 1885 milk separators had been introduced into England, and milk was cheap. Charles Arthur and Leonard then began marketing pure, rich, thick cream in little brown jugs with a label showing a cow looking over a gate. In 1895 this was advertised as supplied to His Royal Highness the Duke of York and in 1896 to Her Majesty the Queen and a few years later, in 1902, as supplied to His Majesty the King and Their Royal Highnesses the Prince of Wales and the Duke of Connaught. The separated milk was sold back to the farmers for feeding to pigs and calves, or put onto the milk floats for the late delivery pudding milk.

At this time, assisting in the business were Walter, William, and Alfred Gates, brothers of Charles Arthur and Leonard. They were later joined by their sons Bramwell, Ernest, and Stanley. Bramwell Gates, son of Walter, joined the business in 1889 and was chairman of Cow & Gate for twenty-one years from 1936 to 1957, and continued as managing director until he retired in 1958.

Between 1887 and 1895 creameries were started at Wincanton in Somerset, also at Sherborne, and at Beaminster in Dorset, and at Kildorrery in Ireland, where, later, my father was the manager. The year that Queen Victoria died, and with Hitler a schoolboy, our creamery in Sherborne installed the new Just-Hatmaker roller drying machine. After removal of the cream, the separated milk was dried, packed, and sold for use in baking and pudding making. This same type of machine was then installed at Wincanton and Beaminster. In 1904 the West Surrey Central Dairy Company began supplying large quantities of full-cream powdered milk and half-cream powder. In 1905 dried full-cream milk, dried half-cream milk, and dried separated milk were advertised for the first time under the

Cow & Gate label. Reports from Sheffield Royal Hospital gave most encouraging results from the use of dried milk in the feeding of babies.

In the early days, breastfeeding, which was regarded as a duty, was common. It usually continued for nine months but sometimes much longer. An alternative, the wet nurse, was unpopular because desirable people were not easy to obtain. Artificial feeding with some modification of cow's milk, or with condensed milk of the early twentieth century, was not without its perils, especially in the humbler homes. Seventy years earlier bottle-feeding was almost equivalent to a death warrant for the baby. Even under the very best conditions, sixty or seventy per cent died.

So it was in these comparatively primitive times, and from such humble beginnings, that our family business grew and prospered, becoming a world-wide organization and a household name. When my uncle had finished, I told him I thought it was really great the way the business had expanded and prospered. Later, when it all fell apart, I never did tell him I then thought it sad that so noble an achievement should have such an ignominious end.

The reason I was only half listening to my uncle was because my thoughts were on this great day, the wedding of the Queen's sister. I don't know what it is about Royal days, or anything Royal, but there is always this feeling of excitement and anticipation.

In a much more insignificant but nonetheless real way, there was the same feeling in our business for the family who had started it and now ran it. There was, of course, the drawback of not being able to get on the main board unless you were a member of the family, but I never knew anyone in our business who was not a member who minded; in fact, all our employees found security and stability in its being family. I expect a lot of this secure feeling was because my uncles were very democratic. Even Uncle Arthur, who didn't like talking to anyone, was, in his own way, democratic. With my uncle who was chairman, and Uncle Paul who was in charge of all the creameries, the humblest worker could walk in and see them; and since we were now this very large world-wide group, we had quite a few humble workers. My rich uncle, the one now taking me out to lunch on Princess Margaret's wedding day, had these notices on his office door: DON'T KNOCK, WALK IN. FIVE MINUTES IS A LONG TIME.

He let it be known that anyone could see him because, although he was chairman, in the sight of God everyone is equal: just another soul. I don't think many workers did go to see him, or if they tried they didn't get past his secretary. She had been secretary for a good many years but

88

didn't have the same democratic feelings as my uncle. She just thought workers were workers.

My uncle, although at this time he was sixty, had a very upright military figure. In fact, he was a military fanatic. He had been at Sandhurst with the Duke of Gloucester. He loved the Royal Family and had been photographed with the Queen and the Queen Mother. These photographs, enlarged, hung framed in prominent positions in his office. When, some years later, we built a large modern head office block in Guildford, there hung in the elegant boardroom a lovely painting of the Queen Mother. Although my uncle loved the Royal Family, he didn't think the Duke of Gloucester all that bright because at Sandhurst the Duke played jazz records loudly in his room above my uncle's, which irritated my uncle when he was busy interpreting the Bible.

So even in his younger days my uncle was busy working at his prophecies, and there developed in him this combination of religious and military fanaticism. His visits to our West Country creameries were run on the lines of parade ground inspections. The men would line up on the loading bays, some dressed in white overalls, some in blue. My uncle would inspect them to see if they were properly dressed, wearing hats and that sort of thing. Empty milk churns were set out in rows in front of the loading bays, each churn brightly polished. When he had inspected the men, and some of the girls, and looked at random churns inside and out, he would run his finger over and under ledges for dust, look minutely into laboratories with their white-coated chemists, scan precisely the parked lorries, and, when he had finished his inspection completely, give the assembled creamery staff a pep talk on production, congratulate them on their achievements, and exhort them all to believe in the Lord Jesus Christ.

We went to his club for lunch. It was in Pall Mall and some of the roads were closed for the wedding, but we managed to park the car and got to the club without too much trouble. I thought perhaps he would want to hurry lunch so that we could see something of the wedding. I knew he would be particularly keen on the church service. I studied the menu. He asked me what I wanted. Even a simple thing like this, asking you what you wanted for lunch, had an underlying sense of urgency. There always seemed to be a sense of urgency in anything he said or did. With him it was a sort of nervous thing, compressed energy pushing up all the time. You had this same feeling, that time is not on our side, in his prophecies. And his prophecies were mostly to tell you how the world was going to end, violently, with the collapse of civilization as we know it. All this was to happen fairly soon.

My uncle had worked it out that the Second Coming would happen in his lifetime, and that he was to be in the vanguard of those treading the red carpet to welcome Jesus. Once, when he said Armageddon was round the corner, I really thought he was on to something. He always spoke in this very firm, convincing way which all prophets and dictators seem to have, saying there would be great devastation, blood would run in the gutters, and London would emerge as the new Jerusalem. He was intensely patriotic, so London was the obvious choice. Anyhow, he was quite sure about it and stocked up at home with large tins of biscuits, soups, tinned meats, beans, canned milk, and canned fruits. This was so that he and his family wouldn't starve when civilization was being wiped out. He had ordered the food from our central stores at Effingham. Being chairman, he could probably have got these tins of food for nothing and had them put down as samples, but he was a man of integrity so he paid the lowest wholesale price. He couldn't have paid less without losing his integrity.

At the time my uncle was talking about Armageddon, Russia and China were threatening each other and the Middle East was in turmoil so, from his point of view, it all looked pretty good because the biblical quotations he had used, to back up his prophecies, showed how nation would be fighting nation and blood from the slaughtered millions would run in the gutters. Once this new Jerusalem, in London, had risen out of the ashes, the twelve tribes of Israel would lead the new generation into a brave new world. As well as prophesying all this in his booklets he talked about it. Constantly. Prophesying in this way gave him a sense of destiny and at the same time acted as a soporific to his fear of oblivion. He had been sent not only to run the family business but, just as the first prophets had done nearly twenty centuries earlier, to point the way.

But what made me think my uncle was on to something was not so much that he had, like Rose's husband, this very forceful way of putting things over, nor that his prophetic interpretation of what would happen seemed to be happening, with violence and killing escalating and this only fourteen years after a war that had killed fifty million; it was that he gave the exact date for Armageddon. I can't now remember the day, but I do know that, when it came and passed everything had gone on much the same. It was an ordinary sort of day, clouds skulking in a grey sky, and a little local scandal, the wife of a schoolmaster having run off with a sixth-form pupil; but it didn't seem to worry my uncle too much that he had got it wrong. He worked it all out to his own satisfaction and then replaced his stocks of tinned food so that they would be fresh for the big event still to come.

For lunch, on this day when he had taken me to his club, I decided on soup followed by lamb cutlets with courgettes. I had just finished my soup when he started on religion. I didn't really mind, as I counted myself fortunate in two ways: firstly, that the lamb cutlets with red currant jelly and mint sauce were delicious, and secondly, that he had, at least up to now, delayed talking about Armageddon. I usually found it best and easiest to agree with everything he said, and although in one way this may seem a bit weak on my part, I thought it a small return for all his kindness in helping me get on in the business, and in giving me these very nice lunches.

Not that I have ever been in the habit of arguing. Most of the time I like to agree with whatever anyone says. I don't know why this should be, why it is I have this weak nature. At election time when the Conservative calls, I'm conservative; when Labour calls, I'm labour; and if the Communist called I would certainly be sympathetic. I have found that if you agree with everything they say, they don't stay very long, and this makes me happy and leaves them happy. I know we are supposed to have minds of our own and I know, too, that this is a free country and we can, within reason, express our views, but it gives me a sense of well-being, making other people feel happy. I did once mention this weakness, wanting to agree with everything anyone says, to Patrick. He said it was because I hadn't gone through the normal teenage stage of revolt against my parents.

My parents had separated when I was three. I didn't see much of my father, who was busy drinking himself to death in Ireland, so there was only my mother, and I don't remember wanting to revolt against her although we had quite a few rows. My stepfather, who came along later, was kind and gentle, so Patrick may be right. Anyway, my uncle started on about God and Mammon and violence and the world's sickness. He said that there had never been so much violence; that man had lost his way, lost sight of the truth; that the carnal nature of the corrupt old Adam was abroad again and on the rampage, and that unless we put to death this old Adam, we couldn't be purged by God's purifying holy spirit; that there had never been a time when violence in young people was so much a way of life, a festering sore, with too lenient a view taken of it by those in high places in our present Godless society. On the whole, the future looked pretty bleak. Because of his very assertive manner, I thought in one way he might be right, even though, deep down, I didn't think he was. I mean, you can often get this duel feeling when you are up against strong people. But for all my uncle said about violence at the present time, had I been the sort of person who likes arguing I might have suggested that

91

for mindless violence on a gigantic scale it would be hard to beat the 1914–1918 war, where at Ypres, on our side alone, the killing was about seven thousand a week, while on the Somme we lost twenty thousand in one day.

A young fellow at the next table was staring at my uncle. He may have thought my uncle had something loose somewhere. My uncle had one of these deep, penetrating voices which reach a long way, so this young fellow could hear all that he was saying about Armageddon and violence and so on. The look on the young fellow's face seemed to indicate he thought my uncle a very odd person indeed, but even if my uncle had noticed this, it wouldn't have worried him. He was a great believer in a prophet not being recognized in his own country. In a way I think, being an extrovert, he would have quite enjoyed being crucified. I don't mean he'd enjoy having nails knocked through his hands and feet, although he would certainly keep a stiff upper lip, but if God delivered him to die for the sins of the world, and plenty of publicity went with it, that would suit him very well.

There may be, for all I know, quite a few people who have this feeling of wanting to be crucified. Simon Parker, who was in the same infant and junior school with me at Fulwell, felt this way. He was seven when I was six, or something like that. Simon told me about these dreams he'd had where he was persecuted by the crowds. He didn't use words like persecuted, but that is what he meant. In one of the dreams he was on the path to Calvary walking behind Jesus. In this dream Simon, like Jesus, carried a wooden cross which, though smaller, was just as heavy. The people lining the route were shouting and jeering and spitting. Although he knew he was going to be crucified, Simon was glad he was not one of the crowd. He hated the crowd. So when they shouted and spat, and he felt the spit trickling down the side of his face, it gave him this feeling of excitement, of exultation, because he was not one of them, not one of the mob. The thought of being crucified also gave him a strange feeling of excitement. In the dream Simon never got as far as actually being crucified, only walking along, dragging his cross between all these jeering spitting people and having this marvellous sensation. When we moved from Fulwell, my mother having found a slightly larger house in Sunbury, I didn't see Simon again until I went to Hampton Grammar School, where he was in a higher form than me. I was then coming up to twelve and he was nearly fourteen.

Simon was in the same position as I in that he lived with his mother, but whereas I had brothers and sisters, he was an only child. His mother had moved to a flat in Twickenham and one day Simon asked me over. It was a Saturday. The morning began bright but cold, then the sky became overcast, drifting clouds thickened up, and it started to rain. By early afternoon the rain was torrential. I thought twice about going but in the end decided to, and arrived at his place dry underneath but with my hair and face dripping. It wasn't a large flat — a couple of bedrooms, sitting room, bathroom, and kitchen, just an ordinary suburban flat neatly and pleasantly furnished. His mother was out for the day.

She went out to work, but Simon didn't say what she did, and he never spoke of his father. I did, once, meet his mother. This was at a school speech day. She was very nice, slim, fine features, fair hair, blue eyes, smartly dressed, and spoke with a slightly foreign accent. She had a kind of elegance. Simon, in a way, looked like her with his fair hair and blue eyes, and he had the same shape features. He was taller than me. He wore silver-rimmed glasses. He was very nice with nice manners, but he didn't have the same firmness as his mother. He had this funny way of looking at you, a sort of peculiar look, deep, hard to describe, as if he was mulling over thoughts inside himself which he might or might not share. You would suddenly become aware that he was staring at you in this curiously contemplative way, but to stare back wouldn't achieve anything and could become embarrassing because in the end you would have to give way.

The first time I went to see Simon nothing much happened. We lay side by side on the floor in his bedroom, which seemed the easiest way to look at his books. He had a lot of these, and a lot of games and gadgets too. I could see his mother spoilt him. Not that he behaved like a spoilt person. He wasn't selfish or mean or anything like that. On my first visit I spent the whole afternoon with him. When I was leaving he asked me if I would like to come again and I said I would. So I went two weeks later. Again, it was a Saturday and he was alone. This time, instead of grey flannels, Simon wore a pair of black silk shorts. I mean, they looked like silk because they were thin, shiny, tight, and emphasized the whiteness of his skin, making that much more noticeable his long, slim legs. Because of this whiteness and his fair complexion he didn't look all that robust, but it was when we got to wrestling that I found he could really hurt. I don't know if he knew his own strength, but his grip left deep red marks on my arms.

On this second visit we again lay on the floor of his bedroom and looked at his books. It was comfortable, lying like this on my tummy, cushioned by a thick lavender grey carpet. The window was slightly open and I could hear the noise of high street traffic. It was cosy in the room. Suddenly he shut the book he had been looking at and turned on his side and lay staring at me in this funny sort of way. Then I asked him, and why I should have put this particular question at this particular moment I couldn't say, I asked him if he still had these dreams where he was carrying his cross, walking behind Jesus on the way to Calvary. He said no, he hadn't had a dream like that for a long time, not since he was quite small — in fact, not since we'd been together at the infant and junior school. He said he had all sorts of other dreams now, and there was one to do with Jesus and this was when they whipped Jesus and put the crown of thorns on Jesus's head. This dream was very vivid, and Simon could feel the pain and feel, if that was the right word for a sensation, the blood trickling down Christ's face from where the thorns had pierced the flesh. Just as his other dream excited him, Simon seemed curiously stimulated by recalling this one. All the time he was talking, his hand was deep down inside the front of his shorts.

I didn't altogether like the situation, so I said could I have a look at his sailing boat, a large model with everything exquisitely made, the sails, ropes, tiller, and so on. He got up, took it from where it stood on top of his bookshelf, and put it on the floor in front of me, and it was then he said: "Willie, would you like to wrestle?" I said no, it wasn't something I particularly wanted to do. Actually, I have never been keen on wrestling or fighting, or any of these manly activities where you stand a chance of getting hurt. So I told him again I didn't want to wrestle and I would much rather go on looking at his books or watch him work his electric train set. He said I could work his electric train set myself if I would first wrestle.

He was still staring at me in this very peculiar way, but I didn't take too much notice until he started to undress. He took off his shirt, vest, socks, and sandals and stood there slim and smooth in his black shorts. He took off his glasses, knelt down, put his arms round me, and pushed me flat on my back. He pressed himself into me, which I didn't like at all, and said: "Come on, Willie," and he was drawing in these quick sharp breaths. This jerky breathing wasn't because he'd exerted himself too much, but because he was excited. I could tell he was excited the way he pressed himself into me and the way he clutched my arms. His grip was hard and cruel and hurt in an unmerciful way; then, still breathing in fits and starts, he said: "Come on, Willie, push me away. Push me away, Willie. Try and get me off." I wanted to get him off, so I pushed him hard, and he gripped me tighter and it hurt like hell; then I lost my temper and told him to pack it up, but he took no notice and went on pushing and torturing me with his grip, and I could feel his breath on my face and I thought it was never going to end when suddenly he groaned, then went limp, and I slid away from under him. On the leg of my trousers was a large damp patch, and I must say I felt more than a little fed up; so I told him I had to be going. I mean, I was a bit bored with all this violence; also, I could see the damp patch on my trousers had soaked through from his shorts, which were messy in front.

When I said I had to be going he didn't seem to mind. He just got up, put his glasses on, put the boat back on top of the bookshelf, put on his vest, shirt, socks, and sandals, and came with me to the door. He didn't ever ask me back. When I saw him at school he didn't talk any more about his dreams, only about cricket and football and, on one occasion, about the suicide of our science master, who left behind a wife and three children when he threw himself under a train.

I finished my lamb cutlets, which, as I have said, were delicious, and was thinking about what I might have for pudding when my uncle said: "You may remember MacDonald. I think you trained under him." I said yes, I did remember him very well. It was in 1950, when I had started my training on the milk rounds, that I was sent to MacDonald. This was at Bethnal Green, where horses were still being used. MacDonald's horse was a bit temperamental. At places where it had been frightened it would suddenly break into a gallop and tear along, everything rattling on the float, until just as suddenly it would quieten down into a normal trot. I liked MacDonald. I think he took to me, too, because not long after I started with him he showed me how to fleece customers. He also showed me where the best pub was for beer and the pub where all the queers went, and he showed me the house where Ada lived.

Ada, in her own way, was a kind of celebrity. This was because she hadn't bathed for forty years. This is what MacDonald said, although I don't know how he could have known unless she told him. But he said, also, that although she hadn't bathed for all this time, she didn't smell or anything like that. Her place smelt a bit because she didn't clean it very often, but not Ada herself. MacDonald said there wasn't anything wrong in not bathing if you didn't want to. He'd read somewhere that Queen Elizabeth 1 had only bathed three times in her life. Then MacDonald asked me if I'd like to see Ada, and I said I would. I thought I might not get the opportunity again to see someone who hadn't bathed for all this time. I said was he sure she didn't smell, only I am not all that keen on smells — that is, the sort of smell you could expect from someone who has this rather disagreeable habit. You get these smells in some of the doss-houses. I discovered this when I went to see those bums who were tapping my rich uncle for money. But MacDonald was adamant and said no, it was a very funny thing but she definitely didn't smell, and I could take his word for it because he'd served Ada for quite a few years. In any case, as far as he was concerned, she was just another customer, and he didn't mind whether customers smelt or not as long as they paid their bills. Ada was never any trouble; she always paid promptly.

MacDonald also told me that Ada wasn't badly off. She went out French polishing. Sometimes she had a few days at home when she'd been too much on the gin bottle, but she was a good French polisher and never without work. She kept her money in stockings under her bed. He'd not mentioned this to anyone else because he didn't want her robbed. He'd told her to put it into a building society, but she liked it where she could put her hands on it. How many stockings she'd got under her bed stuffed with notes he wouldn't like to think, but it would probably run into a few thousand pounds.

The morning we went to see Ada I followed MacDonald in. He didn't knock but pushed open the front door and yelled out for her. He called out again and I heard a stirring from upstairs. The house had once been at the end of a terraced row. It wasn't now because a bomb had flattened the two houses next to hers, so Ada's little place stood by itself, with the rubble and weeds on the ugly bomb site dividing her from the rest of the row of late nineteenth-century workmen's cottages. The small sitting room we had walked into was in the most appalling state. When I say it was a sitting room that is putting it politely in terms of Western civilization. As a matter of fact, it seemed to be the only room downstairs, for against the far wall was a greasy gas cooker with chipped enamel and stains down the side. Underneath the cooker was a cardboard box, and in the box, lying contentedly on a piece of pink cloth covering the bottom, was a black-and-white cat with a litter of three kittens. There was a greasy patched armchair, a wooden table covered with a torn piece of white-and-blue oilcloth, and on top of the oilcloth a plate with the remains of a meal. Also a dark-brown teapot and a George V coronation mug with stale tea in it.

The windows were so cemented over with grey dirt that you couldn't see properly through them, and even a long brown velvet curtain across the door was stained and had a tear down one side. I found it quite incredible that I could see nothing that wasn't grimy or chipped or torn. Only the cat and its kittens seemed wholesome. Then there was this awful stale smell of grease. Old, dried grease. So I thought that when I saw Ada, in spite of what MacDonald said about her not smelling, she would match these surroundings. But when Ada came treading cumbersomely down the uncarpeted stairs, her appearance was not what I had expected.

She was wearing a heavy, moth-eaten black fur coat and looked at me with this plump, smiling, nice-looking face and said in a pleasant voice that it was lovely to see us and would we please sit down and she'd make us a cup of tea. Unless, of course, we'd rather have a little drop of gin. MacDonald said: "We won't stop, darling. Willie, here, wanted to meet you." I shook hands, relieved that I would not be drinking from her china. Then she lit a cigarette and left it dangling from between thickly rouged lips, occasionally puffing and letting smoke drift out from the side of her mouth that was not holding the cigarette. Her bunched-up, untidy fair hair with its brown roots showed heavy peroxide treatment. She had a little smoker's cough, clearing her throat every now and again. MacDonald said in his brusque Scots voice: "Willie here is one of the family. He's starting at the bottom." He looked at me and I confirmed that this was so. Mac-Donald went on: "He'll be doing the round on his own for the week I'm away. You'll look after him, Ada. Give Willie some breakfast." She said yes, if she was at home she'd be very pleased to give me breakfast. The thought of having breakfast in this room made me feel quite ill, although none of this, Ada not bathing and living in squalor, seemed to bother Mac-Donald. I thought this funny because he was so spruce and clean, his nails, as opposed to Ada's grubby finger ends with the red varnish flaking off, carefully trimmed.

Outside, and we didn't stay much longer, MacDonald explained to me that Ada was a real tonic, and he didn't know of anyone who had a kinder or more generous nature. She would give you the coat off her back, except that she wore it all the time. She put it on when she got up and took it off when she went to bed. She did this in summer, even on very hot days. Then MacDonald explained that when Ada went to bed she didn't undress completely like most people; she just took off her coat and her dress and slept in her underclothes. I found this quite interesting and asked: "Doesn't she change her underclothes? I mean, she can't have the same ones on all the time." MacDonald said yes he was sure she changed her underclothes, but he didn't know how often. He said he didn't think that even Ada could have spent forty years in the same underclothes.

When I did the round by myself, I made a point of not going to see Ada, except on the Saturday when I had to collect the money for her milk and eggs; then I stood just inside the door and saw that the kittens were playing by themselves. MacDonald said Ada loved animals and she'd take in any stray and find a home for it; in fact, Ada had this great love for everyone and all creatures. She was one of these rare people, MacDonald said, who would give her last pound note from one of her stockings to help anyone in need. That is what MacDonald said, and I have no reason to disbelieve him. Ada was certainly warm and friendly, and she was the sort of person, when you first met her, you would instantly like. But if you are fussy like me, you wouldn't want her to give you breakfast.

When my uncle asked me if I remembered MacDonald and I said yes I remembered him very well, my uncle looked straight at me and went on: "Did you know that MacDonald has found the Lord Jesus?" I said I had heard he'd been converted and what I'd heard was that MacDonald, one day on the round, had met up with this evangelist who read to Mac-Donald from the Bible and had then handed over some tracts, and from that moment MacDonald became a changed man. I must say, when I heard about it, I found it difficult to believe that after this, when he took round the milk, MacDonald was also delivering tracts entitled "The Man They Can't Get Rid Of," "What I Have to Do with Jesus," "Lift Up Your Heart to God," "God So Loved the World That He Gave His Son," and a pamphlet written by my rich uncle called "The Divine Gift of Life."

Where he could, although it usually meant at the last moment sticking his foot in the door, MacDonald gave news of the glad tidings of his conversion, and I suppose if proof was needed of this startling change, it was that he not only stopped calling in the pub where he got beer on the house in exchange for a fiddle on eggs worked with the manager but, and this seemed to me the strongest and most compelling evidence of the power of Jesus, he immediately stopped fleecing his customers. Then my uncle said, and I knew it was coming: "I've had a letter from MacDonald. He's asking for help. Could you look him up and send me a report." My uncle passed me the letter. It was on cheap yellow writing paper and had a Hounslow address. He continued: "And if you wouldn't mind, Willie, could you make your own way back. I have another appointment."

So I decided against pudding and just had coffee; then we left the club. In the street, after I told him I would see MacDonald and Dunleavy and give him a report on them both, he said: "God bless you, my boy," and I thanked him for the very nice lunch, then went to look for a taxi. In Whitehall I saw a group of people outside a shop window watching television coverage of the royal wedding, but I walked on, thinking about MacDonald and wondering how soon I could visit our Hounslow branch when I would be able to see him at the same time.

Although I hadn't seen MacDonald since we were on the round together, I had heard about him. This was when I went over to our Bethnal Green branch not long after I'd been given my first executive appointment as an assistant to the London sales director. The same manager was there, a good-humoured Cockney in his early forties with a square jaw and perpetual grin. We were sitting in his office discussing sales and talking over future plans when I mentioned MacDonald. I said how odd it was that MacDonald had, suddenly, become so religious. The grin on the manager's face widened as he pulled open a drawer of his desk and took out a small tract which I saw had been printed in America. On the front page was a black-and-white head-and-shoulders drawing of a woman who looked something like Joan Crawford. She had her arms crossed in front of her, her chin resting on the back of one hand. She was smiling, her eyes gazing upwards. Above the drawing were the words: *DOES ANYONE LOVE YOU?* I found the answer on the second page, where a drawing showed Jesus nailed to the cross with the words: *HE LOVES YOU! HE DIED FOR YOU!* Underneath the drawing and in pinhead lettering were these lines from Isaiah 53: "All we like sheep have gone astray". The other pages were written in a similar way, with quotations from Isaiah and Corinthians and Hebrews, and there were more drawings ending with a young man in a white smock and the words: *WASHED IN THE BLOOD.*

I gave the pamphlet back to the manager, who screwed it up and threw it into the wastepaper bin. I remarked again that it really was very odd that a canny Scotsman like MacDonald should be handing out pamphlets like this one, but obviously MacDonald believed in it all, took what was said as gospel — all excellent stuff, good teaching and preaching that he could pass on with complete confidence, hopeful that not everything would fall on stony ground.

Whether there was any fertile ground around in Bethnal Green I couldn't say, but from what the manager told me it seemed that most of the customers, at any rate to begin with, thought it was some sort of joke. When MacDonald called on Saturdays to collect the money and hand out pamphlets, some of them would stand looking at him quizzically, then try and shut the door in his face. This is what his politer customers did. But there were those who took a more straightforward approach and told him to stick his pamphlets up his arse.

When my uncle was telling me how MacDonald had found the Lord Jesus, the last thing I wanted to do was prolong the boring discussion, but this is not to say I was against MacDonald's conversion. At least it would have meant, had he continued on the round, that his customers would have been better off financially. I can't truthfully say, even now, now that I have got into old age, that I am able to go along with people like my rich uncle, or Rose's husband, religious people who really think that someone, somewhere, is keeping an eye on us. Yet there have been these occasions when it has really seemed like this, and my meeting up with MacDonald in Hounslow, not at the address he'd given in his letter but, quite by chance, almost opposite 20 Clare Road, was the most extraordinary coincidence.

It was this coincidence, together with being, also by chance, outside Wandsworth Jail six months later, on the morning of Forsyth's execution, that gave me this strange feeling of an unseen hand resting firmly on my shoulder, pushing me forward into writing this biography which, had I been a writer and not a dreamer, I would have written long ago. And even when I think of excuses for not having written it, when I tell myself that a biography of this nature would never work because, generally speaking, you can't get people all that interested in the working-class, and that not even the working-class themselves would be interested, when I tell myself this as a sound and valid reason for not doing any work, the hand grips tighter and pushes harder. Also, and I might as well come out with it now, in spite of my disbelief, but because, in my hour of need, I was given indisputable proof I cannot disregard completely the power of prayer.

On the Monday following the lunch with my uncle, which was Monday 9 May 1960, when I was in the office, I asked Janice to arrange a visit for me to our Hounslow branch as I wished to take the opportunity to call on MacDonald at the address he'd given in his letter. Janice, of course, was still bubbling over about the wedding. Had I been able to watch it? Wasn't the television coverage marvellous? Spectacular in colour.

Oh, the beauty of it all. Breathtaking! Didn't Her Royal Highness look lovely? So happy and so in love. And Mr Armstrong-Jones. What did I think of him? Wasn't he nice? She was sure he'd make her happy. But the coverage, it was unique. Just imagine, an estimated audience of three hundred million. It had been seen in Austria, Belgium, Denmark, Finland, France, West Germany, Italy, Luxembourg, Monaco, the Netherlands, Norway, Sweden, Switzerland; also America and Canada, Australia, Nigeria, and Hong Kong.

The papers had said the wedding had been a Cinderella-like occasion, and that's just what it was. The dazzling pageantry, the sparkling procession, and a marvellous summer's day with great crowds lining the streets. Then, in the Abbey, all those distinguished people: our own beloved Royal Family and the world leaders. Didn't I think Princess Anne looked sweet, such a lovely little bridesmaid. And the Queen, too, so lovely in that beautiful dress with its exquisite turquoise hue. Also the Queen Mother, so gracious and kind, and Prince Charles, very grown up in the way he smiled and waved at everyone. But of course, it was Princess Margaret's day, and Janice had never seen anything like it. All those tens of thousands of cheering children waving their Union Jacks as the bride, with the Duke of Edinburgh, left Clarence House. The Duke is such a handsome man. The gallant way he helped the Princess into the coach. She looked radiant. Absolutely radiant. And the gorgeous bridal dress of foaming white silk with that gorgeous diamond tiara and the veil waving about her head. She was so happy, smiling, waving graciously to the thousands and thousands lining the route, all shouting their good wishes. When the glass coach passed under the huge arches of red and pink roses it was just like a fairy-tale picture. Again and again, as the Princess passed by, you could hear gasps of wonder from the crowd, and you could hear quite clearly some of them calling out: "Oh, isn't she lovely! How beautiful!" Had I noticed, too, how those normally gloomy old government buildings along the route had been decorated, looking glorious with arrays of white hydrangeas and scarlet geraniums and azaleas?

Then there was the Abbey, with the Princess in her wedding dress of white silk organza, moving gracefully on the arm of the Duke of Edinburgh, walking slowly up the long stretch of vivid blue carpet. And had I noticed how the bridegroom was standing thoughtfully rubbing his forefingers across his lips while the Royal Family, headed by the Queen, sat in three rows of chairs on the south side of the sanctuary? In a chair of the same elaborate design as that used by her daughter sat the Queen Mother, with the young Prince of Wales in his royal kilt beside her. On the north side of the sanctuary sat the bridegroom's parents, Mr Ronald Armstrong-Jones QC and Lady Rosse. There, too, sat the foreign guests, making up a scene rich in colour. Five of the royal ladies were dressed in shades of gold, the gold blending with varied tones of blue, and all of this blending in with the rich vestments of the clergy. Among the many distinguished guests, distinctive in his grey morning suit, was Sir Winston Churchill with Lady Churchill.

The bridal procession was led by the Queen's Scholars of Westminster School; then came the Canons of Westminster and the Dean of Westminster, an impressive figure in his crimson cope, followed by the high bailiff of Westminster; then the picturesque figures of the Queen's four almsmen, traditionally the bodyguard of the dean and walking immediately in front of the bride. Following the bride were the eight little bridesmaids led by Princess Anne, who, as the procession reached the sanctuary steps received from the bride the bouquet; then the royal bridesmaid stood behind the bride when, a little later, Princess Margaret moved forward with the bridegroom to the altar.

I could see by the way Janice was talking, in a rather breathless voice, that her emotions were not only stirred by the lovely and impressive setting of the royal wedding, just as the emotions of millions of others who had been watching had been stirred, but that ideals and dreams had filled, almost to bursting point, thoughts of her own marriage. Janice not only saw the Princess in the role of the royal bride but saw herself in that setting, and, as she told me later, she had already made up her mind to have Psalm 121 and the passage from St. Matthew's gospel, which includes the Beatitudes, for her own wedding. So she went bubbling on and, because royal weddings don't come every day, I listened to her attentively as she recalled every little detail: the sacred vows, for better, for worse, for richer for poorer, in sickness and in health, to love, cherish, and obey until death, and the close of the service with the choir and vast congregation singing the national anthem; then the Archbishop of Canterbury, also impressive in a richly decorated cope and mitre on a cream-coloured background, walking ahead of the bride and bridegroom, who were attended by Princess Anne and followed by the Queen, the Queen Mother, the Duke of Edinburgh, Mr Ronald Armstrong-Jones and Lady Rosse as they went into St. Edward's chapel behind the altar for the signing of the registers. After everyone except the bride and bridegroom had returned from the chapel, the fanfares sounded once more as the Princess and her husband came out and passed in front of the Queen, the bride making a graceful curtsey, her husband bowing in homage, and Princess Anne smiling and curtseying so prettily. I thought Janice might have left it there, as we had work to do, but she seemed determined to go on to the end, to recapture every wonderful moment of that marvellous day. So I sat listening as she spoke of the procession when the bride and bridegroom came down the steps of the sanctuary between the choir stalls, a thousand gilded chairs turned inward, the happiness of the Princess there for all to see, for Janice, for the huge congregation of distinguished people in the Abbey, for the thousands lining the route and for the millions watching it on TV. The service over it was back to Buckingham Palace, the appearance on the balcony, then the finale to this beautiful royal wedding day, with the royal yacht *Britannia* sailing by, down the Thames, in the sunshine, to begin her honeymoon cruise to the Caribbean.

More than a thousand cars and four thousand sightseers had crowded into Greenhithe between Dartford and Gravesend, and one of the biggest crowds Gravesend had known packed the promenade, which had been decorated with bunting, while hooters sounded up-river. The cheering started as *Britannia* came round the bend and continued as the royal yacht went down Gravesend Reach. Tugmen sounded their sirens while sea rangers on Gravesend customs jetty sent a greeting with semaphore flags. Boys of the National Training School lined the front of the riverside establishment; ships at anchor were dressed overall with gaily coloured flags; two hundred and fifty cadets, manning HMS *Worcester* at Greenhithe, gave three cheers as *Worcester* dressed overall, flashed a message of good wishes. Crowds at Canvey Island lined the sea wall, while the royal bride and her husband came on deck to wave in response to the tremendous cheering, as local yachtsmen sailed out in small craft to wish the royal couple 'bon voyage'; then more cheering at Southend from ten thousand people on the pier-head, and fishing craft and more yachts packed with sightseers going out to greet *Britannia*, while from the pier-head coastguard station the Mayor of Southend flashed a message: SOUTHEND WISHES EVERY HAPPINESS TO THE BRIDE AND BRIDEGROOM, to which the flag officer of the royal yacht replied: THANK YOU VERY MUCH FOR YOUR KIND MESSAGE, MARGARET. This was followed by a message from the Coastguards: LOYAL GREETINGS AND BON VOYAGE, to which came the gracious reply: THANK YOU VERY MUCH FOR YOUR KIND SIGNAL. Three miles from Southend an admiralty barge took off the RoyalMarines band. Then, with the happy couple on board, the royal yacht sailed away:

Through the shadows and the sunshine
As in sunshine gleam the ripples
That the cold wind makes in rivers
Smiles the earth, and smile the waters
Smile the cloudless skies above us

So passed into history a great and memorable day.

One thing I am really scared of is death. I try not to think about it. I don't like the idea of cremation or rotting away inside a coffin. If, when I die, it is a freezing cold winter's day, cremation might be acceptable; but if it is a warm day in spring, or one of those lovely English summer days, not too hot and not too cold, then a country churchyard beneath a secluded tree would be best, and for my tombstone these lines from *The Song of Hiawatha*:

Saw the rainbow in the heaven,
In the eastern sky the rainbow,
Whispered, What is that Nokomis?
And the good Nokomis answered:
'Tis the heaven of flowers you see there;
All the wild-flowers of the forest,
All the lilies of the prairie,

When on earth they fade and perish,
Blossom in that heaven above us.

On the whole, thinking about it, whether it is winter or summer I think I'll go in for being buried. I like the idea of a gravestone with those lines on it. It is something, sometime, that I will talk over with Arthur.

I was thinking about all this sitting halfway down on the bride's side of a pretty Hertfordshire church, and then I got to thinking how nice it must be if you are really religious — that is, to have deep convictions like my rich uncle, or like Rose's husband, whom I had met eight months previously outside Wandsworth Jail, or like this nice upper-class vicar now officiating at Janice's wedding. I mean it just seems to me that if you are like they are, then rotting away inside a coffin or just being a handful of dust wouldn't worry you.

Janice, whose June wedding was, all but two days, exactly one year and one month after Princess Margaret's, came up the aisle on the arm of her father, and she looked stunning in her wedding dress, with a wisp of a veil dropping over her pretty nose and her few freckles. The bridegroom, standing at the front of the church with the best man, glanced round as the bride approached. He was tall, in his early twenties, light brown hair, grey eyes, a scarcely noticeable red birthmark on his left temple. He wore a light, fawn summer suit, rose-coloured tie and had a white carnation in his lapel. He was a handsome young man, and I liked, too, the look of Janice's father, a middle-aged man of medium height with dark brown hair neatly parted and a neat moustache. Janice once told me that he was a Socialist and a strong union man. She said he was like this because his childhood had been very hard. There were a lot of brothers and sisters and very little money. Her grandfather had started off as a coal miner, then run away to sea, married an Austrian girl, stopped going to sea in order to be with his young wife, but could only get navvying jobs for a few shillings a week so that often the family were on starvation diet, which had made her father very bitter. He had worked his way up to foreman in a car assembly shop but had never lost his dislike of inherited wealth and privilege, which seemed to be reflected in the firm set expression of his face, an expression stern and uncompromising. He was a man who knew his rights. In a dark navy suit and with a white carnation in his lapel, he walked slowly up the aisle, his chin tilted slightly upwards.

There were about sixty or seventy guests, many of them young people, the girls in bright-coloured dresses, the lads in suits ranging from conventional blue, brown, and grey to light pastel shades, but all of them looking smart in what was fashionable for the young working-class in the 1960s.

There was no choir but the organist was excellent, and the vicar, tall and aristocratic, a man in his mid-thirties, led everyone into the singing with great enthusiasm. He spoke the prayers beautifully. He enunciated each word clearly and precisely without in any way losing the overall rhythm, so that even the Our Father, which can be a monotonous, repetitive chant, sounded new and fresh. The sun lit up the stained glass windows and it was all very pleasant. I was glad Janice had followed Princess Margaret and chosen that passage from St. Matthew containing the Beatitudes. It has all these lovely things about the meek inheriting the earth and the pure in heart seeing God and everyone being the salt of the earth, except if the salt loses its savour it becomes good for nothing; and although I think this business about the meek inheriting the earth applies only to the very poor, the whole passage sounded great the way the vicar, in his wonderfully expressive voice, read it.

Then the vicar went on to ask for God's blessing on these two persons, that they might both be fruitful in the procreation of children and live together in Godly love and honesty so that they would see their children Christianly and virtuously brought up. Of course, it is easier to say something than to do it, but the vicar had this great gift, in the way he spoke, of making you believe that the prayers meant what they said, and he wasn't saying them just because without them you couldn't be married. But again, I have to say that although I haven't got the deep religious conviction which I would like to have and which I envy so much in those people who have it, I certainly believe in the power of prayer. In my hour of need I was not left alone and had this proof which happened during the war in HMS *Malaya*.

Well, here we are cruising along beneath a Mediterranean blue sky accompanied by an aircraft carrier, two cruisers, and four destroyers. We are out on patrol looking for the Italian fleet, but the Italians are about as keen on fighting as I am, so they don't come out very often, which is a good thing as far as I am concerned and which is also one of the reasons I have always liked the Italians.

It is peaceful and calm, with a brilliant blue sky and blue sea. The sun is hot and the upper deck is hot, but I am dressed in cool tropical gear: singlet and white shorts, and with my white blancoed cap tilted back over my head, and I have been given the boring job of washing the camouflage paintwork at the base of the fo'c's'le turret. Under the shadow of the huge sixteen-inch-diameter guns I slap water on and wipe it off, going through the motions mechanically, happy to be by myself and trying to make the job last so that I do not get detailed off for heavier work. I never have been one of these people who is cut out for manual work, which is why I never made a good job of anything I did on the lower deck and got these bad reports.

As a matter of fact, when I think about it, I don't know why I joined the Navy in the first place. It began, I suppose, my wanting to join up, when I saw this very romantic film at the Odeon Cinema in Kingston. I was fifteen at the time, and it was quite a good film about a boy who came from a poor background and went to sea in sailing ships, worked his way up to officer, married the captain's daughter and was killed in action. I thought it really fantastic the way he lay dying, with bodies lying about and the masthead blown off and everything around him wrecked. I mean, when you see it all from a comfortable seat in the cinema it seems marvellous, guns recoiling, belching flame and smoke, men falling all over the place, carnage and blood and death scenes; in fact, I was so moved by it all that almost before I realized what I was doing I had gone to the recruiting office, accepted the king's shilling, and found myself at HMS *St. Vincent* being kitted up. My mother wasn't very happy about it but had reluctantly given her permission. The funny thing is, though, that when I found myself in action, and it is even easier to see this in retrospect, it wasn't at all the same as watching it on a cinema screen, and to be truthful, I don't think I've ever fully recovered from the shock.

Fortunately, however, the Italians, when they did meet up with us, realized they had made a mistake in coming within range of our guns and turned quickly for harbour, so that the engagement lasted only a short time. All the same, it was pretty scary with death and destruction all round, and great spouts of water rising up as bombs and shells, whistling eerily, dropped wide of their targets; but the Italian shells came pretty close, and we scored a direct hit on one of their cruisers, killing some of their crew. And that is another stupid thing with me: I can never think of this as killing the enemy, but only of Italian telegrams going out to parents who will never again see their sons.

Stuck in the pom-pom range-finder turret on the port side of the bridge, I could do nothing but crouch down, shivering and shaking, hoping that the shells and bombs aimed at us would go on dropping into the ocean. It was all high-level bombing so that the enemy aircraft were out of range of the pom-poms, which is why I had nothing to do, but no one saw my cowardice because I had this little circular range-finder turret to myself and was crouched down inside the tall protective shield; but when I say protective I am not so sure, because as soon as the action was over when I was able to stand up and breathe again, there was this jagged hole, just to my left, in the steel plating where a lump of shrapnel had come through, and had I been crouching a few inches to the left it would have gone through me; and I must say that although I was relieved to have got away unscathed, the thought of that piece of shrapnel coming so close didn't make me feel very happy.

During this action when, on odd occasions, out of the corner of my eye, I saw the captain, he was standing calm and serene on the compass platform, in his white uniform, wearing his tin helmet, four little white stripes denoting his rank painted on the front, his binoculars hanging down against his chest as he stood quietly giving orders. After the action he was still standing there, quietly, and for all the emotion he showed he might as well have been at a cocktail party. The other officers on the compass platform were the same, unruffled, unafraid, or if they felt fear showing no sign of it. I wish I could have been like them, because although I am a coward, I admire those who aren't, or if they are, those who have the courage not to show it.

It was with this Italian action in mind, the fright it gave me, and the fervent prayers I sent up shortly afterwards that it should never happen again — it was with this in mind, the scariness that death and destruction inevitably brings, that one morning, not all that long after the Italian action, I again heard the loudspeakers crackling, this time followed by the captain's dramatic announcement that the *Scharnhorst* had been sighted and we were steaming at full speed to engage her. I felt damp and sticky and found it difficult to breathe, not from the heat of the sun but from fear and panic, the panic that comes from being trapped in a terrifying situation from which there seems no possibility of escape.

The *Scharnhorst* was one of Germany's two modern battle cruisers, fast, effective, reputed to be unsinkable, whose guns were able to outrange *Malaya's* so that she could pick us off before we could get within striking distance. I summed up the situation as if it was the Home Guard with 303 rifles going in against a German Panzer division: a situation dear to the heart of the British and marvellous for the history books, but not for me when the chances are that one minute I am alive and well and the next minute a spaghetti-like mess of blood and flesh and bones spattered against the bulkhead. I mean, I just like being alive, which is something that has been born inside me and a feeling I've never got rid of. It isn't that I wanted Hitler to win or anything like that, far from it; but I suppose I lacked those qualities of guts and endurance so precious to people like Miss Page, who had inherited a large estate in Ireland and another smaller estate in England, and who was really keen on the

British Empire and who thought, right to the end of her life, that the natives were missing out by not keeping it going.

Miss Page lived in the largest house I had seen until I went to stay at Rhinefield, the home in the New Forest of the Walker-Munros. She was rich and aristocratic and had been left the house, part of a huge estate, by her father. The estate was so large that it had its own deer park. It was also from her father that she had inherited the estate in Leicester and a beautiful house in Belgravia.

Whenever I was in Ireland, visiting my father, I would telephone Miss Page and go and see her. Although she had all these houses and land and vast wealth, I sensed that she was lonely. She was tall, slim, autocratic, her hair swept back and done up in a bun, reminding me of pictures I had seen of the young Queen Victoria. Not that Miss Page was young, for she must have been then, when I first met her in the early 1930s, in her fifties, and she died not long after the Second World War. But she reminded me in many ways of Queen Victoria, not when the Queen was middle-aged and stout, but the young, slim, attractive Queen; for Miss Page had kept her youthful figure and like the Queen was punctual, exacting, concerned for her servants and the lower orders, often going into the villages near her mansion to take food and comfort to the poor and the sick.

Like all aristocrats, except with her friends, Miss Page stayed at a distance. People who came to stay, who dined at her great table or sat in the large beautiful drawing room with its priceless paintings and exquisite furniture, were often from wealthy, titled English and Scottish families. I had heard that, in her grandfather's day, the Prince of Wales, who became Edward VII, had been to stay. Why Miss Page took to me the way she did I couldn't say. My father was on friendly and sometimes intimate terms with eminent people — Edward Sackville-West, Lord David Cecil, Sir Isaiah Berlin — but this was because of his friendship with Elizabeth Bowen. When Elizabeth and Alan were in Ireland, my father went often to Bowen's Court to see them, and guests from Bowen's Court came often to our house to bathe; this was because Bowen's Court, a large, lovely house, wasn't sufficiently modernised. It had just got past the stage of the maid bringing up jugs of hot water for the master's or mistress's hip bath.

One day, when I went to see her, Miss Page lent me a very interesting book on heroic deeds in which her father was mentioned. He had been a British general attached to the Indian army in days when discipline was kept by a rifle butt on five little brown toes. In this book, as well as her father's heroic exploit, there was a short account of Jackie Cornwall. It seems that Jackie, who was only sixteen, had stayed at his post while a great naval battle was raging. He was mortally wounded and was posthumously awarded the VC. I was fourteen at the time I read about it, and I thought it really great that Jackie, who was only two years older than me, should have won the VC; also that at such an early age his name should have gone down in history. I mean, it is not easy, at any age, to go down in history, let alone when you are only sixteen. So after I had read about Jackie, I thought it must be the most wonderful thing to do, to stay at your post with a battle raging all round; but having experienced that action with the Italians, and being so close to death, I can't honestly say I was all that keen on doing my duty once more. Even if the *Scharnhorst* wasn't modern and fast and almost unsinkable and able to outrange and outdistance us, I would still rather have left the German warship alone.

But of course the Admiralty were very glad to have caught up with her as she had been around for some time, picking off our merchant ships, then vanishing at high speed. Our captain also seemed very pleased at the prospect of an engagement; that is, he sounded very happy about it when, at 1100 hours, he made the announcement that the *Scharnhorst* had been sighted, that we would close up for action stations at 1300 hours, and that he expected to commence firing at 1430 hours. I mean, it all sounded marvellous the way he said it, and if I'd been sitting in the cinema watching it on the screen, I know I would have been deeply moved.

What was to happen was this: a destroyer would be sent ahead to reconnoitre; then, when the *Scharnhorst* was nearly within firing range but not near enough to see the strength of the British fleet, a smoke screen would be laid, and the cruisers and our old battleship would charge through and engage the enemy at close range before the *Scharnhorst* realized what was happening. The idea, of course, was to sink the *Scharnhorst*, although, as I have said, she had a reputation for being unsinkable, having been built with an intricate structure of watertight compartments. But the British are always optimistic and confident of victory, even if it leaves quite a few dead and wounded lying around.

Being British, I know I should have felt pleased at this opportunity to follow in the footsteps of Jackie Cornwall; that I should find it exciting, closing up at action stations dressed for battle, which meant putting on anti-flash gear to cover our faces and hands and wearing tin helmets; that I should be proud I was able to play even this small part in the defence of our country; and that if I now had to lay down my life for what is right and just, I should regard this as an honour and a privilege, knowing, too, that I would be remembered, gloriously, with millions of others, each year, until the time comes when, as has happened with other great battles, the need for remembrance goes; and because of this it makes me even more ashamed to have to mention this feeling of abject terror which took hold of me, and which might not have happened had I not already experienced the horror of the Italian action.

So it was at this moment, at 1400 hours give or take a few minutes, when we were steaming at full speed towards the enemy, the battle ensigns broken at the mastheads, and I was standing closed up for action stations at the pom-pom range-finder in hot Mediterranean sunshine watching the destroyers in V-shape formation followed by the cruisers, then our old battleship, and, well astern, the aircraft carrier; it was at this moment, standing beside my range-finder on the port side of the bridge, and with that same sickening feeling Forsyth must have had when, with the noose dangling in front of him, he took his last few steps out of this world, it was at this moment I made my heartfelt plea.

Fervently, with implicit faith in His goodness and compassion, I asked God to deliver me from this hell-hole, from the battle that was about to take place once we were through the smoke screen and in range. And I told Him that if I could be delivered from the carnage — for in my mind I was already in action in an eruption of total violence, seeing heads blown off and guts and bowels strewn about and spilt blood staining the deck with the strong possibility that my own head, guts, arm, or leg would be part of the mess; or even worse that we would suffer the fate of HMS *Hood* when, in a similar engagement with the Germans, that mighty battle cruiser got a direct hit in the magazine, blowing her and, except for three survivors, the crew of about two thousand, including my young neighbour of childhood days, Victor Papworth, into extinction — that if I could be delivered from all this and He would see me through, if somehow, anyhow, He would get me out in one piece so that I could go on breathing, I would never again complain about anything. I would never complain about not having been born rich and not having gone to Eton, or having a dissolute soak for a father, or being an ordinary humble person with dreams of greatness and immortality; and not only would I not complain but I would be prepared to do the humblest job, to be a dustman or a road-sweeper, anything, as long as I could see again green fields and hear the cuckoo in springtime, lie in the long grass beside the sand-pits where Rose and I read to each other, or just stand near Wilson's boat-house by the Thames at Sunbury watching the river flowing on its way to the tumbling silver water of the weir farther down.

In a way I know it is selfish to pray in this way, because if there weren't battles and brave people, you wouldn't have these marvellous services of remembrance, with the great hymns swelling the Albert Hall, and the red poppies, and war heroes with their rows of medals and the Royal Family in black; also the beautiful Cenotaph service, with the guns booming out for the two minutes' silence and that beautiful lament "Flowers of the Forest" and the "Last Post" and those fantastic words from Binyon's poem: "They shall not grow old, as we that are left grow old: age shall not weary them, nor the years condemn. At the going down of the sun and in the morning we will remember them". Also, that marvellous line, part of a lovely ancient Latin anthem: "Let light perpetual shine upon them".

In another way, too, when I look back now that I am a pensioner, when I look back from the comparative tranquillity of old age, I think it was very wrong of me to have been like this, to have been so scared of going into battle, to not want to defend unto death all that we value in our great democracy, but this is how it was.

So I told God that although I fully recognized the value of dying for King and country — particularly when the enemy was the archetype of total evil, and that it would be nice to be like Jackie Cornwall and be a hero among heroes, and that I should put my trust in Jesus because, if by bad luck I am blown to bits, God's son will be there to welcome me, holding out a guiding hand to lead me through dark places — that although this is how it should be, for me it didn't work because all the time I had this yearning, a longing for those quiet days of childhood:

In the green and silent valley
By the pleasant water courses

Then I told God that if I had the choice of war or peace, I would even put up with being back in Portsmouth Barracks as it was before the war, back to the crumbling brickwork, the dingy, dusty dormitories with rows of iron beds and coarse, hairy blankets, the pig swill for food, the filthy heads where sensitive people like me crept into the latrine at some godforsaken hour, hoping there would not be added to the indignity of sitting in the open the farts and rising stench from messmates squatting alongside, emptying their bowels as their stools drop with little splashes into the pans beneath their straining bums. Even this awful decaying pre-war barrack life seemed like paradise now that I was about to be called on to defend our great and noble British heritage. And once more I promised God, cross my heart and throat, that I would never again complain, that I would never show the slightest resentment at being given the most menial of tasks, that I would look upon it as a privilege and pleasure if I had to continue the humble, almost working-class, way of life into which, unfortunately as I have thought up to now, but through no fault of my own, I have been born. I told God that I could talk in this way only to Him, and to Him alone, because only to Him could I open my heart and explain my reasons for wishing to be a live coward rather than even risk becoming a dead hero.

But God understood. I know that now. He understood and listened to all I had to say, and even now, forty years later, I still feel a deep sense of gratitude in what He did for me; for there we were, all dressed up heroically, guns loaded and pointing towards the enemy, the battle ensigns flying at the mastheads, the destroyers, the cruisers, our old battleship, and the aircraft carrier cutting through the blue Mediterranean water, their bows throwing up little white crests of waves, a stirring and noble vision; then, at the last moment, the smoke-screen failing, failing miserably, for instead of thick black smoke pouring from the funnel of the screening ship, something went radically wrong in the engine room, and wisps of transparent grey drifted about, soon to be sucked up by the sun so that nothing was hidden, and the *Scharnhorst*, seeing the British fleet steaming at full speed towards her turned and ran. And when our planes, taking off from the aircraft carrier failed to find her, we stood down from action stations leaving one watch closed up and the ship in a semi-alert position.

It was then, with an enormous feeling of relief and sudden well-being, that I told God I would never again doubt His existence, that I would never forget what He had done for me, and that I would never miss one day in saying my prayers. If I have missed, it has not been intentional, but because sometimes, having just started Our Father, or having begun to ask for God's blessing on everyone everywhere, I have fallen asleep.

It is for this reason, because I have had proof of His existence, I take seriously what is said in church. I mean, I don't often go to church because I get bored; but with this wedding, watching Janice and her bridegroom making their solemn vows and listening to the reading of the passage from St. Matthew containing those Beatitudes, and seeing my pretty secretary and her young bridegroom so full of joy, happily accepting their responsibilities, coming away from the service as man and wife, joined together not to be put asunder — well, you could see from the look in Janice's eyes when they stood together outside the church in the sunshine posing for photographs, you could see by the way she looked up at her smiling husband, intensely, lovingly, that the marriage was for life. I stood watching from between two gravestones, silver-grey mossy stones, the wording on one almost obliterated, the other showing part of a name and a date: HANNAH ... WIFE OF ... LUCAS ... SHE ... ARMS ... IN JESUS. B. 1884 D. 1914, both gravestones at crooked angles. Amid the long grass a dog rose made a pretty splash of pink and green against the grey stone, and a butterfly, a large white, fluttered past. When Janice and her husband had finished posing for photographs and were then driven away, I followed on with other guests to a nearby hall for the reception.

After shaking hands with the young couple and getting a warm kiss on the cheek from Janice, I took a glass of sherry from the waitress, then went to the back of the hall and stood, glass in hand, watching the happy couple surrounded by laughing friends and relations. Three long tables were loaded with cold food and bottles of wine. Janice, in her flowing bridal dress, the veil tucked back, looked flushed and animated. Her young husband stood with a few friends not far from the magnificent four-tier pink-and-white wedding cake, while Janice, bubbling over with happiness, did the rounds. Except for her, I knew no one there, and no one came up to talk until just before the cutting of the cake when Janice, seeing me standing alone, rushed over and said excitedly: "You were sweet to come. It wouldn't have been the same without you."

My mind went back to the dairy dance and the dark corner, my hand inside her dress as she pushed her tongue into my mouth, and I wondered momentarily, with the silly ego that takes hold of an older man when he thinks a girl half his age is infatuated, whether Janice was in love with me as well as her husband; but I quickly dismissed the thought and said: "It's the loveliest wedding I've been to, and you look gorgeous."

She said teasingly: "Oh, thank you, sir," and dropped a little curtsey.

Before Janice and I could go on talking the vicar came over. Janice introduced me, and he said: "I think we've met before." He paused, smiling. "At Oxford, in the Bach choir, with Thomas Armstrong."

I said: "Of course. I do remember."

Janice left us to talk, and we spoke about people we knew who were up at Oxford just after the war. I said: "The world's a small place," and I told him how I'd bumped into Rose and her husband outside Wandsworth Jail the previous November and explained that it had been thirty years since I'd seen Rose when, as children, we used to read together. Of course, I didn't want to tell him we'd stolen some of the books, so I just said that Rose and her husband, who was also in the church, had gone to protest about the hanging.

The vicar said: "Yes, I remember the case well. It was widely reported. Weren't there two young men hanged?"

I said yes, four young men were involved in the murder; two were hanged, one was too young to hang and was detained during Her Majesty's pleasure, the other was found guilty of non-capital murder and sentenced to imprisonment for life. Then I said: "But the protests were over Forsyth, who was only eighteen, just eighteen. Had he been a couple of months younger, he wouldn't have hanged."

The vicar, who was holding a glass of white wine, drank some, frowned, and said: "I'm against hanging myself. I can't see how it solves anything. You don't bring back the victim and you kill the person who most needs help and understanding."

This attitude on his part slightly irritated me. I felt it was going too far, treating the criminal as the sufferer. So I asked him if he thought that the punishment should fit the crime. He fingered his dog collar and said: "Certainly, within reason; but always with compassion."

I asked: "Whatever the crime?"

He said: "Yes, whatever the crime."

A waitress came over with a tray. On it were glasses of champagne. The vicar put down his wineglass, took a glass of champagne, and I also took one. I said: "The Forsyth murder was a particularly brutal one. The victim was a decent young chap who had got engaged the day before. One of the gang struck him in the face and knocked him to the ground. While he lay there groaning, Forsyth put the boot in, kicking him repeatedly in the head. It was a savage attack. But the worst part was that when, later, he was charged with the murder, Forsyth showed no remorse whatsoever. He showed not the slightest compassion for the victim or the victim's fiancée, but thought only of how long he reckoned to serve before he was a free man again. He reckoned that, with a bit of luck, he'd do five years and be out by the time he was twenty-four."

The vicar said: "Yes, but killing Forsyth wasn't the answer."

I asked: "Then what was the answer?"

"To forgive him. Punish him but forgive him. Because when a person is on the path of forgiveness, he is on the path to redemption. If you kill as a means of retribution, you are committing the same violence as the person you are seeking to punish for doing just that. It doesn't work."

I nodded but felt we couldn't go on talking about a hanging at a wedding, so I looked over to where Janice and her husband were standing. They had just cut the cake and, rather sweetly, were holding hands. This was a time of happiness for all of us: for relations, for friends, for the vicar who had been with me at Oxford. Apart from the choir I had met him a couple of times at smart parties given by Etonians who had been at school with him. His father was a baronet, but he was not the eldest son so would not inherit the title. He was tall, slim, with fine firm lips and a long nose. His brown eyes were friendly and he was slightly thin on top. The way he talked about hanging, not wanting Forsyth hanged, showing compassion where the brutality of the crime seemed to allow for no compas-

114

sion, a man from a background of privilege and wealth, yet sympathetic to this young working-class murderer now nearly six months dead; a man of God for whom the path of forgiveness and redemption was the only way forward, his were the feelings of pity and concern which must have been in the mind of Rose's husband when he made his more positive protest on that bleak November morning; and they must also have been in the minds of the many distinguished people, politicians, bishops, artists, and peers of the realm, people from a class that in every respect was the opposite to Forsyth's, whose letters of protest against the hanging were published in *The Times* a few days before Forsyth's execution.

As well as these letters of protest, a petition of two thousand signatures asking for a reprieve was presented to the Home Secretary, but many of the ordinary people of Hounslow, sick of the violence, the thuggery, the gang brutality, felt only a sense of relief when Forsyth, caught in his own web of violence, was no more. The two executions, Forsyth's and that of the other member of the gang of four who was hanged at Pentonville the same day, came as a shock to other hooligans in the Hounslow area, and the deterrent effect was seen when a period of comparative calm followed, when the mugging, thieving and vandalism dropped dramatically. The violence returned later, but at the time things looked good.

For myself, I have never been able to decide who was right: the many ordinary folk in Hounslow who had to put up with violence on their own doorstep and, because of this, refused to sign the petition for clemency brought round from door to door by the families of the condemned men, or those who, in signing letters of protest against the execution, showed compassion to a teenage boy who, himself, was completely without compassion.

I can't truthfully say I was all that keen on seeing MacDonald again. Not that I disliked him in any way. I had enjoyed the milk round and had many happy memories; also, when I was with him he hadn't seen the Light and become religious and started giving out tracts and doing all the boring things which a lot of very religious people seem to do. But I just think that when something's over, it's over.

As my uncle had asked me to go and see him, I thought the sooner I got it over with the better so I told Janice to arrange a visit to our Hounslow branch, and I told her that I would see MacDonald at the same time. It was about a week after Princess Margaret's wedding, when she was still on her honeymoon, that I drove over to the address MacDonald had given in his letter.

Although this address was in the poorer part of Hounslow, the house, small, semi-detached, was neat and clean. The window frames and the door were freshly painted a pretty primrose colour, while the tiny garden in front of the house had a neat little lawn about three feet square with a border of rhododendron bushes flowering red and pink. There were also some green rose bushes. It all looked pretty on this pleasant spring day, the same warm, sunny weather that we had had for the royal wedding. It was pleasant and peaceful.

I went up the to door of the house and knocked. No one answered. I could hear no movement, no sound, so I knocked once more, waited a minute or two, then left. I drove off feeling relieved that MacDonald wasn't at home; I could now truthfully tell my uncle that I had tried to see him but without success. I drove away from the house and made a right turn, with the intention of going on to our Hounslow branch, which, as I now know, meant another right turn, but I lost my sense of direction, turned left, and saw Mac-Donald coming out of a house in a road that was strange to me, a long curving road of small semi-detached houses with bay windows. Here also the front gardens were not very large, most of them tidy, some with figures of gnomes, or a stork, or pixies colourful in the green grass, grouped round an artificial pond. I was tempted to reverse away, or drive quickly by, pretend I hadn't seen him, but I wasn't certain that he hadn't seen me, so I drew up and got out, and the obvious joy on his face as I approached made me feel, for a moment, glad that I had stopped.

In his terse, genial Scottish voice he said: "Why, Willie, this is a surprise." He shook hands warmly, then added: "What brings you here, Willie?" I explained that my uncle had asked me to come over to see if there was any way in which we could help. He said: "Ah yes, I did want some assistance." He held up a tract and went on: "I need some more of these wee pamphlets. That's what I need, Willie. They come from America." I was pleased he wasn't asking for money. I liked MacDonald and didn't want to think of him in the way one thinks of bums when they send their begging letters.

Physically MacDonald hadn't changed much. He was still spruce, neatly dressed, a little thinner but upright, energetic as he always had been, no difference really in this respect. But it was the way he spoke, the way he looked at me with this gentle expression of welcome in his bright blue eyes, the expression of certainty that I had seen in Pete's brown eyes when I went to the doss-house to enquire about Dunleavy; it was this inner change in MacDonald that I immediately noticed. He had lost the aggressiveness which, in the old days on the round, when he was fleecing his customers, was an amusing part of his personality; but there was no lack of strength and determination in doing what he knew to be right.

Although seeing MacDonald again after a lapse of seven or eight years brought back some of the associations of our milk round days, I soon found that I might as well have met up with a complete stranger. And once I got over the initial pleasure of his warm welcome, I wanted to get away before we got too involved in a religious discussion. So I said politely: "It's nice to see you again. You're looking well."

He said: "I feel well, Willie, I feel well. It's hard work. Some listen to the Word. A lot falls on stony ground."

Thinking of his old milk round days I said: "But you can't force people."

He shook his head. "I don't force them, Willie. That's the last thing I'd do. Certainly not. No, I wouldn't do that."

Again thinking back to the old days and how he behaved to customers who were behind with their payments, I said light-heartedly: "You don't keep your foot in the door?" He grinned, and I saw, fleetingly, the old milkman's expression. "Now and again, Willie. Now and again." He paused, then said: "It's the young people who need to know about Jesus."

I asked: "Only the young? Why not everyone?"

He smiled. "Of course, Willie, everyone. But the young people particularly. You get more trouble among the young, especially in these sort of areas. Depressed areas. There's a lot of trouble here. Violence. There's a lot of violence. They go around in gangs. They don't know what to do with themselves. They go round vandalising, terrorising people. Destruction for the sake of destruction. Of course, they're not all like that." He paused again. "Take this road, for instance. Clare Road. Just ordinary working people. I don't have any trouble here. I talk to a lot of young people about the Lord Jesus. A seed drops, takes root. If just one lost soul comes to know the Lord Jesus!" He looked at me intensely, then said again: "No, I don't have a lot of trouble."

We stood looking along the road. A short distance from where we stood, the road curved out of sight. Because it was early afternoon and a weekday, there were few people around. A white van with the name of the local butcher on it in gold letters flew by. An elderly couple came shuffling towards us.

I said to MacDonald: "Are you able to get out during the day?"

He nodded. "Yes, I do nights. I get up at midday and go out afternoons. I didn't have to work last night so I came out this morning."

I said: "But surely you don't find many people at home this time of the day, not on weekdays."

He pursed his lips, then answered: "If there's no one in, I leave something for them to read. Then I call back the next time I'm round."

"So there's plenty to do?"

"Yes, Willie, plenty." Then he said: "Not far from here there's a large council estate. This side of the Bath Road near Hounslow West station. You know where I mean?" I said yes, I knew where he meant. MacDonald went on: "It's a very large estate and that's where a lot of the trouble-makers are. I spend a lot of time there. Many of the young people don't have work or they're in and out of jobs. There's a lot of unemployment. Usually the trouble starts when they've been drinking. They get violent. There's a lot of violence in Hounslow, because they are unemployed and bored. As I told you, Willie, they go about in gangs and they show off in front of each other. I tell the young people about the Lord Jesus and how he is waiting for them with outstretched arms."

It was as MacDonald was saying this that the door of No. 20, near to where we were standing, opened, and a slim, fair-haired, good-looking teenager walked down the short path. He glanced curiously at us, and I thought MacDonald was going to speak to him and give him a tract, but perhaps because I was there MacDonald said nothing, and the fair-haired youth, with one more glance in our direction, walked off down the road. I stood watching until he got to where the road curved and disappeared. The elderly couple reached us and shuffled by.

It was time for me to go. I took ten pounds from my wallet and gave it to MacDonald. I told him it was from my uncle and was to help in buying more tracts. MacDonald said it was too much, he didn't need that amount, but I told him to take it. Then, looking again to that part of the road where the youth had disappeared, I said: "He seemed a nice young man." I was not to know then, because I did not find out until later that, at the age of eleven, the young man had been put on probation for two years by Brentford Juvenile Court for two cases of larceny; that five years later, when he was sixteen, he was sent by Middlesex Quarter Sessions to an approved school for shop-breaking, larceny, and attempted shop-breaking; that about a week after I had seen him leave No. 20 he was again at Middlesex Quarter Sessions, where he was fined, with an alternative of six months' imprisonment, for garage-breaking with intent; and that four months after this he would stand trial for murder.

Yet what remains in my mind is not the curious coincidence of seeing young Forsyth so shortly before his trial and execution; it is the reply MacDonald gave when I had said that the fair-haired teenager seemed such a nice young man. Looking in the direction I was looking, to where Forsyth had disappeared, MacDonald said: "We all belong to Jesus, Willie. All of us. We all belong to Him."

A BOOK WITHIN A BOOK — II

REFLECTION

This is another bad thing with me. I make notes on old pieces of paper and on the back of envelopes; then I mislay the notes, and sometimes, when I come across them, I can't remember why I wrote them in the first place. That is what happened today. I found this envelope on the back of which I had written:

Equal in the sight of
1. Both had a sunny day
2. Both married commoners
3. Both used the Beatitudes
4. Both had 2 children
5. Both were divorced
6. Both husbands remarried and kept their marriage titles: (a) Mr, unchanged. (b) Earl.

It's annoying when this happens. I ought to keep a notebook. But then I might mislay the notebook and that would be worse. After a lot of reflection, and when I couldn't think why I had made these notes, I tore up the envelope.

I suppose I inherited something from my father, but I haven't yet worked out what it is. Everybody liked him — everybody, that is, outside the family. We had this house in Ireland that was two cottages knocked into one. When I say cottages I don't mean the pre-war hovels of the Irish peasants which you could see dotted all over the place, one stone-floor sitting room with a smoky peat fire, straw in one corner for the chickens, and pigs running in and out. I am talking about two reasonable buildings that, although tiny when compared to the very large houses or mansions where people like the Montgomerys, the Camerons, the Cooke-Collises lived, gave my father five bedrooms, a study, drawing room, dining room, and servants' quarters.

The reason a lot of people outside the family liked him was because he spent so much money entertaining them. After he got through the money left by his father, which was not inconsiderable, he used money he took fraudulently from the Kildorrery creamery. He mixed with a few of the landed gentry, people like Miss Page, but mostly the people he knew well were those with large houses in and around Cork, the idle, wealthy, upper middle class. In return for his kindness and generosity, many of those he entertained so lavishly satisfied his ego by letting him think he was their friend. There were a few, like Elizabeth Bowen, who genuinely liked him, and some, like Miss Page, who were kind, charming, and polite but never really came close.

When I say my grandfather left a not inconsiderable amount of money, it might not seem all that much if you compare it to the wealth of people like Miss Page, but it was enough to make life comfortable. Grandfather was not only a director of our family business, but a practising dentist. He had fitted up a modern surgery in his home, and from that beginning grew one of the largest practices in Ireland. He then opened branches at Mitchelstown, Fermoy, and Mallow. He was on the teaching staff of the Cork Dental School and was honorary dentist to several hospitals. He also farmed. In character he was the opposite to my father. He smoked a pipe but didn't drink, and gave free dental treatment to the poor. An obituary in the British Dental Journal for July 1933, giving a brief history of his life and work, ended by recalling the deep love Grandfather had for the simple folk among whom he lived, and how he never forgot the poor, distressed, and sick.

I was fourteen when Grandfather died. I knew he was a good man and helped the poor and needy and that he and my Grandmother had lost their eldest son, Alfred, on the Somme. Uncle Alfred was a captain in the 2nd Battalion South Lancashire Regiment. I never knew him, because he was killed before I was born. He had trained as a cadet in the old sailing ships, boxed for his ship, and in the war won the MC when he went out into no-man's-land and cut German wire. On 3 July 1916, in a dawn offensive, he went over the top and was never seen again. I think it a pity my father couldn't have done this, gone over the top and got himself killed and never seen again; then he would have left this world with everyone thinking what a fine young man he was and how sad it was that the flower of England should have to be sacrificed in this way, and that the cost of what the country had lost by his death would never be known. As it was, he survived to squander the family fortune, quite a feat since he spent so much so quickly. As well as defrauding the family business, he got rid of most of the property owned by his father; he then mortgaged the house — altogether forty years of lying, cheating, and unhappiness before his pickled body was lowered into that quiet Farahy grave.

I thought it sad, too, that when my father was buried not many people turned up. I don't know why this should have been, because in the bars of the Fermoy, Cork, and Dublin hotels he was always the centre of everything: drinks on him and a hand on his shoulder with just that slight pressure to show the affection felt for him and to show how everyone felt what a good chap he was, a raconteur of wit, a popular friend. But he is not now alone: the Camerons are there and my stepmother, all sleeping peacefully in that pretty little Irish churchyard.

If anyone should ever ask me the basic division between the upper and lower classes, I would say *space*. After my grandfather died, except for the two years I spent on the China station, I went to Ireland every year, and in Ireland I found a different world from that of the London suburbs where I had been brought up. Instead of the long, dreary roads of squashed-up semi-detached houses, with their narrow gardens and neighbours gossiping over broken fences, there were these large houses and mansions that at this time seemed very secure within privately owned meadows, woods, streams, and farms that made up each large estate.

In those days, the days that I remember best, in between the two wars, the Irish workers seemed quite happy. That is, generally speaking, they seemed happy. At any rate, the ones I knew, who worked for us as servants or in the creamery, and others who lived round about, those who had been given free dental treatment by my grandfather, they seemed happy. I suppose this was because they were a pretty ignorant lot. I mean, to become dissatisfied with being poor and lowly, you've got to become educated. In England the poor were becoming educated and had grown dissatisfied, but in Ireland it wasn't so bad because the Catholic Church, unlike the Church of England, hadn't lost its grip and was able to keep the illiterate illiterate, so that those born in hovels, who were quite a few of the population, were mostly content to go on living in them, happy with what God had provided. I say mostly because this didn't apply to Cleary, Miss Page's young butler. Not that when you met Cleary you would have suspected that beneath an inherited servant's manner of compliance and willingness to please there lurked a bitterness and resentment that was to explode, unpredictably and surprisingly, on that never-to-be-forgotten evening when Miss Page was at dinner with her guests, one of whom was a British cabinet minister and another a duchess.

Under Miss Page, Cleary had, so to speak, risen from the ranks, something he accomplished twice, since during the Second World War, he got up to the rank of flight lieutenant and won the DFC before being killed in action. One of nine children, he came from a crowded Irish hovel to the Pages' huge place, where, under the General and Lady Cynthia, he settled down with a quiet intensity to his menial tasks. He was a good pantry boy, and from then on everything he did, he did properly, so that after the death of Miss Page's father, her mother already having died, and with the old butler retiring, it was no surprise to anyone that Cleary was promoted. When I knew him, in those years just before the war, he was in his late twenties, married, with two small children, and lived in a cottage on the estate.

My father and Miss Page weren't on close terms. I don't think she liked him very much. Not that she showed it; it was just a feeling I had. He didn't go there in the way he went to places like Bowen's Court. Almost invariably, when I went to Ireland, I would telephone Miss Page, borrow his car, and drive over by myself to see her. I had lunch with her once; otherwise it was tea, brought into the spacious drawing room by one of the maids. Cleary was around mornings and evenings, which was when I usually saw him, except on that one occasion when, one afternoon, we met up near the walled garden and he came out with this very strange remark. I suppose it would not have seemed so strange if Cleary had not been Miss Page's butler, but the way he spoke, and knowing how she thought, I felt that what he said was not only odd but also a bit disloyal.

By this time the number of Miss Page's servants had dwindled, although not to the extent you would notice. As well as Cleary there was a cook, an assistant cook, six maids, her chauffeur, and four gardeners. I don't know why she kept a chauffeur. He seemed to do little more than polish the Rolls, which was used mostly to meet guests and return them to the station. There were two smaller cars, but Miss Page, when visiting the poor people in the village, went out in her pony and trap. She went often to the villages round about, taking groceries and clothes for the children, visiting and comforting the sick. In her younger days she hunted, but had given that up. Now she spent a lot of time managing her investments and estates; she managed these well, adding to the millions left by her father. I couldn't say exactly who would inherit from her. I think there was a titled cousin somewhere.

What I liked about Miss Page was that she was not only rich and aristocratic, but she had this profound love of the British Empire. She had met King George V and Queen Mary on as near equal terms as is ever possible for a commoner, and this alone, for me, in the days of my youth, when I found out about it, added to her aura. I couldn't say, even now, how Miss Page regarded me. When I had tea with her, or on that one occasion when we had lunch together, she treated me on equal terms, but it was always just the two of us. In spite of her vast wealth and wide social connections, she was a lonely person, of this I was sure. I can't say why I felt this, and I can't say why it was she never married.

Another funny thing is that I could never get round to treating Cleary as a servant. It wasn't because I didn't regard him as one but simply that it didn't seem right. I liked him because he was always kind and polite; I mean, that is how he appeared, although you could never tell from the expression on his face what he was thinking, if he was thinking at all. He wasn't, in the accepted sense of the word, an educated man, which is why it surprised me when I heard, later, that he'd been given a commission. He left school at fourteen, but had a quick brain and could read and write. His butler's uniform suited him, gave him dignity. He had a deep voice, spoke quietly, and I found his soft Irish brogue attractive.

The afternoon I met up with Cleary, near the walled garden, he was dressed casually in a brown tweed jacket, flannels, and white-and-yellow-striped shirt open at the neck. When he saw me, he stopped and looked at me with this little whimsical smile he used for all guests. He was taller than me. He had a compelling face, sallow, lean, good-looking, dark eyes and dark hair, brushed neatly back.

I said: "It's a nice afternoon, Mr Cleary."

He said: "Indeed it is, sir, a very pleasant afternoon." I couldn't think of what more to say. I didn't talk all that much to Cleary. Then I thought that because Miss Page was so keen on the British Empire, Cleary must

feel the same way. The reason I thought this is because of the way servants go about wanting to please those whom they serve in this kind of in-
gratiating way, which makes you think they haven't got minds of their
own; and with Cleary, because he owed so much to Miss Page, who had
got him to where he was, I thought the young butler would be totally committed. So thinking to stir up loyal feelings within him, I said rather pompously: "I've been reading about the General, Mr Cleary. A very
distinguished career! We owe a great deal to him." I wasn't sure what I
meant by this; in fact, I wasn't sure that we owed anything at all to Miss
Page's father, but it sounded good. Cleary stood quietly and nodded. Not
far from where we stood were large rhododendron beds; behind us the
park with its avenue of trees and deer wandering about; beside us the
walled garden and, away to the left, in front of the house, the large rectan-
gular pond with its marble fountain, carp and goldfish, and pretty red
and white water lilies. The April air was warm, and there was no sound
except the odd bird call and, now and again, a rustling as a soft wind
stirred the leaves of trees and bushes.

Having started pompously, and because I didn't think it right that
Cleary, as a servant, should see through the front I had put on, I felt compelled to continue in the same way. So I went on to talk more about the
British Empire, for I have always thought it quite fantastic what we
achieved, not only in India, but everywhere. I told Cleary how our conception of the Empire had changed, because the Empire itself had changed in
form and character sometime before Bright and Gladstone went; how, in
the beginning, we were against expansion; then another change, with the
Oriental character of the Empire shifting its strategic centre to Egypt,
Cape Town, and Colombo, and how this made security for trade and
defence impossible without annexation. I mentioned the full development of British India completed by wars with the Sikhs and Sind, and I
touched on our acquisition of Penang and Malacca; I spoke about Sin-
gapore, how we had brought it from a squalid fishing port to a thriving
city of a hundred thousand people and how, under our rule, Australia, although then still divided into rival states, had, in twenty years, increased
its sheep by sixfold; how gold, coal, and copper had been found in abun-
dance, with South Australia rich in wheat, and tropical Queensland
building a substantial sugar trade; but, I said, the outstanding achievement of empire building in this early period had been the making of
Canada. Through Canada's confederation and absorption of the West, it
had become a great state running from sea to sea. We had built a free
democratic civilization, putting down barbaric Burma and making safe,
from piracy, trading routes through Chinese waters, with safe har-

bourage at the end. As well as this, we had combated sheer savagery in native states like Ashanti, and in the Arab and Negroid tyrannies scattered by history from the Sahara to Somaliland, a vast interior of which little had been known except that it was rife with man-hunting, disease, and war, and into which the British came, establishing a chain of factories on the west of the Gambia river and the Gold Coast. In the face of almost insurmountable difficulties there was often talk of evacuation, but we stayed, determined to break slavery, trying to embody Livingstone's vision, his passion to raise humanity from persecution by Arab and Portuguese half-castes who had made central Africa hell with their cruelty and what seemed an endless procession of slaves chained or clenched in wooden yokes; everywhere ruin, death, and lust, the tsetse fly, fever, and leprosy. In 1873 the slave market was closed; four years later Queen Victoria was proclaimed Empress of India.

Happy with the sound of my own voice, I could have gone on for longer, but Cleary, who up to this moment had stood impassively, nodding occasionally, his dark eyes fixed on me, his handsome face expressionless, began to fidget. It was only a little movement as he started rubbing with his thumb and forefinger the handle of the egg basket he was holding, but I noticed it. I was sure enough of my own position not to think that he could, in any way, be bored, so that it came as more than a shock, I can tell you, when, after I had so confidently assumed that he felt as I did about one of the greatest of all institutions that was to have lasted a thousand years, he then said in his pleasant Irish voice, saying it so quietly that it seemed to come from under his breath: "Fuck the British Empire". For a moment I thought perhaps I had imagined it; then I felt bruised and shaken and felt, too, that I would never again have the same regard for Cleary. It wasn't so much his image that was destroyed as mine, the image I had of myself as belonging to Miss Page's world. Cleary, smiling and clutching his basket of eggs, said: "Goodbye, Master Willie". He walked away, and I stood where I was, looking after him, still wondering if I had heard him right, if he really had used that word. I might forever have gone on thinking about it in this confused way but for the other incident, which involved Miss Page herself.

I can now understand why Cleary had shown resentment towards me, but I can't see why his attitude to Miss Page should have changed so drastically. She had treated him well and was, in her own autocratic way, a kind person. To do what he did and leave her with no alternative but to get rid of him immediately seemed strange. Even if you look at it from a butler's point of view — a butler like Cleary, who had come from a crowded hovel into a bright world of wealth and privilege and, in this way, was forced to make the comparison — even if you take all this into account, it was still no excuse for his behaviour, not only towards Miss Page but towards her guests who were sitting at dinner, including the British cabinet minister and the duchess.

What made it harder to understand Cleary's behaviour was that although I had not spoken to him all that much, he had always behaved so courteously towards me, and it was for this reason one evening after tea, Miss Page having gone out to pick strawberries for me to take back, and when Cleary came into the drawing room where I was sitting alone, that I suddenly found myself confiding in him. In his pleasant voice he said: "All by yourself, Master Willie?" I explained that Miss Page had gone to get me some strawberries, and I sat staring up at him, thinking how nice he looked dressed formally and elegantly in his black coat and striped trousers, and thinking, too, how fortunate he was to be able to go on here when, in two days' time, I would be back to crude shouts and blasphemies, sitting at a wooden table, eating a rushed meal, feeling the sting of the whistle chain on the way up to polish the dormitory floor. As if he sensed a little of what I was thinking, he said: "You like the Navy, Master Willie? It's a good life, I'm sure."

I said: "It isn't all that good." I said this impulsively and he looked surprised. I went on: "As a matter of fact, Mr Cleary, I don't like it at all."

He asked: "Why not? Why don't you like it?"

I shrugged. "I don't know."

He said: "But you must have a reason, Master Willie. Why don't you like it?" Although Cleary's voice was friendly and pleasant, he stayed at a distance, and considering I was then only seventeen, it was nice of him that he should show this respect. Of course, I didn't know at the time that his interest was not so much in my predicament as in his own.

But it was Cleary giving me sympathy when I most needed it that drew me out. Feeling wretched at the thought of going back to HMS *St. Vincent*, I suddenly found myself talking to him as an equal, a friend, someone who would understand. I said passionately: "I hate it, Mr Cleary. I hate it." I felt weepy and felt myself trembling as I told him how I loathed the indignities and crudeness of life on the lower deck, and all the time having to pretend that the crudeness was manly and the indignities noble, because this is what society wants to hear.

A boy of fifteen couldn't know what he was doing when signing on for twelve years from the age of eighteen, a contract in those days almost impossible to break. So I came out with it all, telling Cleary how awful it was in this boys' training barracks in Gosport, the beatings, the bullying, the whole sadistic treatment that passed for discipline; I told him how, on freezing winter's mornings, with the light just breaking in from the east, we clung in terror with frozen hands to the narrow flapping Jacob's ladder a hundred and sixty feet up while screaming oaths from below ordered us to get a fucking move on; I described the punishment of jankers, being whipped round with the whistle chain across our backs, having to hop like kangaroos with an iron bar held under our legs, trying not to over-balance for fear of greater reprisals; I told him how I had run away, been caught, spent a night in a police station, and got twelve cuts of the cane, the blue-and-red weals covering my arse looking like a cubist painting by Pablo Picasso; I told him how some boys were driven beyond endurance and thought of suicide, but that there were nice petty officers who liked us boys, and liked kissing boys, and would go farther if they could, and that if the boys didn't let them do what they wanted, they, too, could turn nasty, so that even if they didn't indulge in beatings like the sadistic petty officers, they would stop the few small privileges that meant so much in that fixed, restricted routine.

I finished and felt an immediate sense of relief which comes from confession, but this was quickly followed by fear, the fear that I had behaved badly, that I had betrayed Miss Page by treating Cleary on equal terms, and I was terrified Cleary would behave differently towards me and Miss Page would find out. But Cleary didn't appear to change in any way. He just said: "It's not right, is it, to treat people like that?" I now know that there was more meaning to his few words than I then realized. But he had covered up well, giving no indication that he himself felt bitter, although he did say something else that was quite strange and which did occur to me as being a little odd when he said it. I was sitting staring at the marble fireplace when Cleary, standing sideways to the door so that he could see me and watch out for Miss Page, said: "Why don't you keep a diary, Master Willie? It helps a lot to get your thoughts down on paper." I didn't think to ask Cleary if he kept a diary. I thanked him for the suggestion, and not long afterwards Miss Page came back with the strawberries. I stood up as if nothing had happened; then Cleary spoke to her about some expected visitors and left the room.

It was when I was back in barracks, back to the dawn wakey-wakey, the mug of steaming pusser's cocoa and the thick dry hard pusser's biscuit, the greasy, unappetising meals, the bullying, the parades, the oppressive confined existence, the homosexual orgies, and the misery of it all — it was then that I thought of that lovely spacious drawing-room with its elegant furniture and the polite young butler who had shown such sympathy and kindness, and from then on I kept a diary. Later, when I heard what Cleary had done, I felt sorry not so much for him as for his mistress. I mean, he could have gone quietly, not embarrassed her in the way he did, yet I suppose to do what he did, although he had this marvellous calm exterior, he must, underneath, have been as mixed up as I was.

The end was quite simple.

There was this very long passage leading from the dining room to the kitchen and pantry, or from the kitchen and pantry to the dining room, whichever way you like to look at it. The house, built in the mid-seventeenth century, at the beginning of the architectural Renaissance, showed Italian influence in its symmetrical galleried plan, and showed Dutch influence in the elaborately detailed gables and dormer windows executed in cut and moulded brick, this beneath a romantic roof line displaying pedimented gables and varied groups of chimneys. It was a lovely house, but no thought had been given to the comfort and convenience of servants, and in those days, when the house was built, there were plenty of servants. It was quite a walk carrying and wheeling heavy dishes. This shouldn't have mattered, but often it is a triviality that assumes gigantic proportions, the triviality being out of any reasonable relationship to the disturbance it creates.

So Cleary, like most people who harbour a grudge, brooded over a tiny inconvenience until it became an obsession which he then used as a focal point for all his troubles until, on that disastrous evening, when either he chose deliberately to use the special occasion to cause maximum impact or the distinguished guests sitting at Miss Page's dinner table and being served with delicacies and vintage wine, surrounded by all the trappings of the rich, became too great an imposition for the angry young butler.

Cleary disappeared from the dining room. A few moments later a startled Miss Page and her guests, including the British cabinet minister and the duchess, watched as Cleary returned riding a bicycle, balancing plates in one hand, stopping by the side table to put them down, then riding round and round the dinner table ringing the bell loudly before cycling out again. Had he done this on the stage, the dexterity he showed in not breaking a plate would have got him prolonged applause; but apart from an initial moment of surprise, there was not the slightest indication that Miss Page or any of her guests thought it anything but normal that a butler should enter and leave in this way. A maid took over, and no reference was made to Cleary, who, the next morning, packed his bags and left, taking with him his wife and two children.

When I was told about it, I did ask if Cleary had been drinking, but my father said he didn't know about that. He said that after Cleary left his tied cottage, pamphlets were found, all about the rise of capitalism, the clash of social forces, the status of the worker, the relationship of the rich and the poor to religion, that sort of thing. My father related it all back to me in considerable detail, obviously enjoying the recounting of it. He said a notebook was also found, half full of extracts from *Das Kapital* and other socialist writings, and there were lengthy observations on British colonial rule.

In view of Cleary's behaviour that afternoon I met up with him, it was no surprise to me to find that his outlook on this particular subject was, to say the least, jaundiced. He had made no mention of the civilizing influence of Western standards, only given a blinkered account of atrocities with particular reference to the slave trade: slave ships crammed with men tightly packed in two rows, since the more men carried, the more economical the shipment; beatings, tortures, and sexual indecencies; slaves imprisoned in cellars to be brought up in chains and sold, often a whole Negro family coming under the hammer, with the individual slaves priced out like cattle, so that a slave subject to sores would go at a reduced price while an old, infirm man would be thrown in for nothing; children taken from their families and formed into grass gangs until they, too, were ready to be sold.

Cleary had also made a list of prominent Englishmen whose vast fortunes, derived from this slave trade, had been used to build manors, castles, museums, and art galleries, magnificent buildings containing priceless collections of art which were to become Britain's heritage. There were people like the Duke of Chandos, who had a slave ship named after him; William Beckford, Lord Mayor of London, renowned for his lavish life-style; Sloane, married to a wealthy heiress who owned slave plantations; Tate, whose money from sugar plantations provided England with the Tate Gallery; and Christopher Cottrington, who gave to All Souls College, Oxford, its magnificent library from money provided by his slave estates in Barbados.

It seemed, for Cleary, there was nothing good about the colonial system. The benevolence of some of the slave owners portrayed graphically in paintings of the mother country with her children, and in the painting of Queen Victoria showing Her Majesty presenting the Bible to a black man, was, in Cleary's eyes, a veneer that only thinly disguised the starkness of black existence, for underneath a cloak of patriotic endeavour was a heartless commercialism, corrupt colonial wealth, harsh work and harsh punishment, the poor people all the time brutalized by their superiors. This slave trade in itself, as far as Cleary was concerned, was a sufficient example of British depravity.

I didn't see Cleary again, so I couldn't say what happened to him from the time he left Miss Page's stately home to when he joined the RAF on the outbreak of the Second World War. I suppose, in the RAF, as he got on so well, he must have kept his views to himself. I did learn later, that he had been promoted to flight lieutenant and had won the DFC before being killed in action on a bombing raid over Germany.

My father thought the incident with Miss Page very funny, and he was not only happy to go on spreading it around, but he enlarged on it. I think the way he did this there was some underlying vindictiveness, probably because he never really got close to her. He was one of those people who needed everyone's complete approval, which was why he entertained the way he did, spending so much money. It made him feel good.

I think often of Miss Page and the pleasure my visits gave me. Tea in her drawing room; sitting together at luncheon, just the two of us waited on by Cleary; those sunny afternoons when I wandered by myself in her spacious grounds. She was kind and nice, and she was a good person. I would in no way go along with my father in laughing at what Cleary did. I have some sympathy for Cleary, but I have never been able to forgive him completely the embarrassment he caused to Miss Page and to her guests, especially the cabinet minister and the duchess.

Of all the people we knew in and around Cork, I enjoyed most of all going to see Miss Page, but I also liked going with my father to see the Camerons. I saw the Camerons not only when they were staying at Bowen's Court, but in London, where they had a very nice ground-floor flat in Clarence Terrace. One of their neighbours, H. G. Wells, came often to lunch on Sundays.

Elizabeth Bowen and my father were very close, which seemed funny to me at the time because, although he had gone to a good public school, he wasn't all that bright academically. In a letter to Virginia Woolf, Elizabeth had written to say that she had been cruel to him because she had made the mistake she so often made of idealizing at the outset a stupid person. And in her book *Portrait of a Writer* Victoria Glendinning said that, compared to Elizabeth, my father was coarse. I think he was stupid, but I wouldn't say he was coarse. I mean, I didn't ever see him like that. Even when he wasn't feeling too good, he was always charming, always polite, and although there were mounting debts and creditors, his manner was never anything but friendly and happy. It wasn't until I grew older that I understood his basic problem and felt sorry for him; then it was too late because he was dead. I don't think Elizabeth knew what was happening. He was liked by all of her friends — those he met at Bowen's Court, those who came to our house for baths.

The only way in which he came near to Elizabeth intellectually was in the stories he told. He was very good at story-telling, conjuring up a fantasy world convincingly, piling everything on quite effortlessly, so that even he felt he was telling the truth. This often happens with people who lie automatically, and they are dreadfully hurt if they think you think they are making it all up.

Going over to Bowen's Court was particularly pleasant in the summer, when on bright days and in the light warm evenings we drove through lovely country, the villagers waving to us as we went through Kildorrery or when we passed them in the narrow country roads as they plodded along with their donkeys and carts.

Sometimes, when we were driving in this way, he would talk about our family business, and to listen to him you would think he alone was responsible for its progress and expansion; that it was his decision, and his alone, to buy creameries at Newcastle Emlyn, Northallerton, Garstang, Lostwithiel, Aller, and Haverfordwest; that it was through his foresight and business acumen that we had then, in 1938, an authorized capital of one and a half million pounds; that it was because of him Torridge Vale Dairies in Devon, Daws Creameries in Saltash, Alfred Rowntree and Sons in Caversham, and Keith Wright in Fenstanton were now in the group. At the time I was nineteen and what he said sounded good. I wasn't to know, of course, that he was bleeding his own little section to death.

Bowen's Court, which was completed in 1776, had been built of limestone from a nearby quarry. It was three storeys high. There was also a basement. Two avenues led to the house, the main one lined with lime, ash, and beech trees. Often in the early evening, when the sun was low and flooding the house with light, the only sound to be heard was the cawing and flapping of rooks. In the late nineteenth century Robert Cole Bowen built a tower at the back of the house which marginally improved the facilities. In 1949 Elizabeth made further improvements.

Once, when I was at Bowen's Court, and it happened to be on my fourteenth birthday, I danced with Elizabeth. This was in the Long Room at the top of the house. The Long Room had a blue-white concave ceiling and ran the whole length of the house from back to front. There were two imposing fireplaces with brass, and at each end were three windows set low near the floor. It had been intended as a ballroom but was left unfinished and empty. As soon as the Long Room had been completed, it was found that the floor would never stand the vibration of dancing, and for this reason balls were always held in the drawing-room. But it was in the Long Room that we danced, Elizabeth and I. Although my father was an excellent dancer I wasn't all that good, but Elizabeth was light on her feet and followed faultlessly my unsure footsteps. It had been Elizabeth's idea to go to the Long Room to dance, and she used her old gramophone, putting on ancient 78 RPM records of foxtrots and waltzes. My father danced with Elizabeth occasionally, but for much of the time he stood at the window watching. There were only the three of us. Alan, Eizabeth's husband, was in London at Clarence Terrace. As my confidence grew, and with the spring light dying outside, we danced on and on. It became a lasting memory, and for this reason alone I feel sad that Bowen's Court is no longer there.

After Alan died, Elizabeth sold the house to Mr O'Keefe, a wealthy American, hoping that he would take care of it, perhaps improve it. But Mr O'Keefe demolished the house, and when the rubble was cleared away, all that remained in the disturbed earth was a transient imprint of the foundations; and when even this vanished under rough grass and weeds, it was as if all the planning and brilliance and eccentricity of generations of Bowens had never been.

Elizabeth grew old, the London flat in Regent's Park was sold, and after some years of lecturing in America, she went to live in a cottage in Hythe, near Folkestone. There I went once to have tea with her, and she told me about the book she was writing, and how she had met up in Germany with Graham Greene when he was researching for *The Third Man*. As I hadn't seen her for some years, I noticed the change. She had become smaller and slightly bent. We sat gossiping, and although I was listening to her I was thinking, at the same time, about another visit to Bowen's Court when, one summer afternoon, I had gone there, as usual, with my father. He and Elizabeth disappeared, leaving me alone in the drawing-room. A cool Irish breeze came through a half-open window as I stood looking at the faded white, grey, and gold wallpaper.

After a while, when Elizabeth and my father had not returned, I went out into the hall, then wandered into the library. It was an airy room, pleasant and very high. It smelt of dry calf bindings and polish. For a moment I stood by the door looking at the arrangement of tables, armchairs, and sofas; then I walked round, scrutinizing the bookcases, until I noticed, on a table by a window, a small portable typewriter with a half-typed quarto sheet sticking out. I went over and saw that the sheet was part of a novel or short story. I didn't read it properly. Perhaps I shouldn't have read it at all, but looking back now and working out dates, it was probably *The House in Paris*. Elizabeth was a careful writer who worked from 9:30 to 5:30 but preferred the mornings, when she was able to think more clearly. She wrote slowly, often laboriously, not waiting for inspiration, rewriting and redrafting, taking out the dead wood.

After the Hythe tea I saw Elizabeth once more before she died. This was at Maurice Bowra's memorial service in Oxford, where Isaiah Berlin spoke so eloquently and movingly. Elizabeth, grown small and with that slight stoop but still dignified, dressed in black, sat in the front pew with old friends, and with her memories.

Six months after the royal wedding, the day of pageantry still fresh in the minds of millions, I met up with Pete. I was walking along the Strand when he came out of Southampton Street. We stopped and I said: "How's the major?" He stroked the bottom of his beard, and I thought I saw a puzzled look in his deep brown eyes. I waited for a moment then said: "Major Dunleavy. How is he?"

Pete said: "I thought you'd called in to see him. I was told you'd called in." I explained that I had gone again to the crèche, which was on a day not long after my first visit, the day I heard from Mr Solomon that Bert was doing time; but again, on this second visit, there had been no sign of Dunleavy. Pete said: "He might be there now. I'm sure he'd be pleased to see you. Or you could try Bruce House. He often goes there for a meal." Pointing along Southampton Street, Pete said: "First turning right, down Tavistock Street, into Drury Lane, turn left and it's on the corner of Drury Lane and Kemble Street. About five minutes from here."

I started up Southampton Street, then turned back and called out to Pete: "How will I recognize him?" Pete said: "He's tall, thin, upright, grey eyes, grey hair thinning on top, a small grey moustache. You'll recognize him all right. He has a military appearance and will probably be reading or have a book tucked under his arm. He loves history. Especially military history."

I thanked Pete and once more made as if to go in the direction of Bruce House, but as soon as Pete was out of sight I went back to the Strand and on to the Waldorf Hotel, where I was taking to lunch a customer coming up from Manchester. I had plenty of time, and could easily have gone to the crèche or to Bruce House, and sometime I would have to go, to report back to my uncle that I had, at least, made some effort to see Dunleavy. But to be truthful, at this moment, I'd had enough of bums, even the ones who were majors.

Although the poor have never appealed to me, I admire people like Pete who can hug bums without any feeling of revulsion. And I have to say, in fairness to him, that although these drop-outs on the whole were a pretty depressing lot, his doss-house was clean. In fact, it was spotlessly clean, which surprised me because not all doss-houses are like Pete's. I mean, if you go into Bruce House in Covent Garden, which I did eventually, you would find it hard to believe you were in twentieth-century England.

In Bruce House the first thing you come up against is this tangy smell of urine. Bits of food and other droppings are on the floor. There are old men and young ones, seedy-looking, too, in dirty, ill-fitting clothes, many of them unshaven. There are large rooms, more like halls, with bare floors, sectioned off by high walls. In one section is a TV. Some sit watching while others are fast asleep, their heads collapsed downwards onto their chests.

Another very large section is the kitchen. It has a huge iron stove in the centre of the room. The stove is at least thirty feet long and four feet wide, with hot plates spaced out on top where bums are boiling chicken or lumps of bacon in decrepit-looking saucepans. The smell here is even more pronounced. It is a stale, unwholesome smell, the same sort of smell which I found in Ada's sitting-room. In this large kitchen section, around two sides of the room, are grouped long tables and stools, like those we had at HMS *St. Vincent.*

A wireless, high up on one wall, is blaring out. A lot of derelicts are sitting at the tables, playing cards, smoking, eating. The tables are stained and scratched. What are called washing and bathroom facilities are dingy-looking loos that stink to high heaven, cold, raw — a fitting place I suppose for these human wrecks.

In another section is a store cupboard where cast-off clothes can be bought, cheap shirts, trousers, shoes. One man, medium height, slim, about thirty-five, is trying on a blue-and-white-check shirt. A pair of shoes costs a pound. You can also buy a cheap razor, razor blades, shampoo, and other household things. Looking at the condition of the inmates, I didn't think there would be much of a sale for these.

Most doss-houses have fixed meals, but at Bruce House you can choose from a number of dishes: different meats and two veg, bread pudding that is bulky and filling, also, in the morning, bubble and squeak, sausages and quite good porridge. The service and bedding arrangements are haphazard. The bedrooms are tiny cubicles, with very little room to move. There is a chair by the window and on each bed is a rubber mattress. If you aren't careful, the mattress slides off, taking you with it. The mattress is there because these poor wretches often wet their beds. There is no lighting in the cubicles, so that when darkness comes there is nothing to do. It is noisy at night, difficult to sleep, unless you are flat out on meths. But you can't buy alcohol; drink is forbidden. In the morning you are called at 7:30 by the ringing of a bell like the one the town crier uses.

Bums, like other humans, are different in character. One Irishman is called the Professor. He talks a lot, mostly about socialism. Big Steve and Big Jock never have any money and are often turned out. Another, Joe, is a union man, experienced in politics, and he gives talks. There is one with a beard who is schizophrenic. He gets angry suddenly, very violent, and will start to fight. At night a whistle is blown every half hour. This is for men to go up to their rooms. You can choose which half hour you go up, but in the bedroom cubicle with nothing to do it is boring, just lying in the darkness. A long night. No women. Nevertheless, Bruce House has been going for fifty years and has kept all the traditional atmosphere of a Victorian workhouse.

Pete's crèche is a lot different. You see this immediately. In Pete's place, halfway down the stone steps leading to the basement, there is a short passageway where a large notice board with a new green baize base has neat notices pinned up in an orderly manner. Each notice is carefully written or neatly printed on a clean piece of paper. One notice says that tea can be had at all times for a penny a cup; another says soup is served at twelve o'clock for the same price, and another that there is a singsong every Tuesday with Melanie O'Mulligan. A photo of pretty Melanie in semi-profile shows her smiling and happy. Beneath this notice about the singsong is one that says Nurse Williams will be in attendance on Monday, Wednesday, and Friday afternoons.

The steps go on down to the basement section, where there is a kitchen on one side and a large rest-room on the other. In the rest-room are about three dozen bums flopped around small circular metal tables. The room could accommodate fifty or sixty people without being overcrowded. The metal tables and chairs look new, the walls have been freshly painted bright green, the floor swept and polished; there is no litter, no mess, no untidiness. The bums themselves look, as they usually look, pretty decrepit, and some of them are arguing with each other while others peer at newspapers collected from garbage dumps of one sort or another. These men are all ages and sizes, some clean-shaven, some stubbly, a few bearded. One large fellow with a long, lean, stubbly face is wearing three ragged overcoats, one on top of the other. Underneath the overcoats is a buttonless torn jacket, held together by a piece of string tied round his waist.

At the bottom of the steps another passageway separates the kitchen from the rest-room, and here a young man, not Pete, dries piles of cups, saucers, and plates. He is slim, clean-shaven, with a white face and expressive blue eyes. He is dressed in pale blue jeans and an open-neck Canadian lumber-style shirt. It was Pete who told me that most of the people here were from the deprived section of the community; but there were also those who couldn't cope with the pressures of life and became drop-outs, people you wouldn't normally think of: a successful chemist, a doctor; also the son-in-law of a parliamentary private secretary.

A BOOK WITHIN A BOOK — III

NAVY DAYS

MURDER IN HMS *Dorsetshire,* 1936

We were all sorry when our nice Leading Seaman was found dead. He was found lying in his hammock, in the remote locker room below decks where he slept. He had been shot through the head. We were sorry not only because he'd been shot but because he was nice. The *Dorsetshire* was a cruiser on the China Station, and at this time, the time of the murder, we were based at Wei-hai-Wei.

As well as our nice Leading Seaman, we had this nice assistant divisional officer, a tall, gangling sub-lieutenant who was later drowned in some accident or other. So we were lucky. Our nice Leading Seaman was not only nice but good-looking. He had blond hair, blue eyes, a slightly tanned skin, and a marvellous smile. He always seemed to be smiling. Not long after we arrived he had his twenty-first birthday.He gave the birthday party in the locker room where he slept. He wasn't entitled to the locker room for his own use, but he'd been in the *Dorsetshire* for quite some time, and no one said anything about it. He just said in a general way he was having a birthday party, and any boy who wanted to go would be welcome. I went with my friend Peter, who had come with me from HMS St. *Vincent* to the China Station with eight other boys.

When Peter and I got to the locker room there were half a dozen boys already there, drinking cans of cold beer which our Leading Seaman had brought in. We weren't supposed to drink beer on board, but he'd got them for this party, and we enjoyed it. We sang happy birthday to him; then we sang sea songs, putting in silly words, such as a life on the ocean wave is better than going to sea, and we sang also "Waltzing Matilda" because one boy's parents had emigrated to Australia.

The locker room had plenty of space. There were shelves on one side with ropes coiled down and bundles of pusser's rags and sailmaker's tools, that sort of thing. In one corner was a small table and chair, both pretty tatty but good enough to sit in privacy and write letters home. We all sat round in the middle of the locker room while our Leading Seaman smilingly handed out the cans of beer. We couldn't go on very late because boys had to turn in earlier than the rest of the ship's company. When the party was over Peter and I returned to the mess in a happy mood.

It was a relief to get to the *Dorsetshire.* We had come out in this old troopship that had been used in the First World War and was even then pretty old. If the cargo had been live pigs instead of ratings, animal lovers would have protested. I can't remember how long the journey to China took, a few weeks, but it was pretty awful; when we were not on the over-crowded upper deck, the only other place was the mess, where we were cramped together with bad ventilation, and with sweat soaking through our tropical shorts and singlets, making them clammy. Often it was sti-fling hot and, as well as the bad ventilation, there was this sickly stench of oil.

In charge of our mess, in this troopship, was a young leading seaman. He had a broad Glasgow accent so that you couldn't understand half of what he said, but he was easy to get on with and had a happy, outgoing nature. He also had toe rot, and at mealtimes he would sit perched on one of the long wooden stools, cutting up loaves of bread, two slices for each boy, and he would sit with his bare, thin, hairy legs tucked under him and, every now and then, in between bread cutting, he would reach down and pull out pieces of moist dead skin from between his toes, then flick the skin away and sniff the tops of his fingers before continuing with the bread cutting. I can't say why it was he sniffed his fingers after each scratching, but this is what he did, and it was for this reason, even the times I felt quite hungry, I would leave my portion of bread. Sometimes I left everything when it was really rough, with the troopship creaking and groaning and things rattling and the ship heaving and plunging and roll-ing from side to side; because when it was like this I was sick, retching and retching and eventually bringing up green bile, and the stench of oil always there, that thick, sweet nauseous stench.

We hadn't gone straight to the *Dorsetshire*. When we arrived in Hong Kong we were sent from the troopship to HMS *Cornwall*, another county-class cruiser. We stayed in the *Cornwall* for two months before she returned home, when we were transferred. The day we boarded the *Cornwall* we were told about this boxing match which was to take place the next day. The new boys joining the ship would be matched against an equal number of boys already on board. To call it boxing is putting it politely. You just rushed in for one minute, slogged away, and when the bell went, the next pair came on. The only thing you weren't allowed to do was kick and bite. I wasn't all that keen on boxing. I had tried it at HMS *St. Vincent*. The reason I tried it was because Peter and I were being bullied by this big, tough, aggressive Welsh boy who had come from the slums of Cardiff. He didn't like Peter or me, and one day he blacked my eye. The reason he did this was because I told him I didn't like the Welsh. When I told him this I didn't know he came from Cardiff. He didn't ask me the reason I didn't like them, but just lashed out. I can't remember now why it was I had this dislike. It may have been because one of the petty officers at *St. Vincent*, who was pretty violent, was Welsh. It was the first time I had had a black eye, and for almost a week it was bruised a horrible mottled colour and very tender. After this the Welsh boy picked on me and on Peter who was small and quiet, and we both got beaten up regularly.

When the beating-up didn't stop we decided to kill the Welsh boy, so I picked these deadly-nightshade berries that were growing behind the open-air swimming pool at the back of the parade ground. That same night, with the berries in a little bag, we crept over to the Welsh boy's bed. Usually he would snore with his mouth open, but this night he wasn't snoring, and we couldn't think how to get the berries into his mouth without waking him. So we let it go, and a couple of weeks later, after we had talked it over we decided it would be easier to hang him. I got a rope and found out how to make a hangman's knot; then we decided on the night for the execution.

After night rounds we got up, and I tied the free end of the rope to the top of the dormitory banister. There was a long drop down within the spiralling staircase. The other end of the rope, with the noose, I positioned on the floor where we thought we could most easily slip it over the Welsh boy's head before lifting him up and pushing him over. We thought we would be able to do it quickly so that he would be hanged before he realized what was happening. But when we went over to get him there was the same problem as before: we couldn't think how to tie him up and carry him to the rope without waking him.

Later, during the war, quite by chance, I met up with the Welsh boy. He was then a Leading Seaman and was in the Prince of Wales when she was sunk by the Japanese with considerable loss of life. Whether the Japanese succeeded where Peter and I failed, I couldn't say.

It was because we had no luck in killing the Welsh boy that I took up boxing. I had some lessons and then entered for this elimination contest. I won my first fight because the boy I was fighting had had second thoughts about it and didn't hit back. I didn't hurt him much, but when I was declared the winner I had this fantastic feeling and decided immediately to work hard for a commission and become an admiral. In my next fight I was knocked out in the first minute of the first round and can only remember everything spinning and receding and my knees sagging, then coming to in the dressing room with a split lip, a swollen nose, and aching all over. After being flattened in this second fight, I made up my mind never again to go in for anything where you could be hurt. Later in HMS

Iron Duke, I did try playing rugby for the United Services D team, but I got sat on a lot and kicked a lot, so I only played it once.

Why I have mentioned all this is because, when they spoke about this boxing match, the day we joined the *Cornwall*, I knew what I was in for. To be fair, they did also say that any boy who didn't want to fight could take a pace forward. One boy did. He stepped forward two paces. I thought it funny he should have done this because he was quite big, strong-looking. He had red hair, freckles, and deep blue eyes. Later he became a petty officer and went into submarines. He did well, got some sort of decoration, a BEM or something, but at the time, the day we boarded the *Cornwall* I just thought he was a coward.

The average age of the new boys was sixteen, those already in the *Cornwall* seventeen; so I suppose, when it came to boxing, the *Cornwall* boys had an advantage. I mean, I don't know if age is an advantage in boxing; it just seemed that way. The idea of the match was that once in the ring, you smashed into your opponent and he did the same to you. There were no rules worth speaking about; we just went in for this minute, which proved to be one of the longest minutes I can remember. The boy I had to fight was lighter than me. They had tried to pair us up to about the same size and weight, but there were these discrepancies. He was the same height but lighter and thinner. All I can remember is his bare, smooth white chest and his thin arms as he danced lightly around me, then the blows to the head and chest, blow after blow, until I felt myself floundering as I tried to hit back; but he came through my guard again and again. It seemed to go on and on interminably, and only when I thought I couldn't take another blow the bell went. I saw, in a blur the smiling, handsome face of a young lieutenant, his gold-banded white epaulettes hanging crookedly on his shoulders; I remember so well the face and thinking at the time it must be wonderful to be an officer and an aristocrat. When, after the match, I was given a loser's prize, a round tin of fifty duty-free Players cigarettes, I took it unsmilingly from the boys' divisional officer and didn't bother to thank him.

After two months in the *Cornwall* we went to the *Dorsetshire*, and I was glad we weren't to be involved in another boxing match. But I felt even better when our nice leading seaman, having taken over from the tall sub-lieutenant, told us he wanted us all to be happy, and if we had any problems we could always go and discuss them with him. He said this with such warmth and friendliness that I only remember it happening once before, when the chaplain at HMS *St. Vincent* had us new boys in for a chat soon after our arrival.

This chaplain was young, bearded, enthusiastic and, like our nice

Leading Seaman, always smiling. He told us, just as our nice Leading Seaman told us, that if we had personal problems we could go and see him whenever we wished and had only to knock on his door. He said Sunday morning service was compulsory, that provision was made for Roman Catholics who had their own priest, but that we should never forget we were all part of a very fine service, and belonging to it should be looked on as a privilege; also that there was nothing to stop us getting to the top. A vice-admiral, at present serving, had started as a boy, not here but at HMS *Ganges*, and what he had done any of us could achieve if we had the ambition and dedication. We should work hard and play hard. The Royal Navy was a service of high and noble traditions. Drake, Raleigh, Nelson, Beatty, and other great men had set an example of courage, discipline, selflessness. This was what this service was all about. It was what service meant: to serve, not for oneself, but for one's country, one's king and, above all, for God.

Of course, none of us is perfect, and we would make mistakes, we would slip up from time to time, but that would be no reason not to go on, not to aim for the ideal. The finest example of this, this ideal, could be seen in the persons of our present King and Queen. We should remember, too, that we were the guardians not only of our island home but of the British Empire, a wonderfully organised association of countries with diverse habits and creeds united under the British crown in Christian freedom and tolerance. He went on and on like this, smiling all the time, and I must say, being fifteen, I was very moved.

In fact, I was so moved I felt I wanted to write immediately to the King and tell him how honoured I felt to be a guardian of our little island and of all his lands beyond the seas, and I wanted him to know, immediately, that he could depend on me. I would never let him down, and if it came to fighting for what is right, even if it meant laying down my life, then Nelson's death would be seen as trivial compared to my dying and all the blood I was prepared to shed for His Majesty. I really did feel good, and for the next half hour I was quite glad I had joined up. Also, I decided that, like the *Ganges* boy, I would become a vice-admiral. Thinking about this, I missed something of what the smiling padre had gone on saying. I came back to him just as he was getting to the end of his talk when, in his wonderfully clear cultured voice, he said he wanted to end on a very personal matter. He said that what he was about to tell us might seem very funny, and, if this is how we felt about it, he would like us all to have a good laugh now. We smiled and giggled a bit and waited, and he said he wasn't going to beat about the bush and he would come straight to the point, because it was in our interest that we should be warned of a danger which, when we got to our first ship, we would all have to face. There were other ratings who might try to use us, make advances for immoral purposes, lead us into temptation with seductive words that what they were suggesting was quite natural, otherwise God wouldn't have given us the feeling. Perhaps we still weren't sure what he was talking about, so he would come straight out with it and he wanted us to heed his words carefully. He had given us the opportunity to laugh; now he would tell us bluntly, seriously, that older ratings, if they made this sort of approach, were after one thing and one thing only, our arses. Although the Chaplain said we could have our laugh beforehand, it was then we gave way to almost uncontrolled merriment. After this, except for the Sunday services, or when he was walking about, smiling, we didn't see him again, and he didn't give us any more personal chats.

Often when you take an immediate liking to someone, you then find that, after a time, you don't feel the same. This is because the person turns out to be different from what you at first thought, but this didn't happen with our nice Leading Seaman. Having had this instant regard for him, for his kindness and his pleasant manner, the more we got to know him the more we liked him.

On that first day, when he took over from our assistant divisional officer, after he had said he wanted us to be happy, he told us where to sling our hammocks at night, where to stow them in the morning, what our immediate duties would be, also explaining that boys did not keep night watches but that wakey-wakey for us was a quarter of an hour earlier than for the rest of the ship's company. He also instructed us in the correct procedure for seeing our divisional officer should we have a request or complaint; and he said we were entitled, through our divisional officer, to put in to see the commander and, in exceptional circumstances, the captain. He then asked us again to remember that he himself was always available if any of us had problems to discuss.

The way our Leading Seaman spoke in this pleasant, easy manner, it gave us new boys a lovely feeling, that warm feeling of security which a child gets from a loving home. He had showed concern, and he would always be there if we needed him; this is what we felt. It was the first time since joining up that I felt confident, a feeling of happy dependence, and I never experienced it again quite in the same way, not in all the twelve years I spent in the Royal Navy, in peace or in war. But something happened to change this, and the change puzzled all of us. It was brought about by the appearance of a new boy who joined us not long before the fleet left Hong Kong for Wei-hai-Wei. He was a strange boy, and the way he came suddenly among us was as mysterious as his sudden disappearance not long after the murder.

It was our Leading Seaman himself who told us that the new boy came from a very wealthy family and had been educated at one of our best public schools; also that he had an uncle, his mother's brother, who was titled. I don't know how our Leading Seaman knew all this, but this is what he said. It was also a bit odd that the boy should have come by himself and not, as we did, in a group. He was quite unlike any of us, with his different background, different manner, different attitude. He was extremely good-looking, tall, well built, with grey-green eyes, a fresh complexion, slightly hollow cheeks, full sensitive lips, a slim nose, sandy hair brushed boyishly sideways. He had natural grace in every movement, and he spoke in an articulate pleasant voice. He was friendly, and everything about him added up to what our nice Leading Seaman had told us about the new boy's background, but it was so unusual at this time for a boy like him to join the lower deck that, even if we didn't think there was something sinister about it, we were left with an underlying feeling of uneasiness. Something somewhere didn't add up.

The new boy, however, did all that was expected of him. Holystoning the upper deck, washing paintwork, cleaning out cutters, cleaning out the picket boat, wire splicing, repairing sails, anything that came his way. In the compulsory seamanship and gunnery classes for boys, he learnt quickly and easily. He was also a good rugby player and was put into the fleet rugby team, where most of the other players were officers. He scrupulously obeyed orders, carried out his duties efficiently, and never complained. Nor did he give anything away about himself, so that we could only gossip, speculate, and wonder what had made a boy of his background, a background of wealth, privilege, and influence, come onto the lower deck where, in those days, in the 1930s, recruits came from the working class, mostly from very poor families and from orphanages. And it only added to the mystery when our nice Leading Seaman, always the friendliest and kindest of people, began acting in a way that was completely out of character.

He made it obvious, and for no apparent reason, that he disliked the new boy intensely, and he went out of his way to harass and humiliate him, giving him the most menial of tasks, sending the new boy to clean out a blocked pan in the boys' heads, which meant mopping up puddles of excrement; detailing him for backbending and monotonous chores such as scrubbing out greasy pans and urns in the galley, holystoning the upper deck for long periods, painting the ship's side where it was most difficult to reach and meant hanging awkwardly in a bosun's chair swinging backwards and forwards in the wind, trying to manoeuvre by pushing away with the feet, then coming in again. But the new boy didn't complain and didn't show any resentment. In fact he showed no emotion at all, which made it all the more puzzling that our nice Leading Seaman should go on behaving the way he did.

As well as these obvious acts of repression, our nice Leading Seaman kept up the pressure of persecution more subtly by ignoring the new boy, leaving him out of any friendly discussions with us, or when inspecting us on a Sunday morning parade, just before the divisional officer's inspection, talking pleasantly to each boy on either side, ignoring the new boy completely, which was worse than if he had criticised him and had told him to straighten his lanyard or pull down his blue collar at the back or square off his cap ribbon. In these situations silence is often the most cruel.

Just as we were wondering how all this was going to end, the persecution stopped. It stopped, as it had begun, for no apparent reason. We had put to sea for five days of fleet manoeuvres and were going on to Wei-hai-Wei. I liked Wei-hai-Wei because there were quiet creeks and coves for bathing, with green verges just like England, and in the sunny warm weather you could sit peacefully, finding temporary rest and relaxation in doing nothing. I found a lot of China like this, and even now, a half century later, I can remember many beautiful places, the villages tucked in beside wooded hills and surrounded by rice fields, the homeliness and friendliness of the Chinese. Only in places like Shanghai, with its fast-flowing Yangstse river where, so we heard, unwanted baby daughters were thrown, only in places like this was the white man's influence felt. At one exclusive park was a notice: NO DOGS OR CHINESE ALLOWED.

In those days, on the lower deck, and I can't now say whether this has changed at all, homosexual relationships were accepted as normal. It was a pattern of life found in boarding schools but without the relief of long holidays; for a commission abroad lasted two years or more. Ashore were the seedy brothels and other places where you could find girls and also, if you were unlucky, pick up VD. So, many of the boys acted as wingers to the older ratings, the relationships dependent on an unwritten code of behaviour which, when broken by unfaithfulness, could end in bitter rivalry and sometimes fighting. It was not unusual to see boys in the washrooms grouped under one shower, naked, fondling each other, laughing and giggling beneath the rising steam, or caressing and kissing in the warm locker room below decks where boys stowed their hammocks. Often, too, they would pair up in out-of-the-way places, behind the gun turrets on dark nights, in little-used locker rooms, sometimes when in harbour, when it was not in use, in the commander's sea cabin. On warm nights boys could sleep on the upper deck, spreading out their hammocks alongside each other. At sea, when the water was smooth, the ship gently rolling, you could lie pleasantly gazing at the small bright stars in the dark blue sky, but even with a full moon there were enough dark shadows for boys to slide in together; so it was no surprise when, later, I was told that from the moment the new boy came on board, our nice Leading Seaman had fallen violently in love with him. It seemed peculiar to me, then, that you could treat someone as badly as the new boy was treated if you were in love in this way, but that's how it was.

Although no charges were brought, we all suspected, rightly or wrongly, it was the new boy who had killed our nice Leading Seaman. The day after the killing, detectives came on board and returned each day for the next week. All the boys and some of the senior ratings were persistently questioned. The boys, frightened by what had happened, told the detectives all they knew; they said yes, our Leading Seaman did like boys and a boy sometimes stayed the night with him in his locker room. No, there hadn't been any indication that the new boy was this way, not before our Leading Seaman started boasting about what had happened. Could we say why he did this, talked about the new boy losing his virginity, when the punishment for acts of gross indecency was dishonourable discharge? Surely it would have been better to have kept quiet. Had anyone any ideas?

But no, no one could say why our Leading Seaman had behaved as he did, telling people about what had happened with the new boy as if it was quite an achievement. Nor could we say if our Leading Seaman had felt resentment towards the new boy because he came from a different background. Yes, there had been this rough treatment in the beginning, and it would appear that the persecution only stopped because our Leading Seaman eventually got his own way. Why did we think this, that there had been a sexual relationship between the new boy and the Leading Seaman? Well, we had noticed there were some nights when the new boy was not sleeping in his hammock, and this was at about the time our Leading Seaman's behaviour changed so dramatically. Then there was the revelation which our Leading Seaman had himself made in his boasting, about what had taken place in the locker room; and it was not long after this that our Leading Seaman was found dead.

No one was able to say where the gun came from. The only consolation, as far as we were concerned, was that our nice Leading Seaman wouldn't have known much about it. He must have been asleep when the gun was put to his head and the trigger pressed, so he just didn't wake up, which is not a bad way to go. After the new boy left HMS *Dorsetshire*, we heard that an aunt had died and left him thirty thousand pounds, a lot of money in the 1930s. Then he left the Navy.

Although the new boy was in the untenable position of being a queer who is ashamed of being a queer, we couldn't feel all that sorry for him. We did feel sorry for our nice Leading Seaman because he was so nice, and we thought that never again would we have anyone as nice as he was. We felt sorry, too, for his pretty wife and baby daughter, whose photographs in gilt frames stood on the small table in the corner of the locker room, which is where our nice Leading Seaman liked to sit quietly, and in privacy, when writing letters home.

COALING SHIP: HMS *Iron Duke*, 1937

0400 hours and I awake suddenly with my heart thumping. Thump, thump, thud. I become aware that it is not only my heart I hear but the duty petty officer, who is busy crashing his fist against the side of my hammock. He also has hold of the top of the hammock and is rocking it dangerously from side to side so that I nearly tip out. Pushing his plump face with its swarthy complexion and ferret eyes into mine, he says quietly, ominously: "Get out, you fucking little wanker".

If he would only stop shaking my hammock, just for a moment, I would get out. My throat is dry and I have this tight feeling in my chest. I had forgotten that today we are to coal ship, and I was in this marvellous deep sleep when this madman started banging away.

On ordinary mornings I can anticipate reveille and am already half awake by 0600 hours, but two hours earlier, even if it is for something special, is two hours earlier. It seems as if I have hardly got my head down before I have this rude awakening. How I hate this petty officer. He is an uncouth bastard. I can never think how they get so uncouth. Even some-one as rough as he is must have had parents, or if he'd come from an or-phanage they would have taught him something. I think his mother must have married a Greek. He has a Greek look and is very hairy. He is the hairiest man I have seen. Stripped, he must look like a gorilla. On his arms are thick black hairs through which you can see his tattoos, a blue anchor and a blue naked girl on one arm and, curling round the other arm, a blue-and-red cobra with a protruding forked tongue. Thick black hairs peep over the top of his white shirt. There are black tufts of hair in his nostrils. He is very strong and has this habit of getting hold of your arm just above the elbow where it can hurt most; then with his thumb he will put pressure into the soft muscle, bruising the skin and leaving painful red marks.

Not long after joining the *Iron Duke* I was rated ordinary seaman. I thought then I would get more respect. I mean, promotion is promotion, even if all you have to do to get it is reach the age of eighteen. Anyway, it isn't helping me now with this brute thumping away and pushing my hammock from side to side. I put one leg out and I can see his eyes travelling up towards my bum, which is half revealed on account of my night flannel being all screwed up around my waist. Now he's started yelling at me again, telling me to lash up and stow, and fucking well be quick about it, you fucking little bastard, if you don't want to be in the officer of the watch's fucking report. Then I start thinking to myself: Christ Jesus, how did I come to get myself into this situation, I mean joining up as a Boy Seaman?

But I haven't much time for reflection because this petty officer goes on yelling and cursing. I don't think he's doing it because it's me, which is not to say he likes me, because I don't think he likes anybody. I don't think he likes himself very much. I have never seen him happy, even when he's drunk. I've seen him drunk several times, leaving his pub, swaying, cursing, which is all he ever seems to do when ashore. On board he gets rid of all his aggressions on anyone who gets in his way, as I have done on this morning of coal ship when dawn hasn't yet broken and he is in one of his frequent filthy moods. But he is a good seaman. He can quote from any part of the seamanship manual in the same way that a learned theologian knows his Bible. For him the seamanship manual is his Bible, and there isn't anything about seamanship he doesn't know.

Suddenly he stops the shaking, and I quickly slide out of my hammock, standing in my night flannel waiting for more abuse. I fold up my blankets and lay them neatly in the hammock. I hold my hammock together by putting my left arm round it; then, with the disengaged hand, I lash it up correctly, the lashes equidistant. I have no trouble lashing up my hammock in the proper way because I've been doing it for nearly two years. I am surprised he doesn't yell at me any more, to tell me to get it fucking well stowed unless I want to be on the quarter deck with my fucking cap off, you fucking little wanker. He watches every move I make as I take my hammock down and put it over my shoulder and go quickly to the locker room. I throw it among others and make for the washroom. I stand in front of an empty wash basin, in line with some of my messmates, two of whom are naked, washing themselves all over. I shave, clean my teeth, then go up to my personal locker to get into blue overalls. After this I return to the mess for a mug of pusser's cocoa and two large pusser's biscuits. The cocoa is steaming hot, thick, with streaks of yellow fat on top, and it is sweet and tastes good. It is still dark outside. At 0430 hours we are piped to fall in for coal ship.

The *Iron Duke* must be the last ship to use coal. She doesn't often put to sea. We've been to sea twice the year I've been in her. Perhaps three times but not for long periods. I would have thought more coal would be used in a semi-detached house than in this creaking old battleship tied up for most of the time in Portsmouth Dockyard.

So what is there to be said about coaling ship? The sweat, the filth, seeing the dawn light breaking beneath a red-streaked early autumn sky, but not strong enough to take over immediately from the harsh glare of large arc lamps. And all day long, with short breaks for meals, humping these sacks, carrying them on bent shoulders up the gangway, across the deck to the chute, then back for more and up, across, back again, faces and hands black with coal dust, breathing the dust, tasting it; all day long humping, tipping, aching, sweating.

I know now what Jesus must have felt on his way to Calvary, although in one respect Jesus was lucky. His cross was heavier, the way longer, his yoke greater, but he only had to do the journey once.

MIDSHIPMAN EASEY, 1943

If I'm honest about everything, when telling Simon Easey about the merits of promotion I was really telling myself. Not that I needed to convince myself, because the day I joined the lower deck I knew I should have gone in as an officer. Not everyone else agreed with this. Some of the confidential reports on me from divisional officers weren't all that good. How I knew about these was that I was sent to collect my papers, which included these reports. This was when I was going in for a commission. Of course, I shouldn't have been sent to collect confidential papers, but these sort of things happened in the Navy. Some of the reports were really quite bad. My divisional officer in the *Iron Duke* said I was the worst ordinary seaman he had come across in the history of the Royal Navy. He probably meant that part of naval history which he had experienced, and he probably felt this way because I had failed the examination for able seaman. I mean, to have failed for able seaman was quite an achievement in itself. This was because you could only give one of two answers to any one question, so even when guessing you should get quite a few right, but nearly every time I guessed wrong. Then my divisional officer in the *Glasgow* said I had these grandiose ideas and suffered from the delusion that I ought to be in the wardroom.

As far as he was concerned that was the last place I should be. Although they weren't very good reports, I didn't feel hurt, because in a democracy people are entitled, within reason, to express their opinions.

Nevertheless, I have always been good at telling other people what to do, except that when I gave Simon this sales talk on becoming an officer he didn't show much enthusiasm, so I didn't think he would do anything about it. Also, he seemed quite happy with what he was doing at the time, although it meant living in Portsmouth Barracks, something that never appealed to me. He had this cosy job in the drafting office and looked all set to stay there for the rest of the war. He'd also built up a few perks, extra rations, extra leave not officially given, but the sort of things that just happen when you become established in even a minor position.

When I explained to Simon the advantages of becoming an officer I wasn't, in fact, telling him to do something I hadn't done myself. In the *Malaya* papers had been started for me to get a permanent commission in the Royal Navy, although it was not all that long after they were started that they were torn up. The reason they were torn up was because I got left behind when the ship went to sea. This was in Alexandria, and there was this emergency when the enemy fleet had been sighted and our ships had to put to sea in a hurry.

At the time I was cox'n of the picket boat, so I had to return quickly and get the picket boat hooked on and hoisted inboard, but I got it hooked on the wrong way round, so that when it was clear of the water it fell sideways, hitting the ship, and this happened twice. The commander, who was standing on the quarter-deck, leaned over the guard-rails and yelled something at me, but I couldn't quite hear what he said because the *Malaya* was a battleship and he was very high up; so I waited and he yelled again, this time louder, with a hand cupped round his mouth, and he told me to get to hell out of it and not come back until the ship came in; then the *Malaya* got up steam and set sail with the rest of the fleet, and that's when I got left behind.

I found a place in the harbour to tie up and hung around all day. Late that night I went out to see if the *Malaya* had returned. It was pitch-dark and I couldn't see a thing, and because of blackout regulations we weren't allowed lights. Then I hit the *Prince of Wales* head on. I didn't know it was the *Prince of Wales* until they hoisted me inboard. They weren't all that pleased because it was in the early hours and a whole watch had to turn out to do the hoisting, but I was glad that this time I had managed to hook on the right way round. This was when I met up with the Welsh boy. In the morning, for breakfast, I was sent to the mess where he was leading seaman.

When I got back to the *Malaya*, later that day, I had to see the captain, who told me my papers for a commission had been torn up. He was quite apologetic about it, which was very nice of him. It wasn't all that often you were able to see the captain, and to be sent for in this rather personal way and having him say he was sorry made me feel quite good, even if it was a sad occasion. I don't know how the commander felt. I think he was quite glad. I don't think he had wanted to start the papers in the first place.

Actually it was not the commander but this American heiress who was really responsible. She was not only lovely to look at but had this beautiful nature. I met up with her when the *Malaya* was in dry dock in the Brooklyn Navy Yard. We had gone there under the American lease-lend arrangements brought in by President Roosevelt. Almost on the day the President announced these lease-lend arrangements, we were torpedoed while escorting a convoy to Freetown, and we went straight out to New York, arriving there on a Sunday morning with a gaping hole in the port side. The Americans gave us a great welcome. They were very keen on the British because we were then standing alone against the forces of evil, and they gave us a really fabulous time. I mean, they couldn't do enough for us, and the commander found this beautiful heiress. Her husband, an officer in the American navy, was on duty overseas.

We were in the Brooklyn Navy Yard for nearly three months, and she came on board quite a lot. At this time I was the commander's writer, running his office, making out the daily orders, and, when at sea, working out the time of dawn action stations, that sort of thing; but when we were in Brooklyn he would send me to meet her at the main dockyard gate, where I would wait in a taxi and bring her back. It was quite some way to the ship, and we would sit in the back of the taxi talking. I got to know her well and liked her a lot. What I noticed most were her mouth and hands. She had a large mouth, beautifully formed, full of expression, and she had these delicate hands. She also had this Veronica Lake hairstyle, and spoke in a soft American drawl. She was really sweet. She was about thirty and I was twenty-two, and sitting in the taxi with her I told her a lot about myself.

Once we were so deep in conversation that we drove past the ship. The commander was standing on the quarter-deck watching, but he didn't say anything. I know she liked me and I know she told the commander that the British Navy were missing out by not having me as an officer, which was very good of her. He was wrapped up in her and was a heavy drinker, so I suppose when he started my papers he was in a state of euphoria and didn't give it too much thought. He just mentioned to me briefly the next day that they had been started.

Of course, it was a bit of a blow when, a few months later, the papers were torn up, and I had to wait quite some time before I could get them started again. This was when someone I knew who knew the First Lord of the Admiralty wrote to the First Lord about me. The First Lord wrote back and said I would be given the chance of a commission in the RNVR, which was when I came back to Portsmouth Barracks, went to the drafting office, and got to know Simon Easey.

Simon, being polite and pleasant,listened carefully when I told him it was the duty of each one of us to realize our full potential. I don't think he'd ever thought about becoming an officer until I put the idea in his mind. I told him that now was as good a time as any to make the effort, because you only had to look at what was happening in the war to see who was going to win. In the Middle East a hundred Flying Fortresses had wreaked havoc in Sardinia, the Union Jack had been hoisted over Tripoli, Tunis and Bizerta were captured, and there had been a big advance by the French. Flying Fortresses had bombed Naples, the Cap Bon peninsula had been cut off, and this was followed by the final Axis collapse in Tunisia. Von Armin and eleven other generals had been captured and a total of two hundred and fifty thousand prisoners taken. Entire companies had surrendered to the victorious British, French, and Imperial forces. On the Russian front, which stretched for nearly one thousand five hundred miles, the Red army had captured Krymskaya and was advancing northwards. The Red air force had inflicted heavy damage at the Briansk-Orel salient, and, in spite of some resistance by the Germans at Kovorossiisk, after continuous heavy pounding by Russian artillery, the Russians had driven a wedge into the enemy line and a German counterattack was repelled. Even Hitler, speaking at the anniversary of the Winter Help Scheme, admitted that the German army had been faced with a crisis during the winter.

In the Far East there was heavier bombing in Burma using American fighter aircraft as dive bombers, while the RAF had made two hundred attacks in one month on the Japanese. A group of Japanese, survivors from a sunk convoy, who had been rounded up on Goodenough Island by the Australians, bowed to their captors and in fair English sang "Auld Lang Syne". Back home, aircraft of fighter and bomber command were over northern France and the Low Countries as the RAF's offensive against railway targets in Germany and occupied territory was stepped up. Large forces of Flying Fortresses were bombing Europe, and bomber command made its heaviest attack of the war on Duisberg, Europe's biggest inland port. The attack started at 0200 and was over by 0245. During this brief period fifteen hundred tons of bombs were dropped, including eight-thousand-pound and four-thousand-pound bombs, also smaller high explosives and thousands of incendiaries, all raining down at the rate of about thirty-four tons a minute. Tremendous havoc was caused, great areas were left in flames, and fires were still burning the following afternoon. As well as all this, Germany was finding increasing opposition in the occupied countries. There had been mass arrests in Croatia after an SS colonel was assassinated, martial law was imposed in Holland, and there were mass arrests in France after the discovery of a plot to assassinate Laval. In an article in *Das Reich*, Goebbels had written that the destruction of the Jewish race was of historical importance, and that the most dangerous enemy of mankind must be destroyed.

But ordinary life went on. Prematurely awakened butterflies had been seen in a garden in Bracknell. In the country, where chestnut trees were coming into full bloom, Dr Vaughan Williams conducted his own work, *Pilgrim's Progress*, at Dorking Parish Church. *Arsenic and Old Lace,* which treated murder as a gentle art, was at the Strand Theatre. The poorer clergy were being given additional help by the governors of Queen Anne's Bounty, and at the Albert Hall the Archbishop of Canterbury, speaking to the Boys' Brigade, said many people looked forward to the days after the war, the glorious time to come, but this would only come if we were ready with discipline as real as that to which we had submitted in the war, and we must maintain this self-discipline all through life. There had been some complaints about booksellers using prisoners of war as a rubbish heap for children's books and other unsaleable literature, while in Yorkshire, in the Midlands, and in the South, thousands of busmen and women, their wage claim, based on the increased strain of wartime conditions having been rejected, came out on strike.

Before I left Portsmouth Barracks, on 14 May 1943, I looked for Simon Easey to say good-bye, but he was on leave. I did well at *King Alfred*, coming high up in the final examination for sub-lieutenant. The reason I did well was because the officer supervising the examination told us the answers before asking the questions. The better we did, the better it reflected on him, so he walked up and down whispering the answers before going back to the front of the class and asking the questions in his ordinary voice. It was very good of him to do this. He was one of our instructor-officers, and, up to this time, I hadn't really taken to him. He was a rough Northerner who had been skipper of a fishing vessel before joining the RNVR. Since then I have had a warm feeling towards him, putting out of my mind the times he shouted and sneered when it seemed I couldn't get anything right. I have often wished all the other examinations I took could have been like that one. It makes it much easier if you can have the answers first.

Once I left Pompey I forgot about Simon. I would probably have forgotten him altogether had I not met up with him once more. This was in the autumn of 1944, when I was back in Portsmouth Barracks as a sub-lieutenant. I was walking towards the parade ground when this brown-eyed rosy-cheeked midshipman approached, saluted, and said: "Remember me, sir?"

I said: "Yes, Simon, of course I do."

He said: "I've got you to thank for this. I'm very grateful to you, Willie. I owe it all to you."

I said: "It's nice of you to say so." Then I said, as if mentioning something very secretive: "To tell you the truth, Simon, I didn't think you'd taken much notice of what I told you."

He laughed and said: "Of course I did. I knew you were right. When you said it's our duty to realize our full potential, it made me think." I nodded, and he went on: "If it hadn't been for you, Willie, I would probably have stayed in that job in the drafting office, ending up where I'd started."

I nodded again. He looked handsome in his officer's uniform, on each lapel the RNVR midshipman's mauve cloth square, the gold buttons of his jacket gleaming, his new officer's cap set at a slight angle, a lock of brown hair peeping out above one ear. Rank and authority emphasized his youth, although I didn't need this confirmation. I already knew he wasn't much over nineteen.

It was a brief encounter. He asked me what I was doing, and I told him I had just left combined operations and was passing through Pompey on my way to Chatham. He told me that he had come third in his class and hoped to be promoted soon to acting sub-lieutenant, and he said he had volunteered for motor torpedo boats.

I said: "Well, Simon, it's great news. Your family must be very pleased."

He laughed again and said: "Oh yes, they are. Gillian, she's my sister, couldn't wait to go out with me. She's going round telling everyone her brother is an officer." Then he added seriously: "Of course, she's only fourteen." He stood looking at me, a look of gratitude, of affection. It made me feel good.

I said: "Anything's better than being stuck in this dreary place for the rest of the war." I thought he was going to thank me once more but he didn't. I held out my hand and he took it, holding it for a second in a brief tight grip. I said: "Good luck, Midshipman Easey." Then I left him.

He called out: "Hope to see you again, Willie."

But I didn't see him again. He went into MTBs, was promoted to acting sub-lieutenant, and, not long before the end of the war, in an engagement with German E Boats, he was killed in action.

DEREK MOND, 1943

I liked Derek Mond. He was rich and he was titled. His father was Lord Melchett. Had Derek lived, he would have been the next Lord Melchett. He was one of those people who seem to be able to do everything. Sometimes you meet people like this and they just seem to have everything worth having that life has to offer: position, wealth, good looks, character, leadership, exceptional ability — all of which is a little annoying for people like me who come from a humble background and who aren't much good at anything. I know it's wrong to feel envious, but I just think it's one more example of how iniquitous this business of being born is. Derek was not only rich and titled but he had inherited all that made his family great. There are some families, the Churchills, the House of Fraser, where the children seem destroyed by their famous fathers, but this was certainly not so with the Monds, who, like the Cecils, went brilliantly from generation to generation adding glory to glory and accomplishment to accomplishment.

It was in the spring of 1943 that Derek, aged twenty-two and a half, strode into our cadets' class in Brighton. He was tall, big, bearded, handsome, Eton and Oxford in the background, married to a beautiful girl, and already beginning to distinguish himself in his chosen field of science. His full potential as a leader showed most clearly when he was on the parade ground taking his turn as cadet-captain, giving orders loudly in a deep, powerful voice, a voice full of controlled violence. He was full of aggression, too, which in the past had spilt over when, with a knuckle-duster concealed under a glove, he would go into a sleazy backstreet bar in whichever port his ship happened to be, and pick a fight.

Felix told me about this. Felix said that he had once seen Derek break an AB's jaw. But it was not until ten years later that the Lord Chief Justice of England was to say of Derek Bentley's knuckle-duster: "Have you seen a more horrible sort of weapon? You know, this is to hit a person in the face who comes at you. You grasp it here, your fingers go through, and you have got a heavy steel bar to strike anybody with; and you can kill a person with it, of course."

Felix told me quite a lot about Derek, as he had been in the same ship as Derek before they both came to *King Alfred* to start the cadet's course. I have never quite worked out the relationship. Felix was always hovering around Mond, but I don't think they could be called friends, because

Felix was small and thin and his voice was thin, too, thin and shrill, and he had this constant nervous giggle. I really don't know how someone as small as he was got selected for officer training, although his mind was sharp and he had been to a good public school. His parents were doctors. He had two sisters, one older and married, the other younger. Felix told me all this just as he told me about Derek. He always seemed to be bubbling over with news and gossip and speculation. I think his compulsion to talk came from an inner nervousness, as if he had to be always on the defensive, uncertain of what the other person's reaction would be, not because he wanted to make a friend, but because he wished to avoid the enemy. Although he often appeared timid and seemed eager to please, I quickly discovered that underneath he was sharp, cunning, vindictive, an untrustworthy friend, a dangerous enemy. Felix had a better brain than Derek, academically better, a brain that got him a first-class degree in law, and distinctions in solicitors' finals. I never did wholly take to Felix — I don't think anyone did — and Mond used him because Felix put himself in a position to be used.

The day we arrived in Brighton to begin our training, I was able to help Felix out of an awkward situation. We had all just arrived and were standing outside Brighton station on this clear day in May 1943. The tang of sea air was invigorating and stimulating, in sharp contrast to the musty atmosphere of Pompey Barracks. We had been standing only a few minutes, talking to each other, when, without warning, half a dozen Focke-Wulf 190s flew in out of the sun, raking the streets with cannon and machine-gun fire. The first thing we knew was hearing the bullets splattering the streets and houses. We dropped flat on our faces, staying this way until the firing stopped and the enemy vanished. A few of the cadets got up and the rest followed, and it was as we were standing brushing down our uniforms that Felix said: "Christ, I've shit myself." He was standing next to me and spoke as if talking to himself, which he may have been. I mean, I wouldn't have thought anyone who had done this would want to broadcast it. I didn't say anything and he just stood looking at me in this rather sorrowful way. Then I could smell what he'd done and it was pretty awful.

I said: "If you're quick, you can get cleaned up," He asked me how so I said: "In the station. There's a loo there. I'll show you."

I went back inside the station and Felix followed. I went down the steps into the loo, pulled out some change, and gave Felix a penny to get in. I waited while he went inside. Then I heard the rustle of paper, and a few minutes later he came out smiling and after washing his hands came back to me and said: "Thanks. Thanks a lot." When we got back to where the others were standing, we found that an instructor petty officer had just arrived. He checked our names, fell us in, and marched us off. I found out later that German fighters had made tip-and-run raids over Brighton before, but not for some time. It was just bad luck they should have come the day we arrived.

Although Felix stayed friendly, I never got close to him. Nor did anyone else. I did once have this feeling that there was some sort of bond between us, but I realised afterwards it was a passing experience, common in war, when you share a common danger. You feel close at the time, but it is just the need for protection. Sometimes this experience lasts as a sentiment, with meetings and a veterans' march past and the memories of fallen comrades.

After I helped Felix on that first day, he not only became friendly but often confided in me. By confiding I mean he told me a lot about himself and about Derek, which I don't think he told to others. Almost from the moment we arrived, Felix had firmly attached himself to Derek, running around in this rather subservient way while the rest of the class looked on with amused indifference. Whether Felix had behaved in the same way with Mond before they came to *King Alfred*, I couldn't say, but now he ran around his hero, fetching, carrying, anticipating most of Derek's whims and fancies, and even, on the parade ground, spying for him, reporting back any whispering or other small breaches of discipline in the ranks so that Mond, when cadet-captain, could bawl out the culprits. The officers, standing watching, assessing capabilities, not seeing what Felix was doing, would think this good. Felix, with the need for recognition which is in everyone, seemed to enjoy playing the role of an upper-class servant: the role of an equerry rather than a butler. Nevertheless, Felix, although he got some satisfaction from the reflected glory, remained conscious of his size, so that there was always a subconscious resentment and sense of injustice which meant that his giggling nervous willingness to be, as it were, all things to all men hid vicious, destructive thoughts that could, if anything dented his image, erupt into acts of revenge, which is what happened with Giles.

The time I had this illusory feeling of closeness to Felix was towards the end of our course at Lancing College. Late one night I awoke suddenly with an instinctive feeling of fear. I could hear nothing but must have become subconsciously aware of danger. The large dormitory was in darkness as I got out of bed and climbed onto a window-sill that formed the ledge of an alcove. I pulled the heavy blackout curtains across so that they fell down behind me, then peered out and saw, in the distance, long, slender searchlight beams crisscrossing. Although the air raid was far enough away not to be a threat, I could feel myself trembling. It needed little imagination to picture what was happening, for the full horror of bombing had come with the London blitzes.

I had seen a London blitz and knew what it meant. Bombs raining down all day long, bombing all day long. The suction and pressure of high explosive pushing you, pulling you, and you feel your eyeballs are being sucked out. Smoke like acid, everything going black, everything black and yellow. People praying, crying, crouching in the crib of a church, the crib shuddering, the kids scared. Kids screaming, crying. The bombers coming on and on. Such colossal heat. Steel doors red-hot. The whole road moving. The docks a raging inferno. Fences alight, barges alight. You walk down the middle of the road, so much fallen masonry. Blocks of masonry as big as houses. Warehouses alight. The smell of burning coffee, of tea and rubber. Houses alight. Piles of rubble, bricks. Heads sticking up, heads of dead people. Hours and hours of intense bombing. Convulsed, you can't get your breath. You think you must be dead. The end of the world. Blood, heat, everything red with fire. Heat, blood, the lot. Digging out bodies.

In one raid, four hundred and thirty killed, sixteen hundred seriously injured. Street after street reduced to rubble. Mothers and children hysterical but the bombers keep on coming. Our fighters can't hold back such an onslaught. High explosives whistling down. The shelter shakes. Nowhere is safe. You get out and find the building gone. A bomb has dropped on a shelter in Chelsea. Everyone killed. Eighteen people wrapped in blankets. Mortuaries full up. A school bombed in Lewisham, six teachers and thirty eight children killed, all to be buried in a common grave. But there is a growing sense of neighbourliness as the bombing spreads to the suburbs. Carshalton bombed and everyone helps each other. Everything revolves around the air raid warden. People coming back, coping with the blitz. The firemen face the greatest challenge. Patriotism, purpose, comradeship pull you through. If you die, you die; if you live, you live. You are concerned for others. By the end of the second week of the blitzes Londoners began to feel they wouldn't give in. Taxi drivers by day, heroes by night. The Londoners stayed. Heroes all. Victory for Londoners in spite of destruction. The noise of anti-aircraft guns is reassuring, but the sheer horror of what they faced in death and destruction remained with them for the rest of their lives.

It was not just these thoughts of the London bombing that made me feel uneasy. I had already seen enough action in the war to know what action meant. Men brought out of HMS *Liverpool* after a bomb exploded in her petrol tanks, men burnt, blinded, dying, men with shattered limbs, dead men, too; merchant ships in the Malta convoys, ablaze from end to end, going down in seconds; a drowned airman brought ashore on the Isle of Wight, his body placed gently on the cold stone ground, his stiff arms held out, so stiff that not even the surgeon lieutenant, when he came to confirm death, could bend them. I watched as they carried him away. He was young, his eyes tightly screwed up from drowning, his arms still stuck out rigidly in front of him as if he was trying for one last embrace.

I sat staring at the searchlights, mentally straining to catch the sounds of exploding bombs, although I knew I wouldn't hear them at this distance even if I hadn't been behind thick glass. Then I felt a movement beside me, a touch on the arm, and heard Felix whisper: "Where's the raid, Willie? Over London?" I said I didn't know, but I didn't think it possible you could see as far as London. He said London was only sixty miles, so I said well, it might be over London but I wasn't sure.

Felix, like me, was in his pyjamas. I twisted into a more comfortable position, pushing the blackout curtains behind him, and we sat huddled together. I found the warmth of his body comforting and lost some of my feeling of fear. No one else seemed to have woken. A cadet in a nearby bed grunted and turned over, there was some coughing down the other end of the dormitory, but that was all. I whispered: "They never seem to catch them, the enemy. They never seem to catch them in the searchlights." Felix didn't reply, so I asked quietly: "Have you seen many raids?" He said he hadn't. Of the few he had seen, most of them had been at night. He said he had only once seen a plane caught in the searchlights, but he couldn't say if it had been shot down. We sat not saying very much, and when the raid was over we went back to our beds. This incident, the sharing of a common danger, gave me no special feeling of affection for Felix because he wasn't the sort of person for whom you could feel affection, but I would have been pleased if my last memory of him had been this slightly nostalgic recollection of what happened that night. Which is what might have happened but for the incident with Giles.

Giles was the youngest member of our class, coming up to nineteen, a grammar school boy of medium-build, good-natured, with brown eyes, brown hair, a fresh complexion, and a slightly effeminate manner. He was polite and pleasant but nevertheless had a very strong character and an honest, direct approach to everything, so that, although he was never rude or went out of his way to hurt anyone, he said what he thought. We knew, and Felix knew, that Giles thought Felix a little creep. Felix, for his part, made no attempt to hide his hatred of Giles and looked only for an opportunity of revenge, an opportunity which came the evening of our last day at Lancing College.

On that day, because the main course had finished, there had been a mood of celebration, and in the evening Mond, with Felix and half a dozen other cadets, went ashore, returning three or four hours later after some heavy drinking. I knew that Felix wasn't a heavy drinker, but the rest of them came unsteadily back, Mond ahead of the others, going straight to his bed, where he stood clutching the rail, swaying slightly, his jaws tightly set. It would have been better if he'd gone to bed and slept it off, which he probably would have done if it hadn't been for Felix. In his shrill, giggly voice Felix said: "I hate queers. I really hate them. Don't you, Derek? Filthy, dirty perverts." As he spoke, Felix stood looking down the dormitory to where Giles was reading. Giles was too far away to have heard what was said, but when he saw Felix staring at him he must have guessed something was up, because the next moment he disappeared, which I thought a mistake, since any sign of weakness only provokes aggression in a bully. Not that Giles generally was frightened or weak, but, as he told me later when we met up after we had left *King Alfred*, he saw the danger and guessed from the way Felix was staring at him, and the drunken mood Mond was in, that there was a good chance of a beating-up. It just seemed sensible to slip away and avoid trouble. And he would have avoided trouble if Felix, sharp-eyed and vengeful, had not followed every movement and seen where Giles had hidden himself behind one of the blackout curtains.

Felix was well aware that the aggression in Mond, already at a dangerous level because of the drinking, needed only the slightest provocation to turn into violence. Trembling with eagerness and looking up at Mond's bearded set face, Felix said: "Shall we give him a bath, Derek? Shall we? I'll go now and fill it." Felix walked the length of the dormitory, passing Giles's hiding place, and went into the bathroom, where there were two old-fashioned baths. Soon afterwards there was the sound of water splashing. Other cadets, sitting on their beds or standing around, waited to see what would happen. They didn't have to wait long. Felix came back, went up to Mond, and said: "He's over there, Derek. Over there behind the curtains." Mond strode over to the window, pulled back the curtains, saw Giles crouching on the sill and yanked him down. Someone quickly closed the curtains as blackout regulations were strict.

Cadets gathered round, and there was yelling and chanting; then Felix said excitedly: "It's ready, Derek. The bath's ready." Mond, holding Giles by the collar just under the throat, his fingers curled inside Giles's jumper, his knuckles pressed fiercely against his Adam's apple, was causing Giles considerable discomfort, but Giles just stood there, making no protest, and Mond began propelling him towards the bathroom while the chanting and yelling went on. Everyone had entered into the spirit of the mobbing; it was all good fun, the cadets happy to celebrate in any way this last night at Lancing. It was a relief to have finished the main part of the course, with only three weeks to go before those of us who had passed became officers.

So many cadets crowded into the bathroom that I didn't bother to follow. I heard shouts and laughter and Felix's distinctive shrill voice, the sound of more splashing, then a cry of pain and Giles's voice quickly calling out: "No, don't. Please don't."

It seemed ages before Mond and Felix and the other cadets returned to the dormitory, some of them with water splashed over their uniforms, but Giles's ordeal had lasted only about ten minutes. Mond immediately undressed, got into bed, and fell asleep.

One cadet, who had also been ashore drinking, looked down at the handsome bearded Jewish face and shouted: "It's Jesus! He's back from the dead. Jesus is back!" There was a little laughter, but most of the cadets were by their beds getting ready to turn in. As Giles hadn't returned I went along to the bathroom. I found him sitting on a stool in the corner. He was soaking wet and streaked with blood, most of the blood coming from his nose. Two cadets were mopping away at him, taking it in turns with a wet blood-stained towel. Part of Giles's blue serge jumper had been wrenched away at the collar, leaving a long tear down the front. The bath had been filled nearly to the top. The cold water, still in the bath, was stained red. I pulled the plug, and blood and water drained away, ending with a swirl and a deep gurgling sound.

We left Lancing College the following day and went to *King Alfred* in Brighton. Giles never complained and never referred to the beating-up. Although he avoided Derek and Felix, it wasn't out of malice. He'd never mixed with them anyway. After three weeks in Brighton we were given our commissions. Nearly all the class got through. We left as officers, going our separate ways, most of us never to meet again. After the war Felix became a lawyer and, if he is still alive, would now be in his mid-sixties.

Derek was killed. On 30 April 1945 a light aircraft in which he was travelling fell into the sea off the coast of Scotland; the aircraft, with its crew and passengers, vanished without trace. On 4 July, under the heading Fallen Officers, news of Derek's death was given in *The Times*, followed, a week later, by this personal tribute:

LIEUTENANT THE HON. DEREK MOND R.N.V.R.

Lord Cherwell writes: Derek Mond's friends — and they were many — must all lament his passing. In the fourth generation he showed all his family's talent and enthusiasm for science, and there is no doubt that he would have made a distinguished name for himself in a branch of the physical sciences but for the untimely accident that overtook him when flying on duty off the Scottish coast. He was one of the fortunate people who make a success of anything they take up. Had it not been for the war he would undoubtedly have rowed for his university; his effectiveness as a speaker is attested by his success at the Oxford Union Society. As soon as he was of age he joined the Navy, and saw active service as a rating and later as an officer in the North Atlantic. He specialised in navigation, and put his early training to such good use that he was appointed to an establishment dealing with the development of the numerous scientific gadgets with which the modern ship of war is crowded. The country can ill afford in these perilous days to lose a young man of such promise, who had so much to give. And all those who had fallen under the spell of his charm will long deplore his premature departure from the scene of his many varied activities.

Easter Sunday 1961. And this is where, had I been a writer and not a dreamer, I would have ended this volume on the life and death of Francis Robert George Henry James Forsyth. I would have ended it here because Easter is a good time, a time of joy, of hope, with all the light days and bright days ahead. Adonis, the God of Spring, green buds on the trees, fresh green shoots at the bottom of what I thought were dead fuchsia stalks. Easter, a time of celebration. Flowers in the church and home. Flowers in the garden, in the fields and woods, too; crocus, daffodil, hyacinth, the flowering currant, apple blow, and wild cherry.

Today April warmth has brought out the white dead-nettle on every bank, dog violets everywhere; the first primroses open out on their reddish felted stems, and among the hedges are the delicate flowers of the greater stitchwort. Bees, tempted out, are busy in the cherry trees. There are wood anemones and wild daffodils, also the cowslips and the pasque flower, pasque meaning Easter, the petals so startling that it was thought to grow from human blood.

On the altar white and green, the white of resurrection and green of eternal life. Immortality. All living things come into being from other living things: a basic biological phenomenon. The life-circle. Continuation, as in the wheat smut puccinia graminis, where the pistils red on young plants later turn black and eventually produce spores which cannot live on the wheat plant, but they can live on the barberry, where they grow into fungi; these fungi then produce spores which cannot live on the barberry but, carried by the wind, start the life-circle again on the wheat. Resurrection, reconciliation. It would be nice to think this way. Forsyth has been dead six months, Allan Jee nearly a year.

I think of 1961 in particular because it was then, on this Easter Day, that I walked to the Festival Hall to hear Klemperer conduct the Messiah. If God be for us who can be against us? The previous night I went to midnight mass at Westminster Cathedral and lit a candle for Billy Lundon. Billy was killed in the war, on 6 June 1942, when the aircraft he was piloting crashed into a field in Scotland. He was a pilot officer, just nineteen. When I lit the candle I thought also of two other young officers, Ian MacFarlane and Bruce Robertson, who were in my class at *King Alfred* and who were killed. I forgot about Derek Mond. I don't know why I forgot, but I did. When I left the cathedral it was two in the morning, and the moon

Showed the broad, white road in heaven,
Pathway of the ghosts, the shadows,
Running straight across the heaven,
Crowded with the ghosts, the shadows.

In bygone days it was common custom to rise before the sun on Easter Day and walk in the fields to see the sun dance — an old tradition which said the sun always danced on this day. Many believed the world would end at Easter time, which is why there is gravity and joy and an expectation of the second coming; the earth not utterly destroyed but transformed, restored to a Garden of Eden, of innocence, no more pain, no cruelty, every created thing glad to be none other than itself. Easter peculiar to the English tongue, derived from Eastre or Eostre, the Goddess of Spring, a Christian festival founded on pagan rituals; the dead Christ cradled in the lap of his mother already typified by Greek artists showing the sorrowful goddess with her dying lover in her arms.

Marvellous, really, to think we may live on; and I was thinking this way, with Easter in mind, as I walked over Westminster Bridge on this Sunday evening in 1961 on my way to the Festival Hall and, halfway over the bridge, became aware of thin, plaintive, reedy strains from a mouth organ playing a First World War tune: "Till the Boys Come Home". I didn't take too much notice, except in the back of my mind I had a sense of mud and trenches and shell shock and decay. But no silver lining. I never saw any silver lining in the First World War or any other war, only the misery and the waste and the illusion of glory. The worst thing about all wars must be each army believing it has God on its side. The Japanese had the son of Heaven as their Emperor. Hitler believed he had been sent to wipe out the Jews, so he built those awful concentration camps; but Kitchener had them, too. Kitchener treated the South African rebels with appalling cruelty, burning farmhouses as he advanced and building the concentration camps where large numbers of men, women, and children died; an idea he copied from camps built during the Cuban insurrection of 1895 to 1898 and not unrelated to the latter conception of Auschwitz, Belsen, Buchenwald, Dachau, Mauthausen, Sachsenhausen, Treblinka.

Better to look on the bright side. Today has been a good day, a friendly day, the London sparrows boisterous and chirpy. Also in bygone days, in Sussex, at Easter time, a great delicacy was sparrow pie and spinage The sparrows don't know this, and it's best to let bygones be bygones. I looked up at Big Ben and saw that it was nearly half past six, plenty of time for a quiet stroll along the embankment. The mouth organ had stopped for a moment, then started again. Another First World War tune: "Take Me Back to Dear Old Blighty". I would go along with that. Even if the dream of a land fit for heroes was shattered, anything was better than the slaughter. The thought of dying is unsettling; there is something unwholesome about it, death, decay, mossy graves. You wouldn't catch me walking through a graveyard at night.

I got to the top of the steps where the lion is, then I looked down and saw this bum with the mouth organ. A young couple were walking along hand in hand. They took no notice of him standing by the parapet with his back to the river. As he played he hopped from foot to foot, but every now and then he stopped, came smartly to attention, saluted in correct military fashion, and called out in a clear voice of command: "Over the top, men. Over the top!" The young couple walked on, and he began playing again. There was a professional manner about all his movements, and he manipulated the mouth organ expertly, but I was sorry he was playing it at all because the sound intruded. It was a pleasant evening. The day had been cloudy, with bright intervals and a moderate warm wind. There was only light traffic over the bridge and, as well as the young couple, no more than half a dozen other people strolling along the embankment watching the passing boats. On such a quiet evening the strained notes jarred, and the bum performing his clownish acts jarred.

Instead of going down the steps and along the embankment I could continue on over the bridge and, in this way, dodge him. It's not so much that I actively dislike bums, but I just don't feel the same about the poor as I do about the rich. This is something in myself that I have never gone into very deeply. Sometimes I have thought about it. I thought about it when I heard a broadcast talk given by the Dean of King's College, London, in which he said that the poor are blessed and have dignity and often share what little they have. He went on to quote what Jesus said about it being easier for a camel to get through the eye of a needle than for a rich man to enter the Kingdom of Heaven, and he ended by saying that all this must be true because what Jesus taught has endured through twenty centuries, and we know it to be the way, the truth, and the life. And that is what the Queen said, too. In her Christmas Day broadcast she said the unfortunate and the underprivileged have an equal place in heaven with the rich, which is a very nice thought if you are poor and underprivileged, but it's not something that appeals to me.

After the Dean said what he did in his very impressive voice, I made up my mind to talk it over with Patrick. Patrick likes poor people, and some of his closest friends are lavatory attendants. Or I could ask Pete. There was that time I saw Pete put his arm round a bum when I was visiting his doss-house. Pete pulled the bum towards him in this quite affectionate way, but how Pete was able to do it I don't know, because the bum was old and wrinkled, with grey, straggly hair and a stubble, and he had on these filthy clothes — old, stained, torn trousers and a stained, torn jacket. The stains were dark and greasy, like patches of oil. Most bums look filthy, but this one looked filthier than most, and there was Pete clutching him, and it really made me feel quite ill. Rose was very poor but she was clean, even to manicuring her toe-nails. I was very fond of Rose, so I suppose it's not quite true to say there aren't some poor people I could like. But not very many.

In a way, though, when you think about all this, it is how society works. I mean, although the Church was started by a carpenter, most of the bishops come from the upper classes, and we've never had a working-class king and queen. Also, when the rich do something it doesn't seem the same as when the poor do it. Lord Thynne's son went on the rampage and stole jewellery worth £31,639 from Sir John Stow and jewellery worth £33,020 from Mrs Wyndam and then committed other offences, making a total haul of £313,000, and it didn't seem to me nearly as bad as thefts committed by working-class thieves who get remanded in custody for stealing much less. I think the judge must have felt the same way, because he gave Lord Thynne's son bail on condition the young man stayed at Longleat House with his grandfather, the Marquis of Bath. I expect there are quite a few people who think the way I do, so I don't feel too badly about it.

After some indecision, as I wasn't all that keen on getting too close to the bum with the mouth organ, I made up my mind not to carry on over the bridge, but to go along the embankment. There is something compelling about the river. At night the violet-grey water reflects shimmering white and orange lights from the palisade of buildings, and in day-time, when the tide is out and the river breeze carries the slightly acrid smell from the grey silt, it brings back childhood memories of Sunbury backwaters, fishing with penny nets in clear, smooth streams, looking for sticklebacks and redthroats, scooping beneath weeds in dank ponds for tadpoles and newts.

I walked down the steps, thinking once more of Easter and resurrection. My father is dead and Miss Page is dead. I wonder if there really is life after death, and if there is, would Miss Page know what my thoughts are; that I never can think that servants like being servants, and it is for this reason, when I stay with people like her, I get this feeling of wanting to help the butler with the clearing away of dishes, or help the maids with the washing up, or give a hand with the dusting, making the beds, that sort of thing. Perhaps it is better just to think of the life-cycle where man-made limitations, including time and space, do not exist. The life-cycle is eternity. I know a medium who communicates with Laughing Water. I wonder why so many guides are Indians? If I could communicate in this way I would ask for Hiawatha:

There among the ferns and mosses
There among the prairie lilies
On the muskoday, the meadow,
In the moonlight and the starlight

It was when I got to the bottom of the steps leading down to the Embankment from Westminster Bridge and got close to the bum that I could see, quite clearly, what he was doing. At first he didn't take any notice of me because his eyes were on another couple who were walking towards the steps. As they got near he stopped playing, came to attention, saluted, and again called out: "Over the top, men. Over the top!". The couple glanced at him, smiled at each other, and passed on.

There were a few more people in the distance, but they were not near enough to see what he was doing. I had intended walking quickly by but, because he didn't look like an ordinary bum, I stood staring at him trying to guess his age, sixty-four or sixty-five. He was dressed neatly, meticulously, in a green-and-brown-check change jacket and narrow, military-style, carefully pressed fawn trousers. His heavy brown full-brogue shoes were highly polished, not down at the heel, and with no splits in the leather which you see in the shoes most bums wear. He had on a neat cream shirt and a regimental tie. He was tall, distinguished-looking. I noticed his row of medal ribbons, which included the white-purple-white vertical bars of the Military Cross; then the red, white, and blue watered ribbon of the 1914–1915 Star, the diluted colours blending into each other; the watered ribbon of the 1914–1918 British War Medal with its orange centre, white with black thin stripe and blue outer edge;

also the rainbow colours of the Victory Medal. Your King and country need you. Kitchener had asked for a hundred thousand volunteers and got over five hundred thousand. There weren't enough uniforms to go round. They jammed the recruitment offices, volunteers jostling to get in. Patriotism to the point of hysteria everywhere. Perhaps his medal ribbons were phoney, part of his phoney comic act. You can never tell with bums. What he was doing was harmless enough: playing his mouth organ, prancing around, saluting in correct military fashion, all wrapped around with nostalgic First World War tunes. If I asked him what he'd done, would I catch him out? He looked the part even though he'd come down to this. Pete had told me I might find him with a book tucked under his arm. He is keen on military history, Pete said. I would have to explain to him that this book on Forsyth, the book that is all in my mind, is finished, the final chapter completed long ago; therefore, I could not then have known what he might have to tell me now.

But if he would answer my questions, tell me about himself, explain how he, a First World War veteran of distinction, judging by his medal ribbons, had sunk to this, to prancing around on the embankment — if he would tell me what I want to know, then I could explain also that although the book on Forsyth is finished, there is a way out, because in each one of us is a book within a book, this secret place, where there is no looking over one's shoulder at other people, no thinking about what other people may think, and where you have all the time in the world to write your own book of dreams.

A BOOK WITHIN A BOOK — IV

VALEDICTION

Calais

Dunkirk

Ypres•

Lille•

•Ghent

•**Brussels**

Arras•

Somme

Albert•

St.Quentin

•Mons

BELGIUM

Amiens•

FRANCE

Rheims•

Verdun•

Paris
•

The Western Front   1914~18

0   20   40miles

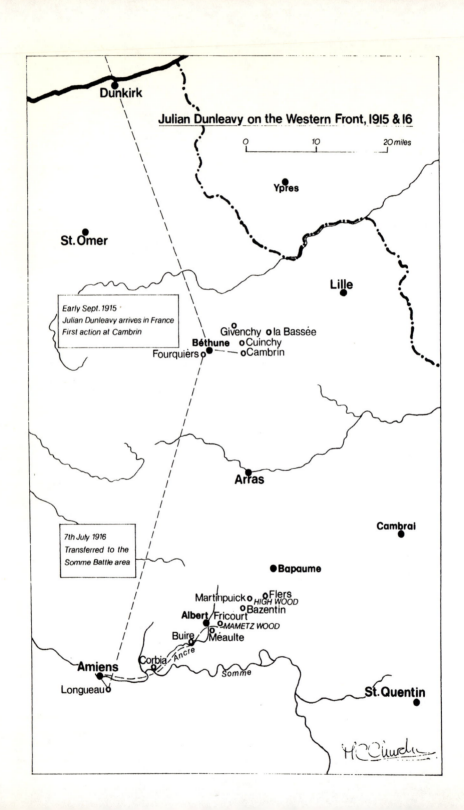

Julian Dunleavy on the Western Front, 1915 & 16

Dunkirk

0   10   20 miles

Ypres

St. Omer

Lille

Early Sept. 1915
Julian Dunleavy arrives in France
First action at Cambrin

Givenchy o la Bassée
Béthune o Cuinchy
Fourquiers o —— o Cambrin

Arras

Cambrai

7th July 1916
Transferred to the
Somme Battle area

Bapaume

Martinpuick o o Flers
HIGH WOOD
o Bazentin
Albert Fricourt
o *MAMETZ WOOD*
Buire Méaulte
Corbia *Ancre*
Amiens
Longueau o *Somme*

St. Quentin

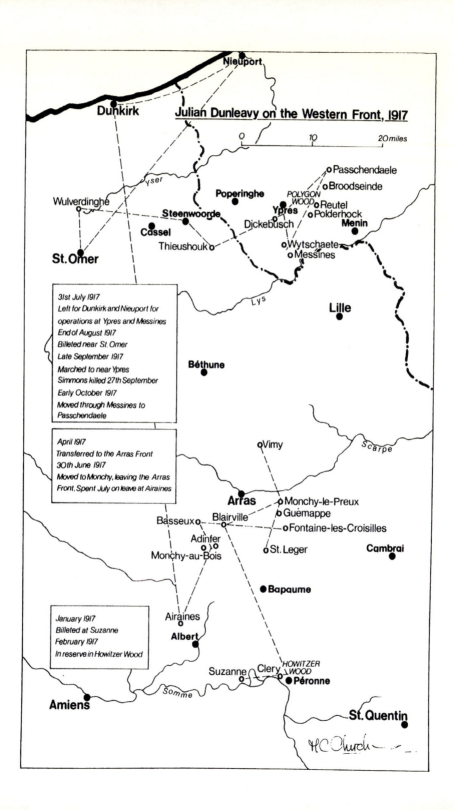

Julian Dunleavy on the Western Front, 1917

0   10   20 miles

Nieuport

Dunkirk

Wulverdinghe

Yser

Poperinghe

Passchendaele

Broodseinde

POLYGON
WOOD Reutel
Polderhock

Steenwoorde

Ypres

Cassel

Dickebusch

Menin

St. Omer

Thieushouk

Wytschaete
Messines

Lys

Lille

31st July 1917
Left for Dunkirk and Nieuport for
operations at Ypres and Messines
End of August 1917
Billeted near St. Omer
Late September 1917
Marched to near Ypres
Simmons killed 27th September
Early October 1917
Moved through Messines to
Passchendaele

Béthune

April 1917
Transferred to the Arras Front
30th June 1917
Moved to Monchy, leaving the Arras
Front. Spent July on leave at Airaines

Vimy

Scarpe

Arras

Monchy-le-Preux
Guémappe
Fontaine-les-Croisilles

Basseux

Blairville

Adinfer
Monchy-au-Bois

St. Leger

Cambrai

Bapaume

January 1917
Billeted at Suzanne
February 1917
In reserve in Howitzer Wood

Airaines

Albert

Suzanne

Clery

HOWITZER
WOOD
Péronne

Somme

Amiens

St. Quentin

HCChurch

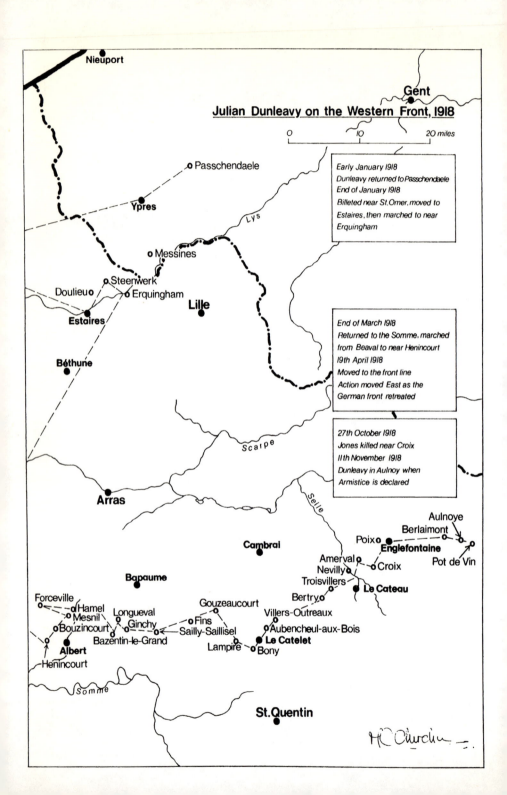

Nieuport

Gent

Julian Dunleavy on the Western Front, 1918

0   10   20 miles

o Passchendaele

Early January 1918
Dunleavy returned to Passchendaele
End of January 1918
Billeted near St.Omer, moved to
Estaires, then marched to near
Erquingham

Ypres

Ly s

o Messines

o Steenwerk
Doulieu o
o Erquingham

Lille

Estaires

End of March 1918
Returned to the Somme, marched
from Beaval to near Henincourt
19th April 1918
Moved to the front line
Action moved East as the
German front retreated

Béthune

Scarpe

27th October 1918
Jones killed near Croix
11th November 1918
Dunleavy in Aulnoy when
Armistice is declared

Arras

Selle

Aulnoye
Berlaimont
Poix o   •
Englefontaine
Cambrai   Amerval o
Nevilly o   o Croix   Pot de Vin
Troisvillers
Bapaume   Bertry o   • Le Cateau
Forceville   Gouzeaucourt   Villers-Outreaux
o   o Hamel   Longueval   o Fins   o Aubencheul-aux-Bois
o Mesnil   o Ginchy   Sailly-Saillisel   o
o Bouzincourt   Bazentin-le-Grand   Lampire o   • Le Catelet
Albert   Lampire   o Bony
Henincourt

So m m e

St.Quentin

Prelude to War

I come from a military family. My father commanded his regiment and his father before him. There has been a Dunleavy in almost every war England has fought. I have always considered it fortunate that in battle I never felt deep fear.

One of my earliest recollections is, at the age of two, hearing the servants talking about Queen Victoria's Diamond Jubilee. It was a splendid occasion, and a tremendous impression was created by the one ruling Indian prince who was dressed magnificently. Almost as colourful were six men from the Sierra Leone artillery, each wearing a uniform of blue with yellow facings, a red fez with a yellow tassel, and red sash around the waist; also knee breeches, with the lowest part of the leg covered by blue puttees. In those days, of course, we had the Empire. The Queen was greatly loved.

I had a happy childhood. My father was strict but fair, my mother gentle. I got on well with my two younger brothers and my young sister; we were a close family. My father had hurt his spine in a hunting accident, nothing too serious, and it played him up a bit in old age. He also had a painful arthritic knee, but he never complained.

We had a small house in Kensington which an aunt had left us, and we went there from time to time, but much of my childhood was spent in the family home in Wiltshire. There we had a lovely old house standing in six acres of good shooting and fishing land. Our Scottish nanny indulged us, but we had to abide by the rules; bad manners were never tolerated.

In Wiltshire the day began with family prayers, and everyone, including the servants, attended. The servants were treated well. Parker, the butler, and the two gardeners had cottages in the grounds; the rest lived in uncarpeted but clean and comfortable rooms at the top of the house. After he enlisted in September 1914, Finch, our pantry boy, wrote several times to my mother and she wrote back. He had not given his true age and was only just eighteen when he was killed in the Battle of Loos. When my mother was told of his death, she wrote to his family and sent money.

When I was ten I was given a pony. I liked riding but didn't follow my father's interests in hunting, shooting, and fishing. Intellectually I was about average, but I was good at sports; I took games seriously both at my prep school and at public school. At my public school I was in the first

177

eleven for cricket, and I boxed for the school. When I was thirteen I joined the Officers' Training Corps. I hadn't long left school when we declared war on Germany.

Although the thought of going out to fight the Germans was exciting, in one way I was sad, because Germany had been our favourite place for going abroad, and even now I can never think of our holidays there without a feeling of nostalgia, particularly for its castles and the smell of the pine forests. In between the wars, my parents having died, I went regularly to Germany with my own children, although these visits had unfortunate consequences because it was there that Jamie, my son, got to know the Wenzels and, shortly before the outbreak of the Second World War, became engaged to Wenzel's daughter. I say unfortunately because Wenzel was not only German but a pacifist; it was his pacifism that had attracted Jamie in the first place.

I have no time for pacifists, whatever the reason, nor for conscientious objectors. I tried to talk Jamie out of it, but he wouldn't listen. He was very obstinate. He got this obstinate streak from his mother, and it was Elizabeth who was responsible for my son's attitude. I thought it shameful, particularly when he persisted in such an irresponsible way even after war had been declared.

Whenever I reflect on my own childhood it is with a nostalgic longing for those more leisurely days of hansoms and broughams and the more clearly defined world where people knew their place in society. We children knew vaguely about Kruger and what the Boers had done, but the Boer War, although very much in the mind of my father, seemed a long way off. In the days of my childhood there were upheavals and troubles, but nothing much disturbed the settled equilibrium until war brought about a drastic change. Those were wonderful times. Great Britain at the height of her glory. Imperial Britain. The emotion shown for the Queen at her Diamond Jubilee was quite unbelievable: one saw this at its best when, in August 1914, we went to war with Germany.

Excitement of War

When war was declared on that warm summer's evening there was such cheering and excitement and everyone was happy. Crowds in the streets were laughing, waving; and most of us with but one thought, to get into uniform and go to the front.

It never occurred to me to do anything else but volunteer immediately. I enlisted six weeks after my eighteenth birthday. Those of us who had been in the Officers' Training Corps could get commissions straight away.

There were temporary officers in the New Army, but I held a permanent commission in a Special Reserve Battalion.

My father being a regular soldier, the army was in my blood. I had grown up with a love and respect for army life, but I had decided against it as a career. I had always hoped to marry and I didn't want the unsettled life for my wife and children which, to some extent, we had experienced with my father. The war, of course, changed everything.

Although, as I have said, I was better at sport than studying, I loved history, particularly military history; also social history because for me the two complement each other. Even before I joined my regiment I had studied in detail its traditions and battle honours.

In any catastrophe there is always a tendency to blame others, but I think it can honestly be said that whoever were the war-mongers, it was not us. Germany has always been an aggressive nation. Prussian military tradition glorified war. It is now known that as early as 1913 a decision was taken in Berlin that a major war was inevitable. At the time we did not know about this, and we were also unaware that Germany had already begun to prepare for the conflict, intending to bring it about in her own time.

The assassination of the Austrian Archduke Franz Ferdinand came as a timely and heaven-sent opportunity for the German declaration. The archduke was extremely unpopular and no tears were shed for him, but his murder was used as an excuse for an attack on Serbia. The great powers then began negotiations which continued until 2 August 1914, when Germany declared war on Russia.

The Foreign Secretary Sir Edward Grey had already warned the German ambassador, on 28 July, not to count on the neutrality of Great Britain. This warning was ignored. On 3 August Germany declared war on France, and on 4 August attacked Belgium. Under the treaty of 1839 we had become one of the guarantors of Belgium neutrality; we therefore set a time limit, expiring at midnight their time, for a German withdrawal.

With me, in Parliament Square, were two school chums: Scott, an all-rounder, a tall, good-looking fellow, killed not long after he arrived in France when he carelessly showed his head above a parapet to take a glance round no-man's-land; and Druce-Williams, medium height, stockily built, who, like me, was good at sports, also boxed well, and would have become a classics master had he, too, not been killed about the same time that my servant, Simmons, was blown to bits in September 1917.

We stood among those singing, cheering crowds looking eagerly up at Big Ben. We were terribly excited and wanted so much to go out and fight the Germans. At that moment I had an awful fear: I thought that something might go wrong, that Germany would withdraw from Belgium and we wouldn't go to war after all. The hands of Big Ben crawled round so slowly; but nine o'clock came and went, then ten o'clock, and, at long last, the sonorous strokes chiming the hour of eleven. As the last stroke died away, the feeling of excitement gave way to one of intense relief, for it was then we knew that we and Germany were at war.

THE GLORY OF WAR — 1

I didn't get to France until just before the beginning of the Allied autumn offensive in September 1915. By the time I got there, Scott had been killed in the Second Battle of Ypres. Druce-Williams, as it happened, was killed in the Third Ypres battle. I have since visited their graves; they are buried in different cemeteries.

When I enlisted, my mother worried a great deal. She was relieved that I hadn't gone to France early on, and would have been happy if I hadn't had to go at all. My father's attitude was quite different: he looked on my decision to volunteer straight away as perfectly normal. Thousands of others had done the same. My brothers, of course, were too young to join up.

It was great fun ordering my officer's uniform. I felt splendid putting on khaki, and an early indication of authority came when I passed some men who saluted smartly. I wondered then, but only for a minute, whether I had made a mistake in not choosing the army for a regular career.

By the end of August 1914, I was in a training camp in the north of England. There I learnt the mechanisms of the rifle and did company drill. Efficient NCOs taught us young officers how to become efficient second lieutenants. Life in the camp did not come as much of a surprise to me, for the Officers' Training Corps at school had been run on strict military lines by a tough ex-sergeant major for whom we all had tremendous respect. I never had any difficulty in making friends and quickly got to know and like the other junior officers in the camp. Although these were only brief acquaintanceships, because, unlike the trenches, we didn't stay together very long, it was always with a feeling of deep sadness whenever I heard of the death of anyone who had been with me there.

The BEF began to land in France on 7 August 1914. The landings were completed by 14 August. You can well imagine how frustrated I felt. I longed to go to France and get to the front. I was quite convinced the war would be over before I could take part in at least one battle. The news in the papers was pretty distorted although there were the lengthening casualty lists, but I had a good idea of what was going on. On 20 August the Germans took Brussels and as they advanced they set towns and villages on fire in retaliation against guerrilla attacks. At this time things looked pretty black: there was the Battle of Mons, which began on 23 August, and the subsequent retreat which went on for eleven days in scorching hot weather ending, from 5 to 10 September 1914, with the Battle of the Marne.

From 15 to 18 September there was the First Battle of the Aisne, also the fighting in Picardy. At the end of the month the first units of the Indian Expeditionary Force landed at Marseilles. The siege of Antwerp went into October of that year, then Antwerp was occupied by the enemy and the Battle of La Bassée began. The Belgians evacuated Ostend and Zeebrugge, Lille capitulated and on 18 October the Battle of the Yser began, ending on 30 November. From 30 October to 24 November there was the First Battle of Ypres. The First Battle of Champagne started on 20 December continuing for nearly three months; also, at this time, there was the defence of Givenchy.

In December 1914 the King, accompanied by the Prince of Wales, visited the regiment, and this was followed not long afterwards by that ridiculous Christmas Truce. I wasn't there, but Wenzel, who then of course was the enemy, saw it all, and he later told me it changed his whole attitude to the war. I'm not so sure about this. From the beginning, although he may not have realized it, Wenzel had been lukewarm. To my mind the 1914 Christmas Truce became a justification for his fundamentally unpatriotic feelings. After the war, when Jamie got to know the family, Wenzel had become a complete pacifist. As I have said, I am sure it was this, Wenzel's pacifism, that, in the beginning, attracted Jamie. It was Wenzel who said to me, when he and Frau Wenzel had come to stay, that war changes many values, both material and moral.

I need hardly say that the reality of war is fighting and killing, and a comparison can be made between ultimate success and total slaughter because the less there is of the enemy the easier it becomes to conquer. Wenzel was quite right: in war moral values do change, almost out of all recognition, for although in war killing is basically a serious business, it has also a superficial sporting flavour.

In any form of violence there is an aggressive need to destroy. Sniping, winkling the enemy out of woods, bombing from the air has something in common with shooting partridge or pheasants, so that there was, at the end of it, the same satisfying experience, the only difference being that instead of finding a dead bird one got a dead German. This is why the Christmas Truce of 1914 was so ridiculous; it was not only unreal but farcical and, to my mind, foolish: a useless gesture. But before I elaborate more on that, let me go over, as briefly as possible, the events that took place before I got to France.

After the Mons show, one could see all the signs of a retreat. Cast-off packs lay by the roadside, there were broken-down lorries and other transport, as well as many wounded. Shells could be seen falling on Bertry and Maurois. The brigade major was wounded and died soon afterwards, and those in the rear guard, marching at night, if they looked back, could see the glare in the sky of places set on fire by the shelling.

For eleven days we retreated in scorching hot weather, covering about a hundred and seventy miles. Most of the march was made at night; there were halts and rests, but all the way the signs and sounds of war. From the opposite direction lorries and buses and other vehicles, full of French troops, were on their way to attack the German First Army as it swung westwards. The Germans got to Lagny, their nearest point to Paris; however, this was the end of the retreat, and at last we were able to turn and drive the Germans back. There was fighting on the banks of the Marne and all up the valley.

Near the Aisne heavy firing could be heard as high-explosive howitzer shells came over. Reinforcements of officers and men were arriving all the time, and the battle of the Aisne became trench warfare. I have already mentioned the sporting aspect of the killing. One officer who was in this battle told me later that driving the woods for straggling Germans was not much different from a pheasant shoot and was great fun. In this way, he said, they shot quite a few Germans.

When the retreat ended and we began to advance, it became harder on the animals, for they were going from rear to front and then back again the whole day and night. In those days there were no night-bombing aeroplanes, but there were spies everywhere; all those caught were shot.

In October 1914 there was the race for the sea, and the massed armies tried, by extending to the north, to turn each other's flanks. The enemy retreated as we advanced, and there were German graves on both sides of the road, which was strewn with dead horses, and a big battle was fought all along the Flanders front. Trenches were dug north of Fauquissart, and we then advanced to Fromelles, occupying French-made trenches in front of Fournes, which was being heavily shelled. The French suffered heavy losses, and a lot of French wounded passed through the line during the day.

There was dispersed artillery fire by field guns and 5.9 howitzers. A salvo of shells came over, and they were pretty frightening. It was the troops' first experience of them. They were nicknamed Jack Johnsons after the boxer and world champion, because of the black smoke. Woolly Bear was the name given to another big shell that exploded with a lot of black smoke. Other names given to different types of shells were Big Willie and Little Willie, after the Kaiser or Crown Prince, Black Maria and Coal Box.

For a fortnight shelling and sniping went on all day and there wasn't much rest at night. Because of the sniping and shelling it was risky to show oneself above ground. There was a good deal of artillery fire, and the bodies of those killed were brought down after dark and friends buried. The Indian Brigade, made up of both British and Indian troops, having relieved the French, suffered heavy casualties. Sniping from both sides killed quite a few men, us and the enemy.

At night star shells lit up everything. Officers and men were all very tired. Pouring rain made it difficult to move because of the mud, particularly at night. German dead hung on the wire. There was a lack of communication trenches as there had been no time to get on with them, and this also caused many casualties. Food and ammunition could only be brought up in the dark and at the same time the dead taken down. Often our own guns caused casualties. Two of our six-inch guns blew one of our platoons to bits. Everywhere lay carcasses of slain animals. One night the German dead, mostly on the enemy's near front, were searched and over four hundred identity disks collected. Quite a few of the disks came from between our trenches and the wire. Our dead numbered much less than the Germans.

In the trenches one lost count of the days and weeks. Often everyone was in the most awful state of filth. If it poured with rain at night, and there was an attack, slimy mud covered everyone and everything. It took ages to rub off. Officers and men would have to go for as long as ten days without being able to get a wash. Although, as I have said, German losses were greater than ours, one of our companies had only two officers left.

Nasty little gullies or depressions which ran up to the company's trenches contained many German dead. After one enemy night attack there were dead Germans on the British parapet and in the British trench, and in the morning a great many more German dead could be seen. One enemy officer had been killed on the last strand of wire. The Sikhs had heavy casualties but finished their job. Some of the enemy were captured, and as the attack continued, the number of German dead increased. One of our officers counted about a hundred and fifty dead in front of him.

A sad sight was houses and villages destroyed by shell fire, with people trudging along the roads. Dozens of cattle lay in the fields, killed by bullets and shrapnel. Many of our chaps, who had been out there for some time, were getting extremely bored by the trenches and were feeling very tired; they hoped they wouldn't be in them much longer and wished they would get orders to advance.

The drawn-out battle had gone on into November, with numbers dwindling and weariness growing. There was no relief and little sleep, yet everyone had to be ready to meet assault upon assault. A lot of fighting at this time was with rifle and bayonet. Both sides were physically exhausted.

The weather turned wintry. There was rain and mud, heavy snow and frost. When the men were relieved and withdrawn to billets in places like Houplines, the greatest luxury was to get one's clothes off, especially boots, and to get the lice out of one's clothing.

Our guns shelled Frelinghien, the Germans shelled Houplines, and there were some aeroplanes in the sky. More reinforcements joined. The Germans put a thousand shells into Armentières, wounding five and killing a woman. Six days before that they had bombed from the air.

As the French in the north were attacking, all the BEF guns were active. More heavy rain set in and the river rose. The constant efforts to exist in water-logged trenches meant finding a practical way of preventing trench foot, which was wasting battalions and filling hospitals. Because of gangrene, which had occurred in the worst cases, toes, even feet, were being amputated.

The German army, prepared and organized though it had been for the past forty years, was staggered by the British at Mons and Le Cateau, and especially by the rapidity of British rifle fire. The enemy had been defeated in the open battle of the Marne and was now entrenched across France, from Switzerland to the Aisne, in previously prepared positions. Far from the war being over in six months, as many had at first thought, both sides had dug in for what Kitchener correctly predicted as a prolonged war of attrition.

The 7th Division disembarked at Zeebrugge on 6 October and, after the fall of Antwerp on 9 October, it fell back with the remnant of the Belgians until it reached Ypres, the old capital of Flanders. By this time the French had made good the line as far north as La Bassée, but between this point and Ypres lay twenty-five miles open to the enemy, the gateway to Calais and all the Channel ports, giving an easy line to Paris.

From its hard-won position on the Aisne, the British Army was rushed north and thrown into the gap with the task of protecting the Channel ports. This movement also shortened the lines of communication, and so began the first battle of Ypres, which lasted for over three weeks, a day-to-day struggle in which numerous minor battles were fought.

The Germans, better equipped than the British, greatly outnumbered the BEF. The trenches we had dug were very shallow, and in short lengths, and were separated by wide gaps extending in places to a width of four hundred yards.

Fighting was continuous night and day. Within a day or two battalions were reduced to companies: just a hundred men and a couple of officers. But we repulsed the enemy with our rapid speed of rifle fire and our field guns.

One can best picture the Salient during this great battle as a map in broad bands, all the fighting being east to west, with these bands enclosing the attack and defence of each sector. On reaching Ypres, we took up a position some five to six miles east of the town, occupying the line Houthem-Gheluvelt-St Julien; our cavalry corps under General Allenby covered the left flank from Zonnebeke to Westroosebeke, while French troops were collecting on the Yser. It was now a race as to which army could concentrate with the greater rapidity, and the Germans got in first.

On 19, 20, and 21 October 1914, fierce and bitter fighting raged around Zonnebeke, where the Germans had made continuous and desperate efforts to force their way into Ypres. The French retired from Houthulst, exposing the flank of our cavalry division. By the evening of 21 October things looked black. Two fresh and unsuspected German corps had appeared from the direction of Coutrai. We suffered continuous losses and were worn to the last stage of mental and physical exhaustion by sleeplessness and by unceasing digging and fighting. We were getting weaker and weaker, while the German attacking force was perpetually augmented by fresh troops.

Then the situation dramatically changed. The 1st Corps was thrown into the fight and took over the whole of our line from Zonnebeke to Bixkhoote. A critical struggle followed north of the Boesininghe-Langermark road where the fight, centring around the Korteheer Cabaret, prevented a German attempt to break through on the northeast of Ypres. From these events was born the Ypres Salient.

On 24 October Polygon Wood was menaced by successful enemy assaults. Our troops fell upon the enemy and in furious hand-to-hand fighting drove him out of the wood. An effort was made to attack Reutel, and our troops, fighting for every yard of the ground, got across the Becelaere-Passchendaele road. The line now formed an acute salient at Kruiseeche, and on the 26th the Germans succeeded in piercing the side of this outthrust point and annihilated the troops in the village. Further loss of ground was checked by our counterattacks. The French troops, now on our north, made small progress.

After more attacks and counterattacks, a mass assault by the enemy opened on the morning of the 29th in dense fog, and German troops attacking from all sides succeeded in penetrating unseen, causing very heavy casualties, but they only succeeded in gaining some five hundred yards of the crossroads at the cost of very heavy losses to themselves. Our weary troops could do little but dig some new fire trenches, which were urgently needed.

The climax of the battle was reached on 31 October when the enemy succeeded in entering Gheluvelt; then a counterattack was launched from the northwest, the Germans were hurled back, and Gheluvelt was recaptured. When the enemy attacks had died down, our troops were withdrawn west of Gheluvelt and the line reformed. Our troops were reduced to a quarter of their strength; they were exhausted with ceaseless fighting and lacked sleep and rest and ammunition. So short had ammunition become that half of the field artillery were withdrawn from the line.

The final great attack came on 11 November. Twelve and a half enemy divisions attacked on a nine-mile front, and of these the flower of the German army — the Prussian Guard, the Pomeranians, and the West Prussians — fell upon the centre sector of the Menin Road; the attack was heralded by the most overwhelming shell fire that had yet been launched. Seventeen thousand five hundred of the enemy were opposed by our little battle-weary force of seven thousand eight hundred and fifty.

The enemy smashed into our front line defence, found positions where they could enfilade our disconnected trenches, and reached the woods north of the road. There our troops met them hand to hand, fought them to a standstill, and drove them back with the bayonet. The German attack failed.

Looking back on all this, there are one or two incidents which I heard about later, and which seem to me to stand out from among all the carnage. On one occasion our men had spotted an isolated farm that the Hun was using constantly as a sniper's lair. It was causing casualties to one of our companies, so our raiders crept out at dusk. The barn was kept under heavy rifle fire until we got to it. A bundle of paper, rags, and twigs, heavily soused with petrol, was put against the side of the barn, and more petrol was thrown over the woodwork. When that was lighted, the wind did the rest.

Another time a man shot himself through the arm. Simmons, my soldier-servant, told me about this. Simmons knew the man well. They had come from the same town and had been in the mines together. According to Simmons, the man shot himself on purpose, hoping it would be regarded as a Blighty wound when he would be sent home to recover. The poor fellow took ingenious precautions to conceal the evidence of a point-blank shot, but soon afterwards he died of a haemorrhage.

A young corporal once told me that what he remembered most about the early part of the war was getting his first German. Hearing a commotion on the traverse, the corporal found some of the others taking pot-shots at half a dozen Huns who were crawling on their stomachs trying to get into a ditch about fifty yards from our trench. The corporal joined in and shot one of the Germans through the head. To try and pretend any friendliness towards the Germans at that time was madness. I remember telling this to Wenzel, when Wenzel and I were discussing the 1914 Christmas Truce.

As I have mentioned, Wenzel took part in that Christmas Truce. He said that on that Christmas Eve it was quiet all along the Western Front, the ground had frozen hard, and Christmas Day started with a thick low fog. When the fog cleared, Wenzel and the others saw a screen, which one of our sergeants had hoisted and on which was painted MERRY CHRISTMAS. The Germans shouted across: "Don't shoot; we don't want to fight today; we will send you some beer." Shortly afterwards they hoisted a cask onto the parapet and started to roll it into the middle of no-man's-land. A lot more unarmed Germans, including Wenzel, climbed out of their trench and began calling over to our men to come out.

A British officer climbed over the parapet on our side and shouted back in German, asking for a German captain to appear. Then a German captain climbed out and walked into the middle of no-man's-land, formally saluted, and, amidst cheering from both sides, introduced himself. Wenzel said the German captain couldn't speak a word of English, but he was a very decent fellow and popular with the men. The German captain called out to his subalterns, and with much clicking of heels and saluting he formally introduced them. All the German officers were very well turned out.

After the German captain had been told that the British were under strict orders not to fraternize, he gave orders for a return to the trenches. Then the captain asked: "Could we not have a truce from shooting today? We don't want to shoot, do you?"

The British officer replied: "No, we certainly don't want to shoot."

So it was agreed not to shoot until the following morning when the British, by firing two shots, would signal that they were going to begin again. The German captain agreed and said: "You had better take the beer. We have lots."

Two of the Germans were ordered to take the barrel to the British side. The British officer sent for a plum pudding and presented it to the German officer in return for the beer. Then the German captain called out an order to one of his privates, who came out with glasses and bottles of beer, and, with more bowing and saluting, the beer was solemnly drunk amid renewed cheering from both sides. After this the Germans had a singsong and so did the British. During the Christmas Truce the Germans were allowed to bury their dead.

That night there was another hard frost. At 8:30 am, on Boxing Day, Wenzel, looking across no-man's-land, again saw a board hoisted with MERRY CHRISTMAS on it. The German captain appeared on his parapet and put up a sheet showing THANK YOU in English. Then the British officer climbed onto his parapet, both officers bowed and saluted and got down into their respective trenches. From the British side two shots were fired into the air, and the killing started again.

THE GLORY OF WAR — 2

War is hell, no one could deny that. It was an experience none of us could have imagined. As I have said, we all thought the war would be over in six months, but, after those first few months of free manoeuvring in Belgium and France, it settled down into a stalemate, with each side dug into a system of parallel trenches stretching some four hundred and seventy-five miles from the North Sea coast in Belgium to the Swiss border. The British held about ninety miles of the line, including the two important sectors of the Ypres Salient in Flanders and the Somme area in Picardy, with about eight hundred battalions of a thousand men each.

The Western Front was not the only theatre of war, but it absorbed more men than any other, and as the memory of the Great War comes overwhelmingly from images of the trenches, perhaps you would like me to explain the trench system.

Trenches were normally three deep: the front-line trench, the support line two hundred yards behind, and further back still the reserve trenches. Perpendicular to the line were communication trenches, and running at right angles from the front line were saps, leading to the most forward positions of all, manned as observation or machine-gun posts. Dug-outs in the sides of the trenches provided deeper shelter for command posts and officers' quarters.

A front-line trench was between six and ten feet deep and four or five feet wide. On the enemy side was a two foot parapet of sandbags, and on the back wall of the trench a corresponding but lower parados. About two or three feet from the bottom of the trench was a ledge or fire-step, on which the defenders stood when facing the enemy. The trench was not a straight line but a zigzag, with frequent traverses, in order to minimise damage from shells and avoid enfilade fire by attackers. The floor was covered with wooden duckboards below which were sumps to collect water.

Between the German and Allied lines was no-man's-land, varying in width from sector to sector, but usually a few hundred yards across. Each side put up entanglements of barbed wire in front of their lines, and sited machine guns to cover them.

Flanders and Picardy have a high rainfall and in parts are low-lying, with the result that the British trenches were nearly always ankle-deep in mud, and often flooded several feet deep. Nor were our trenches, unlike the German trenches, always very well constructed. For ninety miles of our front, and nearly six thousand miles of trenches in all, an army of men lived for four years below ground level in holes and ditches.

Trench duty was normally rotated. After being three days to a week in the front-line trench, a unit would move back to the support trench for a similar period, then to the reserve, and finally spend a week resting and training behind the lines before returning to the line again. The change-over, and indeed the movement of all rations, ammunition, and stores, took place at night.

Once he had arrived in the line, the soldier's day settled into an intense twenty-four-hour cycle which revolved round the ritual of stand-to just before dawn and again at dusk, when everyone mounted the fire-step with his rifle ready to repel an attack. When the Germans did not attack at dawn, the stand-down was given, and everyone began preparing breakfast from rations of tea, bread, and bacon. The bacon was fried in a mess tin over a small fire. During the day there was an endless succession of sentry duties, inspections, repairs to trenches, and fatigues of all kinds. At night, patrols, raiding parties, and wiring parties went out into no-man's-land. Sleep was snatched in short intervals, but throughout the twenty-four hours a majority of the men were awake and busy, and very tired.

While all this was going on men were harassed by enemy shells, which fell almost daily on the trenches, killing, wounding, or burying a few unfortunates. Before an attack the bombardment would rise to a crescendo, with shells bursting incessantly and the whole earth transformed into an inferno of noise and uproar. All hell was let loose, as every account by a survivor testified, but learning to live through shelling was the main business of the infantryman. Some did not manage to do so and were reduced by shell shock to a state of mental breakdown.

Another painful experience was going over the top. This usually happened when a night patrol went into no-man's-land to gain information about the enemy. An officer and one or two men would crawl forward on their stomachs, listening for enemy activity. It was a nerve-wracking business, crouched in a shell hole or lying flat beneath a bursting flare, knowing that at any moment a sentry might be alerted or a machine gun open up. For those who got back to their own trenches, a sense of utter exhaustion followed. On other nights, wiring parties would be out, repairing and reinforcing the protective entanglements.

A bigger and more dangerous exploit was the raiding party, made up of about thirty men whose object was to break into enemy lines with bombs and bayonets and bring back a few prisoners.

But the bloodiest of all was a general attack. Rumours and the inevitable massive preparations first alerted men back in rest positions that a big push was in the offing. Next they would be officially told by their commanding officer that they would soon be in action. Then the order came to dress in battle order with extra ammunition and grenades, and finally they marched up to the front line, occupied the trenches at nightfall, and waited apprehensively for the dawn, when thousands of men simultaneously scrambled out of their trenches and attempted to advance across no-man's-land and capture the German positions. For many, their rough-and-tumble scramble over no-man's-land, with a fleeting picture of enemy trenches behind barbed wire, was their last earthly memory.

THE GLORY OF WAR — 3

England, at this time, seemed unreal. Those who had not been at the front had no idea of what the fighting was like. The papers wrote such rubbish. Politicians and others in safe jobs pontificated. Their talk was mostly of battles won. Reverses were temporary and our brave lads would soon be driving the enemy back; just send the boys plenty of reading matter! At the front there was little time and not much incentive for reading. We sat over braziers, gossiped, played cards, lay down, and snoozed. Reading was difficult enough for an officer; it was far more difficult for the men. Life out there was neither private nor quiet.

At home the only reality of war was the casualty lists. They were appalling, and the public were horrified as family after family lost a husband, son, brother. But I was always glad to get back to France. Dreadful though the fighting was, and in such dreadful conditions, even the constant killing was preferable to the unwholesomeness of being near men smoking fat cigars and drinking champagne, many of whom had become rich because of the war, a war close enough for Londoners to hear the faint rumble of the heaviest bombardment and the distant explosions of the largest mines.

It wasn't long after I arrived in France, at the beginning of September 1915, that I was on my way to the front. I had spent a couple of frustrating weeks in a base camp, but drilling and parade-ground discipline were no substitute for fighting. With five other officers I travelled in the shabby first-class compartment of a jerky, uncomfortable troop train that was so slow I thought the war would be over before I could get into battle.

About twenty-four hours later we stood on the platform at Béthune and were met by our guide. The trenches were ten kilometres away. As well as half a dozen officers there were about sixty men, and as we marched through the unlit suburbs of the town my excitement increased. We could hear the noise and see the flashes of guns in the distance. The men, all of whom were as new to active warfare as I was, sang music-hall songs. The noise of the guns grew louder and we heard shells bursting behind us, then more shells as those from our own batteries hissed overhead into the German lines. You can imagine the feelings of a twenty-year-old at such a moment: I was tremendously elated, for this was what I had been waiting for!

We marched past broken trees, then up a long trench to battalion headquarters. I heard rifle bullets, some of them striking the barbed wire in front of the trenches, giving off a pinging sound. With two other officers behind me, I was taken to headquarters, which was a dugout in a reserve line, where we met the colonel, a regular, who greeted us warmly. The colonel had arranged a meal for us, and considering all things, it wasn't too bad. The meat was tender and the vegetables tasty. Then the adjutant posted us to our companies and another guide took us to the front line, where I reported to the company commander, a captain only a couple of years older than me. He was a striking-looking fellow, tall, angular, with a shock of fair hair. When talking to you he had a habit of twiddling the lobe of his right ear.

The following day Simmons reported to me. He had been detailed as my soldier-servant. He remained with me for the next two years, until he was killed on 27 September 1917. When Simmons first came to me, I was nineteen; he was twenty-one and coming up to his twenty-second birthday. He came from the North. When war broke out he was working in the mines and, like me, he volunteered immediately.

Simmons was from a large family; he had seven brothers and sisters. It took me a little time to get used to him because he had a rather cheeky manner; not disrespectful, I wouldn't have allowed that, but I got to like him, and although killing was a daily occurrence, it was a shock to me when I discovered that, not long after I left him in no-man's-land, a shell had fallen on top of him. His body was never found.

What I liked most about Simmons was his cheerfulness, not easy when death and mutilation were one's constant companions. He had an admirable northern working-class sense of humour. In the most awful conditions he would joke about the rats and lice, about water in the trenches, about things at the front that drove most of us mad. Although he had this somewhat impudent approach to everybody and everything and didn't altogether behave as a servant should, he was never insubordinate, and he followed the rules. He was good at his job and very reliable, which is why I wanted to keep him. Fortunately, even when I moved to another battalion, I was able to do so. I say fortunately because this wasn't common practice; also Simmons was batman to other officers in the trenches.

He physically wasn't anything to write home about. He was small, thin, weedy, with a thin, pale face, hollow cheeks, grey eyes — the same colour as mine — and he had a tooth missing in front. I used to wonder if he'd lost it in a fight, but I didn't like to ask. He had a broad northern accent, which I can't imitate for you; I'm no good at that sort of thing. He came from a very poor background, but although he spoke quite a lot about his family and the conditions in which they lived, it was entirely without rancour.

Actually, it surprised me that Simmons should have felt not the slightest resentment for what, after all, were miserable and deprived conditions. I once mentioned this to my son, Jamie, when he was pontificating, as he so often did, on social injustice and the repression of the working class, and rabbiting on the way extremists do. I didn't altogether blame Jamie since he was corrupted by Elizabeth, my wife. I hadn't realised Elizabeth had strong socialist tendencies which, with the hunger marches of the 1930s, quickly became an obsession.

Simmons's acceptance of his background didn't impress Jamie at all: Jamie thought people like Simmons, who didn't violently protest, stupid. Curious, isn't it, that Jamie, who had a comfortable, privileged, and indulged upbringing — neither Elizabeth nor I had wished to impose on him the more intense rigours my father handed down — curious that he

should feel bitter about this, whereas Simmons had accepted philosophi-
cally poverty and hardship. And another thing about Simmons: he was
the best harmonica player I ever heard. Some of the men played quite
well, but he was the best; he had real professionalism. He organised and
trained others so that on marches they could lead their comrades in full
song and keep good march discipline.

I asked Simmons to teach me. I couldn't play in public as it wouldn't
have been becoming for an officer to do so, but I had many a pleasant and
relaxing hour practising by myself. I never realised there was so much
skill attached to it. And Simmons was very strict. It was quite amusing,
really, for when I was under instruction, our roles were reversed.

He taught me breath control, saying that one should not force air into
the holes because it damaged the reeds and produced bad tone, and would
probably run you out of breath. One had to breathe into the instrument
steadily and gently, using as little breath as was practically possible to obtain a smooth succession of sounds. Actually, it's quite surprising the comparatively small amount of wind one needs to obtain good results.

Simmons also showed me the only correct way to play a melody with
the tongue covering three holes, so that the air which is used for making
the fourth hole sound its notes, comes from breath flowing along the inside of the right cheek, and this passes along the side of the tongue into
the hole. He showed me how to play grace notes, and told me about the
different types of harmonicas.

When I had made myself proficient in playing single notes, he showed
me how to play chords, which require a lot of practice in order to get them
going nicely without fouling other notes. I remember it all so well, Simmons sitting beside me in my billet saying: "Now, sir, don't move your instrument for the two chords at holes eight-nine-ten; now move it to the
left ever so slowly. Do it like that, sir, and you'll get it perfect."

He showed me how to play an accompaniment to a melody, covering
certain holes with the tongue and blowing or drawing, just as you would
if you were playing the melody only, but for the accompaniment you had
to lift your tongue off the notes, so making the notes open instead of
closed. Simmons also offered to show me the chromatic harmonica, but I
didn't bother with that. "Lots of practice is required, sir," Simmons insisted, and I practised.

Once, when Simmons had finished playing "God Bless the Prince of
Wales," Jerry heard it and called across. At some places our trenches and
those of the enemy were quite close, and there was a lot of banter, mostly
good-natured, but all the time we would go on killing them and they us.

193

THE GLORY OF WAR — 4

Any initial experience is invariably the most memorable, and so it was with my first action. Day after day of glorious September weather had passed, with rumours filtering through of a coming offensive against La Bassée. Some days were hot and sweltering, but mostly the evenings were cool to cold. There was daily gunfire, and one afternoon, when our gunfire was particularly heavy, I watched our shoot from the front line at Cuinchy. The German machine guns swept our lines, but at this time casualties were a little down and deaths fewer. Some of our casualties had been caused because of premature bursts from our own shells; this was due to loose driving bands.

One night it rained and thundered and continued to rain. Soon the trenches were muddy. Then the battalion was relieved, and when we returned, the official plans for the attack were made known. These plans were that gas was to lay out all the Germans, after which our leading battalions would have a walk-over, with the supports mopping up.

The next day we spent the morning fitting and preparing, and in the evening there was a battalion dinner, but everyone was too preoccupied with the coming attack to stay cheerful for very long. That same night we left Béthune and marched to Cambrin. It was very dark and poured with rain all the way. There had been a little singing, but spirits flagged and the march was a depressing affair. At about 1:00 pm we reached the assembly trench, some two hundred yards behind the front line, and lay down to await zero.

The assembly trenches were deep and cramped. Everyone was inconvenienced by kit and equipment. Besides his rifle, his bayonet, two hundred rounds of ammunition, and extra ration, every man had to carry a pick or shovel or other tool, also several new and unwieldy bombs called cricket balls. He had to wear on his head a rolled gas helmet, ready to be pulled down at a moment's notice, with a cap balanced on top of it and the whole tied on with a piece of string passed under the chin. But things might have been worse, for although the night was cold, the pouring rain had turned into lighter showers.

Zero hour was at 5:45 am. Simmons had brought me a mug of sweet tea, which was hot and not too bad. I could hear heavy gunfire and some crackling of small arms. Our artillery treated the German front line with rapid fire. The shooting was good. At the same time the Royal Engineers Special Brigade's gas troops opened the cocks of the cylinders, but an unfavourable wind blew gas back into our own trench. Men in the front line got mouthfuls of it and soon became panicky, so gas helmets were adjusted. While the wearers were stifled in them, the German artillery opened up on the crowded trench with well-aimed fire which caused casualties. The first rearward stream of walking wounded began. Some disorder had been caused, but the old line steadied itself. Scaling ladders were put into position and other final preparations made.

The infantry assault was delayed to let the gas act. During the time we were waiting to go over, German shells were bursting on the front line and communication trenches. Some men there climbed out of their trench ahead of the timetable to escape the gas and began a forward movement. Then companies climbed out on time from both front and support trenches, the cover given by craters letting some of the first wave get to the German wire while the second wave dashed forward, to be checked by our own front-line wire. Forty officers and eight hundred men were shot down in five minutes.

When our leading companies had begun to move forward, the support line and communication trenches were being fairly heavily shelled. We could see nothing and knew nothing of the state of affairs in front. I was with the company sergeant-major and a few bombers. We had only gone a short distance when the trenches were found to be blocked with debris, with walking wounded, and with runners and stretcher-bearers, so progress was terribly slow. When we arrived at what was expected to be the front line, but proved to be the support line, one officer found that only twenty of his men had got through the jam and had managed to keep up with him. Hearing a shell coming we dropped flat on our faces. It burst close by. When the dust and smoke cleared there was a fresh shell-hole from a 5.9. I remarked: "That one nearly got us," then we carried on.

We returned to the support line and saw the colonel had a wound over one eye, from which blood was running down his face. I led a small party forward. Six became casualties by the time we reached the front line. The sight of the trench was horrible; it was literally packed with wounded, dying, and dead men; we had the greatest difficulty in avoiding treading on them. And the scene beyond that was the same. The ground was strewn with dead and wounded, and many of the wounded were crawling back through the grass. Gas was still rising from the cylinders in our trench; it drifted up from the right and came back over our line, then fell into the trench for lack of a breeze to displace it. Many of the helpless wounded were gassed.

I made a search for the main body of my company and, having found it, reported to HQ for orders. The CO had gone to hospital, and his place had been taken by another young officer, who told me to get on and advance.

I got the company into line. They had been held up by the wounded working their way down.

The battalion attack was a forlorn hope. The officers blew their whistles and over we went. There were shells bursting over the German trenches but, the morning being bright and sunny, the German riflemen and machine gunners took their toll of us undisturbed. A line of men would go a few yards and fall down. A young subaltern, very popular with everyone for his happy disposition and who had just celebrated his nineteenth birthday, was badly hit, and died later. Another young officer of my own age, advancing not far from me, was badly wounded. He, too, died. Half my company fell in thirty yards. The prearranged plan of advancing by rushes never had a chance to function.

A and D Companies had assembled in Maison Rouge Alley in front of Cambrin Church; their progress to the support and front lines was somewhat similar to that of C and B. We had been ordered to stand fast, ready to take part in another attack which was to be made at 11:00 am, but the further advance of A and D was countermanded by the acting CO, who had watched the useless sacrifice of C and B, and at noon the two companies were relieved. There had been no food for about twenty-two hours.

The companies were withdrawn with difficulty. Men were sent back singly through the long autumn grass of no-man's-land to leap quickly into the trench on reaching the parapet. During these hours the wounded were being helped and were helping each other, and more wounds were being incurred in the helping. One man who had crawled back slowly was laid in the bottom of the trench; there he nearly suffocated with gas before the doctor came and had him moved to a narrow communication trench, where he lay for five hours. No stretcher could be used even if one had been available. Eventually he was carried down slung on his puttees between two rifles. It was an exceedingly painful journey. Once clear of the trenches the medical arrangements were generally good.

As soon as it was dark, parties went out and brought in the wounded and the dead. Work in the dressing-station went on into the night, twenty-one hours in all without food or pause. Lots of men who had nausea from gas remained on duty.

In the morning there was a period of watery sunshine; the rest of the day was overcast and there were hours of drizzle. The following night was dry. On the brigade front it was quiet except for occasional shells, some of them tear gas. The next morning, while the CO A Company was watching the action still going on in front of Vermelles, he was shot dead by a sniper. We buried all our dead in Cambrin cemetery.

Although after Cambrin my first battle was over, fighting continued and casualties mounted. When new drafts came in, it was easy to tell the newly arrived from those who had been out for some months on the move, the older lot crawled, the new marched; the old were content to plod along mostly quietly and seriously, the new sang and whistled and made cheeky remarks to any French girl who took their fancy.

Béthune, where we went for relaxation, was a merry place. Heavy batteries, changing position, moved alongside milk carts drawn by dogs. Townspeople, mostly working people and peasants, together with officers and men from every arm of the service, crowded the streets.

Officers' gatherings were liable to be broken up by a brass hat ordering them to return to their unit, which might be going into action. These round-ups could be made several times a day. Thousands of men had their first glimpse of a society other than that into which they had been born.

The visits to Béthune were pleasant enough, but, following the Cambrin battle, there were also dreary months of trench routine. One misty October morning in 1915 a few of us went out on top to see if any of our September dead had been overlooked. The mist cleared suddenly, the searchers were spotted, and a young officer, who had been with us about six months, was wounded through the lung.

There were days and nights of pouring rain. Men were killed, men were wounded, and quite a few died of their wounds. On one occasion a lad from a new draft found a dud, and wanting the nose-cap as a souvenir, tried to prise it off. The dud exploded, killing two and wounding another five.

The routine of trench life was never so systematized as in this winter of 1915-1916. The line was stable, the enemy marking time, and the trench system a year old. Although there was rain, the Cambrin-Cuinchy-Givenchy front was not the wettest part, but rats and lice were always with us. It was rough when a man was badly hit, but a Blighty wound was a matter for congratulations. At the end of November we were all able to enjoy a week at Gounchem. Football every afternoon and a singsong nearly every night. The weather was fine and frosty throughout. One night brought the first sprinkling of snow.

In late December preparations for Christmas Day began. Heavy gunfire could be heard beyond Béthune, and there was an order to be on the shortest notice. There was to be no repetition of the Christmas Truce. On the second day of January 1916, the Germans blew what was then their largest mine. The total casualties were three score or more. Movement near the front in daylight was, from now on, forbidden.

During January 1916 the ordinary activities of trench warfare increased on both sides, and during the last ten days of the month bombardment and counter-bombardment reached an intensity that had not been known since the battle of Loos at its worst.

Round about 27 January, which was the Kaiser's birthday, there was more activity than usual, and anti-aircraft guns, nicknamed Archies, were blazing away on both sides at aeroplanes. One of our fellows, a captain who was a particularly good shot, sometimes aided our snipers. Once, where the enemy parapet was low, he shot a German officer; the next day he got a pheasant for the pot.

It was an uncommonly active tour and our casualties greatly exceeded the weekly average. An officer, returning off leave, met his company stretcher-bearers carrying down one of the dead. Following them was a man with something in a sandbag. As money, letters, and other personal possessions were taken off the dead and sent home, the officer asked: "Are these his effects?"

"No, sir," was the reply, "it's his pal: he was blown up by the same shell and it's all we could find, two limbs."

In the middle of February 1916 we returned to Cambrin. The Germans had narrowed no-man's-land by connecting up their saps. One night a mystery fireworks display was solved. Fritz had soused with oil the body of one of our chaps hanging on his wire and set fire to it, exploding the cartridges in the pouches.

We moved into Montmorency Barracks, the favourite billet in the area. This was the beginning of six weeks when we could try and forget the trenches. The chief snag was the weather. The winter of 1915-1916 was the least severe of the five winters the battalion spent in France, but there was one continuously trying spell at the end of February and the beginning of March. It was wintry, with snow showers. Throughout March there were quick changes through frost, thaw, rain, snow, and sunshine, with keen wind continuing.

Some nights were bitter, with bright cold mornings; then the weather changed and we would be living in mud and icy water, the trenches falling in. Steel helmets were issued. We called them tin hats. Even in a deep dugout there were few who did not reach for their helmets if shells burst outside. The CO arranged as many singsongs as possible, and at Beuvry there was more opportunity for football than elsewhere.

By the beginning of April it had become milder. Larks sang in the bright sunshine. In the parapet of one trench a German had been buried; it must have been in the autumn of 1914. The weather exposed a pulpy arm with a wrist-watch on it. One of the men passing by wound the watch and it went. Others gave the winder a turn until someone took the watch.

In the middle of April we had a week of glorious days and very cold nights. The genial weather made bathing a popular pastime. Intermittently we and the Germans had been setting off small mines. Our fliers were much more over German territory than the Germans were over ours. New divisions were still arriving in France, and one afternoon I heard a cuckoo sing.

This was another uncommonly lively tour, with shells, minnies, and rifle grenades flying about in profusion, while trenches on both sides were blown in daily. I was glad when we were relieved and went back to Montmorency Barracks; it was pleasant to wander about in the country. Once I thought I heard a nightingale. In the strafed front line, throughout the turmoil, a pair of swallows tried persistently to build under an overhead traverse, and a lark nested amid the wire. In June, at the Béthune theatre, I went to a service for Lord Kitchener who had been drowned in HMS *Hampshire* while on his way to Russia. All the French notables around attended. Chaplains of every variety took part; Handel's march was played and our bugles sounded the Last Post.

When I think back over the first half of 1916, what I remember most is seeing, one morning, some shells falling in no-man's-land in front of our trenches when part of a putrefied human body rose in the spout. It was then, for the first time, I felt sorry for the men there, whichever side they were on.

THE BATTLE OF THE SOMME

Wenzel's account of the Somme fighting is better than mine. He was there on the opening day, when his side killed twenty thousand of our men and wounded twice as many. I don't hold it against Wenzel, of course; it was the stupidity of our own top brass in allowing preparations to take place in the open. When the Somme show started on 1 July 1916, every prisoner taken had known where we would attack, and so fierce was the fighting, and on such a large scale, that the French people round about were quite sure the war would be over in a few weeks.

On the night of the fourth day of the battle, which was my twentieth birthday, I stood watching the rising and falling of Verey lights and star shells along Vimy Ridge against a sky all shimmering with gun flashes.

Simmons, who was standing beside me, said: "What does it feel like being a captain, sir?"

"No different," I said casually. A couple of days before, the CO had informed me of my promotion. He told me it was well deserved. I had shown, he said, a quiet and exemplary devotion to duty; then he poured two large whiskies, remarking that if I was transferred he would be very sorry to lose me.

I was glad I hadn't been required for that terrible opening day; it would have been a sickening sight to see our men, heavily weighed down with equipment, obeying orders to walk across no-man's-land as if going for a Sunday stroll in the park, wave after wave of them dropping as they walked into a hail of German machine-gun bullets. But in any case, I don't want to go into every little detail of the Somme battle; I prefer to keep, as much as possible, to what I experienced personally even when relating Wenzel's side of the story; so if I limit my part in the battle to what happened in High Wood, it should be enough to show you what Wenzel meant when he and the other Germans who fought on the Somme described it as the Bath of Blood.

Up to 3 July 1916 there had been, for us, six really restful days with wonderfully fine sunsets. In the foreground was the canal and the marsh with its flowering herbage and reeds, and the willows and poplars aslant the dykes. On 7 July we went south and in the quiet freshness of the morning marched through Béthune to Fourquières, entrained at midnight for Longueau, then marched through Amiens the next afternoon.

At the beginning of our journey up the right bank of the Ancre, we could see Corbie across the Somme. On the road, we had passed the transport of the 38th Welsh Division coming out after the mauling at Mametz Wood. We got to Buire and settled into tents in an orchard.

The battle front was only seven and a half miles away; gun flashes played brightly on the sky after dark. At night the guns became increasingly audible. A body of cavalry passed up as we were having breakfast, then the CO and company commanders went out to reconnoitre forward areas, so we knew we would be for it soon. With all the marching and changing of scene, at least we hadn't the boredom of trench warfare, where so much of an officer's time was taken up with making returns and reports and reading and noting orders and circulars, which could run to several sheets of type.

On 14 July we moved to Méaulte, a slightly damaged village where we had a haversack lunch. The whole brigade bivouacked on a forward slope one kilometre farther on, passing a lot of prisoners on the way. At 4:00 am the battalion moved down the Fricourt road through a thick mist; crossing where the front had been on 1 July, we saw a few broken wagons, dead horses and drivers, and a dead German who lay on a stretcher by the roadside. The mist cleared. Fricourt had been flattened and we were among the dead of a unit we knew. Friends were recognized and buried.

The task now of the division was the capture of a switch trench which ran from High Wood to Martinpuich — the men called it Martin's Push. The attack began at 9:00. Another short move took us across the road to the southeast corner of Mametz Wood. Some of us went exploring in Mametz Wood and there were nasty sights. German machine guns were artfully placed, and hidden by the long grass and covering the switch were new wire and unreported posts which stopped all progress. Smitten in front and enfiladed, our two broken brigades ended the day where they began it.

After sunset, flights of 0.77 shell came over and burst about us with quiet plops. They were noxious gas-shells and we were encountering them for the first time, although some had been in use for several months. The night was spent close behind our main artillery position and the noise was ear-splitting, more than anything I had known. One of our sapper officers slept beside a several-days-old corpse without noticing anything unpleasant, but all about us the air was heavy with the reek of the dead in Mametz Wood. Throughout the day, batteries rolled into Happy Valley, which was also called the Valley of Death; this was east of Mametz Wood and on the slight rise of Caterpillar Wood. Soon these sites were stiff not with guns but with batteries.

Shelling on both sides was tremendous. Whole brigades sat down en masse in a field, and we bivouacked in close order every night. The show was in the open, guns and all. I slept in my Burberry and we were down to bully and biscuits. Rain came on in the afternoon, and the rain and the noise lasted all night. I wondered whether those at home, in their nice comfortable beds, were thinking of us.

At midnight the battalion moved through a light barrage of explosive and bromine shells to relieve another battalion between the cemetery and Martinpuich road. There were a few casualties going up.

The night was noisy and wet, the morning quiet and fine. An appalling lot of our dead strewed the easy rise of the High Wood-Martinpuich glacis. Most of the afternoon, our position was under a bombardment that caused losses in which HQ details shared largely. Hordes of rats came over the ground.

There was rain for most of the next night, which was 19 July. For the first time since the night of 13th I slept for more than an occasional snatch of a few minutes. The next day was fine and there was more activity in the air than usual. We watched the superiority of our airmen with much satisfaction, for the Germans had, of late, been having the best of it. On the whole it was a comparatively quiet, less stressful day after several days of physical discomfort and broken sleep, of exhaustion through drawn-out waiting, of being in the middle of almost incessant noise and suffering appreciable losses.

High Wood is about a mile east and north of Bazentin-le-Petit, at the waist of a tactically important ridge. By midnight the units of the brigade were moving to their assembly positions. The CO, becoming impatient in the absence of news, sent a subaltern and a sergeant forward to learn what was being done. Everything was chaotic. The hours passed, and about 11:00 am the situation in front changed suddenly. An order to complete the capture of High Wood was delivered to HQ.

Waiting to attack is like what waiting for the hangman to come and do his job must be. Everyone was eager to get going one way or the other, for the uncertainty of being launched into eternity or of coming back in pieces was not comforting in those tense moments. By 2:00 pm all were ready.

It was the quietest part of the day in my corner of High Wood. Simmons was with me. The going was not bad just at the start, but the luxurious July foliage on the low-hanging and broken branches and on the fallen beech trees, which was the result of ten days' shelling, made keeping any sort of alignment or direction more and more difficult.

At Crucifix Corner the CO let his men sit down while casualty reports were made up. The last subaltern from a gallant trio of youngsters, who had joined from Sandhurst in June, was killed. At night his platoon carried him back two miles for burial. Another young officer was brought out smiling, dying. The adjutant, all four company commanders, eight other officers, and a great many rank and file were killed and wounded. In one company there was only one officer left; few engineers were left. In these circumstances, brigade was advised that fresh troops should relieve those on the ground if the holding of the Wood was to be reasonably assured.

Apart from one flare-up, the Wood was a peaceful spot for a couple of hours, cool to walk in on a rather airless afternoon. Then a fresh start was made, the digging and manning of a new line. The day had been warm and still, with a slight haze; the evening was serene. Our air observers and German fliers met over the Wood, manoeuvred, and fought. In the evening a solitary German strolled across the open towards our right flank. Someone shot him, unaware that others hoped to take him for what he might have to tell.

The light faded from the trees. The German guns opened up. At about 9:00 pm groups of Germans suddenly appeared on the front with an intended attack. Some of our men lost their heads and fell back, and could not be recalled by the NCOs. The attackers closed quickly to bombing range; half the remnant of my company became casualties. A lance-corporal spent the whole day lying among dead and severely wounded men. His companions were mostly victims of a machine-gun that had fired through the gap. From daylight, for hours, men and groups who entered the ride along which it fired had been shot down. At about 10:00 pm the Germans plastered the Wood with heavies and with machine-guns. It was a bombardment so merciless that the enemy appeared to be using most of the guns on the Somme. This lasted for an hour or more.

Darkness was a time of strained suspense. The experiences of seven such days and nights as had been ours, and the chagrin at the end of them, made nerves susceptible to trivial impressions. We were relieved unexpectedly and arrived at our bivouac on the southeast of Mametz Wood. Even some of the hard-bitten, now that there was no more need to key themselves up, showed signs of the strain through which they had passed. Everyone lay down where he found himself and slept, though the imaginative shouted, cried horrors, and gesticulated in their sleep.

The next morning and afternoon were spent in peace and quiet, cleaning up, and resting in the warm sunshine. Our casualties the day before, and there were many missing, were the result of a German counterattack at dark. Our disappointment was great that what had been gained so dearly had been lost so easily, but our companies ought not to have been deceived by the appearance of the oncoming Germans at dusk. Many of the men had never seen Germans attacking. By holding the southeast of the Wood, the net gain of its costly operations was the High Wood approach. Of one group in Caterpillar Wood seventy-five per cent became casualties.

On 6 August we marched at 10:00 in the morning to the hillside behind Becordel and bivouacked. For most of the week that we were there, the weather was broiling. Training continued, and recreational training was added to supple unused muscles. In the dark of the morning on 13 August, a short move was made to Fricourt Wood.

The German gunners made our last month's bivouac unoccupiable; they had many more guns and their infantry was well wired in. A German plane came out of a cloud with one of ours on top. About a dozen shots were fired, then the German turned on his side and went down behind us, ablaze. It was a spectacular sight against a deep blue sky, but not pleasant to think about if the German pilot hadn't been shot dead.

For six days we found large working parties to dig a communication trench to High Wood, and to carry from the Bazentin Dumps. The men came in for a lot of shelling. After three weeks of ideal camping conditions the weather broke, and new drafts were having to make their first crude attempts to get themselves some shelter and comfort.

After a chilly and noisy night the grey morning of 18 August broke fine. There was more noise from 11:00 am until noon; 2:45 pm was zero for a push through Wood Lane and High Wood by two brigades. The gunfire was over in little more than an hour. Through it all one of our bands practised. It was a good band and played good music of the popular kind. The great din of guns made a strange obbligato. We moved forward and, after many wearisome halts, arrived in the dark at the Longueval-Bazentin road below High Wood, and hung about.

When daylight on 19 August was breaking, we returned, still more wearisome, through a communication trench near Crucifix Corner. We were foodless and sleepless. A few widely dispersed shells came over at intervals. Three companies held a trench about a hundred yards from the Germans; the fourth was again in support. In the autumn heat the air was fouled with the smell of innumerable dead so lightly covered that, in unsuspected though extensive places, one's tread, disturbing the surface, uncovered them; or swarms of maggots showed what one was seated near.

On the morning of 20 August, a company CO and his CSM were killed by a shell. His successor was later killed in the same place. In August 1916, High Wood and the ground in the rear was an unhealthy place. All the companies were rattled. The old lot showed it, too, although there were some stoics.

At midnight the Germans put up flares all round, threw out their defensive screen of bombers, and dropped all their barrages. At 5:00 am we were relieved and went into support at Crucifix Corner. Ever afterwards these three days were spoken of by experienced officers, NCOs, and others as a nightmare.

There was a tremendous din for two hours in the early morning. One brigade made some progress between Delville and High Woods. We got the overspill of the shelling. At 4:00 pm we returned to High Wood through a barrage, slight but unpleasant enough. Flame projectors and other gadgets were on the ground to ensure a spectacular capture of the Wood. The attack was made a week later, but the rest was tragedy. Although High Wood was attacked in strength 22/23 July, it was not until 15 September, 1916 that it fell to men of 47th (London) Division.

In the second half of September, an attack on a wide front led by tanks with caterpillar tracks and armed with guns, the tanks making their first appearance, carried the line beyond Flers on both sides of High Wood.

The German garrison was cut off from support or escape and surrendered. We were relieved and withdrew to Fricourt Wood in the rain. The mud was inches deep in what, nine days ago, had been a pleasant sylvan retreat.

At 6:00 am we moved to a trench in front of Montauban; the trench, in its first state, had been a ditch. We were lent to a brigade who were nibbling at Wood Lane. There was heavy rain, operations were at a standstill, and our working parties came back through the mud at one mile an hour. Some of the drafts had to be sent to the transport for shelter and rest, but incredibly some of these drafts were singing.

DEATH OF A SERVANT — 1

Where Elizabeth and Jamie went wrong was in trying to compare the lives of the wealthy and powerful to those of the poor. There is no comparison, there never has been, and it is ridiculous to try. In Victorian and Edwardian times especially, the rich and the poor were worlds apart.

Simmons, for instance — and there were many like him — came from a drab industrial town where the men were sketchily educated, often ill-nourished, unacquainted with the world beyond their immediate district, their lives utterly humdrum. For them it was work, early marriages, children, football, boiled cabbage, and Saturday night at the pub. It was a savage struggle for the husbands to keep large families on low wages, if these men were fortunate enough to be in work.

The cheapest material in a fast-developing industrial Britain was the human being, and, in 1914, people like Simmons, since anything was better than the drabness of their repetitive work and the boredom of unemployment, needed little persuasion to rush into the great killing machine where training was exciting. I remember Simmons once saying to me: "You know, sir, the best part of that training was when they taught us bayonetting. That was exciting, sir! Wasteful it is, to plunge the whole bayonet through the body; three inches of cold steel is enough for any man. Jab your bayonet into the enemy's guts, stir around briefly, then quickly swing the butt of the rifle to stun the next Hun while kicking a third one in the stomach." Looking at me with a satisfied smile on his face, he added: "Am I right, sir?" I told Simmons he was right.

When war broke out, in August 1914, Simmons was working in the mines. As a child he'd heard lurid stories from his grandfather, stories of pauper children taken from the London workhouses and forced to work long hours and boarded in dreadful conditions, in dormitories and apprentice houses.

One has to admit that being poor in those days, even up to when Simmons was a boy, had its oppressive side. I told you that I have always been interested in social history as well as military history, and certainly conditions in the early Nineteenth Century were, for a lot of the poor, brutal.

In those early days many of the working class were caught between the relics of the domestic system and the full force of industrial capitalism.

Instead of getting sympathetic help and consideration in times of distress, caused by unemployment, by sickness and old age, there was the building of grim workhouses where prison-like discipline enforced behind high walls spread fear among those caught up in its bestiality. For most of the time in pre-industrial England the labouring poor could be safely ignored, or taken for granted, by the educated classes; only occasionally, in those days, did the poor protest, but any eruption was quickly and ruthlessly put down.

Simmons's family were Methodists. Wesley himself was autocratic and conservative in his social views, but his open-air preaching converted many humble people. In the time of Simmons's grandfather the big downtown Wesleyan chapels in the northern towns were dominated by prosperous mill owners and businessmen, but often the local preacher was a working man and spoke the working man's idiom, so ordinary people like the Simmons family felt at home in a way they were seldom able to do in the parish church with its liturgy, ritual, and a sermon given by a middle-class parson, and where most of the livings were in the hands of the squires. The message given to the working class from the great central Methodist experience of conversion was one of joy and hope; it brought happiness and a cheerful conviction that in God's providence there was a place for everyone, however humble.

DEATH OF A SERVANT — 2

Although more than a quarter of the population lived in poverty, for the nation as a whole those were days of great prosperity. There were the very rich: the great London landlords, Bedford, Cadogan, Norfolk, Portland, and the wealthiest man in Britain, Westminster. As well as possessing ample resources elsewhere, they derived huge personal incomes from metropolitan rents alone. Apart from the King there were twenty-four individual landowners, each owning more than a hundred thousand acres. In the United Kingdom less than seven thousand people owned four-fifths of the land.

For the many poor, in spite of an expanding economy that raised living standards, the housing conditions were appalling, and the weakest and poorest existed like animals, but the vast mass of common people, as they still do, showed great deference towards the upper class.

Contrary to the impression you would get from people like Elizabeth and Jamie, who spoke only of the hardship and the repression suffered by the poor, working-class people enjoyed themselves. They had the local pub where they gathered to sing or discuss politics or talk about local events; they had theatres and music halls; there were holidays centred round religious festivals, and also local fairs and race meetings. In the north and midlands there were the wakes, when all factories and workshops in the locality were closed for three or four days, sometimes for a whole week.

The building of railways and introduction of excursion fares made it possible for all but the very poor to go to the seaside. When Simmons's father was a child, a family of four could go to Scarborough and back for nine shillings. These day trips and excursions did not kill the traditional holidays but gradually transformed them.

State power was almost always wielded in the interests of the ruling classes, but in Edward VII's time a lot was done for the poor. The introduction of old-age pensions by the Liberal government, in 1909, transformed life for aged cottagers; in fact, the Liberals' remarkable programme of social welfare between 1906 and 1911 undermined the assumption that the working class had nothing to hope for from state action. What the Liberals did, in bringing these reforms, was indeed remarkable, and it relieved many old people of constant anxiety, and certainly no one showed more concern for the poor than the King himself; but it had not been until the Reform Act of 1884 that there had been anything approaching democracy.

The Labour movement was the most powerful expression of the common people organized for action, although it did not include all the people or even the majority of the working class. However, by the outbreak of war, in 1914, membership of the trade unions had reached four million and the system of collective bargaining had evolved. For many Socialists the revolt against Victorian society and all that it stood for was paramount.

So Simmons and the others marched to war singing, until their dream of glory ended abruptly among splintered trees, shell holes, shattered trenches, ruptured sandbags, broken gas masks, helmets, webbing belts, rusting small arms and ordnance, shell cases, sodden fragments of paper and unidentifiable bits of cloth, the blackened skeleton of a gun limber, anonymous gnarled pieces of metal, and the various decayed corpses of men pushed hurriedly into shallow graves, some in 1914, some in 1915, some the previous week; rising from the slime, other corpses still strung on fragments of barbed wire, and abandoned dumps looming up like the derelict remains of lost civilisations. Everywhere the smell, a combination of the sweet, cloying odour of rotting flesh and the acrid stink of burnt animal hair and cordite and the mustiness of stale gas, a smell that made the teeth ache and the eyes water, a smell that once smelt was never forgotten.

DEATH OF A SERVANT — 3

The months went by and the end of the war seemed as far off as ever. When I first went on leave I thought I would be glad to be home, but England seemed strange. At my club there was no shortage of food, and the place was full of prosperous businessmen who had all the answers for beating the Hun; but their talk was newspaper talk, empty and meaningless. Those of us who had been in the trenches spoke more realistically, and we weighed up the chances, thought to be pretty slim, of any of us being alive at the end.

In November 1916 I returned to France, an old soldier, taking with me half a dozen young officers who were little more than jubilant schoolboys, babbling away, wanting to take charge of the war and, as quickly as possible, get Jerry on the run. At the end of the war I met up with one of them who had a shoulder wound that had kept him out of most of the fighting; he told me that of the others, one had been blinded and the rest killed. My battalion was still on the Somme, and I was glad to be back and to be sent up to the trenches.

Simmons welcomed me with a cup of hot strong sweet tea. He said cheerfully: "I'm going home for Christmas, sir." I nodded. I felt good even though the conditions were pretty awful. Simmons went on leave; Christmas came and went; he returned as cheerful as ever. For part of January we were in reserve billets at Suzanne; the place was in ruins, with all the houses shelled, so our billets were no more than dugouts and shelters. The winter was exceptionally hard, and the men played inter-company football matches on the river, which was now frozen two feet thick. There were no French civilians around, no houses that weren't in various stages of ruin; the only movement came from soldiers, horses and mules, and a few moorhens and ducks that could be seen on the unfrozen central stream of the river.

During February there was the Anglo-French conference at Calais on the military situation, and in March another Anglo-French conference took place in London. Towards the end of February 1917 the Germans had begun their retreat to the Hindenburg Line, and at the beginning of April — 6 April to be exact — the United States declared war on Germany. In the same month the Battle of Arras began, also the Battle of Vimy Ridge, the First Battle of the Scarpe, the Second Battle of the Aisne, and the Battle of the Hills. May saw the Battle of Bullecourt, 7 June the Battle of Messines, and in June also, Portuguese troops — the men upset them by calling them pork and beans and port and geese — were for the first time in action on the Western Front. Also at this time, the first contingent of United States troops arrived in France. In July the Germans attacked Nieuport, and the end of July saw the beginning of the Third Battle of Ypres, in which Simmons was killed.

To go over all these months in detail would be doing little more than repeating what has already been said about the previous battles I have described; the places differ, there is a variation in circumstances, but that is all. However, there are a few incidents, which happened at this time, that I would like to mention.

In February, when we were in reserve in Howitzer Wood, a German artillery position east of Clery had driven the French from Tortille Valley, and in an attempt to regain it the French had left no-man's-land dotted with their dead. At one place, close to the parapet, I saw a Frenchman and a German lying where they had bayonetted each other, the throat of the one, the chest of the other, pierced.

Another time, it was about a couple of months later, I was walking along with a young subaltern while an attack was being made in Fontaine-lez-Croisilles about three-quarters of a mile away. We passed a lot of yesterday's dead lying in front of the trench. The subaltern, who had been to Winchester, was a sensitive chap, and I could see that having had his first look at the horrors of war, he was trying to behave as if it was all quite ordinary. The dead were lying there in all their equipment, most of them shot in the head. The stretcher-bearers had been identifying the bodies and had arranged them in seemly attitudes, their heads pillowed on their haversacks. I had grown accustomed to such sights. Detached from the fighting, we had simply gone for a short walk, but I could see, in spite of the attempted cover-up, he was deeply affected by the sight of these dead soldiers.

The truth is that infantry soldiering in the battle zone was an overwhelming physical experience. Such human elements as food, warmth, and sleep were the living realities, and it may not have occurred to many military historians that the weather was a more effective general than Foch, Haig, or Ludendorff, or that after a week of some intense experience that added a battle honour to the colours of his regiment, the only thing a man clearly remembered from the ordeal was a bad blister on his heel.

For those whose active unit was company, platoon, or section, physical sensations predominated. Mental activity, detached from feet and belly, was strictly limited by gross physical actualities. Whatever exploits a fighting man might afterwards claim he had achieved, his achievement could usually be recorded in a few short sentences. But how lifeless, how meagre and incomplete that epitome would seem to one who understood but had not shared the experience, unless it was interwoven with those details of discomfort, so difficult to remember, which constituted the humanity of infantry soldiering.

In April of that year, 1917, the Canadians made a big push over Vimy Ridge. I was on the Arras road. The country was white with an inch and a half of snow melting under a drizzle of cold rain. There were detachments of men, some of them wounded, and guns and vehicles of all sorts. Dead and dying horses lay by the roadside. When I got to Blairville I found all the division's transport there. The camp was beside the old German line. On a snow-sprinkled heap of sweepings, on the roadside, sat a robin, a yellowhammer, and a woodlark; there wasn't a twig or spar for them to perch on.

As we continued on in long-occupied German territory we saw that the Germans had razed everything. Buildings and walls had been thrown down by explosive; culverts were broken and great craters blown at all crossroads. Trees, bushes, and posts had been felled. The labour of destruction was immense. Booby traps of most varied and ingenious contrivance were left in both likely and unlikely places, causing casualties. My journey led to the escarpment of Vimy Ridge, which stretched along the whole visible front as it rose from flattish ground.

At this point I must say something about the Hindenburg Line, to which, between 23 February and 5 April 1917, the Germans retreated. It was a truly wonderful piece of engineering, consisting of two trenches two hundred or more yards apart. The front trench, easily ten feet deep with splayed sides, was just in front of the crest of a long glacis. In the parapet were timbered fire-steps of solid construction, and here and there timbered steps led to the front and to the rear, and to concrete machine-gun emplacements along the parapet at varying intervals of fifty to a hundred yards. In front was a belt of stout barbed wire thirty to sixty yards across; this had been flattened in places by tanks during the successful assault. The support, or tunnel trench, was on the reverse slope; it was of the same construction, but the wire and much of the fittings were incomplete. There were communications between the two trenches.

All these surface works had been considerably knocked about by our heavy guns. Beneath the support trench, at a depth of forty feet, was a huge dugout or tunnel some six feet six inches high, and said to be two miles long in this portion. It was fitted down the middle with tiers of bunks and small living rooms and storerooms opening off it, and was wired throughout for electric lighting, but current had not been laid on. There were entrances of solid joiner-work every forty to fifty yards, and wide timber-cased stairways alternated with inclined planes for stores. Above and below ground, the opposing garrisons were separated by blocks or barriers; the latter had been made by blowing in the tunnel. The blocks were just east of the Croisilles-Heninel road.

At this time, the middle of April 1917, we had marched to St. Leger. The companies occupied an outpost line and were detailed for fatigues. HQ was in a fairly intact cottage where there were crocuses and other bulbs in pots left by some German lover of flowers. A plan had been made to assault the Hindenburg Line, so I will just mention briefly the fighting.

There was bombing along the tunnel. At zero a trench-mortar bombardment with thermite shells had practically obliterated the German barricade, thirty yards distant. The Germans began to retreat and persuasion backed by bombs caused some two hundred of them to come up from the tunnel. They were sent to the rear, where one of them described how he had been in a listening post during the night and realized, from the noise in our trench, that we meant to attack, but he had said nothing about it because he wanted to be captured. From the beginning both we and the Germans suffered heavy casualties in killed and wounded. Two of our companies were cut off and had many losses before escaping across country in the afternoon. Other companies lost many more.

In the advance, one of our companies was strung over a great part of the trench, carrying bombs, and with the Germans coming down the trench a bombing fight began. For two hours this company and another had a bad time at the barricade. There was a good supply of rifle grenades and bombs, parties were organised to use them, but it was the turn of the Germans to be in the ascendant. They manned their trench-mortars and sent over a colossal collection of every kind of aerial torpedo, pineapple bomb, and rifle grenade. The position became very unhealthy; casualties increased every moment. One of our captains, who was preparing to lead a party of about a dozen volunteers over the top, was killed by a trench-mortar bomb. A lieutenant was wounded at about the same time, and one of our NCOs was killed.

After a quiet afternoon, another early-morning attack failed badly. Very few of our men got beyond the barricade; those who did were faced by

211

a tangle of barbed wire which was covered by a machine gun farther back. The attack up to the front trench also failed. The only result was that the Germans, beginning at 7:45 am, plastered both our barricades and the neighbourhood with shells and trench-mortar bombs, and the bomb-throwing competition started all over again.

A bomb thrown by one of our chaps hit the top of the trench, fell back into it, and blew into fragments the feet of a young private who had been sitting for hours, imperturbably straightening the pins of Mills bombs. Casualties were increasing, the number of men to call upon was lessening. One officer, who tried to get the men remaining with him to attack again, was mortally wounded. Then a company sergeant major was hit; he died in the tunnel.

The next day I was standing beside a former German gun emplacement close behind the left of the shallow trench. Behind me, to the left, lay a dead officer. The last of the men were shuffling into position when from the right some 18-pounder shells came over, falling a few yards in front of the German line. Then the barrage, what there was of it, lifted. The Germans quickly mounted their machine-guns. Among shell holes and the dead and wounded, our men were dashing forward on converging lines. Many dropped fast, killed and wounded, while others tried to escape the jets of bullets. Two of our platoons scarcely got across their parapet, and some were hit on it; they were on even ground that sloped down to them. Where the slope rose to the flat, they came upon a nearly solid hurdle about thirty yards long, made up of our dead lying where the machine-guns swept the brow of the rise, all shot in the head or chest. Close to the wire others dropped down. All was over in little more than a minute.

The following day was dull, with a clouded sky. I stood watching Monchy-le-Preux being pounded to rubble and dust, and watched also the to-and-fro movement of khaki figures where Guemappe had been and bombs were being hurled. Some Germans gave themselves up. None could have been more scared than those Jerries were during a bombardment, which suggested a counterattack might follow; or so relieved when, at last, they were sent away with a stretcher case. We had a few casualties, including another officer, a subaltern, who was killed. We could see and hear a lot of explosive that was being used at the Tunnel Trench barrier. As darkness fell, some of our men in shell holes tried, too soon, to come in; they were seen and hit.

Simmons, with extraordinary cheerfulness, came up with some food, relieving a famine, and related some of the pandemonium he had seen while coming through Tunnel Trench. As it grew dark some of our wounded were seen looking out of shell holes; then Simmons volunteered, with others, to go out and bring them in. Someone called out that the Germans had gone and the companies were ordered forward at once behind the patrols. One of our officers ran on, searching the ground from side to side in front of the patrols. We went close to where the Hindenburg Line crossed the Fontaine-St. Martin-Copeul road before being fired on; there we stopped to exchange shots with the enemy. The ground from which they had withdrawn was honeycombed with shell-holes; spread about it were a few concrete strong points, the pillboxes of the Hindenburg Line.

We found a few Germans, some of them wounded, but the dead of five battalions of our division lay in front of the abandoned German machine-gun position; these dead were the result of four assaults, and an example of the stupidity of throwing men into an attack after a futile artillery bombardment that leaves the defenders practically unscathed. Ours was the third bull-at-a-gate attack to be detailed in nine days. The occasion was but one of innumerable occasions when a company or battalion was squandered on an attack seemingly planned by someone who, lacking either first or second-hand knowledge of the ground, just relied on maps of moderate scale.

Brigade, as we know it, was remote in action, and ineffectual. Battalion information about local detail was not always taken well. A practical suggestion might be received as if it were a reflection on the higher rank's competence or initiative, so nothing might be thought of but high-explosive shell, which so often gave warning of an infantry assault and failed to aid it. Except quite often for raids, infantry manoeuvre in the BEF had come to an end, or fallen into disuse. It was not unusual for a brigade to reach its objective with only a hundred casualties, more or less, and then have a thousand in falling back because the position was untenable, made so in part by its own failure to help clear its flanks during the advance. If the partly trained infantry cast a look to right or left, it was because it had learned to fear cross fire, not to help by cross fire a flank unit in trouble, and any delay lost it its own artillery cover.

As with brigades in larger operations, so it had been with battalions in brigade attacks. In the smaller operations the use of ground is everything, and an intelligent plan can be carried out even by half-taught officers and half-trained men.

I am afraid I have digressed a little, but I must also add that I have never gone along with the popular view that this war was run by old, incompetent generals — Haig, in many ways, was a brilliant tactician — because those in the top command were limited by what would have been regarded in the Second World War as primitive methods of communication and much less effective armament. I was glad when we were relieved and, a couple of days later, moved to Blairville. Then we marched to comfortable billets in Basseux, where it was a treat to have a mattress.

At the beginning of May we marched to a bivouac of leaking tin shanties between Adinfer Wood and Monchy-au-Bois, where the old front line ran. Rations were never better, the fresh beef and mutton excellent. Early one morning I heard heavy gunfire; another morning I awoke to hear a cuckoo's call and the unrest of rooks in Adinfer Wood. The wood was never part of a battlefield, as it had been left whole when the Germans withdrew. On its front, hidden in the beech hedge, were machine-gun emplacements of concrete and armour plate, like large letter boxes. Within it were gun emplacements and shelters built of large boles, planted over with ferns and grasses for concealment; smaller shelters were woven cleverly of branches, some growing and some partly or wholly cut. Its trees were erect and unbroken. Moss and ivy, violets, bluebells, anemones and wild strawberry carpeted it. The relics of its occupation were unobtrusive and took nothing from its charm.

The weather alternated from sunny and fresh to grey and cold. Greenery was appearing everywhere. One day I watched the horses, turned loose, revel and roll on the fresh young grass. There was a tranquil twilight landscape with a distant border of shell bursts and rockets against a glow of pale lemon and blue. It was a curiously pleasing scene. By the middle of May the only ground the enemy had lost since last we were in line was three to four hundred yards of the Hindenburg Line on the left of Sensée.

The Germans strewed the country with 5.9, 4.2 and .77 shells. Attack, counterattack, and renewed attack ended with our gaining and holding the Hindenburg Line front trench from the Hump to the Sensée. We failed at the Hump itself, also at Tunnel Trench, though it was entered. The German machine-gunners were as good as ever. The usual German tactics now were to take a heavy toll, at the cost of a screen, for giving ground, and then counterattack when we were depleted and disorganized; then their garrison lay out to meet our attack in front of our bombarded objective, instead of withdrawing behind it.

This bit of the Hindenburg Line was far from being as complete as that at Henin. There were no machine-gun emplacements and it had been considerably knocked about by our heavies. No-man's-land, quite three hundred yards wide, might have been on the Somme, it was so ploughed up. On a day that was quiet in front, we were invited to a battalion sports day about six miles away. I took part in an inter-battalion tug-of-war for officers, which we won!

At the end of May we lost two more of our officers, one killed by a shell splinter, the other by a sniper. We were shoulder to shoulder in the trench, there were so many of us. Movement was not easy, and it was discouraged because of German spotters; splinters from German shells bursting in no-man's-land were flying over us ominously. There was the usual random shelling of the country behind us. Whitsun kept its promise of a fine day. Our guns were unusually quiet. It was a beautiful Sunday morning and the untilled fields around us were now fresh and green and filled with flowers; the fallow was pretty with yellow and gold.

The opening of the guns at 1:55 brought two of our officers onto the parapet to call out their two companies. One of the officers gave his men a hand to climb out and again reminded them not to hurry: just stroll over behind our shells as if you were taking a quiet Sunday afternoon walk, and in line with the other officer he led them at that pace. A third officer was waiting on top to direct his company up Plum Lane and make good our flank to the right of it. The fourth company was to form a third supporting wave to the first two waves, and mop up. Everything was going according to plan, with nothing to disturb the advance in the open.

Very soon bombs were flying, and our men advanced well until they were faced by a machine-gun firing down the lane. An attempt to bomb it had to be organized before any more progress could be made there. Our casualties so far, all slight, were owing to some shorts from our own guns. This caused a check, and the rear wave closed on the second.

During the pause, men with rifles still slung and hands in pockets, turned to watch the German barrage. After the check the advance slowed down as the enemy's shell-hole line was approached. The lifting of our guns, and this lag, let its garrison get ready to resist. The two officers who had come onto the parapet when our guns first opened up were killed, not far from each other.

A company officer ran along the Tunnel Trench side of the shell-hole line, shouting to the men to come on. Some of the Germans were leaving the shell-holes and making for Tunnel Trench; others remained and were firing. Some of our company on the right passed through the wire and were fighting with the enemy in the shell-holes at close quarters, but farther to the right the officer couldn't see. He was about the centre of his company, urging his men on. The bulk came up and were approximately in line advancing on Tunnel Trench. Then the officer was hit by a machine-gun and badly wounded. A sapper officer came along the trench and said that things seemed to be going well. Just then a shell burst behind, throwing earth about. The sapper fell, half on the newly broken parapet, and slid to the fire-step, dead.

A brisk small-arms fire, mostly from the German machine-guns, had started up; there had been short bursts from one gun before this. Then some of our men began running back, a few at first, but it quickly became a surge; on they came, but none went beyond the trench. The collapse was stupefying in its suddenness; the manner of it was sickening. Some men said they were stopped by the wire, others that they had orders to retire. There were, however, no officers and very few senior NCOs among them.

Little groups and individuals followed at short intervals. Then among the last came one of our officers, making for Plum Lane, into which he hurried. When the attack in the open collapsed, his concern was for our block in Plum Lane. Another violent exchange of bombs had broken out there. The Germans had come over the top on the right to counterattack. Some of them jumped into the lane and were instantly killed, but some of our men were cut off. The officer took part in the bombing that covered his men's withdrawal and the rebuilding of the block. Until it was made secure, the bombing was fiercer than when our attack in the Lane was launched. A Lewis gun on the right had helped by firing on the Germans who advanced to the crest of the ridge.

I learnt later of what happened in front. We were ringed in by Germans who were well led. From shell-holes and over the top the enemy came and fought at close quarters. With the enemy on all sides, many of our men strove to an end that came quickly. Most of our dead lay beyond the shell-hole line. A young subaltern fell wounded on the parapet of Tunnel Trench; his leg was amputated in a German hospital. Several men reached Tunnel Trench, and a sergeant died fighting in it; he had been a handful of trouble in his earlier irresponsible days.

One officer came in wounded in the arm; another followed, wounded in the foot. Two others were carried in, both badly hit. German shells were dropping in front of and behind our packed trench, but not into it, for which we were more than thankful. The shelling did not last long. A man who had fallen across the wire of the shell-hole line, mortally wounded and helpless, made some convulsive movements for quite a time before becoming still. Our wounded, lying out in front of Tunnel Trench, had seen no stir there. They said our trench-mortar bombs were all over, but they had put the wind up the Germans.

The empty valley in rear was shelled for two hours after the failure of our attack. Providentially, our trench was left alone, for it was overcrowded until nightfall. No one appeared to be in command of the operation; only stretcher-bearers were wanted. At 9:00 pm our guns bombarded Tunnel Trench and killed some of our wounded, none of whom had come in yet. One of our sergeants summed up the failure of our attack as panic among men without enough training and discipline, but he agreed when another sergeant said that the capture of Tunnel Trench only wanted running forward instead of running away. Also, the loss of time waiting to file through the few gaps in the wire, made by the resolute, had allowed Jerry to man his parapet and get up his machine-guns. It became clear that there had been no lack of leadership, but the irresolute mass had been given no proper training. Our battalion casualties in the calamitous affair of minutes were ten officers and a hundred and fifty-five other ranks, almost half of whom were dead. Not long afterwards, another division entered Tunnel Trench by a ruse at a cost of half a dozen. When the wind was favourable, smoke-shells mixed with gas-shells were fired on one or two days; next time, behind smoke-shells only, the infantry walked over and surprised the Germans, who were in their gas masks.

In the late afternoon of 30 June we moved to Monchy. This was our adieu to the Arras front. Then in July we passed three and a half weeks very pleasantly at Airaines. The weather was fine. There was a divisional horse show and the drums provided music, including "Ash Grove" and "Forth to Battle," and on the last day of July we left for Dunkirk, arriving there at 4:00 the next morning. A great strafe had started Ypres' way; it did not quieten down for forty-eight hours.

All the company officers thought more training was needed; our generals said the men were getting stale, but they never came to find out what we were like. On the eve of our departure there was thunder, and a deluge after dinner. We were going up with a trench strength of twenty officers and four hundred and sixty other ranks out of a ration strength of nine hundred. The Yser was rolling rapidly when, having passed through Nieuport, we reached the riverbank at dead of night. The floating bridges and their approaches were being shelled. As I crossed, some biggish shells burst nearby and cries of "gas" were raised.

We got to Lombardzyde Right, a breastwork area in marshy land crossed by dykes and raised stone causeways. Our front had been knocked about in July and was still in disrepair. The line consisted of posts in staggered echelon. It was easy to slip between them; once an officer's orderly put his head round a corner and saw some Jerries at supper; he got away unseen.

No-man's-land was seventy to a hundred yards wide, but our left post, Geleide, on the riverbank was within bombing distance. The Belgians were on the division's right. The operations at Messines and Ypres were begun to clear the way for a combined naval and military push up the coast, and to deny a base for submarines, which were working havoc among our merchant ships. I found that too many of our men were gun-shy; they ducked for any shell, however wide of them.

The bridges over the Yser, like those at Béthune, were named after London bridges. Watching them being shelled was one of my pastimes until it was dark enough to visit the front. I never saw a hit although two hits a day were usual, so good was the German shooting.

The idea of cover acts strangely on the mind. Men will sit calmly under no more than a corrugated-iron sheet, or even a ground sheet, when shells are dropping about; yet in similar circumstances, but without anything over them, they would be terrified. Absolute safe quarters, like the Hindenburg Line, spoiled one, even made one a bit windy in quarters that were less secure.

One afternoon a venturesome German airman flew low along our front, so low that he could be seen working furiously to get his machine-gun going. He was fired on, and a lot of black smoke came from his fuselage; he turned sharply to his right and just managed by a banking movement to clear his own breastwork before his machine crashed and burst into flame.

On our immediate front, things had been pretty quiet this tour, bar some inter-post bombing, although minutes were few when a shell did not swish past. Our artillery got most of the shelling; they were said to be having nearly fifty casualties a day, which seemed a lot. The fall of a shell could be watched by standing aside. Many American medicos had been hired to make up our shortage, as things were warming up on this front. We had a second night-and-day ding-dong strafe with the Germans.

At the end of August we went to billets in farms and cottages at Houlle and Moulle, two adjoining hamlets not far from St. Omer. Houlle and Moulle were enjoyable. There was training and the odd route march; other local activity was on the part of the Germans, whose planes bombed from Cassel to St. Omer, or passed over untrammelled to Dunkirk, Calais, and Boulogne. Our hospital townships on the route were not touched.

We went to St. Omer, about five miles distant, entering it by a road lined with sycamores. Just before we left, a bomb, dropped quite near our billets, killed three RFC officers; they had gone out of their cottage and were lying down in the garden looking up at the raiders.

A man who had joined us eighteen months before as a private was now a sergeant. Before enlisting he had been butler to an officer in the regiment. He declined to be a servant when he came to us, said he preferred duty and hoped for promotion. He was a capable, good fellow and was up for a commission when he was killed at Ypres.

Going forward, we marched north over hilly country to Wulverdinghe.

We reached Steenwoorde at 4:00 pm on 16 September 1917. By the time we got there a lot had sore feet, and not a few were dead beat.

The next day there was short march to Thieushouk, a hop-growing centre, where we rested for a couple of days. About this time, the Germans were lengthening the range of their guns. A year later I was again in this neighbourhood; so great was the destruction that not much of the village was left standing, or of Estaires and Meteren. Bailleul suffered less, but it was doubtful if there was a house fit for habitation.

The rumble and reverberation of gunfire beyond Ypres sounded all day and night. Gun flashes blinked in the dark. From higher ground near us, the line of Verey lights could be followed through Boig Grenier, La Cordonnerie, Neuve Chapelle, Festubert, Givenchy, Loos, and, up to the fall of Lorette Ridge, to Vimy, rising and bursting into brilliance, hovering, fading, falling and burning brightest before flickering out.

We were up early, leaving Thieushouk before 4:00 am on 20 September. The sky was clear and star-spangled after heavy rain. On the way the rain became fairly heavy again, and we arrived at Westoutre all equally wet. At that time we heard nothing of the morning's push, and of the aborted German counterattack that a prisoner had given away. If one could find anything good about the ghastly Ypres show, it was that the capture of one more ridge would give us a good jumping-off ground for the following year.

After lunch I and another officer rode among the dwarf oaks of Mont Rouge to its top. South, west, and north we could see a tumble of hill, wood, and wasteland, all in fine colour. Our curiosity was in the east. Not far off, some of our heavies were firing. The stumps of Ypres could just be seen in a haze that hid everything beyond. At night there was a clear sky, with stars and no moon.

The following afternoon I rode to Poperinghe. A few shells were fired into the town at times, but a large civilian population was doing a roaring trade in many goods, for the place was alive with our troops. When I got back to camp, duty was over for the day and the men were taking it easy, or were busy with their own affairs among rows of tents, or piles of arms and equipment. Beneath a late September evening sun the illusory feeling of peace seemed real.

Now in its third month, the third battle of Ypres had begun at the end of July, following the recapture, on 7 June 1917, of the Messines and Wytschaete ridges. The German front was obliterated by the blowing of huge mines, which cleared the right flank of the Salient. Since then there had been the most dogged fighting; men in thousands and shells in thousands of tons had been expended to advance the line one and a half miles on a small front. Sometimes the weather was fine; at other times men stuck in the mire, and wounded men drowned in shell-holes.

The Australians, on our left, had the east side of Cameron Covert and Polygon Wood as objective; the division was to straighten the line between. The Germans counterattacked in the centre and we lost considerably in men and ground.

Reveille was at 3:30 am. It was clear starlight. We marched by La Clytte, Dickebusch, where the transport remained, and the Café Belge to the Bedford House area, a smelly spot south of Ypres, where the railway bends east round Shrapnel Corner. It was strange to see the volume of traffic at high noon on roads where, for so long, men had hurried in the dark. We occupied flimsy old shacks that gave shelter from splinters when shells came over. Ypres was in ruins; the town would have to be rebuilt, every house, from its foundations.

First by road, then by tracks, we went round the south of Zillebeke Lake, past Hellblast Corner, the Dormy House, and through Sanctuary Wood to Stirling Castle. We arrived just after midnight. Some earlier troops had begun digging; the men were tired; they could not be bothered to carry on and make cover for themselves; they just lay down and slept. I envied them being able to sleep on so chilly a night; I had to walk about for warmth.

Tanks were to lead and cover the attack. A tank clattered up the Reutel road after our men had settled down; it was cursed heartily for turning up, only to draw fire, and went away willingly. It was the only tank of which anything was seen. We were ordered to attack at noon. We were required to deploy on the Reutel road east of Black Watch Corner, to advance and establish a new brigade front facing south of east, its left being near the southeast corner of Cameron Covert, a point about fourteen hundred yards eastwards of Black Watch Corner. A shortage of maps caused some difficulty to begin with. A conference of company commanders was called.

Although a time-consuming detour round Glencorse Wood was entailed, we were screened in great part from observation and we avoided the barrage on Inverness Copse, where the early morning advance lost cohesion and the direct approach north of it. One of the other battalions was said to have had two or three hundred casualties in the copse.

We crossed the Menin road east of Clapham Junction, on the fringe of the barrage. It was boggy behind Inverness Copse, where half a dozen foundered tanks lay, and the bog extended a great part of the way behind Glencorse Wood. Delay was caused by having to cross much of it in single file, choosing bearing footholds and jumping soggy bits. The track was traced by Lewis gun magazines and rifle grenades cast aside by their carriers. I was further delayed by helping a badly wounded man.

Between Glencorse Wood and Nonne Bosschen the ground rises and comes under observation from higher ground in front. The howitzer barrage had to be gone through there; then a track, about which shells were dropping, had to be followed. We had casualties in the barrage but reached our jumping-off ground without serious loss. The ground over which we were to operate was found to be as bare as tidal sand — not a wild flower, not a blade of grass grew on it; the surface was churned-up soil, which nearly mashed the roads and shell-holes. Trees, all of them small, had survived, and there were short lengths of hedge. All the farms and houses named on the map were pillboxes on the sites of dwellings.

Zero hour was noon. Just before then we were forming up under some machine-gun fire. A captain, who had been in France for most of the war, was shot through the throat and died almost immediately. Another of our officers was shot through the head as his company was entering a scraggy orchard enclosed by a scraggier hedge north of Jerk Farm, which was about five hundred and fifty yards eastwards of Black Watch Corner.

I saw one of our companies get clear of a row of pillboxes. Coming into the open, the company was met by machine-gun and rifle fire from the Polderhoek Chateau direction, and brought to a standstill facing southeast, with its left on Jerk Farm. Two more officers and a number of others were hit. A few Australian dead and German wounded lay about; these were the casualties of the earlier operations. Two platoons of another company on the right edged off under the small-arms fire and came to a standstill with their right in front of Lone Farm. Another of our officers was wounded there; he died within a few hours.

It looked as if we were in front of a screen of a few machine guns and rifles, most of them on the higher ground between Polderhoek and Reutel, skillfully hidden among the leafy trees. When the companies lay low, the Germans held their fire, but any movement, even by one man, drew a very accurate fire.

The Australians had their first aid post as well as their HQ at Black Watch Corner. Their many wounded were spread about waiting for removal, and the German observers could not but see the amount of movement there. Two signallers had begun to enlarge and deepen a shell-hole, but finding it far too hot a spot they went to a shallow trench in the rear, where others were already sharing it with some Australians.

A dud shell buried itself close behind us, lifting us clean off the fire-step on which we sat. Within a few yards of us a wounded German was trying to crawl behind our lines. I noticed that one of our officer's hair had turned much greyer during the two days he and others were in that wretched hole. I happened to speak to one of the prisoners during the latter part of the show and was struck by his white and haggard appearance, but on taking a look at some of our own men, I saw that they were no better, and I am sure I was the same.

Finding nothing to do for the time being, and having had no food since last night's dinner, I decided to look for Simmons. At that moment a signaller came and told me that while three of our officers, one the assistant adjutant, were talking to each other, a 5.9 burst among them, killing all three. After I heard this, I went to look for the adjutant about the Reutel road, where I had seen him an hour before. On the way, there was another explosion about a hundred and fifty yards ahead, and two men suddenly rose in the air amid a spout of soil. I found the adjutant, and we went to the HQ area and sat in a shell-hole while he made out a report for brigade. The writing was interrupted several times by the quantity of soil thrown about us.

About 3:30 pm the report was sent off, then a German plane came along the line of the Reutel road low enough to be fired on. It circled round Black Watch Corner and Lone Farm and went back over our companies. It went only as far as Bacelaere and came back, flying on the same course as before, amidst a fusillade. This time it seemed too low to be under control. It turned northeast at Lone Farm and glided unsteadily past our men, who joined in firing at it. The pilot looked over the left side of the cockpit. He was wearing a black flying helmet and goggles. The plane crashed not far away. The pilot was seen to have been shot.

Just as in other battles, hours passed unmarked except by the odd incident. The shelling slackened everywhere. Among a few pillboxes that lined our part of the Reutel road, a rare shell broke long spells of quiet. The day's casualties were a hundred and forty odd; upwards of a hundred had occurred during the hour or so about midday. In a trench at Carlisle Farm were many of our dead.

Twice between dark and midnight the SOS went up in the Reutel direction and was repeated by other units. It was a red-over-green-over-yellow parachute grenade at the time, a pleasing combination of colours hanging above the outline of pines that stood in dark relief against a clear night sky.

The staccato of the machine-guns filled the intervals of the larger reports and of the shell bursts, and the overhead rush of bullets through the nearly still, crisp air was like the whistle of a great wind. A veil of acrid smoke drifted over us, tainting the freshness of the autumn night. About one in the morning of 27 September, an Australian officer arrived at HQ with the news that the Australians had orders to attack in the morning, in conjunction with British troops on the right. At dawn there was a softening up barrage by our artillery, followed by quiet.

Rations were collected from a brigade fatigue party. Before going over the top tots of rum were issued to the men with, usually, whisky for the officers. We then received orders to advance in conformity with the Australians. In anticipation of this, and because the Australians were concentrating in Polygon Wood, the battalion had closed somewhat to the left. While we were waiting there it was lightly shelled. One 4.2 that burst among three men sitting in a shell-hole killed them with no more visible mark than some singeing of their clothing.

At 8:00 am the battalion moved yet farther east. A request was made to have the alarming deficiencies in Lewis gun magazines and rifle grenades made up. At 9:00 am a patrol was sent to learn the state of affairs east and southeast of Jerk Farm. The Australians had been on the move early. Our concern was that we were so terribly short of ammunition. At 11:30 am a brigade message came through to push forward at once, and a report also came from our patrol that the Australians were in Cameron Covert and that German machine-guns were firing into Polygon Wood. Officers commanding companies were summoned to HQ, now in a pillbox north of Jerk Farm. They were told that what loose ammunition lay about was to be collected, and were instructed how to proceed without artillery or machine-gun covering fire.

At 12:30 pm we began to dribble forward by twos and threes. Except for a little small-arms fire at the beginning, there was no opposition. By 1:30 pm the companies had settled in a shell-hole line. The idea was to go forward another hundred yards after dark. Throughout the advance the formation was a loose line. Here, too, there was no opposition to test any formation. Then an acting company commander reported movement on his front which made him uneasy. Two platoons, which were in reserve at Jerk Farm, were moved closer up; the sapping platoon was moved from reserve at HQ out to the right.

The companies continued to enjoy the quiet of their advance. Everything suggested that the Germans had gone back after making their counterattack, and that they were settling into another position. Until the late afternoon, a battery of howitzers was enough for the shelling which was dispersed in and behind Polygon Wood, with bursts about HQ. A couple of snipers cross-firing from Polderhoek and Reutel provided what small-arms fire there was; the companies were in dead ground to them, HQ area got all of it. Beginning near 6.00 pm there was an hour's sustained shelling of HQ, so accurate, so concentrated, that my confidence in a new shell-hole as the safest shelter was shaken. I came to date a failure of nerve from impressions taken then.

Through scattered trees at a distance the sun was seen sinking amid clustered cloudlets barred with red and black. For an hour the gunners on both sides and our machine-gunners did their worst on a pretty narrow front. So far I had not been under such a drumming. As the shells burst redder in the falling darkness, and doubt crept in and grew of what might be happening in front, the fascination to watching eyes and ears became tremendous. At last the uproar lulled for a little, then, as if by agreement, ended. The echoes had barely died down when the head of our relief came along. There being no trenches the change-over was a quick one.

At 10:05 pm we got away. We neared Inverness Copse, then on by Clapham Junction and the Embankment to our destination, four kilometres beyond Dickebusch, a long way to go, ten miles in all, but the surface was good and we were in the spell of fine weather. By 4:00 am on the 28th the last of us was in. Some, including an officer, had to be helped at the finish. After fifty-six foodless hours and seventy-three sleepless hours of almost incessant movement, I could take only some clear soup before sleeping. At 11:30 that morning I was called for breakfast but, for the first time in two years, not by Simmons.

During the previous afternoon, while I was sitting in a half-improved shell-hole which had just been quitted by two others, Simmons and another man, with that coolness and heedlessness of danger so common, had lit a fire on the enemy side of a pillbox and made tea. Then the two of them came over to my shell-hole. Simmons was grinning broadly as he handed me a mug with a quite good brew of his usual thick sweet tea, which he knew I liked. I drank it, then told the two men to wait in the shell-hole for the time being, as I had decided to look for another in the HQ area. I had not long left when I heard a crump, but took no notice because there was shelling going on everywhere.

From information gathered later, it seems that although I had told them to stay where they were, Simmons had decided to go back to the pillbox and collect the tea things. He had just stepped out of the hole when a shell — I am sure it was the one I heard — burst on top of him. Nothing was found of him anywhere. The other man suffered only shell shock.

Personal loss is a little more tolerable when a body, even a torn one, is there to confirm death. But to vanish completely, utterly, not a trace, such an end seems strangely bizarre and unreal. I suppose what I remember most about Simmons, apart from his humour, is his teaching me the mouth organ; also, another time on the Somme, when he came up to me with part of a letter written in French, which he'd found, and which he asked me to translate.

I don't know what the future would have held for Simmons had he survived the war. He was only twenty-four when he was killed. Although poverty and suffering were still widespread, a lot was being done for the poor; and the rich and powerful in this country, unlike the European aristocracy who lived only for pleasure, often performed acts of great public service. An example was set by the King himself when, as Prince of Wales, he accepted nomination as a member of a royal commission on the housing of the working classes.

Simmons was nine years old when Edward became King. Germany was then ruled by the King's nephew, Kaiser Wilhelm II, whose mother was Queen Victoria's eldest daughter. Since Simmons and millions of others like him were caught up in a social system ruled over, in the main, by these two men, it is worth looking in some detail at their characters; also their actions and the influence each had on world affairs, and therefore on the interlocking of those social forces which decreed the fate of my soldier-servant.

THE QUEEN IS DEAD — 1

When Edward VII nearly died of the same typhoid fever that had killed his father, there was a tremendous upsurge of affection. He laid a foundation stone here and there, visited a few factories, and asked to be kept informed of public matters, but his real love was the social round both in this country and on his travels abroad.

His visit to India, in 1875, when he was Prince of Wales, was spectacular. First he visited Baroda, where he hunted cheetah and black buck and enjoyed some pig-sticking; he also enjoyed immensely the wild-beast fights arranged for him where elephants, rhinoceros, buffaloes, and rams were pitted against each other. Then, after a lavish dinner at sea to celebrate Lord Charles Beresford's promotion to the rank of commander, the Prince landed at Colombo and went up to Kandy, where he killed his first elephant. Just before the killing he knocked over another elephant, which lay quietly and looked as though it were dead. The Prince, amused by what then happened, often told the story of this elephant he thought he had killed, because just as he had finished hacking off the elephant's tail, and while Charles Beresford was dancing a hornpipe on its rump, the elephant rose unexpectedly to its feet and tottered off, wounded and bleeding, into the jungle.

In November of that year he left Bombay so that he could shoot elephants in Ceylon, and, by December, he had arrived in Madras, where he was welcomed by the Governor, the Duke of Buckingham. In Madras he went to the races and hunted jackal. The following month, January 1876, he began a tour of north India and stayed with successive maharajahs. Then in February he killed his first tiger, a female eight and a half feet long with three cubs in her womb; the same month he went to a camp formed in jungle country at Bonhussa on the Sardah river, the boundary between India and Nepal, and was met there by the Prime Minister, who was the virtual ruler of Nepal, a man who had rendered valuable aid during the Great Mutiny, but who was reputed to be of low extraction.

The Prime Minister had collected two hundred riding elephants and two thousand coolies, and, in addition to these, on the Nepalese side of the river, there were another thousand riding elephants and at least ten thousand soldiers to act as servants and beaters. The Prince, with the other white sportsmen, and there were less than twenty in all, waited in a camp called Jumoa, a camp covering many square miles of forest.

On his first day in Nepal the Prince, seated in a howdah on the back of an elephant, killed six fully grown tigers. After this, in each of the various camps that were used, he enjoyed a hot bath, changed into evening dress, and gave a dinner party in a large and richly furnished tent.

Writing home to his sons, Prince Eddie and Prince George, he recounted how, the day before, he had killed the six tigers, and then the next day, in fact only a few hours before he had sat down to write this letter, he had killed a tigress that had a cub with her. Then he told his sons about an elephant hunt which he described as the finest day's sport he'd seen.

As well as sport there were a lot of receptions and sightseeing visits. In the throne room the Prince held a durbar. Six maharajahs — Gwalior, Jaipur, Jodhpur, Kashmire, Paliala, and Rewa — bejewelled and bearing rich presents, were presented personally; then he reviewed eighteen thousand troops and attended large-scale manoeuvres. He also went to the gaol at Lahore and had a long conversation with an old prisoner who claimed to have murdered two hundred and fifty people, but whose life was spared when he turned Queen's evidence.

The effects of the expedition as a whole, but particularly the visit to Nepal, were summed up by Sir Bartle Frere, who told Queen Victoria that the wonderful sportsmanship of the Prince of Wales had won the affection of the common people of India, as well as getting the respect and admiration of India's princes and nobles. An impression had also been made on people from a distance — an impression of manly vigour and power of endurance.

Frere told the Queen that just as she would be, in future, Empress of India and not merely the sovereign of India's British conquerors, so the Prince of Wales had infused a new hope into an entire subcontinent, and had conferred a new dignity upon the common people of India by coming, for a time, to share their mundane lives and to dwell and travel in their midst. Frere added that, in all this, the Prince stood to India's inhabitants in exactly the same relationship as that in which he stood to the British. Another member of the Prince of Wales party wrote to the Queen, describing the Prime Minister of Nepal as the most energetic specimen of a native they had met; this quality being so rare, it was greatly admired; the man was a remarkable savage.

But India was not the only place where the Prince showed his magnificent sportsmanship. In August 1885 he went to Drottingholm as a guest of the King and Queen of Sweden. There he took part in an elk hunt, where four hundred beaters served forty-six guns who were extended over a great distance. On one day alone, 10 September, they were able to kill an unprecedented total of fifty-two elks. Then he went on to Hungary for the stalking before the season was over.

At Bergeneze, on Lake Balaton, a party of Hungarian magnates accompanied the Prince every morning to stalk deer. Returning to breakfast at 9:30, he went out again for three hours at 4:00 pm. But on one occasion he devoted an entire day to partridges, when eight guns killed four hundred and nineteen brace.

It would be unfair to give this brief account of the Prince without mentioning his efforts to help the poor in his own country. When the Royal Commission on the Housing of the Working Classes stood adjourned on 5 December 1884, he had attended nineteen out of fifty-one meetings.

Another time, accompanied by Lord Carrington and Dr Buchanan, the three of them disguised as workmen, the Prince drove in a four-wheeler to visit the slums. In one unfurnished room he saw a gaunt, shivering woman lying on a heap of rags with three almost naked children who were too cold and too much starved to make any response whatsoever. After visiting more very bad places the three got back to Marlborough House in time for lunch, and, four days later, in the House of Lords, the Prince described some of the scenes he had witnessed. Unfortunately, although his intentions were good, he was distracted almost at once by the sudden death at Cannes of Prince Leopold. A month later he went abroad for seven weeks, although in the autumn of that year he stayed in England so that he could attend the business of the commission.

In December 1892 he accepted an invitation from Gladstone to become a member of the Royal Commission on the Aged Poor. He gave up his annual visit to the South of France and attended thirty-five out of forty-eight sessions during the two years the commission sat. He addressed many shrewd questions to witnesses and was most affable to his working-class colleagues, the MPs Henry Broadhurst and Joseph Arch.

But he found himself in a difficult position. He was eager to see suffering relieved, but he equated socialist remedies with revolution. He always regarded the hierarchical society, of which he was soon to become head, as divinely ordained; he therefore signed a statement saying he was obliged to observe strict political neutrality, and, because of this, no action was taken to provide state pensions, which eventually Lloyd George brought in with the Old People's Pension Act of 1908. At this time, although our own empire was still intact, the Turkish empire was disintegrating, so that one could not, altogether, blame the Prince for worrying about the implications of socialism.

When he became King, Edward VII's unease over the abuse, as he saw it, of the hereditary principle continued. He disliked intensely the new policy of admitting natives to a share in the government of India, and he vehemently opposed the government's appointment of a Hindu lawyer, Satyendra Prassano Sinka, to membership of the Viceroy of India's council. Two ex-viceroys, Lord Landsdowne and Lord Curzon, warmly supported him.

Edward said his mother would not have approved this new departure, and his son, who would be the next king, held the same views. He also wrote to Minto, the fourth Earl and Viceroy of India, saying that the Indian princes, who were ready to be governed by the Viceroy and his council, would greatly object to a native, inferior in caste to themselves, taking part in the government of the country.

It was natural that he should be concerned about anything which touched his prerogative even remotely. Peers were still worshipped in the countryside and often in the cities, but when change was being forced on the King, he spoke among intimate friends about abdicating; this was during the winter of 1909-1910, but the talk was not taken seriously; it was regarded as a symptom of sickness and depression.

THE QUEEN IS DEAD — 2

Edward VII's routine, which he followed year after year, soon became predictable. He spent Christmas and the New Year at Sandringham, through which, as with Windsor and Balmoral, guests perpetually flowed. He came to London for a night, two or three times during January, and he spent one week shooting with the Duke of Devonshire at Chatsworth and, later, with Lord Iveagh at Elveden.

At the end of January he moved to Buckingham Palace in time to open Parliament in state, and throughout February he entertained guests or went out to dinner, theatre, and supper parties every evening without exception. He left England punctually at the beginning of March for two months' holiday in the sun. He liked to spend a week in Paris, where he enjoyed strolling incognito on the boulevards, followed by three weeks at Biarritz. He would then cruise for a month in the *Victoria and Albert*. He liked best the Mediterranean.

Returning to London at the beginning of May in time to preside over the season, he again dined out or entertained friends every night. He gave famous and splendid suppers in a private room behind his box at the Royal Opera House, Covent Garden, and spent weekends at friends' houses or in his private quarters at the Jockey Club, Newmarket.

Moving to Windsor Castle for the Ascot races in the middle of June, he would then follow this with a three- or four-day visit every July to some provincial centre before going, at the end of the month, to stay with the Duke of Richmond for the Goodwood races. He left Goodwood for Cowes at the beginning of August to preside over the regatta, and used the royal yacht as his headquarters.

Immediately after Cowes, while the Queen was in Denmark staying with her sister, the Dowager Empress of Russia, he went to Marienbad in Bohemia for a month's cure. His very comfortable suite of rooms at the Hotel Weimar was furnished each year in a different style, but he travelled more simply abroad than his mother had done. Queen Victoria rented an entire hotel and took at least a hundred personal servants. Edward seldom took more than thirty servants apart from his suite.

When travelling over continental railroads, the King used three private coaches, built for solid comfort, with three easy chairs, thick pile carpets, bathrooms, and spacious cupboards. One coach was furnished like a clubroom with Spanish leather armchairs, card tables, books, newspapers, drinks, and cigars. Three automobiles and three chauffeurs were dispatched in advance to Biarritz or Marienbad. On returning from Marienbad he liked to spend a few days at Buckingham Palace. This was during the second week of September before he went to stay with the Saviles for the Doncaster races, and then with Arthur Sassoons in Inverness-shire.

When he stayed in the great houses, he had an Arab boy as a servant, just to make coffee the way he liked it. Balmoral, with its grouse and deer, remained his headquarters throughout October, and from there he attended the autumn race meetings at Newmarket, using his royal train. The first week of November was spent at Buckingham Palace, the second at Sandringham, and then, for an entire fortnight, he indulged in a round of Christmas dinner, theatre, and supper parties in London to which he looked forward, and which he enjoyed thoroughly until his health began to fail.

He made friends, quite naturally, with the rich and powerful. Throughout the 1890s enormous new wealth had been found in the gold and diamond mines of South Africa; there the sweat, toil, and death of black slaves made millionaires here.

Another of King Edward's great interests was food. He never tired of caviare, and although for Sunday lunch, as a change from the richer food, he liked a plateful of roast beef and Yorkshire pudding, he adored elaborate dishes. His dinner seldom consisted of less than twelve courses. He was especially fond of grouse, partridge, or pheasant stuffed with snipe or woodcock, when the latter was stuffed also with truffles and the whole garnished with rich sauce. And he loved ortolans, small Egyptian birds cooked in brandy.

In one of my not infrequent discussions with Jamie on the state of society in those years leading up to the Great War, one had to admit the obvious, that the life-style of the King and his circle was almost obscenely indulgent when compared to those starving people whom he, as Prince of Wales, had visited with Carrington and Buchanan; or even compared to people like Simmons who, in comparison, were born with nothing and took nothing out. However, Edward VII was scrupulously honest, quite the opposite of his nephew, who, at that time, ruled autocratically over a country which, more and more, we were being forced to regard as our enemy.

THE QUEEN IS DEAD — 3

Although Edward VII did not have the absolute power of the Kaiser, nevertheless, as King and head of state, and particularly because of close family ties, he, more than any other Englishman, was in a better position to influence the Kaiser, and therefore Germany's attitude to peace or war.

Although there can be bitterness and hatred in families, blood ties are usually the strongest and most effective means in uniting people; so one may well ask what it was that made two powerful nations, whose rulers were members of the same family, slaughter each other with such ferocity and intensity over a period of four years for no very good reason and, at the end of it all, with nothing much gained on either side.

The British public saw what they thought was an early indication of the Kaiser's friendliness towards this country when, on the death of Queen Victoria, he announced that he was remaining in England as a bereaved member of the British royal family and not as the German Emperor.

The sentimental British were enchanted by this attitude, and the Kaiser's bearing was so gentle and modest that King Edward believed a new chapter had been opened. After the funeral the King wrote to say that it was a sincere pleasure to confer upon the Kaiser the rank of field marshal in the British Army, and to invest Frederick Wilhelm, the German crown prince, a charming young man, later known as Little Willy, with the Order of the Garter.

On another occasion, only seven years before the outbreak of war, the Emperor and Empress of Germany arrived at Windsor to begin a state visit. The King said everyone was delighted to see both Their Imperial Majesties looking in such splendid health, and he hoped their stay, however brief, would further benefit our country.

During the visit, the Kaiser came to London and drove in procession to a lunch at the Guildhall. The enthusiasm of the crowds which lined the streets was uninhibited, although many of the cheering youngsters, who of course could not have known their fate, would soon be going to their deaths in the trenches. When the Lord Mayor presented the Kaiser with an address in a gold casket, the Kaiser declared, amid thunderous applause, that blood is thicker than water.

No guests could have been made more welcome. The King personally organized shoots, massed choirs, theatre performances, and banquets for their entertainment; the Emperor and Empress described one of the banquets to be finer than any spectacular display of the kind they had seen, a juxtaposition of medievalism and the twentieth century with the castle itself, the lines of Beefeaters in their gorgeous uniforms, and the splendid gold plate, flowers, and diamonds.

The British government felt that the King's knowledge and judgment of the Kaiser's disposition was much superior to any of theirs, and in 1908 Grey provided the King with two memoranda about the naval building programme; and although it was known that the Kaiser would be sensitive to any attempt to influence German naval expenditure, it was felt it would be best to regard it as a personal matter between the King and the Emperor. At Friedrickshof Castle on the morning of 11 August 1908, the King and the Kaiser were alone together for three hours, but no record exists of their conversation. Edward then saw the Austrian Emperor in Ischl. Nothing came from either of these meetings.

During his official visit to this country the year before, the Kaiser, in two long talks with Grey, had declaimed wildly against the Jews; then, after the official visit ended, and he had stayed on privately for another month, the German Emperor said the English were as mad as March hares in not acknowledging him to be their best friend, as he alone was capable of keeping in check the anti-British feeling of the majority of his subjects; and he said, also, that he was cruelly misunderstood. In an interview with W.B. Hale of the New York World, the Kaiser told Hale that King Edward was personally corrupt, that his court was rotten, that his country was heading for disaster, and that an Anglo-German war was now inevitable.

Yet before this, early in 1906, in a charming letter to the Kaiser which the German Emperor received on his forty-seventh birthday, the King wrote that as they were such old friends and near relations, he, Edward, was sure the affectionate feelings which had always existed between them would continue and that, above all, a friendly feeling could exist between Germany, France, and England because the Kaiser could be assured that England had no aggressive intentions towards Germany.

Replying from Berlin on 1 February, the Kaiser wrote that the whole letter from his uncle showed such kindness and warm sympathetic friendship that it constituted the most cherished gift among his presents. He also quoted the proverb "Let bygones be bygones" before recalling the death of Queen Victoria, describing the silent hours when they watched and prayed at her bedside until the spirit of that great sovereign lady passed away as she drew her last breath in his arms. The Kaiser ended his letter by saying he felt sure that from the home of the eternal light, Queen Victoria was now looking down on them and would rejoice when she saw their hands, that of the King and the Emperor, clasped in loyal and cordial friendship.

In the last years of his reign, Edward's depressions grew blacker and blacker. What troubled him most was evidence of the disintegration all round him of the old social order, and any social disturbance only strengthened his growing awareness of the drastic changes, now taking place, to all that he held dear. The attitude of his German nephew, which was significantly deepening the rift between their two countries, only added to this burden.

For thirty years Kaiser Wilhelm II was the apex of the Reich's social, political, and military pyramid, the all-highest person and the supreme warlord. Although there was no real censorship in Germany, most newspapers were absolutely loyal to the monarchy. To insult the Kaiser was an offence punishable with a prison term. The result of this was a demigod attitude towards the man who controlled Germany's destiny.

The Kaiser kept himself quite apart from the people. Comparatively few ever spoke to him. When he visited a town or any other place, all schools were closed and crowds lined the streets, but they had no more than a glimpse of their Emperor dashing by in a horse-drawn carriage, wearing an army or naval uniform.

The most important constitutional right of the Kaiser was his control over all appointments to the government, the bureaucracy, the army and navy, and the diplomatic service. Gradually, the German Emperor created a government and an administrative apparatus of his own choosing. Pliant tools of the imperial will were appointed to all key offices. Besides the policies for which the Kaiser was responsible, one has to consider also measures which were not put into effect, either because he blocked them or because the German government knew that to propose them would be futile in view of his attitude.

To millions of his subjects the Kaiser symbolised all that was decent and worth fighting for in German culture. His public image, and the propaganda developed to broadcast it, reinforced respect for authority and a feeling of collective solidarity against enemies of the Reich both at home and abroad. He was regarded by his contemporaries as the strongest force in Germany, and the mystical faith he inspired among some of his closest advisers cannot be explained simply as a craving for a supernatural leader who would provide for his people a world of higher meaning; nor can it be explained in terms of opportunism.

Certainly the Kaiser did have impressive qualities: a vivid imagination, quick intelligence, tireless energy and enthusiasm, and considerable charm. Yet he was a man who, in the midst of so much change, did not himself change, did not develop, did not mature; a man whose actions, nevertheless, had grave significance and practical consequences for so many; an emperor with the highest estimation of his own abilities, and who not only believed he was the German Reich and that he was the balance of power but, like his uncle King Edward VII, believed he had been appointed by divine right.

The real facets of the Kaiser's character, as distinct from that presented by official propaganda or conjured up by wishful thinking, were an inability to learn from experience; a restlessness; a grandiose belief in his own importance; a tendency to take all things personally, to regard any setback or obstacle as a personal insult; his consequent rage against those who would not do his bidding; his determination to avenge himself on those who betrayed him; an overriding pathological hatred for his mother and the British royal family; his deeply offensive behaviour towards others, even monarchs and princes; the hurtful practical jokes against his friends and members of his entourage; and, finally, his love of uniforms, of jewellery, of dressing up, and of childish games played in all-male company.

Part of his trouble could have been his withered left arm. This may have been responsible, beneath the trappings of kingship, for a feeling of inferiority. But it may not have been so much this deformity that was the problem as his mother's reaction to her son's disability. Determined that the damage to her son's arm should be repaired, whatever the cost, she sent for the unsmiling Calvinist, Hinzpeter, and one cannot help having sympathy for the boy, nor fail to be angered by the treatment of this sensitive eight-year-old, who, in spite of his handicap, was subjected to almost savage discipline when taught to ride on the orders of his mother.

The closer Wilhelm came to the throne, the more he could behave as he wished. After 1888 he was able to use the whole apparatus of army, navy, and state, the whole arena of world politics, to do whatever he liked. But he continually covered his fundamental internal weakness — his lack of self-confidence — by an agitated and anxious grandiosity. He was boastful, he loved public speaking and display, and he tended towards extreme exaggeration. He also needed to surround himself with charmers and flatterers. He was most sensitive to blows to his pride, and reacted to perceived insults with outbursts of rage and vengeful brooding. He could not admit mistakes or tolerate criticism, and yet he depended on others to provide him with direction and purpose.

The confusion and incoherence of Wilhelm's actions contributed decisively to the confusion and incoherence of German policy towards England. Because of the Kaiser's inconsistencies, neither the English nor the Germans could rely on him. They never understood his motives, and in their uncertainty, both countries came to mistrust each other completely. From the very early days, well before he came to the throne, he had a love/hate relationship with Britain, which was brought about, in part, by a very bad relationship with his mother. This developed into a hatred of England, a country he regarded with increasing intensity as

Germany's archrival and, after 1914, the bitterest of Germany's enemies. In 1881 he married Augusta Victoria of Schleswig-Holstein-Sanderburg-Augustenburg who also had an intense and inflexible dislike of England.

Because of his constitutional position and because of his personal character, Wilhelm repeatedly influenced the course and conduct of Germany's external policy. Constitutionally, the German kaiser was a crucial political figure. He was at the centre of the decision-making apparatus, and all chain of authority terminated in him. Only the kaiser, not the Reichstag, had the power to select and dismiss the chancellor. Ministers were his men, and the entire conduct of foreign policy was in his hands, and only by delegation in the hands of the chancellor.

To most contemporary observers, the Kaiser's policy was German policy, and for this reason his escapades, bombastic speeches, restless travelling, and occasional intrigues were interpreted by other governments as showing that Germany was ambitious, unreliable, and unpredictable. The conclusion drawn differed: some merely thought the Kaiser unbalanced; others took the militant bombast and the constant pushiness more seriously; but the blunt fact remains that the German government was being pushed towards a naval policy in the mid-1890s, not so much from without as from within — that is, from the Kaiser.

All plans were laid before the Kaiser by the chief of staff. Long before 1914 he had approved and wholeheartedly supported Germany's operational war aims, which included the navy's schemes to overrun the Netherlands and Denmark, as well as the Schlieffen plan, with its proposals for a large-scale sweep through neutral Belgium. His view of the distribution of power within his empire was that the military supreme command, both in peacetime and wartime, was his absolute personal prerogative, and, until the war, there was no decline in his power. During the war, although he remained as supreme commander until the end of October 1918, when the constitution of the Reich was reformed, he was only a figurehead. From 1916 to 1918 the most powerful man in Germany was General Erich Ludendorff.

It is a well-known fact that the Kaiser had a turbulent behaviour pattern, and this can be easily understood if an examination is made of his private life; although one has to keep in mind that he was a great public figure and that when he became ruler of the German Reich, a difficult job that gave even Bismarck nightmares, an enormous strain was placed on his shoulders.

The Liebenburg Circle, to which he was greatly attracted, was homosexual. Repressed homosexuality in the Kaiser would explain his restlessness, his friendships, his love of childish jokes, of rings and bracelets, of dressing up in all-male company; but this would only be a part explanation, and, when looking at the causes of the First World War, one has to take into account that within him, there was a deeper disturbance at a more primitive level.

Contemporaries of the Kaiser, the founders of modern psychiatry and psychoanalysis, were themselves provoked into commenting on the curious behaviour pattern of their powerful emperor. Eminent German psychiatrists, including Emil Kraeplin and Robert Gaupp, regarded Kaiser Wilhelm II as pathological in fact, a typical case of periodic disturbedness. What Kraeplin and the other German psychiatrists had in mind when they diagnosed Wilhelm II as periodically disturbed was that their emperor was manic or manic-depressive. So close was the correspondence between the clinical descriptions of mania and what was then known about the Kaiser's behaviour that a number of psychiatrists arrived at this conclusion independently of each other.

Dr Paul Tesdorf, a psychiatrist with a practice in Munich, had been convinced of the Kaiser's abnormality for a very long time. In 1916 he sent his diagnosis to Bethmann-Hollweg, to warn the chancellor of the grave political dangers which the diagnosis showed to exist. Tesdorf had written that he and many of his colleagues were certain that the mental illness known as periodic disturbedness — that is, the alternation of periods of pathological psychic depression — was the cause of numerous words and actions which had emanated for decades from the Kaiser and which were inexplicable except in psychiatric terms, and which had determined the fate of the German Reich and those who belonged to it. Tesdorf's views were widely accepted when he published them after the fall of the monarchy in 1918, though of course one of the reasons for this acceptance was to save the Kaiser from being tried and then hanged as a war criminal. After the war, when the Kaiser was in exile in Holland, the Dutch refused to hand him over to the Allies, much to our relief.

It is often asked how much responsibility the Kaiser had in bringing about the war. What is quite certain is that he did nothing to prevent it, but also it is certainly not possible to write the history of German decision-making for this period without reference to him and his immediate circle.

THE ENEMY — 2

Ma Chérie,

Ici, en Allemagne, il y a des préparatifs au sommet. Les généraux veulent la guerre. Il y a des gens ici qui pensent que L'Empereur est contré. S'il l'est, alors il n'y aura pas de guerre. Mais il semble bien

236

qu'elle va avoir lieu, et si c'est le cas, alors je suis l'ennemi et il sera décrété que je dois tuer ton frère et qu'il me tuera.

Mais je ne peux pas penser à moi-même de cette façon. Je ne peux pas imaginer que là où il y a eu l'amour il y aura la haine, où il y avait la joie il y aura le besoin de destruction. Je ne peux pas imaginer un tel changement. Mais une signature assurera que le changement doit être, et que je dois alors être ce qu'ils ordonnent que je sois. Mais mes cheveux seront toujours blonds, mes yeux bleus, mes pensées pour toi juste comme elles étaient quand nous marchions main dans la main dans les bois de Pozières.

Je n'ai jamais vu de gloire dans la bataille et je ne veux pas tuer de Français. Je ne veux tuer personne, parce que tuer n'a jamais été dans mon esprit. J'ai vu une fois un sanglier sauvage abattu lors d'une chasse. J'étais seulement un garçon et j'ai vu le crime aux abords du bois. Tous ces hommes à cheval lançaient de longues pointes sur la pauvre bête et elle criait et tournait et je fus malade.

Je ne veux pas être l'ennemi; je n'ai pas de haine dans le coeur, pour personne. Quel bien ferait la guerre? Quel bien la guerre a-t-elle jamais fait? Ils disent, ici à Frankfurt ...

THE ENEMY — 3

It was towards the end of the Somme battle when Simmons came up to me with that letter, or the part of it which he'd found in a shell-hole near the ruins of a church. When he asked me if I would translate it for him, I agreed to do so. Although my French wasn't all that good, I could get by.

The letter was botched. I couldn't make out the address or date, although from the contents it had obviously been written just before the outbreak of war. I also had to assume a few of the words.

I first read the letter through to myself. It had been written by a young German to his French sweetheart and was a sad letter. I then read out aloud to Simmons, but made up a translation as I went along. To tell him exactly what was in it wouldn't have been good for morale, not at that time. I made up something, I can't remember what. I kept the letter. The reason that I didn't want Simmons to know exactly what was in it was because it would only have given him a distorted view of the enemy. When one considers it was written by the enemy, it's extraordinarily human.

Of course, they weren't officially the enemy then, but from the way it was written, preparations for war were going on. I didn't show the letter to Jamie. In 1938 Jamie became engaged to Wenzel's daughter, which was against my wishes. Not that I disliked the girl. She came from a good background; her father was a lawyer and they were well off, but they were Germans.

I met Wenzel and his wife over here. Elizabeth had them to stay in 1938. She encouraged the whole business. Wenzel was nice enough, a nice-looking fellow, too. He'd been wounded during the war — the First War — and had lost the sight of an eye. He was the quiet, intellectual sort; he'd read Dickens and Shakespeare in English. If the girl had been English I would have approved. She was older than Jamie, a couple of years older. He was about to go over for her twenty-first birthday when the Second World War started.

Wenzel had two sons. The younger was killed in the Dresden air raid. His wife found the boy's burnt body. The other son, who was not much older than Jamie, served in the German Army. The daughter, Ellen, Jamie's fiancee, was a nurse in Germany during the war. After the war she married a German doctor. When this war was over, Elizabeth wrote to the Wenzels and asked them over again. I didn't like the idea, but as it happened, I was able to have long talks with Wenzel and found him quite interesting, except I didn't like the way he'd turned pacifist. We talked mostly about the First War, which was the one we'd both fought in, the one in which we'd had similar experiences. He was particularly bitter about the Kaiser. I am quite sure an Englishman would never turn on his sovereign in this way, whatever the circumstances. It was very disloyal.

THE ENEMY — 4

For Germany, 1 August 1914 was officially the first day of mobilization. Wenzel, because he'd had the education, and because his parents could afford it, went in as a potential officer candidate. Reservists could be seen everywhere, and the young Germans particularly were enthusiastic and ready to fight the world. Wenzel said that he, and ordinary Germans like him, were under the impression that their country was completely encircled.

Once war was declared, Germany, of course, became the enemy. Our feelings, then, for all of them were impersonal. We respected them as good fighters, respected their courage, but one couldn't get emotionally involved. Alive, they were there to be killed; dead, they were corpses of no further interest; wounded and captured, they were just so many of the enemy out of the way.

On 6 August Wenzel was issued with his field grey uniform; then he was put on a troop train where he met up with some friends. Some had been at school with him and some belonged to his tennis club. After a very short time, out of the eighteen young men who joined up with him, six were dead and five wounded, including one who had his arm blown off. Wenzel later was promoted to officer rank and was blinded in one eye from a shell splinter.

Wenzel's unit crossed the Belgium border on 25 August 1914 and saw the first sign of war: some burned-out houses. Warfare in Belgium soon became a hideous experience. The Belgians, whenever they had the chance, shot down German soldiers. There was little defence against that sort of warfare because the houses and streets were full of civilians. Unless the Belgians shot first, nobody knew where they were. It was nerve-wracking in the extreme, and resulted in savage and merciless slaughter at the slightest provocation.

When the Germans got to Tirelmont, they found it burning furiously. The inhabitants were milling and running around, trying to save their houses. Some dead were lying in the streets. The Germans marched on about fifteen miles to Louvain, an old university town. It seemed as if all of Louvain was on fire, the houses burning on both sides of the narrow streets. Most houses of the villages they had passed through were burning, and dead soldiers and civilians lay everywhere. Some were burned black, their arms and legs sticking out stiff and rigid. Frightened civilians lined the streets, hands held high as a sign of surrender. To see these men, women, and children, Wenzel said, was a terrible sight.

After marching through Brussels, the Germans went west towards Alost-Termonde and found themselves deep in enemy territory. By 6 September Germany's armies had reached the River Marne, about seventy miles from Paris. Tremendous victories had been won, but the French and English armies fought brilliantly with the utmost tenacity and courage. The Germans always referred to us as the English, but when recounting to you what Wenzel told me, I prefer to think of us as the British.

What Wenzel said was true: the Allies gave ground only after inflicting terrible losses, and made counterattacks whenever possible. When it appeared impossible to beat the enemy by clever manoeuvres, the German high command substituted a plan of ruthless, ceaseless attack, hoping to smash and pulverize Allied resistance.

At a critical moment two German army corps had to be transferred from the Western Front to hold back the invading Russians. The French high command detected the weakness caused by this withdrawal, and quickly threw its last reserves into the battle on the Marne. Overtired German troops could not hold back this fresh onslaught. Wherever Wenzel looked he saw dead German infantrymen lying on the ground. The

French 75mm field gun could fire up to twelve thousand yards, while German maximum range was only seven thousand five hundred yards. For much of the time the French stayed carefully out of range, inflicting terrible losses with their accurate fire. This was the situation by the middle of September when Wenzel, with the rest of the German armies on the Western Front, had to retreat to a position, still deep in enemy territory, which they then held for the next four years. By this time the attacking German troops on the Western Front, originally numbering about one million, had lost two-thirds of their officers and two-fifths of their men in dead and wounded.

As soon as Wenzel and the other young Germans — and those not so young — got to the front, their object was to kill as many French and English as possible. Wenzel saw a lot of the fighting. When war broke out he had just begun his studies, and he told me that what remained in his memory were incidents very little different from mine. Although he wasn't religious in the strict sense, he found that prayers were a great relief. On both sides, just before they went over the top, there were men silently praying. Another thing we and the Germans had in common were the rats.

In the beginning, the German trenches were better than ours — better constructed and comparatively more comfortable. But towards the end of the war, they were no longer in good condition, and the rats had become much more numerous. Wenzel said another common denominator among all these human beings who were busy slaughtering each other was fear. He was inclined to talk like this at times; he'd become quite bitter. He said this fear might have been something that could have been built on when peace came, but as it turned out, it was a shaky peace leading to a second gigantic conflict.

The only overriding feeling Wenzel had, during most of the war, was a longing to get away from the fighting and the killing, to leave the trenches and all the horror forever and be back with his family and those friends who had survived. I don't think he changed even after he was commissioned. He said the full horror of the war soon sickened him; he saw this happen to so many young Germans, those same young Germans who had started out with their heads held high and with patriotism in their hearts.

At the front there was no quietness. Even in the remote depots and rest areas the muffled noise of the shelling was always in one's ears. The guns were never so far off that the sound was no more to be heard. I know exactly what Wenzel meant. It was always there, in the back of one's mind, the noise of shelling, there eternally. He said the bombardments, the noise of the bombardments, became unbearable.

In the beginning, Wenzel's thoughts were on patriotism, on killing the enemy, this and nothing more. When he went to war he was young, he and his comrades, most of them teenagers, and although after a time one would have thought they might be hardened by the war and the killing, they all became weary of the interminable pointless slaughter. At the end of a year's killing, two years even, the Germans had moved perhaps a mile, then gone back to where they were, a stalemate all the time. This is what the war proved to be, a stalemate; it was like that until the very end. Knowing this truth, on both sides, didn't stop the fighting, so we went on killing each other.

Wenzel also said that to know fully what the killing meant, to understand completely, you had to be there at the front and see the mutilation, hear the cries of men drowning in mud and slime, see bodies eaten by rats, and all for what? For an advance of a couple of hundred yards, then pushed back, then a small advance, years of stalemate, and the feeling of hopelessness, with nearly all one's comrades killed, and seeing no end to it; the guns, those hideous guns, day and night, night and day, attack and counterattack. You had to be there to know what it meant in all its horror.

Once you have been in action there is usually a complete change — a reversal actually — from the feelings you had before. It's an experience that can never be adequately described. Young men on both sides couldn't wait to get into uniform, to be in France, go to the front and face each other, play their part in this great war. The Germans and the Allies went marching into battle, each having God on their side, marching smartly, buoyantly, singing patriotic songs, laughing, joking, bright and confident; young soldiers excited by the prospect of conflict, these Germans, English, and French, and those from the other countries who joined in, most of them just out of school, young men from every class united in a common cause, their patriotism and a vision of glory and honour urging them on. How were they to know it would all quickly change, become a nightmare from which it seemed they would never wake up — and from which many didn't? In this way, of course, the Germans were no different from us: ordinary people feeling fear just as we did, caught up in a war not of their own choosing.

Not all German casualties were youngsters, but most of them were, and after the war, Wenzel said, Germany's leaders would then pretend. There would be solemn services and acts of remembrance and exquisitely kept cemeteries, but the deaths and mutilation of these young German soldiers were worth nothing, really. When a boy died he would be just another corpse, a name in a war cemetery, at best a bitter memory for as long as those who loved him lived on. Then the whole horror would be no more than a generalized account in the history books of battles won and battles lost.

The only people to weep over a soldier's death would be his parents, brothers, sisters, and, if he had them, his wife and children. And, Wenzel had asked himself, to whom else would it matter? To the Kaiser? To the generals? To the German government? No, to none of them, least of all the Kaiser.

DIE SCHLACHT AN DER SOMME

By January 1916 Wenzel was on the Somme, where the German command on the Western Front had concentrated all its energy and all its available strength in manpower and gunpower for the attack on Verdun. For this attack the Crown Prince had demanded men and more men, until every unit that could be spared from other fronts along the line had been thrown in. Divisions were called in from other theatres of war, increasing the strength on the Western Front to a total of about a hundred and thirty divisions. But the months passed and Verdun still held out above the piles of German corpses.

But, Wenzel said, it was the British offensive that the German command feared most, for the Germans had no exact knowledge of our strength, or of the quality of our new troops; they only knew that our army had grown considerably since the assault on Loos nearly a year before. The Germans had also heard of Canadian reinforcements and the coming of the Australians, and the steady increase of recruiting in England. Wenzel said that they knew, too, of the steady, quiet concentration of enemy batteries and divisions on the north and south of the Ancre.

After the bloody losses before Verdun, orders of the day were issued to the German battalions, counselling them to hold fast against the hated English, who stood foremost in the way of peace. This was the gist of an order of the day from Crown Prince Rupprecht of Bavaria, promising a speedy end to the war.

The British attack had begun with a great bombardment and was a revelation to the German command, and to the soldiers who had to endure it. The German gunners found that in heavies and expenditure of high explosives they were outclassed. They were startled, too, by the skill and accuracy of the British gunners whom they had scorned as amateurs, and by the daring of British airmen who flew over German lines with the utmost audacity, spotting for the British guns and registering on batteries, communication trenches, crossroads, railheads, and every vital point of organization in the German war machine opposite the British lines, north and south of the Ancre.

Wenzel found that food and supplies of all kinds could not be sent up to the front-line trenches without many casualties, and sometimes could not be sent up at all. Telephone wires were cut and communications broken between the front and headquarter staffs. German staff officers, who were sent up to report, were killed on the way to the lines. Troops moving forward from reserve areas came under heavy fire, and lost many men before arriving in the support trenches.

At 7:30 am on 1 July 1916, the British infantry left their trenches and attacked on the right angle southwards from Gommecourt, Beaumont Hamel, Thiepval, Ovillers-la-Boiselle, and eastwards from Fricourt, below Mametz and Montauban. For a week the German troops, Bavarian and Prussian, Wenzel among them, had been crouching in their dugouts, listening to the ceaseless crashing of the British drumfire.

In places like Beaumont Hamel, in the deep tunnels, some of them large enough to hold a battalion and a half, the German soldiers were safe as long as they stayed there; but to get in or out was death. Trenches disappeared into a sea of shell craters, and the men holding them, for some of the Germans had to stay on duty in the trenches, were blown to fragments of flesh.

Many of the shallower German dugouts were smashed in by heavy shells, and Wenzel saw officers and men lying dead. Those still alive below ground, under the tumult of bursting shells, tried to keep up their courage, but wrote pitiful letters to their people at home describing the horror of those hours.

Thirst was one of their tortures. In many of the tunnelled shelters they had food enough, but the water could not be sent up. The German soldiers were maddened by thirst. When rain fell, many of them crept out and drank filthy water, and they were killed by high explosives. Other men crept out, careless of death, but compelled to drink; they crouched over the bodies of men who lay above or in the shell holes, lapped up the puddles, then, if they were not hit, crawled down again.

In those early days of the struggle there was no sign of cowardice or low morale among the German troops, even though, after the first week of battle, the German general staff had learnt the truth about the qualities of those British new armies which had been mocked and caricatured in German comic papers. They learnt that these amateur British soldiers had the qualities of the finest troops in the world; not only extreme valour but skill and cunning, not only a great power of endurance under the heaviest fire but a spirit of attack which was terrible in its effect. The British were also great bayonet fighters. Once they had gained a bit of earth or a ruined village, nothing would budge the British unless they could be blasted out by gunfire.

German losses were piling up. Wenzel said that the great agony of the German troops under British shellfire was reaching unnatural limits of torture. German generals had to fill up the gaps, to put new barriers of men against the waves of British infantry, and to fling into the line new troops called up hurriedly from the reserve.

Now, for the first time, the German staff showed signs of disorder and demoralisation. When the Prussian guard reserves were brought up from Valenciennes to counterattack at Contalmaison, they were sent onto the battlefield without maps or local guides and walked straight into a British barrage. A whole battalion was cut to pieces, and many others suffered frightful things. German prisoners later told their British captors that the Germans had lost three-quarters of their number in casualties, as British troops advanced over heaps of killed and wounded.

Wenzel said that, owing to the ceaseless gunfire of the British, they could get no food supplies and no water. The dugouts were crowded, so that the Germans had to take turns to get into these shelters, and outside, British shells were bursting over every yard of ground. Another prisoner told the British that those Germans who went outside were killed or wounded. Some had their heads blown off, and some their arms, but they went on taking turns in the hole although those who went outside knew that it was probably their turn to die. Many of those who came into the hole were wounded, some of them badly, so that they lay in blood.

The German command, Wenzel said, was not thinking much about the suffering of its troops. It was thinking, necessarily, of the next defensive line upon which the Germans would have to fall back if the pressure of the British offensive was maintained: the Longueval-Bazentin-Pozières line.

On 15 July 1916, when British troops broke the German second line at Longueval and the Bazentins, great loss was inflicted on the Germans, although they fought courageously until British bayonets were among them. A day or two later, the fortress of Ovillers fell, and the remnants of the garrison, a hundred and fifty strong, after desperate and gallant resistance in ditches and tunnels where they had fought to the last, surrendered.

Then began the long battle of the woods, which continued through August with most fierce and bloody fighting and gradually but steadily forced the Germans back, in spite of terrific German bombardments which filled these woods with hellfire prior to constant German counterattacks. Wenzel heard time and again this order from the German staff: Counterattack! And battalions of men marched out obediently to certain death.

The losses of many of the German battalions were staggering, and by the middle of August the morale of the troops was severely shaken. So far as Wenzel could ascertain, the greater part of the reserves had been absorbed into the front and support trenches, leaving, as the only available reserves, two exhausted battalions.

Wastage was faster than the arrival of fresh troops. It was also noticeable, Wenzel said, that German divisions were being left in the line until incapable of further effort, when it would have been better had they been relieved earlier so that, after resting, they might again be brought onto the battlefield. The only conclusion to be drawn from this was that the Germans had not sufficient formations available to make the necessary reliefs.

The British and French offensive was drawing in all the German reserves, and the Somme was being called the Bath of Blood by German troops, who waded across its shell craters and ditches that were heaped with German dead. But what Wenzel had described so far was only the beginning of the battle. This name, the Bath of Blood, had been invented before the first phase of the battles of the Somme; the second phase, for Wenzel and his comrades, was the great British advance on 15 September from the Pozières-Longueval-Guillemont line.

This name, the Bath of Blood, and the news, could not be hidden from the German people, who had already been horrified by the losses at Verdun; nor from the soldiers of reserve regiments quartered in French and Belgian towns like Valenciennes, St. Quentin, Cambrai, Lille, Bruges, and as far back as Brussels, waiting to go to the front; nor from the civil populations of those towns held for two years by their enemy, these blond young men who lived in their houses and marched along their streets.

The news was brought down from the Somme front by Red Cross trains arriving in endless succession, and packed with maimed and mangled men. German military policemen formed cordons round the railway stations and pushed back civilians who had come to stare with sombre eyes at the blanketed bundles of living flesh, but when the ambulances rumbled through the streets towards the hospitals, long processions of them, with the soles of men's boots turned up over the stretchers on which they lay quiet and stiff, the tale was told without any words being spoken.

The bad news was also spread by divisions taken out of the line and sent back to rest. The German soldiers reported that their battalions had been cut to pieces; some of their regiments had lost three-quarters of their strength. They described the frightful effect of British artillery: the smashed trenches, the shell craters, the great horror. This was not good for the morale of men just about to go up there to take their turn.

So it was in no cheerful mood that the German soldiers went away to the Somme battlefields. Battalions of grey-clad men, most of them in their teens and early twenties, entrained without any of the old enthusiasm with which the German soldiers had gone into earlier battles, and their gloom was noticed by the officers. "Sing, you sheep, sing!" the officers shouted, and the men were compelled to sing, by order. On the way back to their billets they were told to sing "Deutschland über Alles," but this broke down completely. Soon, Wenzel said, songs of the Fatherland were heard no more.

The journey to the Somme front for the Germans was a way of terror, ugliness, and death. Not all the imagination of morbid minds, searching obscenely for foulness and blood in the great deep pits of human agony, could surpass these scenes along the way to the German lines round Courcelette and Flers, Gueudecourt, Morval, and Lesboeufs. British long-range guns were hurling high explosives into distant villages, barraging crossroads, reaching out to railheads and ammunition dumps, while British airmen were on bombing flights over railway stations and rest billets and high roads down which the German troops came marching at Cambrai, Bapaume, in the valley between Irles and Warlencourt, at Ligny-Thillon, Busigne, and many other places on the lines of route.

On the march in open country the German soldiers tramping silently along, not singing in spite of orders, were bombed and shot at by British aviators, who flew down very low, pouring out streams of machine-gun bullets. The Germans scattered into ditches, falling over each other, leaving their dead and wounded in the roadway.

Sometimes a regiment on the march was tracked all along the way by British gunfire directed from aeroplanes and captive balloons. One German battalion, ordered up hurriedly to make a counterattack near Flers, suffered so heavily on the way to the trenches that no attack could be made. The stretcher-bearers had all the work to do. German soldiers walked now through places which had once been villages, but were ruins where death lay in wait for them.

Again and again men lost their way up to the lines. Reliefs could only be made at night in case they should be discovered by British airmen and gunners, and even if these German soldiers had trench maps, the guidance was of little use when many trenches had been smashed in, and only shell craters could be found. One young German wrote home: "In the front line of Flers the men were only occupying shell holes. Behind, there was the intense smell of putrefaction which filled the trench almost unbearably. The corpses lie either quite insufficiently covered with earth on the edge of the trench or quite close under the bottom of the trench, so that the earth lets the stench through. In some places bodies lie quite uncovered in a trench recess, and no one seems to trouble about them. One sees horrible pictures — here an arm, here a foot, here a head, sticking out of the earth. And these are all German soldiers — heroes!"

Another young German soldier wrote home to his mother: "Not far from us at the entrance to a dugout nine men were buried, of whom three were dead. All along the trench men kept getting buried. What had been a perfect trench a few hours before was in parts completely blown in. The men are getting weaker. It is impossible to hold out any longer. Losses can no longer be reckoned accurately. Without a doubt many of our people are killed."

These German soldiers, sitting in wet ditches or, as one of them described it, up to the waist in mud, scribbled pitiful things which they hoped might reach their people at home; but they had little hope of escape from the Bath of Blood, and all that these young Germans wrote was what Wenzel himself had experienced.

The German general staff were becoming seriously alarmed by the declining morale of their infantry under the increasing strain of British attacks, and adopted stern measures to cure it. But, Wenzel said, they could not hope to cure the heaps of German dead who were lying on the battlefields, nor the maimed men who were being carried back to the dressing stations, nor bring back prisoners taken in droves by the French and British troops.

All through July and August, German troops fought with stubborn courage and obstinacy, defending every bit of broken woodland, every heap of bricks that was once a village, every line of trenches smashed by heavy shell fire. It is indeed fair to say, and I told Wenzel this, that throughout the battles of the Somme and throughout the war, the British fought against an enemy hard to beat, grim and resolute and inspired, sometimes, with the courage of despair which is hardly less dangerous than the courage of hope.

The Australians who struggled to get the high ground at Pozières did not have an easy task. The Germans made many counterattacks against them. All the ground about there was so smashed that the earth became finely powdered and it was an arena of bloody fighting at close quarters which lasted not for a day or two but for many weeks. In the tunnels of

Mouquet Farm, German soldiers hid and came out to fight the enemy in the rear, long after the site of the farm was lost.

Delville Wood was a living horror which could not, for a long time, be cleared. The Germans fought against an enemy who slashed through its broken trees and fought their way over its barricades of fallen logs, and over the bodies of German soldiers; but the German soldiers crept back with machine guns and would not give up. It was not until the beginning of September that it was finally captured from the Germans.

The Germans never could be sure of safety at any hour of the day or night, even in the deepest dugouts. The British varied their times of attack. At dawn, at noon, when the sun was reddening in the west, just before dusk, in pitch-darkness even, the steady regular bombardment had never ceased all through these days and nights, and would concentrate into the great tumult of sudden drumfire; and waves of men, English, Scottish, Irish, Welsh, Australians, Canadians, South Africans would be sweeping onto the Germans, rummaging down into their dugouts with bombs and bayonets.

In this way Thiepval was encircled so that the German garrison there who had held it for two years knew they were doomed; in this way Guillemont and Ginchy fell, so that in the first place not a man out of the two thousand Germans escaped to tell the tale of horror in the German lines, and in the second place there was no longer fight against the Irish, who stormed it in a wild, fierce rush which even machine guns could not check.

The German general staff was getting flurried, grabbing at battalions from short parts of the line, disorganising its divisions under the urgent need of flinging in men to stop this rot in the lines, ordering counterattacks which were without any chance of success, so that thin waves of men came out into the open — I told Wenzel I had seen this myself — to be swept down by scythes of bullets which cut them clean to the earth.

Before 15 September the Germans hoped that the British offensive was wearing itself out. It seemed to them at least doubtful that after the struggle of two and a half months the British troops could still have spirit and strength enough to fling themselves against new lines; for the German reserves of strength were failing to keep pace with the tremendous strain upon the whole machinery of their organisation. Many of their guns had worn out and could not be replaced quickly enough. Many German batteries also had been knocked out in the emplacements along the line of Bazentin and Longueval, before the artillery was drawn back to Grandcourt and a new line of safety. Battalion commanders clamoured for greater supplies of hand grenades, entrenching tools, trench mortars, signal rockets, and all kinds of fighting material enormously in excess of all previous requirements. The difficulties of dealing with the wounded, who littered the battlefields and choked the road with the traffic of ambulances, became increasingly severe owing to the dearth of horses for transport, and to the longer range of British guns which had been brought forward.

The German general staff studied its next lines of defence away through Courcelette, Martinpuich, Lesboeufs, Morval, and Combles. They did not look too good, but, with luck, and the courage of German soldiers, and, as the Germans thought and hoped, the exhaustion of British troops, these lines were good enough.

On 15 September 1916 the German command had another great shock. The whole line of British troops on the Somme from south of the Ancre rose out of their trenches and swept over the German defences in a great tide. The defences broke hopelessly, and waves of British dashed through. Here and there, as on the German left at Morval and Lesboeufs, the bulwarks stood for a time, but the British pressed against them and round them. On the German right, below the little village of the Ancre, Courcelette fell, and Martinpuich; then High Wood, which the Germans desired to hold at all costs, and had held against incessant attacks by great concentration of artillery, was captured and left behind by the London men.

A new engine of war had come as a demoralising influence among German troops, spreading terror among them. It was the first day out of the tanks, very deadly in their action against machine-gun emplacements, not stopped by trenches or barbed wire, or tree stumps, or refuse heaps of fallen houses. For the first time, Wenzel said, the Germans who had been foremost in all engines of death, were outwitted in this invention of destruction. It was a moment of real panic in the German lines, a panic spreading back from the troops to the high command.

Ten days later, on 25 September — and all this time the French, too, were pressing forward — the British made a new advance. Combles was evacuated without a fight and with a litter of dead in its streets; Gueudecourt, Lesboeufs, and Morval were lost by the Germans; and a day later Thiepval, the greatest fortress position next to Beaumont Hamel, fell, with all its garrison taken prisoners.

There was a great deal of real sickness, mental and physical. The German ranks were depleted by men suffering from fever, pleurisy, jaundice, and stomach complaints of all kinds; they were twisted up with rheumatism after lying in waterlogged holes, lamed for life with bad cases of trenchfoot, and their nerves were so broken that they could do nothing but weep. The nervous cases were the worst and were the greatest number. Many German soldiers went raving mad. The shell-shock victims clawed at their mouths unceasingly, or lay motionless like corpses with staring eyes, or trembled in every limb, moaning miserably and afflicted with great terror.

For Wenzel and many other German soldiers, the Somme battlefields were not only shambles, but a territory which the devil claimed as his own for the torture of men's brains and souls before they died in the furnace of fires. A spirit of revolt against all this crept into the minds of men who retained their sanity, a revolt against the people — in particular, Wenzel said bitterly, the Kaiser — who had ordained this vast outrage against God and humanity. And into the letters of German soldiers crept bitter burning words against millionaires who had grown rich out of the war, and against high-up people who lived in comfort away from the fighting.

Behind the German lines, deserters were shot in batches. By the end of September the German command was hard pressed. From 1 July to 8 September 1916 it had been reckoned, from what Wenzel believed was trustworthy information, that fifty-three German divisions in all were engaged against the Allies on the Somme battlefront. Out of these, only fourteen were still in line on 8 September. Twenty-eight had been withdrawn, broken and exhausted, to quieter areas. Eleven more had been withdrawn to rest billets. Under Allied artillery fire and infantry attacks the average life of a German division, as a unit fit for service on the Somme, was nineteen days. Since the end of June 1916, more than two new German divisions had to be brought into the front line every week to replace those smashed in the process of resisting the Allied attack. Of course, one has to remember that Wenzel, who at heart was a pacifist, when recounting his experiences, tended to make much of the horrors of war. It was not until October 1918, over two years later, that German morale and discipline broke.

Wenzel said it was reckoned, by competent observers in the field, that well over one hundred and twenty German divisions, this number including those which had appeared more than once, passed through the ordeal of the Somme, the place they had named the Bath of Blood.

THE GLORY OF WAR — 6

Funny, in a way, to hear the Hun talk like this. It was not how we had been taught to regard the enemy. Wenzel was young then, as most of us were. He said that having seen only death, fear, and sorrow, and seen how the Kaiser, with the blood of millions on his hands, had escaped into a safe and comfortable retreat, it was a relief to have got away from the falseness, the phoney patriotism and treachery with which he Wenzel, and all the others, including the many young Germans left rotting on the battlefields, had been seduced. I can't say I admired Wenzel for this attitude, and in my opinion, if he couldn't help having these views, then he ought never to have accepted the commission he was given towards the end of the war.

Of course no one in his right mind would wish to say that war is enjoyable, or that fighting, particularly as we had experienced it in the trenches, is anything but hell on earth. Nevertheless, one did one's duty, and with honour.

After the death of Simmons, the rest of 1917 and most of 1918, up to the Armistice, passed in the usual way: marches, shelling, rest periods, leave, bombing, killing, and wounding. The battalion casualties were one-third of the trench strength with which we had gone in, and more than sixty were dead.

At the end of the first week in October we went through Neuve Eglise to the foot of the Messines Ridge by road, then on uneven and greasy single duckboards in the dark, the very dark, then more rain. We were all partly or wholly wet through on reaching the support line just north of Messines. The village was only foundations, brick rubble, and a few stark pillboxes. The ridge had been captured early in June at heavy cost to the Australians, and to the Germans, who counterattacked again and again. The dead of both were still where they fell. From their attitudes it was easy to reconstruct the fighting round the pillboxes: it had been a fierce affair at close quarters, mostly with bombs.

No-man's-land was crawling with German patrols. The next afternoon an officer strolled over from his company and put his head past the door. There was no time to offer a drink as a shell burst in front, then one behind. The CO and others sat still. For over an hour 5.9s rained down, two every minute. There were several direct hits. To the end the servants squatted against the lee wall in a huddle of crockery, pots, pans, and stores. The CO moved HQ.

We had now all the high ground in the north except one or two spurs. At the end of October we were still in a succession of unsettled days: rain, sometimes heavy, at some part of the twenty-four hours. A draft of seventy of our new conscript class joined, eighteen-year-old boys. About ten days later, just as my leave warrant came in, another draft of about two hundred paraded for inspection. All but a score were eighteen-year-olds, although many thousands of men were being kept in the camps at home. Orderly room reckoned that of the drafts of two hundred and forty boys, fewer than forty were left by May of the following year.

Shortly after I came back off leave we moved, at night, to Passchendaele support line. We were shelled going up and had casualties. The men would go about, contrary to orders, until a shelling and the resulting casualties induced immobility.

There was no real cover, only a few badly constructed dugouts. But there were other things to think about, for with the Russian Revolution this was a time of dramatic historic events.

The Pop-Ypres road carried, as always, a procession of vehicles. There was death, desolation, ruin, and decay. The whole country round was waterlogged waste, barely passable except on raised footboard tracks and corduroy roads. A lonely wounded man might perish in a shell hole, or in the mud beside a track, before help arrived. After dark we scrambled to the front at the apex of the Salient, winding our way among shell craters until the Broodseinde-Passchendaele *pavé* was reached. There were only bursts of shelling. At dawn I went with another officer round part of the line. Many scarcely recognizable dead lay about, a few of them Germans. The fields of Passchendaele were a shell-crater swamp. Mud flowed through entrances of cellars; rain dripped through the cracked cemented-brick floors roofing the cellars and onto the occupants. Some of the cellars were crowded to suffocation. Where the position was overlooked, the men were pinned down by day and numbed with cold day and night. In places, as behind Crest Farm, freedom to move about unseen was paid for dearly.

In the morning some of our planes came over, and in the afternoon a German plane was shot down in flames near HQ. One of our lieutenants helped to take out the dead pilot, who wore the Iron Cross, 1st Class, given him by the Kaiser. The guns were active all day. A rapidly filling cemetery nearby was a most unrestful place. It took the labour of a squad to keep the dead in their graves. A sapper officer was killed and buried in the morning; he had to be reburied twice during the day.

On our front German-held Moorslede was separated from Passchendaele by a hollow that was an almost impassable sea of mud, and by the flood water of a meandering stream. In that hollow a few German posts somehow existed, but until the ground dried or froze neither side could hope to advance.

One officer, a young captain, had rejoined the battalion when it was at Ypres before going up to Passchendaele. His company occupied a freshly dug, and very narrowly cut, strong point near Passchendaele Church. There was heavy shelling, often for hours at a time. At times the shelling was like a bombardment before an attack. Under this ordeal one of the officers lost his nerve and had to be sent away. A draft of young soldiers who had just joined were, naturally, very nervy. Standing up hour after hour under heavy shellfire, unable to move about in extremely trying weather conditions, was a severe test of anyone's morale, and this was their first experience of war conditions.

Ration parties were not regular; most of the food arrived sodden with mud and water. Dealing with casualties was pathetic. In that part of the Salient, at that season, many of the wounded died from exposure and inattention owing to the difficulty in getting them away; stretcher cases had to remain until night, and four bearers were required for each stretcher. The second morning the company had casualties from the machine-gun fire of two aeroplanes that flew over less than a hundred feet up. In the afternoon of the third day, an officer and the CSM, who had shared a hole covered with a waterproof sheet, were buried; they had had a minor experience of the kind the day before, but they were then dug out little the worse, although the same shell had killed and wounded some of the others.

To approach Company HQ in daylight was forbidden; to find it in the dark was not easy, as a wire fixed on stakes had to be found first and followed. The relief took place about midnight; it was a quick one because there was nothing to hand over but a few boxes of ammunition and the battered trenches. I heard afterwards that the relieving company had lost fifty per cent of its strength the first night of its tour.

Our casualties since Polygon Wood had exceeded those there. For those three days there were forty-seven killed and forty-three severely wounded, while eighteen slightly wounded remained on duty. Not all was owing to shell fire, and many were newly arrived boys. No one fired a rifle except at an aeroplane, or saw a German except the dead pilot. For the men, Passchendaele was perhaps the most disheartening period of the war, of which some of them had seen a good deal. It was bad enough in support, but that was a tea party compared with the village itself. The mud, the shelling, the inadequate protection seemed to them to point to the hopelessness of the situation. On the first day in December two men were killed and two wounded by a shell bursting in a shack, but another shell landing in the signallers' tent hurt no one.

Russia was now out of the war, and German troops were being transferred to the west, to strike before the American Army could become a decisive factor. For the next few months intensive work was in hand along and behind the British front preparing for a new phase of the war. By this time my new servant, Jones, had settled in. He was an exceptionally good servant. A few years older than Simmons, Jones was nearly thirty when he came to me. He had a fresh country complexion and looked younger than his years. Like Simmons, he was on the small side, but not so thin.

He wore rimless glasses and accepted his orders meekly but with an eager-to-please smile. He wasn't very bright; he hadn't Simmons's intelligence or lively personality, which is probably what made him an even better servant. Also, he had been trained in attending to the needs of others: he'd been employed as a pantry boy in an earl's country house and was satisfied with the cleaning and scrubbing which went on from early morning to late at night. He applied his diligence to my needs, and, once he got used to me, I had to tell him very little.

Jones, poor fellow, was killed a week before the Armistice when a sniper got him. Only the day before I had told him that the chances of living to a ripe old age were distinctly rosy for those of us who had come through this last show. The fighting, by then, in early November 1918, had looked like being the Germans' last despairing stand, and collapse seemed near.

I was still practising my mouth organ regularly. Simmons had been a good teacher. I mastered it well and got a great deal of pleasure playing to myself whenever I got the opportunity.

At the beginning of January 1918 we had returned to our former position at Passchendaele Village. The wind was back in the east and the weather was clear and freezing. Between seven and eight inches of snow fell. One morning, during a two-hour strafe round HQ, I realized my nerve was failing. Any confined space under shellfire had always been hateful; now, sitting in a pillbox, the entrance of which faced the enemy, I became possessed by a picture of each oncoming shell bursting in it, and shrank within myself. Two months later, this loss of the sense of placing and timing shells had become a horrible worry. A period of enforced absence from the shelled area, but not from a sometimes bombed area, restored self-confidence, and by the start of our last long action against Fritz, which was to lead to his defeat, and to the Armistice in November, I felt perfectly all right.

THE GLORY OF WAR — 7

By the middle of January 1918 snow had become sleet, and it was dripping off the roofless broken walls of Ypres when we got into the icy cellars in the Rue de la Boucherie. We had come in for a fair amount of shelling, and had just over a dozen casualties during that tour, half of whom were dead.

One afternoon, at the end of January, we entrained at St. Jean for St. Omer and marched in bright moonlight to billets at Longuenesse, which was within half an hour of St. Omer. Everyone was cheerful. In February there were some frosty moonlit nights and beautiful days. An American aeroplane, the first to be noticed, flew over the area. At home the engineers were on strike. For us there was reduction and reorganization, and we were transferred to another division.

At Estaires the front was five miles away. Points of defence were dug five miles in rear of the town. Officers poured in from disbanded battalions. By mid-February we had over fifty, but this situation with officers wasn't to last. We marched in a drizzle via Doulieu and Steenwerck to a good camp of huts at Hallebeeke Farm near Erquinghem.

At home staple food, such as sugar and meat, was now rationed. There were slight frosts at night; days were clear, sparrows and cats all round. On the last day of February I heard a blackbird. Winter had gone, although Jerry was coming. In March I went on leave and, passing through Steenwerck, saw the latest class of French conscripts leaving home for their depots. Dressed in their Sunday best, beflowered, beribboned, beflagged, befuddled, they were calling on friends' houses and being given liquor. Poor boys!

I came back from leave to a mixed explosive and gas shelling of the area. For the next two days the front and rear areas were shelled, with gas and heavy stuff being used. For all this I was glad to get back to the wholesome humanity of the front. London was never so unpleasant.

We were back on the old Somme line. The German offensive on the Somme had begun on 23 March 1918, so the Germans had recovered in two or three days what we had needed months of toil and slaughter to take from them. By the end of March everyone was feeling a bit done in. The companies in front had been affected by the long suspense, and by frequent warnings that Fritz was coming over.

One night at the beginning of April, as we marched off from Beauval, a large factory village, in starlight, the moon not up, we saw the navigation lights of a procession of our bombing planes going on their baleful mission. The next morning we passed eighteen dead horses and two broken limbers, the result of a direct hit which exploded the ammunition in a limber. For much of the way we passed country people clearing out. Ground that cost the sweat and blood of months the autumn before had been lost in a day.

We marched by night and bivouacked in the open between Henincourt and Millencourt. There was a magnificent dawn, with an azure sky and sunshine all day, a glorious April day. Birds were singing and the sprouting crops were brilliant, spotted with red or slashed with white where shelling or trench digging had thrown up surface soil or underlying chalk.

Our spinney was bursting with leaf; there were catkins on a willow, a blackthorn brake was in flower, and anemones decked the ground.

There were six hundred to a thousand yards of no-man's-land, and both sides were wiring themselves in. The line was much as it was before July 1916, but villages were being shelled that we had spared then. By now they had been cleared of their inhabitants. According to the orderly room, of our eighteen-year-olds who had joined in October-November, the largest number now left in any company was nine. Then, on 19 April at 10:00 pm, we moved to the front line.

The German line was the Ancre and the steep bank on the other side. At 7:30 am on 22 April 1918, our artillery opened fire and the infantry went over. The German barrage dropped within seconds of our own. The first walking wounded soon arrived. The slighter early wounded came in the usual rush and the first stretcher case was brought down in forty minutes.

At 10:00 am it began to rain. For want of stretcher-bearers, a dump of wounded had to be made on the Albert road. By midnight thirty lay there. The number rose to fifty and remained at that for three hours, although German prisoners and our pioneer squads worked unceasingly. Stores and ration limbers clattered up and down the road, which was never shelled, but there were no blankets or dressings. The width of no-man's-land had become from six hundred yards to thirty or forty at Lone Tree, on our left. Brigade casualties were said to be about seven hundred. From among the prisoners one very youthful German officer talked to our equally youthful officers.

At dawn five enemy planes shot out of a low cloud and flew close and boldly over our lines; the Lewis gun fire that opened on them was a feeble effort. In the afternoon a German pilot flew high just behind us, then his wings folded over his head and he dropped like a stone.

Our casualties for the tour were about fifty, a large proportion from snipers and our own guns. I was lousy, and so were the men, for we had had only one bath in five weeks and no change of underclothing. Our health kept good despite the discomforts, broken rest, and not quite satisfactory feeding; rations were no more than enough for the demands of temperature and work. Quite a lot of men were only nineteen or twenty. Our tired division couldn't get rest, but there was quiet confidence that we could wear Fritz down.

On the first day in May it was still grey and raw and the mist chilled us. The second day the sun came out and I saw the first swallow; the air was filled with the song of larks. There was a shortage of officers in the line. One of our companies had only two officers on a front of about four hundred yards. Heavy rain came and there were inches of water in the trenches, with streamlets on roads and tracks. Forget-me-not was the favourite flower, and there was a lot of the white variety. We had some fine days in May but were too near the big guns to have anything but noise at night. We relieved on the left front of Bouzincourt as German planes came bombing in the moonlight. At the beginning of June we took over the Mesnil sector.

Then we moved to the reserve line. The weather was fine. The battalion was warned for a big raid on returning to the line. The area to be raided was a half mile of road and railway embankment immediately north of Aveluy Wood. For six days we practised the raid; after this we had to spend five nights laying guiding tapes in no-man's-land.

As the appointed day approached, the weather turned wet. On the afternoon of our move there was a colossal thunderstorm with torrential rain. At 9:00 pm we moved off. Everything was soaking wet. Throughout the seemingly interminable march of several miles a cold drizzle fell. Sometimes, because of blocks caused by stretcher cases coming down or stores going up, we had to wait for twenty minutes, up to our knees and higher, in water and mud.

About two hours were spent huddled in the front line, standing in water, shivering with cold, wet and dispirited, with our bombs and Vickers gun equipment sunk into inches of mud and slime, and with the rum ration arriving too late to be dished out. Nearly a minute before zero, at 2:00 am, the trench mortars opened fire, and when our artillery opened up the enemy guns replied instantly. My part of the trench was cut in chalk, very narrow and deep, and there was over a foot of water in it. In spite of some shells and an infernal din, the company started across as if on parade. Going down the slope it accelerated to the double and found the sunken road. The road was empty, having obviously been unoccupied for weeks. Every section was accounted for and the second wave sent on.

Within five minutes we were enfiladed by machine guns firing from Aveluy Wood, and later a most accurate trench-mortar bombardment commenced. About twenty casualties were incurred in the road and on the railway. The second wave went through the trees to the river and still found nothing. When it was time to return, the trench mortars had ceased firing, but the Germans started traversing machine-gun fire along our line.

The worst of a raid is not always felt in front. One officer, whose observation post was in a trench immediately behind our front line, told me afterwards that, when the guns opened up, he found himself in a German barrage, and there he spent the longest hour of his life. Four or five men were crouching in the trench as flashes, smoke, and earth filled the air, while the raided area to be observed and the raiders' light signals were completely blotted out, and all rearward lines were broken. The trenches around crumbled under terrific counterbombardment. Every second he expected a direct hit on the spot where he and the men were imprisoned. He said that every moment seemed an hour, every minute an age. He feared to look at his watch for it seemed to be motionless. One of his men fainted under the strain. The relief they experienced when the guns lifted is unbelievable to any but those who have lived through a similar experience.

After the raid we returned to Forceville. It was a thoroughly bad show from start to finish. It was futile in its aim and the organization was bad, for the guns and trench mortars did not start together. The men were left in ignorance about things and were, therefore, very windy. Finally, the raid should have been postponed because of weather conditions. From another company two officers and a strong patrol went out on their own, but beyond finding a few corpses they achieved nothing.

At the end of June we moved up to the front again. The foliage and the undergrowth in the wood were still dense. Jerry seldom used heavy stuff; he realized that spraying a wood with shrapnel produced better results from flying pieces that cannoned off the trees and caused ragged wounds. Shrapnel striking the leaves was not a pleasant sound: it was as if an almighty rainstorm was going on. Sniping was one of the usual pastimes. Generally, there were a couple of our men sitting up in the trees, but we thought the Germans were better at the game. They scored several direct hits.

Often, in that closely planted wood, stretchers could not be handled, and the clearing of the mangled was a long and distressing affair. A hammock was improvised by tying jackets together; this was then used to move a corporal with a painful and hopeless-looking belly wound, whose struggles must have lessened what little chance of life he had, a chance that wasn't realized.

Another raid was ordered, a battalion affair. Its objective, Hamel. Another terrific thunderstorm broke over the area and the support line was knee-deep in water. In the evening the weather cleared, then there was a fine starlit night with just enough light to pick up landmarks.

At 11:00 pm, with a sudden terrific uproar a hurricane bombardment, together with intense overhead machine-gun fire perfectly timed, fell on Hamel. The battalion rose to its feet and started. Hamel was a mass of red flames and flashes, and one began to feel a tremendous exultation. In two minutes all approaches were barraged, communication trenches to

Beaumont Hamel being specially dealt with. Our main line of advance was northeast.

Realizing that the sooner we got to our objective, the safer we would be, I made for the junction at the double, leaping over half-filled trenches, stumbling, falling over wire. The final rush was over an old British cemetery in which wooden crosses loomed up white in the lurid glare of the artillery. We found nothing.

A Verey light was put up from the road about a hundred yards on our right, and a machine gun opened fire with tracer bullets over the ground we had crossed; then more lights were put up. It looked as if the battalion was being enfiladed. We could see the Germans, five of them, working their gun for all they were worth. Before we could get near enough to rush them, we were attacked in the flank by a bombing section. Some quick work with bomb, revolver, and bayonet made casualties on both sides. At that moment the sergeant's party attacked with bayonet. The Germans bolted. We chased them into the road, killing some and capturing others, and we became so excited that we roamed over no-man's-land looking for victims, but forgot all about the machine-gun which was not brought in.

The company's right party went too far and got into trouble beyond the village; the platoon commander was killed and his corporal wounded and captured. In a wrecked churchyard there were broken tombstones everywhere. From among the tombs suddenly rose two very frightened little Jerries; they were only seventeen or eighteen years old. With hands above the head they kept up a perpetual chant of "Kamerad". We took them along while we explored farther; they trotted beside us, causing no trouble at all.

The din had become indescribable. By now the sappers were blowing up the strong points and dugouts; some twenty were demolished; they dealt with the village thoroughly. One bungling sapper blew himself up together with some of our men. Trench mortars across the river had also started up and were making the village unhealthy for us. These were the two main sources of our casualties.

When Hamel had been combed front to rear, from the railway to its western limit, and no more Germans could be found, the companies were withdrawn. Over fifty Germans were estimated to have been killed; many were found dead and dying in the village, especially at the crossroads. We had one officer and three other ranks killed, three officers and forty-four other ranks wounded, and eight missing.

An active German withdrawal was taking place. Locally the Germans had recrossed the Ancre. We were in what had once been their support line. A great many dead, especially Germans, lay in no-man's-land; most of them had been there since the spring. Americans were again attached for instruction; what was chiefly impressed on them was that they were a bit late in coming over.

For the first time companies were supplied with carrier pigeons. An old and a young bird had to be released together. It was understood that they would fly to corps HQ. Not many of the pigeons seemed to survive. The mess cook probably knew most about the last phase of the pigeons. We had entered a tremendously busy time. The impulse eastwards which the Western Front had been given was gathering mass and momentum. Night operations were held up a good deal by the dropping of brilliant Verey lights of greatly improved pattern, which were effective over a wide area and burned for a long time, compelling us to stand still until they went out.

One of the surest signs that a large-scale operation was impending was the settlement of officers' mess accounts. Albert was being heavily shelled, and there were large fires in the town. We had orders to send a patrol over the river. A lieutenant, a cheery round-faced Lancashire boy, took out three or four men. We watched them cross. The Germans began dropping heavy stuff about, and the lieutenant was hit on the head. He was brought in, but nothing could be done for him.

There were isolated instances of hand-to-hand encounters. After the capture of the main German position there was no organized opposition. Over two hundred prisoners were taken. The CO ordered me to remain as guide until we caught up with the advance. While waiting there I used the men that were with me to collect some thirteen of our dead. As no padre appeared handy, and as I had a prayer book in my pocket, I read portions from the burial service over them as their common grave was being filled in.

A general move was being made beyond the original objectives, against a line the Germans were understood to be holding a thousand yards east of where we were. It was hoped to get astride the ridge on our front at High Wood. When we did move off at 2:30 am, progress was difficult because of intense darkness, the shell-pitted ground, narrow-gauge railways, innumerable trenches and dugouts, trees, and road screens. Added to all these there was, ahead of us, a very heavy bombardment of roads and other spots vital to the Germans. All most of us remembered of that march was blundering and stumbling along interminably, and having a vivid impression of men marching in extended order, silhouetted against the light from burning huts and dumps.

We went forward, following the general direction of the obvious battlefront. The going was rough as there was no road or track of any continuity; detours had to be made frequently owing to crossroads having been blown up. Later on in the night, progress with wagons became impossible, the roads and tracks were so broken up. All available men manhandled as much water and rations as they could, and we carried our loads in this way for what appeared to be many weary miles. Before us it was as if the battle was waging all night, with much shell fire and noise, flashing explosions, burnings; and tremendous activity was apparent in a general move forward of guns and ammunition, all cross-country fashion. The battalion reached Contalmaison without any opposition.

We took position just east of Mametz Wood, having Bazentin-le-Grand, Longueval, and Ginchy as the successive objectives. Zero was 4:00 am on a very misty morning. Before daylight we came up against serious machine-gun opposition, which gradually increased. Because of the mist and early-morning darkness, we veered out of line in the direction of Caterpillar Wood; soon realizing this, we worked inwards towards our left over some ruined buildings, damaged emplacements, and the stumpy undergrowth of Flat-iron Copse. Here we stumbled on some very recently killed and wounded Germans.

I then followed the Longueval-Contalmaison high road. In a quarry on the left of this road we saw the aid post up to the eyes in work, dealing with casualties of all units of the division, as well as of attached troops. At approximately midday the division seemed to have come to a halt. On taking stock we found our numbers considerably depleted of both officers and men. Enfilading machine guns on the ridge above Montauban, outside our area, had done a lot of mischief.

The Germans had assembled in Trones Wood and were streaming out of it, moving parallel to our front and towards our left. They were harassed right along by machine-gun and rifle fire from our line. We went forward to meet them with the bayonet but opened out to let through the cavalry, who had an exciting dash at the counterattacking enemy. The Germans broke and cleared back before doing any great damage, but there were quite a few casualties among the cavalry.

The night passed without incident for us. In the morning another officer and I visited High Wood. Like Mametz Wood it was in a much worse state than when a few of us saw it in 1916, having been more fought over since then. Its tree stumps were fewer, and the ground was a tangle of undergrowth, shell holes, and wire. We found the graves of several men of ours who had fallen there in 1916.

It was now the end of August, and we had been in the line since the first week of the month, moving forward and fighting for six days, and the strain of this more or less active warfare was beginning to tell on those of us who had been in it the whole time. Fortunately, the weather had been good although the nights were cold, and rations and water had never failed. But the Germans were making good use of cycle machine guns, and companies had casualties. Heavy shelling continued. Our strength was considerably less than when we crossed the Ancre: there were only two officers for each company, all of them subalterns.

Overnight on 1 September, which was a Sunday, the Germans withdrew from Lesboeufs. The road leading to the assembly was being shelled when we went forward. From 4:45 am we lay under an intense barrage; then, when we had gone about a thousand yards, we began to be really troubled by Germans about five hundred yards away on our left, who kept up a continuous fire, enfilading us. All had gone well until we came suddenly face to face with an inferno of machine-gun fire while we were yet in open country. We scattered and took cover wherever we could. I dropped into a shell hole in the middle of an open field, and signallers near me did likewise. Then suddenly there was an appalling and withering outburst of machine-gun and rifle fire from the front and left-front, the west and northwest of Sailly-Saillisel. Our fellows went down like ninepins, and soon all was confusion.

To stay was to be slaughtered. I shouted to the men to rush the railway. I could see the survivors making their way back. Counterattacking Germans were all about. Isolated shooting, bombing, and some hand-to-hand fighting took place over a fairly wide area. The German counterattack drove us to the right and, as best we could, we organized a withdrawal along the railway line. All companies reported disaster and the loss of their officers. One sergeant, who was known as a tremendously forceful talker, was shot through the mouth. Our senior signaller, in tears, told me that he had just found his nephew dead, bayonetted in several places. In just under two weeks his nephew would have celebrated his nineteenth birthday.

I came across the padre, who had collected a number of wounded, ours and German. He was walking along a road on which were some dead horses. The day had been disastrous to the battalion; thirty-six were dead and our company had been almost wiped out. Afterwards, the causes of the disaster became clear: the battalion had advanced with both flanks uncovered and found itself in a cul-de-sac, and there were still Germans who were well led, and who had plenty of fight in them.

Officers and men were dead beat from fatigue and want of sleep. The battalion had a strength now of about ninety. The weather was fine but the desire for relief became an obsession. The men as a whole were patient but listless, having almost reached the limit of endurance. A youngster, one of a group of thirty among whom a shell burst, became violently mad with shock; he was like a hysterical child and had to be restrained forcibly from running wildly towards the enemy.

Relief came at last, and the battalion enjoyed a well-earned rest for three days. Since we had gone into the Aveluy Wood sector, early in August, there had been practically a continuous performance of trench warfare, followed by more or less open fighting. None of us had taken off our clothing during that time, and we had been wet many times since we waded the Ancre. Our casualties had been nearly three hundred and sixty, and we had come out of action reduced to less than one company.

THE GLORY OF WAR — 8

I will go as briefly as possible through the next few weeks, which led up to the Armistice, but while doing so there is a particular incident I would like to mention concerning my servant, Jones.

One morning in the middle of September, which turned out to be a perfect early autumn day with bright sunshine, it was very quiet and still and not a shot was fired along the whole front. We thought the quiet rather ominous. We had finished breakfast, and our cook, an old soldier, was in his shirt sleeves washing up. Jones was sitting nearby talking to him. Suddenly, at 9:20 am, we heard in the distance what sounded like a long ripple spreading in a wide arc along our front, and almost simultaneously a hurricane of shells descended on us. We lay down in the shelter, biting the dust. We realized at once that this was something quite different from yesterday's shelling, and was almost certainly the prelude to an attack. Where we were, the shells were falling as on the day before, about twenty yards behind the trench. This intense bombardment lasted forty minutes; then it lifted as suddenly as it had started.

No one in our post had been hit. We scrambled up and heard shouts from the trench: "Here they come."

The Germans were coming over the skyline in extended order, in sections, on each side of the communication trench which entered our line at this point. Two Germans were carrying a light machine gun, one firing the gun from the hip as he walked, the other holding the box with the cartridge belt. There were two others away on the left, but in front of us the first lot was quite close.

On our left the nearest part of the unit had disappeared along the trench, leaving a long stretch empty, and leaving our flank in the air. A section or so of the Germans got in there, but one of our young sergeants picked up a Lewis gun, jumped out on top, and, getting a position for the gun, shot eight of the attackers.

I was told to go quickly to the far end of our line and see what was happening, so I ran off down the trench and found it had been almost completely blown in. I picked my way over masses of broken earth and could not find a man alive. Three of our posts had been wiped out. At the far end one small post had survived and was firing away, just as the Germans on this part of the front were beginning to appear in an extended line on the crest.

Our artillery was now putting over a very effective shrapnel barrage. The raiders began to waver, then ran back. I could hear firing and bombs bursting at the end I had come from, but after a time that ceased and all was quiet. I listened intently but could hear no sound. It was impossible to know what had happened. The post at my end numbered eight or ten sound men. A few wounded, who were able to move, had joined them from the next post, but all the rest had been wiped out.

The main part of the raid had been repulsed, thanks mainly to the young sergeant and a few others of the old army in the post. When I got back to them they were sitting in a group, calmly cleaning their rifles and discussing the morning's shooting. Our cook, still in his shirt sleeves, had gone back to his pots and pans. Jones was there, and I thought he looked a bit shaken. On the parapet lay a dead German NCO. Our losses had been heavy: one company was reduced to about twenty men all told.

Then we ran into a perfectly hellish bombardment which covered the whole of our front and support lines. It was impossible to seek shelter forward, so we had to try and work our way back to HQ. We went in pauses and dashes to dodge the shell fire. We found that HQ area also had been severely shelled and all the support companies had suffered under the shelling. Besides some half dozen prisoners, the Germans left thirteen dead among us, whatever other casualties they may have had. Our losses proved to be greater under their bombardment. A company commander was very upset that another company had failed to move all their dead; he said it was bad for the morale of his men, which was no doubt true, but the company of which he was complaining had all it could do to get away its wounded.

A week later, a march to trenches on Fins Ridge took us through our heavy artillery positions. We were part of a brigade in reserve during a full-dress show. As darkness fell, the stupendous volume of the bombardment for this attack was apparent. It was the greatest show of fireworks I had yet seen. The front was a line of flame, the explosions so numerous that they combined into one continuous ear-splitting crash. At 8:00 am, with this going on, we were side-stepped to the left into trenches north-east of Dessart Wood. Our recent Gouzeaucourt trenches were just over the ridge in front of us, but the enemy had been driven back since we were there. Rations were late in coming because the transport officer's party, on the way up, had had a particularly bad time from the shelling. It was then I asked Jones if he was feeling all right. He thanked me and said there was nothing wrong, so I put it down to tiredness and strain brought about by more or less continuous action with so few short rest periods. We were under orders to be relieved, and it was rumoured we were going a long way back into corps reserve. The men in my party were singing lustily; then an order for the front line came in and the singing stopped.

One night I went out on patrol with a sergeant and one man. On the way back we came across several wounded men lying out in no-man's-land, and took them in. It was beginning to get light when we reached the trench. During the day several more wounded men found their way back into our lines. In the evening there was again a heavy strafe of our front line; however, that night, at last, we were relieved.

On Fins Ridge the cookers were waiting for us with a meal of porridge. I don't remember ever tasting anything so good. We marched on most of the night, to good huts at Lechelle. The men were in tremendous form, singing hymns all the way. We were glad to have seen the last of Gouzeaucourt and district. We were on the road most of the day and passed the GOC on the roadside; he offered congratulations on the Gouzeaucourt show and shouted to the men: "Well done, did you get the bayonet to work?"

A week was spent refitting, reorganising, and training. The arrival of large drafts, including nine officers, almost brought the battalion up to strength. We had time to ramble about with excursions into Doullens, and there was basketball. Jones continued to look after me as efficiently and punctiliously as ever, although he was quieter than normal and seemed preoccupied. At the end of September 1918 we went by bus to a hut-and-tent camp at Sorel-le-Grand, southwest of Gouzeaucourt. Stirring events were taking place a few miles ahead. The Hindenburg Line had been broken through on the 27th, to everyone's surprise, and Jerry was on the run again. But there were rumours of disaster to the Americans on our right.

One evening, at the beginning of October, the battalion marched via Epehy to trenches near Lampire. Our route was on top of a high bare plateau which was being shelled with bursts of 5.9s. The enemy must have had a line in front of his main position there, because the ground was thick with American dead. We had come on a long line of tanks, twelve or fourteen, all blown up and out of action; they had been manned by American crews and had run onto one of the antitank minefields laid in 1917. Deprived of the cover of fire from the tanks, the Sammies had come in for heavy casualties and had to be extricated from their difficulties by the Australians.

The Hindenburg Line was about a mile in front; it extended like a long snake as far as we could see in either direction. Three thick broad belts of wire, with a space between each, protected it. Far away in the distance we could see the smoke and bursting shells of the battle in progress. In the late afternoon we moved on again, came to Bony, and spent the night in part of the Hindenburg support line.

Our next move to a line west of the outskirts of Le Catalet-Gouy was a short one. The position was well wired and covered by a highish cliff, on top of which had been a line of machine guns which had taken a heavy toll of the attackers; but there were also a great many of our dead on, and in front of, the wire. We felt that the enemy retreat was being accelerated to a point when it must fairly soon become a rout. A pillbox that had been used as a dressing station was full of dead; when the bodies were removed it made very comfortable quarters. Some parcels arrived, and we settled down to enjoy quite a good dinner from the contents.

A short march in the morning brought us up to south of Basket Wood near Pienne. We were now beyond the old Somme battlefield. The countryside was a pleasant contrast to the much-fought-over ground that had been our habitation and our outlook for so long.

Well before this, the Germans had prepared the reserve line, their next main line, two and a half miles behind the Hindenburg Line. Not all trenches had been dug, but concrete machine-gun emplacements had been built, deep dugouts had been prepared, and a thick, double barbed-wire entanglement ran along the whole length. For the most part the line was in open country, so it had a wide field of fire.

A night attack had been decided on. Zero was at 1:00 am, but we failed completely against undamaged wire and heavy machine-gun fire. The sunken road just south of the east end of Aubencheul-aux-Bois was choked with advanced parties and machine-gunners, all seeking cover from the rain of machine-gun bullets which swept over the top. There seemed to be a complete deadlock.

We had to march through Aubencheul, which is built on an eastern slope overlooking Villers. The night was very dark and wet. As we came over the ridge and through the main street, we saw many lights going up from the direction of the German trenches in front of Villers and on our left front, and a good deal of machine-gun fire was coming into, or going over Aubencheul. This was our first indication that all was not well.

We were met at the end of the sunken road by a colonel who told us that the attack had failed, that our supporting tank had not turned up, but that we were to go ahead and do our best to get into the village. Leading to the village was a long straight road, so we marched up the road in fours, fixing bayonets as we went. Suddenly, German SOS rockets went up all round and we were fired on heavily from a trench just ahead. Almost at the same moment our tank came lumbering up behind, firing into us. We scattered in all directions, taking cover as best we could. The tank came right into the middle of us and circled round, shooting at anything moving seen against the lights of the show. A lot of our men were hit. At the same time, Fritz was barraging the road heavily with howitzers and trench mortars. Shells burst with tremendous crashes on the road; happily, one hit our tank and put it out of action.

It was beginning to get light. We were fired on from Pierre Mill on the left, and from trenches directly behind us which had been unsuccessfully attacked earlier. Taking cover behind a railway embankment, we returned the fire with our Lewis Guns. A number of the enemy came out of Pierre Mill and ran away across the open, and we could see others slipping away down communication trenches in the direction of Angelus Orchard.

We were fired on by a field gun on the rising ground just behind the village. We had several casualties from the first two or three shells before we got back into the sunken road between the brick field and the station. Very soon one of our planes came over, so we lit a ground flare to show where we were. It replied by dropping bombs into the brick field; then our own artillery started shelling us, so things were not too comfortable. A runner was sent to the CO. Soon a message came back to say he was having the artillery stopped and directing it onto the enemy, and that another tank was coming to help by working round the north of the village; also that he was returning to us thirty-two men who had absconded at the time we were given the orders to do our best to get into the village. One of those who had absconded was my servant, Jones.

When I questioned him, he seemed in a state of shock, and was shaking and almost in tears. He said he'd had a letter from his wife and his little boy hadn't been well. He said he hadn't deserted, he'd only gone back to see if the rations had arrived. I hadn't time to do more than tell him to pull himself together. Those thirty-two were fortunate in having a humane CO. A charge of desertion in the face of the enemy meant the death penalty, which was almost invariably carried out. Jones was lucky, for excessively nervous soldiers at the front were a constant problem. Cowardice in a male was regarded, at that time, as one of the worst types of degradation.

According to the official records of the British army, between the outbreak of war and the end of March 1920, a total of three hundred and forty-six officers and men were tried by courts-martial and sentenced to be summarily executed by firing squad. The details of their trials and executions were closed to the public.

The first British soldier to be executed was court-martialled a month after war had broken out. He was eighteen and was found hiding in a barn on Baron de Rothschild's estate at Tournau. The gamekeeper asked him what he was doing there, and the teenager replied: "I've had enough of it. I want to get out."

He was tried for desertion by a field general court martial, the members of which were a colonel, a captain, and a lieutenant. When the court martial sentenced him to death, no address in mitigation of sentence was made on his behalf. That afternoon Sir John French, the Commander-in-Chief, confirmed the sentence. Two days later, a captain in the provost marshal's branch visited the young private in the guard room of his battalion just before 6:30 am. The captain read out the findings of the court martial to him and told him that the sentence of death had been confirmed. Within the next forty-five minutes — sometimes, as in this case, the condemned man was informed of his execution the same morning — the youngster was taken before a firing squad and shot. The boy had made a soldier's will in the back of his army pay book, leaving what few worldly possessions he owned to his girl friend.

Another private was tried on two charges of desertion. Both offences had taken place when he was seventeen, and when he really should not have been on active service at all. The boy's corps commander said the death sentence should be commuted because of this soldier's extreme youth. The army commander and the commander in chief had no hesitation in saying he should be shot. He was executed during the last week of February, when he was just over eighteen years old.

In 1916 one of my own men was accused of cowardice. I knew him well and was among many officers who pleaded to have the death sentence commuted. The accused man was a private and came from the north of England. A stockily built quiet fellow in his mid-thirties, he was in reserve when war broke out and, like Simmons, who got on well with him, had been in France from early on. The man had been detailed as member of a patrol led by a lieutenant and which was to go out under cover of darkness.

No-man's-land in that sector was about two hundred to two hundred and fifty yards wide. The lieutenant said afterwards that the whole party had been in an extremely jittery state, as they'd been at the front for some time without relief. When the moment arrived to move forward from the British line, the private refused to go, saying it would be certain death and that he had a wife and five children at home to consider.

For the defence it was explained that the man's nerves had been affected by an experience five months before when a shell burst close to him in the trench, splattering into his face the head and brains of one his comrades. Before this his conduct had been impeccable, and he had shown great courage under fire, but after the incident he'd changed completely and was continually reporting sick.

The court not only recommended mercy but suggested a thorough examination by a medical board. Nevertheless, sentence of death was confirmed and, as usual with most of the condemned men, he was informed of his impending execution the evening before he was taken out and shot.

Before the end of 1914, Sir John French confirmed more death sentences. The approach of most senior officers to the accused was autocratic and stern, and the medical officers, with few exceptions, were no less brutal than the generals in making sure that the death sentence was carried out.

Towards the end of 1916, the strains of interminable battle were having an appreciable effect on the troops, and men who had formerly been courageous soldiers were sometimes yielding to the impulse of uncontrolled panic. Sometimes also, at courts martial for desertion, accused soldiers revealed in their inarticulate ways the eternal suffering of their loneliness, and their hopeless despair of ever seeing their homes and their families again.

Although it was customary for a firing party to be supplied from the condemned soldier's own unit, there was no inflexible rule to this effect. Sometimes the men were taken from another battalion in the same brigade.

The night before his execution, the prisoner was kept at a camp or in a billet as near as possible to the place where he was going to be shot. If the death sentence had already been promulgated to him, he could receive, if he wished, a visit from a chaplain of his own religious denomination. Meanwhile, the last preparations were put in hand. A grave was dug and the necessary stores were collected. A message from brigade to a condemned soldier's battalion in April 1916 told them they must provide a chair, a blanket, and two ropes, and that their medical officer must have available in the morning a bandage and a piece of white cloth to mark the heart. The message also said that two men were to be standing by with spades to fill in the grave after the prisoner's body had been put into it.

Executions were ordered to be carried out, according to various divisional orders, at daybreak, or as early an hour as might be found convenient, or as early as possible after the first light of dawn. On the final morning, a chaplain was always at hand to support and try and comfort the prisoner.

An execution was sometimes carried out in private. Sometimes it was carried out before an audience of compelled spectators. In September 1915 a divisional commander directed that the whole of the accused soldier's own battalion should be present to watch. So great was the natural dread of the firing squad that many men awaiting trial by court martial, on capital charges, endeavoured to escape from custody. One private managed to abscond three times before being executed in April 1915.

Before the firing party was marched to the scene of execution, an officer, a sergeant-major, or a senior NCO would probably impress on them the importance of shooting to kill from motives of sheer humanity. The majority of men detailed for the firing parties carried it through to the letter, and the executions towards the end of the war differed in no way from those at the beginning.

The generals who had to make the fateful decision as to whether the prisoners were going to live or die were inured to the paltry value of the lives of the men they commanded. These generals were, of necessity, dealing out death warrants in the abstract almost daily. It happened each time they ordered an offensive operation; it happened each time they sent a battalion up the line. To terminate the existence of some remote and numbered soldier at such a time was scarcely a matter of very great significance. Death was no stranger in the forward lines of battle, and the total number of soldiers in the British Army who were executed by firing squads during the First World War is utterly insignificant compared with the massive carnage at the front.

Most soldiers were sustained in action by an innate belief in their own invulnerability. For the condemned man the certainty of proximate death to be suffered ignominiously at the hands of his own comrades must have been a horrifying prospect. The few who lost their nerve were, at the time of their condemnation, branded as shirkers, funks, and degenerates whose very existence was best forgotten. But death did not come to them, random and abrupt, in the field of battle; it came with measured tread as the calculated climax of an archaic and macabre ritual carried out, supposedly, in the interests of discipline and morale. Therefore, you can see what I mean when I say that Jones and those others who absconded were lucky not to have been put on a charge of desertion. I think he realized this himself, because there was no further trouble.

Anyhow, we pushed into the village again and took some prisoners. In a cellar we found a half-demented little Jerry, a boy who looked no more than sixteen and who gave himself up readily enough. The prisoners were so docile that only one man was sent to HQ with them, as escort. On one occasion, our chap taking back prisoners fell down a shell hole and the prisoners arrived carrying their escort.

A decision to work through the remainder of the village had been made. We did this without meeting any further opposition. Going forward there was a view from the crest over a big stretch of open country on the right, with a disordered crowd of the enemy retiring. There were gun limbers, horse-drawn wagons, and motor lorries. The sight of this gave our company a feeling of exhilaration, and we opened fire.

By 4:00 pm the day was over as far as the battalion was concerned. We had been at it for twelve hours. An occasional shell from a long-range gun was all that came over; so, by penetrating the village, we had turned the German defence on both flanks and turned an awkward situation into a great success. Our aid post was busy with a great many wounded, both our own men and the Germans. Our losses during the day were heavy. An outstandingly good officer was killed, as was our non-conformist padre, who, in the early morning, had insisted on going forward with us.

The night was spent in Villers-Outreaux. I could not help contrasting this kind of warfare with that we had been used to during the preceding years. I never believed that we could lose the war, but I knew, like many more, that Jerry could hit very hard, and I expected that he would do so again. Here we had been advancing from the Ancre, and the opposition was becoming weaker at every scrap. His readiness to give in that day showed his morale was gone.

We marched to Bertry, and were the first Allied troops to rest there since the fight at Le Cateau on 26 August 1914. The villages had been occupied by the Germans as rest billets for four years. In general, hatred of the Germans was deep; a man would spit on their dead who were laid out for burial. The villagers were friendly and kind to us, but they seemed as yet too dazed to realize that the German occupation was actually a thing of the past. They were badly clad and looked sadly emaciated.

The German retreat was speeding up. We were about midway between Montay and Neuvilly. Battalion HQ shared Rambourlieux — the men called it Rumblebelly — Farm with brigade HQ. The farm was on high ground, a landmark for miles around. Traffic about it was hazardous, for it was shelled constantly with gas and high explosive. The railway embankment was hit by our heavies and gas projectiles. The Germans replied with an unusually heavy volume of fire, for these days, on our river positions. A shell burst on one of our posts, killing or wounding everyone in it. After dark the battalion returned to Troisvilles. Baths had been fitted up, so we became clean and rested. Troisvilles had been shelled continuously since first we came to it, and casualties were of daily occurrence.

The crossing of the Selle was accomplished against stout resistance. The high railway embankment, not the river, had been the enemy's main line. It was held by numerous well-placed machine-gun posts, which our artillery and machine guns smothered. An exceptional number of machine guns were found abandoned, both damaged and undamaged, along the embankment, and the large number of German dead beside them was eloquent testimony to the high total of the defenders' losses.

We were relieved, returned to Troisvilles, and were ordered to be ready to move in the morning. The next day the whole third army moved forward. We left Troisvilles at 5:30 am for the assembly position at Amerval Ridge. At midday we advanced in artillery formation.

An enemy aeroplane swooped on us, but his aim was so bad that we had no casualties then; later we had a few from long-range shelling. At dusk we reached the neighbourhood of Croix and settled in for the night, but were on an hour's notice. Companies were disciplined for untidiness and untidy billets. Special orders were issued about saluting.

At the end of October a very heavy strafe at 6:00 in the morning looked like the prelude to an attack, but nothing happened on our section of the front. Sniping from housetops, street corners, and cellars was the chief activity in villages through which the front ran. In places there was safety on one side of the road and sudden death on the other. Winkling these lairs and little strongholds was a popular pastime.

It was altogether a queer sort of warfare for troops bred to war in trenches, but the technique, in its essential, is as old as warfare. It consisted in creeping up to a post and watching for a favourable chance to surprise it; the gain was then used to attack the next enemy post in reverse, or threaten it, so that one's own next post could come up into line. Sometimes there was stout resistance. Posts and patrols were encouraged to let pass enemy patrols they could cope with, who did not see them, and then to close on them from behind. A prisoner was refusing to give his particulars when one of our officers, known for his blunt manners, handed to the man a German wooden cross and a pencil; after that there was no further trouble.

The chief opposition to our forward movement was about three hundred yards in front of company HQ, where the Germans had a barrier on the main road beyond the centre of the village. As Jones was peeping round a corner to observe it, a sniper shot him through the head, killing him instantly. I went quickly round to the back of the house and found in the cellar twenty civilians who shouted excitedly, "Anglais", and embraced us. They had been crammed in that cellar for several days. Next day, 28 October — it's strange that both Jones and Simmons were killed on the 27th — was a quiet day.

I was amused by the issue of an order instructing our trench mortars to blow a gap in a garden fence but insisting that all care was to be taken not to damage anything beyond the needed width of the gap. It made strange reading to anyone who had seen the destruction of everything, regardless of its use, value, and associations, on every front from the Somme to Nieuport.

Poix and Englefontaine were shelled heavily by the Germans, who always fired in front of their posts with great confidence and accuracy. Villages shared by the Germans and the BEF were being shelled by both artilleries, so the clearing out of all the remaining civilians was ordered. As the desire of refugees to take the most needed of their chattels tied them to the roads, and the roads were always liable to be shelled, instances of loss of goods and of life were not uncommon in those days.

In the evening we were relieved and returned to Croix, being heavily shelled on the way. The operations had cost the battalion two subalterns, of whom no trace was then, or since, discovered.

Bulgaria was already out of the war, having signed an armistice and surrendered on 29 September. Turkey signed and surrendered on 31 October. Now Austria-Hungary was suing for peace, so we felt our prospects were brightening. On 2 November the battalion returned to line.

The morning of 3 November 1918 was lovely, a quiet day of preparations, inspecting rifles, ammunition, and bombs, and giving instructions. At HQ, maps and aerial reconnaissance photographs were studied. One of the subalterns went sick and was sent down the line; in the evening a substitute reported, a youngster who had come to the front for the first time.

Zero for our brigade was 6:15 am. Our artillery opened on time. Almost as the action began we became enveloped in thick fog. Although it made the keeping of direction difficult, it helped the attack and hampered the defence. The second stage of the advance was through the Forest of Mormal. It started off behind a fresh barrage. The mist had lifted, but part of the line was held up by trench mortars. After the mortars had been scuppered there was no real resistance. The German defence had broken down during the morning, and the enemy was in rapid retreat. On relief we returned to our billets in Englefontaine. Our casualties during the operation were one officer and ten other ranks killed, four officers and sixty-five other ranks wounded or missing. The next day we cleaned up and reorganized.

On 6 November, in cold and heavy rain, we marched to a bivouac in the heart of the forest: everyone was soaked to the skin. Movement in the forest was a hazardous business, since booby traps for the unwary abounded. Passage for transport was also a problem because the main tracks were mined, or blown up. Much RE reconstruction work was necessary before heavy vehicles and guns could use the rides and tracks.

The battalion moved on to Berlaimont, where we halted for four hours. Then, under considerable shell fire, we crossed the Sambre to Aulnoye, a mile or two beyond the river, and billeted. Huge coal dumps along the sidings had been fired by the Germans.

Early in the morning of the 8th, the battalion moved out in the direction of Pot de Vin. My last impression of the war is the advance across fields, and the enemy fighting a rear-guard action with rifles and machine-guns. At noon we returned to our billets. The transport, which had been at the village of Sart-Bara, came up. It was plain that the war was fizzling out. Rumour of an Armistice was, from now on, the general talk. By the 10th, operations had become a pursuit. A few reinforcements joined.

The last two and a half months had seen nearly as many changes in the battalion as all the months on the Somme two years before. There had been so much talk of an Armistice; then a brigade message on the morning of the 11th told us it had been signed at 8:00 am and that hostilities were to cease at 11:00 am. When the news got about, that the war was over, there was spasmodic cheering, and the general atmosphere was a slacking off for the day and the notes of a lively band in the afternoon.

A voluntary service of thanksgiving was held in a cinema the Germans had requisitioned. The spacious building was quite full. Local civilians were overjoyed, but for me the most remarkable feature of that day and night was the uncanny silence that prevailed: no rumbling of guns, no staccato of machine-guns, nor did the roar of exploding dumps break into the night as it had so often done.

PEACE — 1

When, soon after the Armistice, I resigned my commission, I did so with some reluctance. Not long after I left the army, Elizabeth and I were married. Jamie was born in 1921, Lucy two years later. When the Second World War broke out, Jamie was eighteen, about the same age as I was when the First War started. But Jamie had very left-wing views. He said he would refuse to join up. There was conscription. The first class of militiamen called up on 1 July 1939 were the twenty- and twenty-one-year-olds. But with the National Service Act, passed on 3 September in the same year, the age was dropped to eighteen with an upper limit of forty-eight. Even so there were ways and means of ducking it. When Jamie said he would never enlist he refused to say why, so either he would not, or could not, give any good reason.

Elizabeth didn't help. I blame her more than I blame Jamie. She was always talking about the 1920s and early 1930s, the land fit for heroes that was promised after the First World War. Everyone knows there was a lot of poverty; places like Jarrow, where two-thirds were permanently unemployed; but not only Jarrow, for there was mass unemployment in most of the industrial areas, with villages in Durham, South Wales, and Lancashire, where the entire male population was out of work. In those places unemployment had become a way of life.

Chamberlain tried to help. In 1934 he restored the cut in unemployment benefit. He also reduced income tax to 4s 6d, which made the rich richer. There have always been the very rich and the very poor, that is nothing new; but there was no need for Elizabeth and Jamie to be so vindictive about it all. Unfortunately, their views, which had been the views of only a minority, became more widespread.

At the end of the 1920s came a sudden rush of war books. Practically all the books on the First World War, those we remember most and still read today, novels, memoirs, and plays like *Journey's End*, were published between 1928 and 1930, and all preached the same lesson: the futility and dreariness of war and the incompetence of generals and politicians, with ordinary men on both sides victims of this incompetence. These lessons were reinforced on an academic level by British and American historians who had studied the diplomatic origins of war.

At the time, few educated people believed that war had been caused by deliberate German aggression, though there were some who held that Germany had been too militaristic. The general opinion was that wars start by mistake, and this was the view of Lord Grey. It was also felt that the negotiating machinery of the League of Nations would prevent these mistakes in future. Lloyd George believed that wars were caused by armaments; others believed the cause was grievances, and therefore Germany should be redressed. Jamie's view was that the private manufacturers of armaments had a lot to answer for. Needless to say, this idea came from Elizabeth!

In 1935 there was a royal commission on war armaments traffickers; also, a Senate inquiry had started in the United States. When I mentioned this to Elizabeth, she said that neither she nor Jamie was interested. She said these sorts of royal commissions were simply capitalists whitewashing capitalists. They had funny ideas, my wife and poor son.

But people like Elizabeth and Jamie, people who are always talking about the exploitation of the poor, seem to forget it was not only the poor who fought for their country. The soldiers who fought and died and were wounded came from every class. I lost most of my chums. There were those who became rich because of the war; there were some who became richer. Jamie said these were the only sensible ones, but I ignored his remark. It was too stupid even to try and refute. The majority of people fought, and fought for what they believed in, although many, like Wenzel, ended up disillusioned.

Another of Jamie's hobby horses was the incompetence of the generals. He said they used men simply as fodder for the war machine. He also said that the generals had no concern for the millions they sent to their deaths. As a matter of fact, I think it was Field Marshal Robertson, who resigned as Chief of Staff, who said he couldn't get emotionally involved, otherwise he wouldn't have been able to prosecute the war.

Our generals weren't all that incompetent. As I have already told you, it has to be remembered that in those days communication was primitive compared to what it was in the Second World War. So often, in the 1914 war, the generals didn't know immediately what the results of their strategies were, and whatever criticisms are made of our generals in the First War, we did win! Also, if one talks in terms of cost, that question can be asked of any war. If the 1914 war was particularly costly, it was because it was that type of a war.

PEACE — 2

For a long time I couldn't talk about Jamie. I can do so now. His views worried me. He seemed to become even more extreme than his mother. But we are a democracy, and he was old enough to have a mind of his own. Marxist views attracted him, and in the 1930s there was the creation of a new element in the Labour Party: the left-wing intellectual. This new development was basically a revolt of social conscience by intellectual members of the educated class who were ashamed of all the poverty in the midst of so much plenty. Elizabeth and Jamie were in sympathy with this.

Many of these intellectuals had learnt their Marxism in Berlin during the struggle of the Communists and National Socialists; this was before Hitler came to power. Theoreticians were also directly inspired by the example of Soviet Russia, where the Five Year Plan, started in 1928, appeared to show a way of escape from what Jamie called the evils of our capitalist society.

Jamie was not a Communist, I'm sure of that; but he sympathized, as did the other Marxist intellectuals, with Soviet Russia. Not many of these middle-class Marxists joined the Communist party, certainly not openly; instead they formed a new organization, the Socialist League, which was completely intellectual and was all leaders and no followers. When this movement began, the thinking was almost entirely on economic questions.

In a way, I suppose, one could say that Jamie was a caring young man. There was a great deal of poverty, and unemployment became the spur towards a more aggressive socialist policy and provided the opening through which Communist influence broke into the middle classes.

The Communists controlled the National Unemployed Workers' Movement, and it was a Communist called Harrington who hit on the device of hunger marches. Select bands of the unemployed from the depressed areas marched on London where they demonstrated to little purpose, although their progress through the country was a propaganda stroke of great effect.

These hunger marches were able to portray graphically the failure of capitalism. A lot of middle-class people felt the call of conscience and set up soup kitchens for the marchers, and accommodated them in local schools. Jamie was always saying that capitalism had broken down, that a class war fought to a finish would, automatically, end capitalism and all its evils, but I didn't take too much notice; he was only thirteen or fourteen at the time Hitler came to power and established a National Socialist dictatorship in Germany. Marxists here thought the British capitalist government was aiding Hitler.

Although a lot of people were concerned about unemployment, they were even more worried about the tyrannies of Nazi rule. In fact, these two emotions merged into one. Hunger marches filled the street one day, demonstrators against fascism followed on the next. But economic discontent was still the main driving force, with anti-fascism feelings growing; in fact, there was a change of tone and emphasis. Social questions, though still important, slipped into second place, and those who had begun by applauding the hunger marchers now wished to arrest capitalism's march to war.

At this time I had frequent arguments with Jamie and Elizabeth; Lucy was more interested in boyfriends and parties. It was when we got onto the subject of disarmament that these arguments became rather heated. Not so much when Hitler came to power, because then there was still an anti-war feeling in this country; it was after this, when Labour and Liberals wanted disarmament as the main element in British foreign policy, and the chiefs of staff, quite rightly in my opinion, recommended rearmament. They did so because they had in mind the Japanese invasion of Manchuria in 1931 and there was the threat of the Japanese Navy in the Far East. With Hitler as chancellor there was also the growing threat of the German Air Force.

In October 1933 Germany withdrew from the disarmament conference and a week later left the League of Nations. The year before, in 1932, the chiefs of staff had increased their warnings. They said that Japan was the more immediate danger, though Germany would ultimately be the greater one. It was easy to see that Hitler was a brutal man, using brutal methods, particularly in his treatment of the Jews; yet the defence estimate barely moved, and when we issued a white paper explaining that German rearmament made British rearmament necessary, Hitler used this as an excuse for restoring conscription in Germany.

It was obvious we had to rearm, but there were many — and Jamie was one — who would not see this, and were advocates of disarmament. Whether at this time Jamie was, as Wenzel had become, an outright pacifist, I couldn't say. Certainly Jamie had strong pacifist leanings.

In October 1935 the Italian armies attacked Abyssinia. Our reaction to the Italian aggressor was weak. Italian credits were cut off, and all imports from Italy, and some exports to her, were banned by almost all members of the League. We were resisting the aggressor by all sanctions short of war. In my opinion, we should have gone to war. It's a mistake to let a bully get away with it. Appeasement with people like Hitler and Mussolini meant disaster. Jamie didn't agree with war whatever the reason, but as I have said, he was young, fourteen at the time of the Abyssinian crisis, and still greatly influenced by Elizabeth.

Although the national government wanted a mandate for re-armament, and in theory asked for it, their approach was a carbon copy of what Lloyd George had done over reparations in 1918: they spoke the truth in an undertone, hoping no one would hear. In any case, there was little interest in rearmament. We had an election in November, and the National Government supporters, except for a few extremists, were saying the same thing: all sanctions short of war, for no one was thinking about war. The important matters were houses and unemployment.

We didn't stand up to Mussolini, but the Abyssinian affair was eclipsed by greater events. The first of these was in 1936, when Hitler sent German troops into the Rhineland. We did nothing, nor did the French. Jamie, like the majority of the British public and the British government, favoured appeasement. He, of course, wanted total abolition of war. Any sane person wants that, but not at any price.

As I have said, Jamie and Elizabeth regarded the 1914 conflict as a capitalist war. The strange thing is, Elizabeth didn't have these views when I married her; or if she did, she kept very quiet. I don't know what it was that changed her, no more than I know what it was, later, that so radically altered Jamie's view of war, unless it was my son's reaction to my calling him a coward.

One expects the Left to think of any national disaster as capitalist-inspired. It is true that there were those who became rich because of the war; those who made millions out of armaments; those who stayed behind enjoying their champagne and cigars while men in France, floundering in the mud of Flanders, slaughtered each other; and it is true that those men who profited from war were glad, no matter what the reason, that they were able to make their fortunes; but most of us did our duty as we saw it, and when the threat to individual and collective freedom was again apparent in Hitler's aggressive policies, especially his brutal treatment of minorities, and when the moment for a decision had to be made, there weren't many who held back.

Our policy of appeasement was stupid and cowardly. We should have gone in against Italy over Abyssinia; we should have stood up to the Germans when they reoccupied the Rhineland. Nevertheless, by the end of 1935 our armament plans had been recast, not merely to fill a few gaps but to prepare for a great war. The following year, 1936, the air defence of Great Britain was divided into bomber command and fighter command, with Dowding at the head of the fighters. In the summer of that year came the Spanish Civil War; Germany and Italy sent aid to Franco, Russia sent military aid to the republic, and volunteers from other countries went there to fight.

On the Spanish question, Jamie again followed Elizabeth, whose sympathy was with the Communists and the republic. I can make allowances for Jamie. He was young and impressionable, and one has to remember that the young tend to see everything in terms of black and white with not too much logic. He was still in his early teens, so I didn't worry too much. I thought and hoped he'd grow out of it. He was a sensitive and impressionable boy but — and I know this may sound like a father's bias — tall, physically strong, and extraordinarily good-looking. He had Elizabeth's deep brown eyes and her dark hair, and he had a fine complexion. His looks were more hers than mine. If his character wasn't quite as strong as hers, he was every bit as obstinate. Elizabeth, when she'd made up her mind on anything, was immovable, so it was pointless arguing with her, although I often did so, up until the time I made that unfortunate remark to Jamie.

With him there were frequent arguments and heated discussions. I tried to show him the error of his ways, how muddled he was in his thinking. I pointed out that one's duty to one's country and loyalty to one's sovereign overrode almost all other considerations. I stress almost, because one has to be sure that what one is being asked to do is morally right. Elizabeth and Jamie said it was not morally right to rearm, but in my opinion they were wrong; it was our duty, in the face of aggression, to stand up and be counted, for this was the spirit of the Empire and it was how Britain became great.

When Germany began to overrun her weaker neighbours and continued, with them, her evil practices of repression and extermination, I found Jamie's pacifist views not only distasteful but intolerable. I don't think Elizabeth fully realized the damage she'd done, but it resulted in Jamie saying that even if war broke out he would refuse to join up and that he wouldn't go even if he was conscripted.

I found his attitude disturbing and his repudiation of a basic loyalty and sense of duty abhorrent and, as far as I was concerned, totally unacceptable. By this time we had very little in common, but the great tragedy was that time had run out for any chance of a reconciliation. If only I had known. But I lost my temper and said what I should not have said, what I have always deeply regretted having said, and what I shall, for as long as I live, wish I had never said, for once said it could not be revoked. I called him a coward. I said he was yellow. It had made me so angry that people like Jamie couldn't see what was happening, or if they could see, that they should be so blind to the danger. Elizabeth never forgave me for what I did, and it was never the same afterwards.

PEACE — 3

The Abyssinian crisis and Germany's occupation of the Rhineland had shattered the easy security of post-war years. It was obvious that Germany was intent on becoming again a great military power. Even at this late stage the British people weren't fully aware how dangerous Hitler had become. Churchill and his few supporters were convinced that Germany was set on a great war, and that Great Britain must prepare to resist her.

Efficient and conscientious though Chamberlain was, he headed a humdrum government; yet he, more than any other man, laid the foundation for British fighting power during the Second World War. At the same time, he also resented the money wasted on armaments and the way in which foreign affairs distracted him and his government from their projects of domestic reform.

Chamberlain's asset was his sharp rationalism. Churchill tended to talk as though Great Britain and France could still lay down the law to Europe, but where Chamberlain went wrong was in his belief that Hitler and Mussolini were, like himself, rational statesmen, or at any rate that they could be treated as such and that their discontents could be appeased by rational discussion to get Europe resettled on new lines. He believed that a great war would last for years and tear all Europe to pieces; such a war he and nearly all Englishmen wished to avoid.

Anyone who knows what war means couldn't wish for another, so I wouldn't altogether have blamed Jamie, up to the time we went to war, for feeling as he did. It was after war broke out, and when he then refused to even consider enlisting, although in any case he would have been liable for call-up, that his cowardly approach — or this is what I thought it was — angered me.

Germany under Hitler was a reversion to barbarism. But though Chamberlain shared the revulsion of feeling against German brutality, he still believed that appeasement was the best way of bringing Germany back to civilized behaviour. The great majority of people shared his view. Australia and New Zealand were especially anxious to see Europe settled so that more British power could be built up in the Far East against Japan, and their anxiety was increased when, in July 1937, there was renewed fighting between Japan and China.

Eden, the Foreign Secretary, instead of showing resolute action, relied on moral disapproval, strong words, and no acts. He believed that sooner or later Hitler and Mussolini would come begging for forgiveness if he, Anthony Eden, continued to wag his finger at them; so the dictators got what they wanted and grew increasingly confident that, by threats, they could get more.

On 20 February 1938 Eden resigned and Halifax took over as Foreign Secretary. On 13 March Hitler entered Vienna and incorporated Austria with Germany. In September the Czechoslovakian crisis exploded. President Benes reluctantly gave in to Hitler's threats and agreed to the separation of the Sudetan Germans from the rest of Czechoslovakia. Most people hadn't noticed the Czech affair until the middle of September; now they saw the bullying of a small democratic state. Preparations were made for war.

On 29 September Chamberlain flew to Munich again and signed an agreement with Hitler emphasizing the desire of Great Britain and Germany never to go to war with one another again. Later, at the airport in England, Chamberlain stood waving the agreement and, in the evening, appeared at the window of No 10, telling the cheering crowd: "This is the second time that there has come back from Germany to Downing Street peace with honour. I believe it is peace in our time."

The overwhelming majority of ordinary people approved of what Chamberlain had done; nevertheless, rearmament went along quietly. In November 1938 Hitler launched a sharper pogrom against the Jews. In January 1939 Chamberlain and Halifax visited Mussolini. They came away fairly confident that Mussolini would exercise a moderating influence on Hitler. In February the British government recognized Franco as the rightful ruler of Spain. In March President Hacha, who had succeeded Benes after Munich, gave in completely to Hitler. German administration, including the Gestapo, moved in and established the same Nazi dictatorship as in Germany. Hitler dismembered his small neighbour without warning or provocation, and carried off the most valuable industrial part for himself. It was clear proof of planned aggression.

Chamberlain still believed that appeasement was the wisest course but, on 30 March 1939, fearing a German attack, an Anglo-French guarantee was given to Poland, and to Greece and Rumania. The government also announced its intention to set up a Ministry of Supply and bring in compulsory military service. In August Ribbentrop went to Moscow, and he and Molotov signed the Nazi-Soviet pact when Russia promised to stay neutral if Germany became involved in war. Two days later, on 25 August 1939, an alliance was made between us and the Poles.

On 31 August Hitler gave the order to attack Poland. At 4:45 am on 1 September German troops crossed the Polish frontier. At 6:00 am German aeroplanes bombed Warsaw. The Poles appealed to us, and the Cabinet decided that if Germany would suspend hostilities and withdraw her troops, a solution without war would still be possible. A message stating this was sent to Hitler.

On the afternoon of 2 September there was a unanimous Cabinet decision that the ultimatum for this withdrawal should end at midnight, but it was not until 9:00 am on 3 September that the British ultimatum was delivered to the German government. The Germans did not reply, and at 11:00 am, when the ultimatum expired, Great Britain and Germany were again at war.

THE GLORY OF WAR — 9

The French declared war at 5:00 pm. The British declaration had automatically brought in India and the colonies, just as it had done in 1914. This alone should have shown Jamie where his duty lay; it should have taught him what was honourable. But Jamie had such peculiar views. He even said that the evacuation of the London children — about a million and a half were sent away — showed how the wealthier classes manipulated the poor.

When the city children reached evacuation areas, they had no warm clothes or strong shoes, let alone rubber boots, to protect them against country mud, while the overburdened rural authorities had no funds from which to make clothing grants. Foster parents were themselves usually too poor to help, and many children, far from home, were upset.

I suppose it's true to say that these troubles fell upon those least able to cope. The poor housed the poor. But Jamie seemed obsessed with this sort of thing. People like Elizabeth and my poor son seem to think that the destitute are the only people who matter; that the rich have no feelings, no compassion, no problems; that there is something not quite human about the wealthier classes.

Contrary to what we all thought, no bombs fell on London for many months, and a lot of people returned home. The country people, who included some of the wealthy, were able to learn, for the first time, how the city poor lived. English people had become more mixed up than ever before. When the air raids eventually came and produced a second evacuation, this time unplanned, there followed another great upheaval. But Jamie would only see what he wanted to see. He was, as I have said, very obstinate. Lucy had no strong feelings. She married a stockbroker. They have four children, three boys and a girl. I haven't seen them for some time. They live in Oxfordshire and Elizabeth lives near them. I don't see any of them now.

In the beginning, when Jamie said he would refuse to join up, or if called up he would register as a conscientious objector, it didn't bother me too much. Military conscription moved slowly, and there was no point in calling up men until the army was equipped to receive them; also, I hoped Jamie would eventually come to his senses. But when, even after the start of hostilities, he persisted in saying he wouldn't take part in a capitalist war, it made me very angry.

The division between civilian and combatant in the Second World War was less sharp than in the First World War, but in war, whatever the reason, I see no place for conscientious objectors. It was then I called him a coward and told him he was yellow. It wasn't long after this — I was away at the time — that he joined up; then in 1942, a week before his twenty-first birthday, in the battle for El Alamein, his tank was hit and caught fire. There were no survivors.

Whether it was our quarrel that made Jamie change his mind and volunteer for the army, I couldn't say. Elizabeth wouldn't discuss it. I asked Lucy, but she had no idea. At the time I had a lot on my mind. There was Dunkirk, then France fell and we were standing alone, waiting for an invasion which never came.

The governments of Poland, Norway, Holland, and Belgium were on British soil with their fighting men. These governments also brought their financial resources and over three million tons of shipping. General de Gaulle was organizing the Free French movement, and although the Americans at this time were neutral, they were helping us.

In 1940 we had the Battle of Britain, when the Germans, using fleets of bombers protected by fighters, began their full attack on southeast England. Then the enemy set out to destroy the fighter bases in Kent, nearly succeeding but suddenly turning aside to bomb London. Again we thought an invasion was imminent. The blitzes brought much destruction because a major German raid meant a hundred tons of bombs, although later we were dropping one thousand six hundred tons a night on Germany. The blitzes devastated London, the East End particularly, and many provincial cities, destroying or damaging more than three and a half million houses.

Then there was the war at sea, lease-lend with the Americans, the German invasion of Russia, the Japanese attack on Pearl Harbor — so that it was no longer a war between Great Britain and Germany; a world war in a very real sense had begun.

THE GLORY OF WAR — 10

El Alamein, fifty miles from Alexandria on the coastal railway to Mersa Matruh, is nothing more than an ordinary little station. The battle fought there has often been thought of as decisive, but in terms of actual fighting it was insignificant compared to other theatres of war. In Russia two million soldiers were on active service, while at Alamein there were fifty thousand

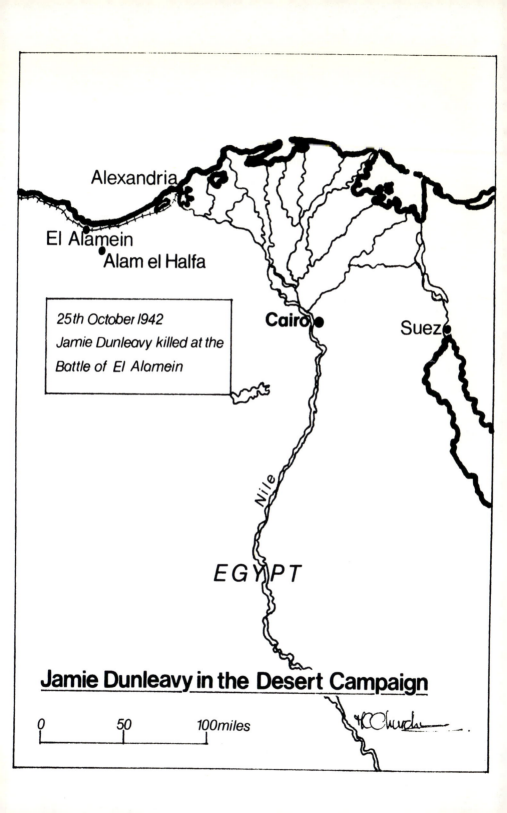

Alexandria

El Alamein
Alam el Halfa

25th October 1942
Jamie Dunleavy killed at the
Battle of El Alamein

Cairo

Suez

Nile

E G Y P T

Jamie Dunleavy in the Desert Campaign

0   50   100miles

But the Alamein victory helped clear the way for our ultimate successful prosecution of the whole war, and not only this, after a series of failures, it restored confidence to the British people and strengthened their one indestructible characteristic: an irrational optimism in ultimate victory.

Although our material superiority over Rommel's resources was so great that it would, in the end, have been more than strange had we not achieved victory, Churchill was right when he said that El Alamein would always make a glorious page in British military annals. What is particularly interesting for me about the battle, not simply because it was where my son fought and died, is that, in many ways, it was similar to the First World War.

Bearing in mind the slogging and futile offensive of the First War, a comparison can be made between Alamein and some of the actions in Flanders, particularly with Montgomery's insistence on mass artillery to kill men, although a new feature in this battle, one which presented immense difficulties throughout the campaign, was the huge shield of minefields laid by both sides.

The Battle of Alamein has been termed pure warfare. There was no cluttering up of the battlefield with houses, roads, or churches, no farms or animals, no people other than the soldiers themselves. In the desert, by and large, there was not a great deal to destroy. The very vastness and emptiness of the desert made it important that there should be some clear and offensive purpose, which was to take airfields or ports or tactically important features so that the ultimate goal of destroying the enemy forces, or denying them the ability to operate against you, could be achieved. To advance great distances could only compound administrative difficulties, unless you could take all the desert and either kill or capture or kick out your opponents once and for all, which, in the event, it took the British three years to do.

The North African campaign was, in fact, a shuffling backwards and forwards between Egypt, Benghazi, and El Agheila. First the British knocked the Italians about, then Rommel brought blitzkrieg to the desert and pushed the British back to Egypt; next Rommel was himself forced to withdraw only to spring back and defeat the 8th Army so heavily that Tobruk fell, and the enemy were stopped only by Auchinleck's personal generalship at Alamein. Finally, Montgomery pulverized the Afrika Korps and sent it off to the west for the last time, to be sandwiched between the 8th Army following up behind it and the 1st Army advancing east from French North Africa. During most of this shuttling backwards and forwards there were certain constant features: the interdependence of land, sea, and air operations, the overriding importance of supplies, and the dominance of the tank.

I don't know what attracted Jamie to the Royal Armoured Corps. Fighting in the desert, more than in any other theatre, was dominated by the tank and the anti-tank gun. El Alamein was unusual in that it more closely resembled a set-piece battle, and it was attrition rather than mobility that proved to be the decisive factor; nevertheless, tanks still played a vital role in the battle.

The number of crew varied according to the type of tank. Lees and Grants each had two main guns and had a crew of six or seven, whereas Crusaders had a crew of only three. Jamie was in a Sherman, which had a crew of five — commander, gunner, loader/wireless operator, driver, and co-driver/hull machine-gunner. He was the loader/wireless operator.

During the second Alamein, which was when Jamie was killed, six hundred Allied tanks were knocked out. Only a hundred and fifty of them were beyond repair, although some regiments suffered devastating losses. The 9th Armoured Brigade lost most of its tanks. The Royal Wiltshire Yeomanry, both on 24 October and again on 2 November, lost virtually every tank.

Even if a tank was hit by the much feared 88 anti-tank gun, it could be that one or two members of the crew might be killed, another one or two wounded, while the remainder escaped relatively unscathed; and crewmen could escape when a tank brewed up, although it was harder for some like the driver and loader. However, it was not uncommon for all the crew to be killed either by blast or burnt alive, and Shermans were particularly notorious for catching fire, often within ten seconds of being hit.

Casualty returns were completed each Saturday and passed to GHQ 2nd Echelon. Returns would be processed at Middle East HQ and then passed on to the War Office, which informed relatives by telegram. A letter from an officer would probably follow. We had a letter from Jamie's squadron commander which said that at all times Jamie showed a devotion to duty and fearlessness in battle worthy of the highest traditions of the British soldier; one couldn't ask for more than that!

Until the final turning point came in the middle of 1942, almost three years after the outbreak of war, the British campaigns had been indecisive and ponderous, with one consistent and redeeming feature: perseverance — a kind of gallant doggedness in defence and unimaginative slogging in attack. The one notable exception to this had been O'Connor's brilliant offensive, but this had been against the Italians. Otherwise, on the British side, there had been none of the flair for fluid and mobile battles, the personal leadership, the implacable drive and opportunism that so coloured all the operations commanded by Rommel.

It was Rommel who dominated the scene from the time he brought a new set of rules to the desert, confusing and confounding the British. Backwards and forwards the struggle had gone, the dreary Italian advance to Sidi Barrani, their utter routing by O'Connor, Rommel's first drive into Egypt, his withdrawal to El Agheila because of Auchinleck's Crusader push, his final fling to Tobruk and Alamein, and the 8th Army beaten and in a perilous position from which it was rescued only by Auchinleck's personal leadership; but it had to wait for Montgomery to apply his own brand of generalship before indifferent troops were turned into competent ones.

The character of Montgomery suited his army, just as Rommel's character had inspired and moulded his. Within an astonishing short space Montgomery imposed his will on his officer corps, and his personality on his troops. It was a feat of generalship to instil a new sense of purpose and confidence into a puzzled uneasy multitude and into a jaded army of such diverse origins: Australia, New Zealand, South Africa, India, and Great Britain. Between Alamein and Tunis the charisma of Montgomery's personality never waned, and his iron will never relaxed, so that when the 8th Army linked up with the 1st in Tunisia they arrived in the spirit of conquerors, backed up by numerous victories.

In August 1942 Montgomery began his work on the 8th Army to get it in trim for the coming battles, and he did this in savage conditions: static positions under a fierce sun and with the adjacent unhealthy delta that brought out swarms of flies so numerous it was often impossible to raise food to the lips. The Afrika Korps had an added discomfort. Its units were close to, and sometimes intermingled with, the Italians, whose peasant style of sanitation was a paradise for the flies; and this at a time when gastric illnesses in the Middle East were eroding the strength of fighting men so that only the strictest sanitary discipline could stop an epidemic. This applied to the British as well as the Germans, for any carelessness and indiscipline bred disease — gippy tummy or jaundice — and just as frequently men were troubled with the purulent desert sore. Very rapidly the slightest scratch would extend into a wide suppurating circle which might take months to heal, and even then would leave a nasty scar. Rommel himself was ill, and was told that recovery could only be expected with a long stay in Germany under proper medical supervision.

Montgomery moved his own headquarters to a pleasant position by the sea near Burgel Arab, where it was next door to the headquarters of the Desert Air Force commanded by Air Vice-Marshal Coningham.

Montgomery's whole attitude to war, so different from Rommel's, which was chivalrous, was to go out and kill Germans wherever they were to be found. Rommel did have a magic that others didn't have, and he came to represent, to the British soldiers, the Axis forces in Africa as a whole. Rommel, unlike Montgomery, was not a vain man. If Montgomery had any shortcomings as a soldier, benevolence was not one of them, but what mattered about Montgomery was his clarity, his conviction, his confidence, all of which permeated throughout what became his army, together with a thoroughness and the determination to see an unromantic and slogging battle of attrition through to its only possible conclusion — final victory.

It was by mastering the mechanics of the battle of position that Montgomery set the seal of his authority on the army. His sense of certainty, his simple eloquence, the obvious grip he exerted over his subordinate commanders and, through them, over the soldiers, his flamboyant press conferences and personal signals to Churchill — all these things made up his style of leadership. As the days of 1942 advanced, the shadows were lengthening for Rommel and his Afrika Korps.

Several reasons can be found for Montgomery's ultimate victory: mistakes by Hitler, one of which was refusing to allow a plan to attack and capture Malta; Rommel's precarious situation with supplies, particularly petrol; Operation Torch; the Allied landing in Northwest Africa which would hit Rommel in the back; the information on all of Rommel's movements and intentions given by Ultra; and not least the personality of Montgomery himself.

The first battle which Jamie found himself in was that of Alam el Halfa, more usually called Alam Halfa, which Rommel launched during the night of the 30/31 August. Almost at the outset things went wrong for Rommel. The minefields were far denser than had been expected and were stubbornly defended. Flares turned night into day, artillery fire was heavy and continuous, mortar bombs rained down, the Desert Air Force bombed, machine-guns raked the lines of advance, and all this while the Germans were trying to clear paths through the mines. General von Bismarck, commanding the 21st Panzer Division, was killed by a mortar bomb; General Nehring, in charge of the Deutsches Afrika Korps, a part of the Panzerarmee Afrika which included Italians in whose overall command was Field Marshal Rommel, was wounded. Rommel's attack was bogged down before it had got under way. On the second day of the battle the weather cleared, and the British tanks and artillery that were massed on the ridge opened fire. After dusk the bombers came. Rommel called it off and withdrew.

It must have been a proud and happy moment for Jamie. The new German 75mm had taken a heavy toll and many of our tanks were on fire. Alam Halfa could not be called a major battle, but it was a defeat for Rommel. The fact that no important ground was gained or lost by either side, and that the casualties were relatively minor, is not so important; what mattered was that the battle had gone as predicted.

For the British there were to be no more failures and there was to be no more retreating. The Axis losses were 50 tanks, 400 lorries, 55 guns, and 2,900 killed, wounded, and missing. The Allied losses were 67 tanks, 15 guns, and 1,750 killed, wounded, and missing. Each side lost about a hundred aircraft. The battle of Alam Halfa ended in the way we wanted.

By the autumn of 1942 the German advance at Stalingrad, as well as the Caucasus and North Africa, had been brought to a standstill. This time it was more than a temporary interruption; it was the end of Hitler's offensives. Up to this moment, Hitler was undisputed master of the greater part of continental Europe, with his armies threatening the Volga, the Caucasus, and the Nile. But now the tide began to turn, and this is nowhere better demonstrated than at El Alamein.

Montgomery, who planned Alamein in a wholly deliberate manner, was an absolute master of the set-piece battle. His intention was to pound Rommel until Rommel could stand the pounding no more. Clearing paths through the mines was as important as having masses of men, guns, tanks, and aeroplanes, for unless the mine clearing was done quickly and effectively, everything else would falter. Practice and rehearsal for prodding and lifting mines, using the new Polish mine detector, the flail tanks, the gap-marking parties, the traffic control organization, all these were necessary as a first step to success. There was a touch of grim humour in the very code word, Lightfoot, chosen for the first part of this operation.

One essential feature of Montgomery's plan was to deceive the enemy into believing that the main attack would be in the south. Dummy supply dumps and camps were built; bogus water-pipe systems, which seemed to be timed for completion in November, were set up; a complete armoured division motored to the south, only to return at night to a position north of Alam Halfa, leaving realistic dummies in its place; and patterns of wireless traffic were designed to confirm this emphasis on the south.

Montgomery's advantage over Rommel was considerable: the 8th Army had everything it wanted — men, armoured cars, tanks, artillery pieces, anti-tank guns — while the enemy had scarcely sufficient of these for routine operations. Furthermore, the Desert Air Force dominated the skies. In a personal message to all ranks, Montgomery made it clear that all that was needed from the army was the determination to fight, to kill, to win.

On the night of 22/23 October the infantry quietly moved back north and took up positions already dug for them just behind the front. Strict orders were given that after dawn there was to be no movement, and for a whole day they had to lie cramped in temporary slit trenches waiting for night. They could not move out, even to relieve themselves, and one can imagine the discomfort they suffered. An officer said the tension was almost unbearable and the day dragged terribly. He spent the time going over and over again the plan of attack, memorising codes and studying the overprinted maps which showed all the enemy positions, the result of weeks of patrolling and air reconnaissance.

After dark there was tremendous activity: last-minute visits by commanders, and minor adjustment to plans. Then a hot meal was brought up, but most of our men were too restless to eat much. Before the order was given to move forward to the start line, the CO came round and wished everyone good luck.

At 9:00 pm, when the infantry moved forward to the start line with a taped line stretching across the open desert just in front of the forward positions, it was deathly still. A full moon lighted the bleak sand as if it were day. Suddenly, the silence was broken by the crash of a single gun, and the next moment a mighty roar rent the air. The ground shook as salvo after salvo crashed out from hundreds of guns while shells whined overhead in a continuous stream. Soon the enemy line was lit up by bright flashes. One or two fires broke out and the ground became clearer than ever. The starry sky appeared to echo with the thunder of the barrage as the night was filled with the blinding light of flares and, at the same time, bombs rained down on strong points and defensive positions, on tracks and crossroads, on huddling groups of tents and huts.

It seemed a long time before the enemy started to reply; then, as the Allies approached, enemy machine guns and mortars began. Tracers streamed about and men began to fall, groaning and shouting. A sergeant tripped over a strand of wire and was blown to pieces. Our men were now running, and dim enemy figures appeared from the trenches. The line had broken up into blobs of men all struggling together. Some men in a trench in front were standing up with their hands above their heads, screaming in terror. Some of our NCOs were rounding up prisoners and kicking them into some sort of formation. A terrified Italian was running round and round with his hands above his head, screaming at the top of his voice. One of the enemy came out with his hands up, then threw a grenade. Behind him were two others crouched on the ground at the bottom of the square trench; as they went to get up they were bayonetted. There were many sights of bayonetted men around.

Another enemy position surrendered without fighting. I was told later that some more of the enemy near this position scuttled down the trenches to the left, and remained in the gap where our unit should have been but had failed to keep up, and this cost us dear, because when we had passed, the enemy filtered back and shot up the reserve companies and battalion HQ, who were coming up behind.

Our side was in firm position, and everyone was pleased that things had gone so well. Tanks nearby were firing away and shells were whistling about. A signaller, back in his own trench, tuned in to the BBC and heard the news that the 8th Army had attacked, and the battle was progressing favourably and according to plan.

The night began to resolve itself into scores of apparently unrelated tiny battles between sections and platoons and isolated posts; five men against two with a machine gun; two platoons against a wired and reinforced strong point; six men desperately trying to extinguish the flames of a blazing ammunition truck lighting up the night, and attracting a storm of enemy fire.

Dust and smoke reduced visibility despite the bright moonlight. Groups of men were unsure where they were or where anyone else was or what was happening. By this time the whole area was enveloped in dust, there were masses of vehicles all over the place, and the marking of routes and gaps was very hard to see. It needed only a vehicle or two to stray off the side to remove all the signs and lead everyone behind into confusion. Tempers got as heated as the engines, while the tanks and other vehicles ground along at a snail's pace in the billowing clouds of dust. Three Shermans were disabled, two on scattered mines and the third, which I now know to be Jamie's, was hit and caught fire.

On the evening of 25 October, in brilliant moonlight, the Crumbling Operations began. Our men started to advance, this time with no artillery support, for the object had been to surprise the enemy. An officer in a reconnaissance car had earlier reported that the position was only lightly held by frightened Italians, who had tried to surrender to him. This was cheering news, and our soldiers advanced confidently, but they had only gone a few yards when streams of machine-gun tracer bullets whistled across the front, intersecting at a point about a hundred yards directly ahead. The enemy were firing across our front on fixed lines; some mortars added to the discomfort of our men, but we pressed on.

It is a strange feeling approaching the first almost continuous stream of machine-gun tracer, knowing that the next step will take you into it;

our side crossed it with a few casualties and continued to advance. Ahead was barbed wire; breaking into a trot, our men jumped over and started to rush the positions they could now see. They saw German helmets and cursed the reconnoitring officer for his misleading information.

A machine-gun opened up not more than fifteen yards half-left from an officer, who saw the tracer bullets coming straight for him. He was hit, spun round, recovered his balance, carried on, but after going a dozen paces his leg suddenly collapsed under him and he fell forward. We took the position but had a thoroughly uncomfortable and dangerous day ahead, with the battle raging all round. It was learnt later that the enemy, whom our fellows had encountered there, was an Austrian unit with German officers who had taken over from the Italians shortly before we attacked.

Describing the action, an Italian lieutenant wrote in his diary: "On all sides I could hear the groans of the dying and the wounded. We fired rockets at a group coming at us with fixed bayonets; a few of the men surrendered, but the first few were shot down. All around there was the usual scene of battle; men writhing in agony, some squealing like stuck pigs over a scratch, others suffering atrocious wounds in silence, some vomiting, others messing their trousers. We had seen it all before."

By 26 October our side had lost some six thousand men killed, wounded, and missing. About three hundred tanks, including Jamie's, had been put out of action, although many of the tanks were recoverable and could then be repaired. When Jamie's tank was hit and caught fire, he and the rest of the crew perished. Those not killed from the blast were burnt alive, although it would have been over almost instantaneously, of that I am sure.

What the depth of Jamie's religious conviction was, I don't know. His socialism had Christianity at its base, so I am not so puzzled about that side as I am about his reversal in attitude, which changed him from a pacifist into a brave and loyal soldier.

He came from a long line of soldiers, and it could have been, in the end, that my son found redemption at Alamein in a way described by another soldier who was there, a young poet later killed in Normandy and who, not long after D day, wrote: "I never lost the certainty that the experience of battle was something I must have. Whatever changes in the nature of warfare, the battlefield is the simple, central stage of the war, for it is there that the interesting things happen. We talk in the evening, after fighting, about the great and rich men who cause and conduct wars. They have so many reasons of their own that they can afford to lend us some of them. There is nothing odd about their attitude. They are out for something they want, or their government wants, and they are using us to get it for them. Anyone can understand that: there is nothing unusual or humanly exciting and amazing to see thousands of men, very few of whom have much idea why they are fighting, all enduring hardships, living in an unnatural, dangerous, but not wholly terrible world, having to kill and be killed, and yet at intervals being moved by a feeling of comradeship with the men who kill them and whom they kill, because they are enduring and experiencing the same things. It is tremendously illogical — to read about it cannot convey the impression of having walked through the looking-glass which touches a man entering battle."

THE GLORY OF WAR — 11

The climax of the Alamein battle was Operation Supercharge. The tactical idea was that this would be a repetition of what had gone before, another kind of Lightfoot — that is, a further infantry assault which would open the door for the armour; and although there were heavy casualties, it worked.

The timing of the attack was eventually settled for 1:05 am on 2 November. Soon Montgomery was in full pursuit of Rommel's forces, which were streaming westwards. Four parts of the battle of Alamein were over: the initial attack on the night of 23/24 October; the Crumbling Operations of the next two days; the Axis counterattacks of 26/28 October and Montgomery's change of plan; then Supercharge, which wore down the enemy to the point where they could no longer prevent a break-out. Now the break-out was under way, and Montgomery had turned his attention to pursuit, but it was pursuit only in name, not effect; in effect it was a following up.

The battle was finished, and from now on, except for brief forays like Mederine and Kasserine, Rommel remained on the defensive. Of some hundred thousand Axis forces which began the battle, about half were either taken or were casualties, and the enemy had left on the battlefield about one thousand guns and four hundred tanks. The 8th Army's losses were thirteen thousand five hundred men killed, wounded, or missing, one hundred guns destroyed, and six hundred tanks knocked out or damaged. Three hundred and fifty of the tanks were able to be repaired. Right up until the end, that is the final stage of Supercharge, it had been a conflict of attrition, with Montgomery to step even further into blood and, as he himself said, prepared to accept a hundred per cent casualties in order to achieve victory.

After twelve days of heavy and violent fighting, the 8th Army had inflicted a severe defeat on the German and Italian forces under Rommel's command, and there was great excitement in Britain, with Churchill discussing the question of ringing the church bells. These had not been rung since Dunkirk, as their ringing was to be the signal that a German invasion of this country was about to begin.

The battle of Alamein had been won; the battle of North Africa was moving into its final phases; in the Pacific the Americans had, despite heavy losses, turned the tables on the Japanese at Guadalcanal; at Stalingrad the Wehrmacht, having been encircled since 19 November 1942, surrendered on 1 February 1943. The final victory was still a long way off, but Alamein was a stepping stone to that final victory.

Compared with what was happening at the same time in the dreadful carnage of Stalingrad — which one young German officer described as eighty days and eighty nights of hand-to-hand struggle, the street no longer measured by metres but by corpses — compared with that, Alamein was puny. But for the British it was all-important. It was the turning point of our fortunes, and, from this time forward, as Churchill subsequently recorded, victory was to be the order of the day.

There were many individual acts of gallantry. One section leader stood up and, with his rifle at high port, walked calmly towards an enemy tank. He did not walk far before he was killed. Another member of the section was shot through the leg and still crawled forward; a third had his leg blown off, and another soldier remembered something that flew past his head; it was a leg with a boot on it. A platoon commander recalled the appalling din of guns firing and of shells bursting, the grim sights of mangled men and twisted corpses, the nauseating smell that was a mixture of sulphur and rotting human flesh, the mental strain from sleeplessness, and, for an officer, the added strain of responsibility.

Then there was the desert itself, the swirling, driving sandstorm which penetrated everywhere, the irritation of sand in and with everything, and, for those like Jamie, the furious heat which inside a tank was doubly uncomfortable.

When the battle in Egypt began, Churchill sent a telegram to Roosevelt, telling the American president that all the Shermans and self-propelled guns which had been given to us by America would play their part. The infantryman, in attack or sitting it out day after day in his slit trench in the front line, played his part; the sappers clearing the mines played their part; the anti-tank gunners played their part; the Desert Air Force played its part; and Jamie, in his Sherman tank, grinding forward in the dark and dust among the mines, or trying to edge forward by day towards the ridge from which the anti-tank guns were firing, played his part.

On 15 November 1942 the church bells rang out for the famous victory at Alamein. They rang out for the men of the 8th Army, for the heroes who survived, and for those, like Jamie, never to return.

PEACE — 4

After Jamie was killed, Elizabeth changed out of all recognition. She blamed me for everything. Our marriage broke up. For a time Lucy kept in touch; then I lost all contact. I don't know why. It just happened. It was my fault, I know.

I loved Jamie so much, and I wrote and told him I was sorry. I said that I was sorry we'd parted as we had, that I wanted to be friends. I wanted that more than anything. It's strange how petty incidents can cause such wounds in a family; those little things, stupid little things, blown up into such gigantic proportions so that there is no room for common sense.

Jamie and I differed on fundamental issues, but I was brought up to believe in those values that made our country great. We had our wonderful empire, and I couldn't accept the way Elizabeth and Jamie felt; they seemed so obsessed by what they believed to be the suffering of the poor and oppressed. Of course there was hardship and oppression, and human nature being what it is, there undoubtedly always will be.

But we are not born equal. Equality was not intended. We are not equal in the sight of God, and it is when you pretend that society is anything but a fraternity of unequals that you run into trouble. You always get trouble when nature — the natural order of things — is disturbed. Elizabeth and Jamie castigated the rich, as if people born into great families can help being what they are, any more than can those who come into the world poor and underprivileged. We don't ask to be what we are. We are what we are.

I suppose Elizabeth, feeling as she did, couldn't help herself, but she should not have done what she did to Jamie — corrupted him. I didn't have to tell her how strongly I felt; she knew it. When I called Jamie a coward, told him he was yellow, it extinguished a spark in her. I realized this afterwards, and with Elizabeth it was never the same again.

After war broke out, Jamie's attitude and behaviour greatly offended me. I couldn't believe a son of mine would act as he did when, alone and with our backs to the wall, we were fighting for all that makes life bearable; fighting for toleration and understanding, for civilised rules that govern compassionate societies; fighting evil incarnate and not only fighting to protect ourselves, but defending, against total extinction of liberty, those in Europe already under the heel of that monster.

How could Jamie have not seen Hitler for what he was? And in the face of all this, how could I not feel bitter and ashamed when my son acted as he did? But even if Jamie hadn't had a complete change of heart, even if he had persisted in his pacifist views, and even if I had continued to feel angry and ashamed, I could not have loved him less. I loved him so much, and his death was a terrible shock.

I wish I could have seen him to tell him how much he meant, that no matter what happened he was — I don't know how to put this properly — everything in the world to me. If I could have seen him just once, I know we would have been friends. I didn't want him to go with bitterness in his heart. But I did try. I wrote and told him that if, after the war, he wanted to marry Wenzel's daughter, he would have my blessing. I couldn't do more than that when twice I had fought against Wenzel, when twice Wenzel was the enemy.

All I wanted was to forgive and forget, that Jamie and I should be friends. I wanted that so much, but he didn't answer, and then he was killed. My poor boy was killed. If only he'd written, just once, just to say we were friends: I wanted that more than anything, but it wasn't to be. I've seen his grave and I know he is at peace, out there in the desert, with his fallen comrades. The graves are beautifully kept: one must be thankful for that.

A BOOK WITHIN A BOOK — V

FINALE

It's a dull day. I suppose you can't expect anything else in January. It's almost the middle of the month and already my New Year's resolutions for 1988 have crumbled. One of the resolutions I made was to make a start on this book about Floss Forsyth. I gave it quite a bit of thought, then decided to begin with the last chapter. I know most writers write the first chapter first, but I came across this scrap of paper on which I had scribbled the words: 'Mummy,' said the child, 'can I have something to give that poor man?'

The piece of paper had fallen down at the back of a drawer, which is where I found it. It had been there for some time, nearly four and a half years, to be exact, because it was shortly after I had returned from taking the three Weinel youngsters to Honolulu that these words came to me as a possible opening for the finale.

Anyway, I made an effort and pulled open the desk drawer where I had left the piece of paper, glanced at the words, then began mulling over all the lousy news I'd read in the morning paper, including an account of the My Lai massacre, and a report by Washington researcher Ruth Legar Sivard on the cost of belligerence in 1986.

In the article on My Lai no mention was made of cost. This may have been because, in terms of warfare, the whole operation, which was over in four hours, wasn't all that expensive. The massacre itself, the slaughter of almost five hundred villagers, took only half an hour. For twenty years the Americans had tried to cover it up, which is not surprising when you read about what happened.

And what happened was that on the morning of 16 March 1968, nine War Lord helicopters, accompanied by Sharks, helicopter gunships, and aeroscout helicopters flying reconnaissance, flew Charlie Company into My Lai landing at 0730, just as the villagers were preparing their early-morning breakfast. Within twenty minutes all hundred and twenty men and five officers had dispersed. The first and second platoons spread out, firing as they went. The GIs attacked anything that moved, animals and people. Women and children were dragged away, some to be raped, then butchered, often with knives; some were scalped, some had their hands cut off, others were disembowelled. One young GI clambered onto the back of a water buffalo and stabbed it repeatedly with his knife until the beast collapsed.

An hour later Bravo company landed on the opposite side of My Lai. A land mine killed one man, and several more were injured. Within thirty minutes the first platoon had made its way into a small hamlet called My Khe, about a mile and a half away from My Lai, where mass executions were already taking place. The GIs at My Khe began their own slaughter. Fleeing peasants were cut down by raking machine-gun fire which poured into the village; then the GIs mopped up, going from house to house, tunnel to tunnel, lobbing in grenades, bayonetting old men, women, and children. As the inhabitants tried to escape, pregnant women had their stomachs slashed open and were left dying in the hot sun. Whole families sheltering in makeshift tunnels were quite literally blown apart.

An eleven-year-old girl ran from tunnel to tunnel trying to find members of her family. Earlier her grandmother had tried to approach the American soldiers and had been shot in the chest; a hand grenade then dismembered her completely. Both entrances to the tunnel where the girl and her grandparents had been sheltering were blown up by TNT and had collapsed; the girl was later dug out by the few survivors the Americans had left in My Khe. Of the ninety-seven killed there, thirty-three were part of the girl's family. Women and children were stripped naked, some raped, others stabbed in the vagina.

Back in My Lai the mass executions were being conducted in an orderly and efficient manner, mostly by men from the first platoon, but the other two platoons helped. Villagers were shot in their homes, on paths, and in paddy fields, while others were rounded up by soldiers who gathered the people together and marched them off to a central point. Many of the women of My Lai were stripped, raped, or sodomised; some were gang-raped, then they were killed, either shot or bayonetted. The simple straw-covered homes where the killings had taken place were afterwards set on fire by zip squads, the name given to GIs with cigarette lighters.

Soldiers of the first platoon were ordered to kill a large group of people gathered at a ditch; some GIs refused, but one young soldier obeyed and opened fire with a machine gun. More than fifty Vietnamese went down in one go, and old men, women, and children began falling into the ditch, most of them dead but some mortally wounded, leaving very young children crawling along the edge of the ditch.

One woman had died trying to push her twelve-month-old baby into the mud at the bottom of an irrigation ditch in a vain effort to save it. Several villagers were pleading and begging the soldiers not to shoot, but the Americans, using their rifle butts, pushed these villagers into the ditch, shot them, then began shooting more and kicking them down.

Other villagers, frantic at seeing their family and friends killed in front of them, jumped into the ditch on top of dead bodies as well as live people; then they too were shot. Many of the children of those shot dead were left standing crying; the soldiers heard the crying, came back, and shot the children. In that dyke alone, a hundred and seventy people were killed. It is no exaggeration to say that the earth ran with blood.

Nearby, an officer ordered a GI to fire into women and children lying in a ditch, some of whom were still breathing, but the young soldier couldn't do it and threw down his machine-gun. The officer picked it up and fired himself into the women and children.

Although badly shot up, one small Vietnamese boy, about four years old, stood by the trail with a gunshot wound in one arm. The child stood clutching his wounded arm with his other hand as blood trickled between his fingers. He stared about in shock and disbelief at what he saw; he just stood there staring, as if he didn't understand or believe what was happening. Then the captain's radio operator put a burst of M16 fire into him.

The killing continued. One GI shot twenty to twenty-five people lined up near a ditch. Like most of the shooting carried out that morning, it was the Nazi-type execution. Some villagers were killed by hand grenades thrown into huts. The GIs found one of the hut doors hard to open, so they crashed through it and saw, inside, an old man shaking with fear. The old man waved his arms and shook his head, pleading with the GIs not to shoot him, but he was shot.

Some GIs refused to take part in the massacre, and of those who had carried out the executions, there were many, later, who had doubts about the killing of women and children. For these Grunts* there were haunting memories of women huddled against their children, hugging the children, putting their bodies over the children to try and save them. But it did no good.

Many terrible things were reported from both sides of the Vietnam war. Nobody could forget, certainly nobody in Vietnam could forget, the wholesale slaughter of civilians by the Vietcong during the Tet offensive the previous year. But now that the truth of what happened in My Lai was revealed, it eclipsed, in sheer barbarity and mindless cruelty, all other acts in that barbarous and cruel war.

After reading about this, it was quite a relief to turn to Ruth Legar Sivard's more generalised account of the cost of belligerence in 1986. In that one year there were twenty-two wars, which killed 2.2 million

* Grunt was the nickname the US troops in Vietnam called themselves (Imperial War Museum)

people, 64 per cent of them civilians. Global military spending soared to a record $3580 billion, more than $31,000,000 a minute. The United States spent $320 billion more than the Soviet Union, and together they put up 59 per cent of all military investment, and, in that same year, in 1986, there was a world total of 26.6 million people in military uniform.

After reflecting on all these wars, I then got to thinking more about Honolulu, those happy memories of sunshine and laughter. Dreaming about the past in this way and wanting to escape from further contemplation of the world's sickness, I reached for my 1983 diary and sat for some time reminiscing over these entries:

Sunday August 7, Gatwick Airport

The airport is crowded. The three youngsters are excited and we are all looking forward to the trip. We have just boarded and are waiting for take-off at 4:45 pm. Fiona, Andrew, and Alastair are sitting together in the row behind me.

I don't know what the time is, but we have not long ago passed over Frobisher Bay. Looking out I can see bare brown rock with blue patches of water. This is a long flight — about 11 hours. We are flying into daylight all the time.

Monday August 8 ,Anaheim

We got into Los Angeles on time. We had a good night's rest. It is hot and sunny. We spent a good part of today in Disneyland. We went on the Caribbean Tour, the Haunted House, the Space Travel, and others, and they are very good indeed. America is having a heat wave at the moment. This evening we went to watch the Angels play baseball. They lost to the Minn. Twins 4-2.

Tuesday August 9, Anaheim

We have been at Disneyland for most of today and thoroughly enjoyed it. We went on the Submarine, the Jungle ride, the Train, went into the Tiki room, and so on. We came back to the hotel this afternoon and went swimming. We are going back to Disneyland for the night parade.

Wednesday August 10, Anaheim

We spent all day at Magic Mountain and got back to the hotel at about 8:15 pm. We went swimming in the hotel pool and then had dinner at the restaurant across the road. We all enjoyed the day.

Thursday August 11, Anaheim

We are flying to Honolulu this evening, expecting to arrive there about midnight.

Yesterday, at Magic Mountain, the three youngsters did quite a lot. Alastair went on Free Fall, which is dropping at body speed from about eight storeys. It shook him up a bit, and he said he wouldn't go on it again. He also went on the Giant Coaster, which can be pretty scary. But it was an enjoyable day. We have been very lucky with the weather. Rather hot, but cooled off a little now, and no rain.

We took a Gray Line coach to Magic Mountain, and this was interesting. We all managed to get front seats, and on the way the driver, who was very nice, gave us a running commentary on all places of interest together with some of the history of Los Angeles. We saw the L.A. river, went through Hollywood and Beverly Hills, which from a historical point of view was interesting, and we went into Universal Studios. Magic Mountain being near San Fernando Valley, it was 10 degrees hotter there.

Friday August 12, Honolulu

We left Los Angeles at 9:15 pm and arrived in Honolulu about midnight.

We all went down for breakfast at about 9:00 am. It is sunny and hot. We have a lovely view from the hotel (Waikiki Village — 17th floor) over the white sandy beach and bluest of blue seas and lush green palm trees. Honolulu is exactly what you see on postcards. Very lovely, even if commercialised. Fiona, Andrew, and Alastair have gone to the beach and are thoroughly enjoying themselves swimming and snorkelling.

Saturday August 13, Honolulu

After breakfast I met Mr Roy Kelley, the owner of this hotel, a multimillionaire, and we had a long chat. He told me briefly his history and what it was like when the Japanese bombed Pearl Harbor.

Sunday August 14, Honolulu

Sally and Ed Sheehan collected us from the Waikiki Village Hotel and we drove to Diamond Head to look at the Kimballs' house. It is the most lovely house with a breathtaking view of the Pacific Ocean. In the house are lovely treasures — the Kimballs are very wealthy. We went to Sally and Ed's beautiful apartment next to the Kahala Hilton; then we watched the dolphins being fed at 2:00 pm in the hotel pool. Fiona was given a fish to throw to one of the dolphins.

Mr Kimball has the only salt water swimming pool — fed from the ocean — on the island.

Tuesday August 16, Honolulu

Today we went to Pearl Harbor in the admiral's barge.

We saw a film of the actual bombing of Pearl Harbor from captured Japanese war films. This made our tour all the more poignant.

Thursday August 18, Honolulu

The days are gloriously sunny and hot, the trade wind refreshingly cool. The youngsters spend most of the day on the beach.

Sunday August 21, Honolulu

I saw two U.S. Army policemen with a young man in shorts and nothing else, but his hands handcuffed behind, being led towards the barracks. I took a photo but I don't know if it will come out.

Monday August 22, Honolulu

Last night I watched *A Bridge Too Far*, on TV. It was very good and it reminded me of Tui Montgomery, who was killed at Arnhem.

Tuesday August 23, Honolulu

Today we went to the hula dance show. We saw some Hawaiian dancing which was lovely. We went on to Hanauma Bay. The youngsters went snorkelling and saw a lot of fish. Andrew saw an eel.

Wednesday August 24, Honolulu

I finished reading *The Ugly American* this morning.

Thursday August 25, Honolulu

Yesterday Sally and Ed took us to the older part of Honolulu. We went where there is the most marvellous high view over a part of the island, mountains and the ocean in the distance; then we went into the Pearl Harbor base, as Sally and Ed have VIP passes, and they showed us warships close up, including two nuclear submarines.

Friday August 26, Honolulu

This is our last day in Honolulu.

Saturday August 27, On flight

We were late taking off from Honolulu. I got an excellent view of Waikiki Beach and Diamond Head as we took off. Bright, sunny day and blue sky, white, fluffy clouds beneath us.

Sunday August 28, On flight

We landed at Los Angeles when it was dark. As we were coming in I could see a vast maze of yellow lights and streams of small white lights from car headlamps.

We went straight to our connecting plane, took off, and have now been flying for just over six hours. It is light now, bright outside, and beneath us is a blue-and-white mottled carpet made up from the ocean with fluffy white clouds floating high above it. We are due to land at Gatwick in just over three hours.

I put back the diary and thought again about all those wars; then I wondered what the future would hold for Andrew, Alastair, and Fiona and whether, in their lifetime, there would be any less of the world's violence?

"Mummy," said the child, "can I have something to give that poor man?"

"No," she said crossly, not so much because she didn't want to waste money on a tramp, but because it wasn't good that children should talk to strangers.

Another First World War tune had started up: "Goodbyee, goodbyee, wipe the tear baby dear from your eyee." I watched as he played and hopped around. He went on playing until he saw me looking at him; then he stopped, came to attention, saluted, and called out: "Over the top, men. Over the top!" He remained at attention, smiling, showing fine white teeth.

Taking twenty pounds from my wallet, I went over to him. I was about to tell him who I was and who my uncle was, and to say that my uncle had asked me to give him the money. In the end I said nothing and just handed him the notes. He looked at me quizzically, then made as if to give the money back, but I pushed his hand away and said: "Please take it, sir."

I don't know why I addressed him in this way. It wasn't because I thought of him as anything but just another bum, even though he was clean; so it must have been because I believed in him, believed in his medal ribbons, knew that he'd fought in the First World War and, later, had been at Dunkirk.

Or if it wasn't simply this, it could have been because he'd written that intelligent letter to my uncle when asking for help; or that when he tried to give back the money I saw, in spite of his antics, that he hadn't lost all sense of dignity. Then again, it might have been that I have, in the back of my mind, a picture I am never without: that of the poor persecuted Jew squashed into the wooden cart being pulled along by young laughing Nazis.

Or if it was none of these things then it could only have been that, as he stood there smiling whimsically, clutching his mouth organ in one hand and the money in the other, I saw, briefly, in his grey, troubled eyes, the sadness of the human race.